"There are no easy answers to these and other questions. But
questions in the right way, to sift through the information we ~~already know, and to conduct the~~
research necessary to learn more. These skills aren't just essential to college professors and researchers. They're essential to your success as a criminal justice practitioner and to just about anyone who
wants to succeed in an information economy," I explained. Nearly immediately, a student raised his
hand and asked, "Dr. Withrow, you were a cop for a long time before you became a college professor, right?" "Yes," I responded. "So, are you telling us that cops use research methods?" he asked.
"Yes. That is exactly what I'm telling you. All criminal justice practitioners use research methods –
probation officers, FBI agents, correctional counselors," I explained.

"Let me give you a final example, this one from personal experience. A little more than 30 years
ago, when I was a state trooper in the Texas Panhandle, I noticed an increase in alcohol-related
motor vehicle crashes in a part of my beat. Using a red felt tip marker, I put a dot on a map for each
alcohol-related crash over the preceding six months. This told me where the accidents were happening. I then made a bar graph, by hand because Excel didn't exist at the time, showing the number
of alcohol-related crashes each month for those six months. Finally, I read the narratives from each
crash report, paying particular attention to the day of week, time of day, and any other important
information that I and my colleagues had gotten from the individuals involved in the crashes. The
other troopers and I came to the conclusion that the intoxicated drivers involved in these crashes
were traveling in the same direction and seemed to come from the same place: a new drinking es-
tablishment just across the border in Oklahoma. So, along with troopers from the Oklahoma Highway Patrol, we met with the bar owner. He agreed to monitor his patrons more closely, to refuse
service to inebriated patrons, and to stop serving alcohol one hour before the bar closed. We then
increased patrols on the border during the days and times we had previously determined were the
most dangerous. Driving while intoxicated arrests increased and, eventually, alcohol-related traffic crashes decreased. I am convinced that there are people alive today because of the research my
colleagues and I did back then," I explained. As I finished, I looked at the student who had originally
asked me about the point of the class. "Did I answer your question?" I asked. She smiled and said,
"Yes, professor. Thank you."

Since that day, I've often wondered whether criminal justice students enrolled in research methods
classes at other colleges and universities are also asking, What's the point of this class? I know that
most of you have no intention of becoming a university professor or professional researcher. I certainly did not when I was in your shoes. But research skills are just as valuable to the criminal justice
practitioner. As such, you deserve a research methods book that will teach you how to apply these
skills to a career in criminal justice. And that is the point of this textbook, its website, and its ancil-
lary materials. So sit back, enjoy the ride, and rest assured that the skills you learn here will make a
difference in your professional lives. They certainly have in mine.

Brian L. Withrow

Brian L. Withrow, Ph.D.
Texas State University
San Marcos, Texas

"Brian Withrow breathes life into what can be a difficult and confusing topic that many undergraduates have trouble understanding. His use of real-world examples, many from his own life and career, makes the text useful and popular."
—*Geoffrey P. Alpert, Criminology and Criminal Justice, University of South Carolina*

"It is not difficult to endorse *Research Methods in Crime and Justice* as it is one of those rare research methods books that are a page turner. Brian Withrow's use of story-telling to engage the reader is superb! This is an important book that has accomplished what many research methods books have not, illuminating the importance of applying research techniques to both real-world and criminal justice scenarios."
—*Henry Jackson, Jr., Criminal Justice and Criminology,*
Metropolitan State University of Denver

"A major travesty in our rapidly emerging field has been our obsession with quantitative strategies. The vast majority of our undergraduate and masters level students who go on to work as practitioners in Criminal Justice rely on training that is qualitative in nature. This text addresses that need and helps fill a void in our evolving pedagogy."
—*W. Wesley Johnson, Criminal Justice, University of Southern Mississippi*

"Brian Withrow has written a research methods textbook that is sure to be welcomed by those of us who teach methods to criminal justice students. *Research Methods in Crime and Justice* is a refreshing look at the many methodologies available to research-ers via real life examples embedded throughout the book's chapters. Instructors and students alike will be well served by his efforts to help students understand why studying research methods is important to them and their future careers."
—*Barbara Sims, Criminal Justice, Mars Hill College*

"I really like this manuscript. The contents are unique and excellent."
—*Bitna Kim, Criminology, Indiana University of Pennsylvania*

"I agree with Brian Withrow that it is a very good idea to rely heavily on storytell-ing as a teaching method and it is important to show students, in a convincing and powerful way, why and how learning research methods is quite relevant to their future work as criminal justice practitioners."
—*Yuning Wu, Criminal Justice, Wayne State University*

"What distinguishes this manuscript from all others on the market is the down-to-earth approach, written in common language, which will undoubtedly appeal to typical undergraduates who traditionally struggle with methods."
—*Gaylene Armstrong, Criminal Justice, Sam Houston State University*

"I like the aims of the book relative to the kinds of things I am trying to accomplish. Focusing on the 'story' of research is a useful tool. I also like all the additional mate-rials that focus on giving students a roadmap to produce their research papers as well as research more generally. I also like the exercises at the end of each chapter and elsewhere in the book (or online)."
—*Thomas Stucky, Criminal Justice, Indiana University–Purdue University Indianapolis*

Routledge
Taylor & Francis Group

Research Methods in Crime and Justice

This fresh and innovative blend of text and online materials uniquely addresses the fundamental question asked by many undergraduate students: why do criminal justice majors have to take research methods? The author Brian L. Withrow, a former Texas State Trooper, widely published academic researcher, and teacher of the undergraduate research methods course, consistently demonstrates how research skills aren't just essential to university researchers, they are essential to student success as criminal justice practitioners, and to all who want to succeed in an information economy. More than 80 short, sharply focused examples throughout the text rely on actual research that is conducted by, on behalf of, or relevant to criminal justice practitioners. *Research Methods in Crime and Justice* presents a balanced treatment of qualitative and quantitative approaches to criminal justice research. The book engages students' interest like no other.

The online materials also offer a unique feature, *The Researcher's Notebook*, which provides students a series of structured exercises. These exercises enable students to develop a viable research question, complete a comprehensive literature review, and design a research method that, if implemented, would provide the data necessary to answer the research question. This practical learning can be implemented with a minimal commitment of instructor time for assessment.

Research Methods in Crime and Justice

Brian L. Withrow

Routledge
Taylor & Francis Group

NEW YORK AND LONDON

Whether you are an instructor or student,
go to **www.routledgecj.com/withrow**
for a wealth of support materials for this text

First published 2014
by Routledge
711 Third Avenue, New York, NY 10017

Simultaneously published in the UK
by Routledge
2 Park Square, Milton Park, Abingdon, Oxon OX14 4RN

Routledge is an imprint of the Taylor & Francis Group, an informa business

Library of Congress Cataloging in Publication Data
Withrow, Brian L.
 Research methods in crime and justice / by Brian Withrow. — 1 Edition.
 pages cm. —(Criminology and justice studies series)
 Includes bibliographical references and index.
 1. Crime—Research—Methodology. 2. Criminal justice, Administration of—
Research—Methodology. I. Title.
 HV6024.5.W58 2013
 364.072—dc23
 2012050046

ISBN: 978–0–415–88436–5 (hbk)
ISBN: 978–0–415–88443–3 (pbk)
ISBN: 978–0–203–76882–2 (ebk)

Typeset in ITC Stone Serif and Frutiger
by Swales & Willis Ltd, Exeter, Devon
Printed and bound by Courier in Westford, MA

This textbook is dedicated to my late mother Faye Withrow,
Founding Librarian of the DeSoto Public Library,
in appreciation for introducing me to the story.

BRIEF TABLE OF CONTENTS

DETAILED TABLE OF CONTENTS

PREFACE

On an unremarkable Tuesday morning two university professors were preparing to deliver lectures in adjacent classrooms. It just so happened that both of them were scheduled to lecture on experimental design research to their undergraduate students.

Professor Smith walked into a quiet and nearly empty lecture hall. Had the students not spread out throughout the room it is unlikely there would have been enough of them in attendance to fill the first two rows of seats. "Good morning class," Professor Smith began. "Today we are going to discuss experimental design research methods. An experiment is a research method that allows researchers to identify and measure the effect of an independent variable on a dependent variable. I refer you to page 235 in the text …" he continued. Some of the students dutifully turned to page 235 and a few began taking notes. More than a few took out their cell phones.

Professor Jones walked into a crowded lecture hall. Nearly every seat was taken. Aside from the usual pre-class banter most of the students were ready for class. Nearly all of the students had turned to page 235. Their notebooks were already open and their pens were poised ready to take notes.

"*Good morning class,*" Professor Jones began. "*Can anybody tell me why it is mandatory in this state for a police officer to arrest a person he or she suspects is guilty of domestic violence?*" he asked.

"*Because if domestic abusers are arrested then they are less likely to recidivate,*" one student said.

"*No, it is a dumb idea. The mandatory arrest law only deters victims from calling the police in the first place,*" argued another student.

A few other students offered opinions before Professor Jones interrupted and asked, "*How do you know what you think you know?*" His question was greeted with near complete silence. "*Do we have any evidence that mandatory arrest laws reduce domestic violence recidivism or that they deter victims from seeking help?*" he asked. Again, the room was silent.

"*Would it surprise you to learn that prior to the 1990s many American police departments expressly prohibited their officers from making arrests in domestic violence cases? Many of the departments that did not prohibit these arrests altogether required officers to get permission from a supervisor prior to taking a domestic violence suspect into custody,*" Professor Jones explained. He smiled as the students looked at him in disbelief.

"Then, beginning in the late 1970s, advocacy groups and other organizations took on the domestic violence issue and raised it to a national issue," Professor Jones explained. *"Then along came two university professors who thought they'd like to do a little experiment to see if arresting domestic abuse suspects would deter them from repeat offending or, as some at the time suggested, make them even more dangerous. Let's talk about how they did this experiment,"* the professor continued.

Over the next hour Professor Jones told the students the story of how Lawrence W. Sherman and Richard A. Berk conducted the Minneapolis Domestic Violence Experiment (Sherman and Berk, 1984a). In doing so he talked about independent and dependent variables, experimental and control groups, pre-tests and posttests, random group assignment, group equivalency, and all of the other concepts that are important for a thorough understanding of the experimental design model. He even found time to discuss the controversies that surround this research and offered ideas on why some of the subsequent research in other cities has failed to produce similar results.

Professor Jones' teaching approach is not a gimmick. Storytelling is the oldest and most effective communication tool in human civilization. For thousands of years human civilizations have relied on stories to communicate social values, religious traditions, cultural lessons, and yes, even knowledge. Storytelling even predates the development of the alphabet.

Storytelling is an effective educational tool because it engages learners at a personal level. Stories create enduring personal connections to a subject matter and, in doing so, enhance recall. Listeners are able to identify new perspectives and imagine alternative solutions to old problems. When we listen to a story we develop empathy for the characters and understand how the worlds they live in affect how they behave and influence the decisions they make.

As a teacher I learned this lesson many years ago. I noticed that my research methods students seemed more engaged when I told them stories about how actual researchers overcame challenges. They seemed to understand methodological concepts more completely when I presented them in context. I also came to the realization that I was much more motivated to teach when I moved away from merely lecturing on methodological concepts devoid of illustrative contexts.

Several years ago, I learned something else. My students had stopped reading the textbook I had adopted for the course. Some didn't even bother to purchase it. Frankly, who could blame them? Most textbooks are not 'page turners' and they are very expensive. Instead the students relied on the visual presentations during lectures and the stories I told them about how actual researchers applied methods to answer important questions. Their ability to critically analyze research methods improved substantially as did their performance on examinations. Eventually, I became so disenchanted with the lack of context (i.e. story) in the available research methods textbooks that I simply chose not to adopt one. I have not used one since.

So in 2009 I set about the task of producing a very different research methods textbook. Rather than merely define methodological concepts and discuss procedures I chose to tell the stories of how other researchers overcame challenges as they sought answers to important questions. While telling these stories I devote sufficient time to introduce relevant methodological concepts and procedures. When first introduced and defined in the textbook, key terms and concepts are in bold type. These key terms and concepts are also formally defined in the glossary. My method is neither a pedagogical trick nor a thinly veiled attempt on my part to write a textbook that is 'more appealing to the younger generation.' Instead, my objective is, unapologetically, to breathe life into research methods through storytelling.

The stories I use to illustrate methodological concepts and procedures appear throughout the text in one of two forms. First, Chapters 9 through 13 in Part Three (Acquiring and Analyzing Data) contain set out boxes called *Developing the Method*. Within this feature the steps that actual researchers followed during specific parts of the research process are analyzed. Telling the researchers' stories achieves two important teaching objectives. It reinforces the research process that is previously introduced in Chapter 2 and, more importantly, provides the students with illustrative contexts that better explain the decisions these researchers made, or were forced to make, as they sought answers to their research questions.

Second, every chapter contains numerous set out boxes called *Making Research Real*. This feature includes short, narrowly focused vignettes that are relevant to the methodological concept or procedure that is being discussed at the time. This feature provides students with tangible contexts of how methodological concepts and procedures are applied during the research process. It is important to note that the stories within this feature are far more than mere examples. Many of these vignettes include characters, plot, conflict, and other characteristics a reader would expect to encounter while reading a story.

Very early in my scholarly career I observed that most of the undergraduate students in my research methods classrooms had no interest in becoming researchers. It is an open secret that some students' motivation for enrolling in a research methods class is based primarily on the fact that it is required for the Bachelor's degree. Given the choice they would likely prefer to take another elective. These students have no scholarly appreciation of the nuances of a well-written question on a survey or for the importance of equivalency between experimental and control groups. For the most part they want to be criminal justice practitioners. I understand their motivation; however, I do not accept the notion that research methods are irrelevant to them. In fact, having been a criminal justice practitioner prior to becoming a scholar, I know just the opposite to be true.

The students graduating with Bachelor's degrees in criminal justice today are entering an industry that is far different from the one I became a part of more than three decades ago. The knowledge base is much larger and information is more readily available to them. When I started we were encouraged to accept the ways of our predecessors. In fact, we were often told not to question why we did the things we did. It is very different now. Innovation and change are more than buzzwords. They are a way of life for contemporary criminal justice practitioners. We approached the job in ways that 'made sense' to us. Contemporary criminal justice practitioners must approach the job in ways that are justified by the results of well planned and executed research. This requires a solid understanding of research methods and an ability to use that knowledge as a consumer of research. Those of us who teach research methods to undergraduate criminal justice students are more relevant than ever. *Research Methods in Crime and Justice* makes the case to these students that learning research methods is important to their success as a criminal justice practitioner. The examples used throughout the book are, with rare exceptions, relevant to criminal justice practice. Moreover, the previously mentioned series of set out boxes called *Making Research Real* relies upon actual research that is conducted by, on behalf of, or relevant to criminal justice practitioners.

Another important pedagogical feature in *Research Methods in Crime and Justice* is called *Getting to the Point*. This feature contains short summaries of the information the student should 'take away' from each section or subsection. These set out boxes appear at the end of nearly every section or subsection throughout the book. This allows students to find and review the critical lessons contained within each chapter. The information in this feature is repeated in the chapter summaries.

Like many other textbooks each chapter in *Research Methods in Crime and Justice* includes review questions and exercises. These materials are organized into two main categories. First, each chapter contains a series of review questions that provide the students with an opportunity to test their knowledge of the material contained in the chapter. Students who are able to respond correctly to these questions are reasonably assured of their familiarity with the material contained in the chapter. Second, each chapter refers to two or more research application exercises. These exercises require the students to read peer-refereed articles from the scholarly literature (accessed for free through the textbook's website) and answer specific application questions. These articles and application questions are relevant to the subject matter in their corresponding chapters.

The instructor's manual and test bank for *Research Methods in Crime and Justice* (available online) contains the features one would expect to find in a resource of this type – lecture outlines, test questions, visual presentation aids, and so on. More importantly the teaching materials are arranged independently so as to allow professors maximum pacing options during a semester or quarter. For example, some professors may prefer to lecture on variables and the levels of measurement prior to lecturing on hypotheses and the structure of research, or vice versa. Rather than being forced to pace subject matter in the way they happen to be arranged in the textbook, lecture materials and their corresponding student reading assignments are organized by concept or procedure rather than by chapter.

The student workbook, titled *Research Methods in Crime and Justice* (available online) also contains the features one would expect to find in a resource of this type – learning objectives, key points, practice test questions, learning checkpoints, and so on. There is an additional feature that is unique to *Research Methods in Crime and Justice* – a structured method by which students can actually practice research methods without requiring a professor to devote an inordinate amount of time to assessment.

Many professors assign students to write semester research papers. In most cases these are not much more than literature reviews, but they can be far more. Imagine a system that would enable students to create a research question, conduct a literature review, and then design a research method that would provide the data necessary to answer the research question. Assigning students such an ambitious project requires an inordinate amount of time for assessment, particularly at the end of a semester when time is a limited resource, and likely focuses too much on the product (i.e. the final paper) rather than the process of research.

Through a series of structured exercises called *The Researcher's Notebook* (available online in the instructor's resources section of the companion website) the students will:

- develop a research question;
- write the introductory section of a research report;
- develop an outline for the literature review;
- access the available literature;
- learn how to recognize the most authoritative literature available on a subject;
- annotate their literature review outlines with information from the literature;
- learn how to know when they have accessed 'enough' literature;
- write a literature review, and;
- develop a research plan that, if implemented, would produce the data necessary to answer the research question.

Each of the assignments in *The Researcher's Notebook* has a clear learning objective and an objective grading standard. In other words everybody knows what is expected of them. In addition, evaluating the students' work in this format distributes assessment throughout the semester or quarter *and* reduces the amount of time that a professor must devote to assessment overall. Completing a semester-long research project in this way allows professors multiple opportunities to evaluate the research process rather than wait until the end and 'hope' the students figure it out. It also reduces the opportunity for plagiarism and deters students from producing a semester-long assignment the night before it is due. I have personally used this system for more than a decade in several teaching contexts and I am convinced that by the end of the semester my students have a greater understanding of research methods and, in turn, are more informed consumers of the research. I also go less frequently to the office supply store to buy more red pens!

Research Methods in Crime and Justice tells the story of research, and in doing so, provides the students with a deeper understanding of how research gets done. Students who learn about research methods within the contexts of actual research projects are more likely to remember the concepts, use them when they are asked to conduct research, and appreciate them when they evaluate the research of others. *Research Methods in Crime and Justice* makes the case to undergraduate students that a solid understanding of research methods is essential for their success as criminal justice practitioners. As criminal justice practitioners these students will be asked to conduct research. Sometime, maybe several sometimes, during their careers they will be asked to conduct a survey, evaluate the effectiveness of a criminal justice strategy, or conduct some type of data-gathering project. The results of these 'research projects' will, in all likelihood, influence decision making at the policy level. Their professional success will depend on their ability to apply generally acceptable research methodologies to solve real-world problems. Finally, through *The Researcher's Notebook* feature, *Research Methods in Crime and Justice* provides students with an opportunity to apply what they learn to a research project of their choosing. While it is not likely that the students will have enough time to actually complete the research project they develop, the mere process of planning a research project that will produce the data necessary to answer a research question is highly instructive.

ACKNOWLEDGMENTS

There are always many people to acknowledge for their contribution to a textbook. In my case there are hundreds. I am a better teacher and hopefully a better author because of the hundreds of students who have sat in my research methods classrooms. I am indebted to them all for their attentiveness. I am especially appreciative to the students who raise their hands to ask questions. Responding to well asked questions makes one a better teacher. I am forever in my students' debt for what they teach me.

This textbook is dedicated to my late mother Faye Withrow. In 1965, she founded a library in our small town. During the early years the library collection consisted mostly of donated books, magazines, and obsolete encyclopedias housed in a small lean-to building attached to a nursery school. Today the DeSoto Public Library resides in a 30,000 square foot facility and serves one of the most diverse communities in Texas. More importantly, at least to me, is that my mother introduced me to stories. She insisted that my brothers and I read every day – even during the summer. I admit that there were many times I would have preferred to be at the park playing baseball, but because of her perseverance I grew to appreciate a good story. My happiest memories of her are the times we talked about the books we read together. I still read every day and this textbook's pedagogical use of stories to teach research methods is in no small part due to my mother's influence.

During the years I spent developing the materials and writing this textbook somebody else maintained our home and tended to the needs of our family. That person is my wife, Lisa Withrow. For the past 30 years we have shared a life that far exceeds that which we could have imagined. Lisa was patient with me as I struggled to 'find just the right word' or when I rewrote entire passages because they 'just didn't read right.' She listened attentively as I read aloud the difficult passages and was honest in her assessment of them. Lisa is an exemplary public school teacher and I am proud to say that nearly everything I know about teaching I learned from watching and listening to her.

I am convinced that professional success depends in a large part on the guidance one receives early on in one's career. In this regard I have truly been fortunate. I began my professional career as a State Trooper for the Texas Department of Public Safety in Childress Texas. My first supervisors – Sergeant Bill Ricks, Lieutenant Jerry Tucker, and Captain Gene Turman – taught me the values of mutual respect, public service, and a sense of duty. Later, while preparing for a scholarly career, I learned from Charlie Friel and Rolando del Carmen the values of preparation and authenticity. Whatever professional success I enjoy is the result of these five men and their willingness to invest in my future.

A special relationship exists between authors and editors. In many ways it is very much like a marriage – full of ups and downs. In 2009 Steve Rutter braved a Texas thunderstorm to meet Lisa and me in San Marcos to discuss 'my idea' for a new kind of research methods textbook. I liked him immediately. I am sure over the past four years Steve has been frustrated with me many times. I have likely caused him more than a few sleepless nights. As we near the release of *Research Methods in Crime and Justice* it is important for Steve to know how much I respect and admire him for supporting the concept of this book and for investing so much time into its production. It is a better textbook and I am a better writer because of Steve.

Research Methods in Crime and Justice would merely be words on pages without Dr. Susan Mannon. Through a conference call early on in the project Steve introduced me to Sus and instructed me to routinely submit my written work to her for editing. I was pleasantly surprised. Few publishers anymore commit substantial editorial resources to textbooks. I was excited about the prospect of working with an editor. What I did not know, at least at first, was that Sus is far more than a wordsmith. She is an accomplished scholar who possesses a thorough knowledge of social research methods. And, perhaps more importantly we share an appreciation for social research methods instruction. I am not sure if another textbook is in my future. I am, however, quite sure that should I agree to write another, I will insist on working with Dr. Susan Mannon.

I would be remiss if I did not take a moment to acknowledge the individual and collective contributions of the many scholars who reviewed previous versions of *Research Methods in Crime and Justice*. Their thoughtful and sometimes frank comments made the manuscript better. These scholars are:

Bitna Kim	Indiana University of Pennsylvania
Gaylene Armstrong	Sam Houston State University
Gregory M. Zimmerman	Northeastern University
Christopher Sullivan	University of Cincinnati
Lee E. Ross	University of Central Florida
Evita G. Bynum	University of Maryland Eastern Shore
Thomas D. Stucky	Indiana University–Purdue University Indianapolis
Tina L. Freiburger	University of Wisconsin, Milwaukee
Rosemary Barberet	CUNY, John Jay College of Criminal Justice
Huan Gao	California State University, Stanislaus
Jennifer Wingren	Metropolitan State University
Elizabeth Stassinos	Westfield State College
Tiffiney Barfield-Cottledge	University of North Texas
Taiping Ho	Ball State University
Eric Jeffries	Kent State University

| Nancy Morris | Southern Illinois University |
| Robert Tillyer | University of Texas, San Antonio. |

Finally, you would not be reading *Research Methods in Crime and Justice* without the contribution of the production team. These dedicated professionals transformed a nondescript manuscript into a product that students will use to improve their knowledge of research methods. These professionals are Emma Håkonsen, production editor at Routledge; Kate Reeves, copy editor; Anna Carroll, proofreader; and Susan Park, indexer.

Brian L. Withrow, Ph.D.
San Marcos, Texas

ABOUT THE AUTHOR

Dr. Brian L. Withrow is Professor of Criminal Justice at Texas State University–San Marcos. Prior to joining the Texas State University faculty in 2009, Brian was an Associate Professor and Director of the Forensic Sciences Program at Wichita State University. While on the faculty at Wichita State University, Dr. Withrow served one term as Mayor of Bel Aire Kansas. From 1993 to 1999, Dr. Withrow managed a police leadership development program at Sam Houston State University in Huntsville, Texas.

Prior to his scholarly career Brian worked for the Texas Department of Public Safety. He started this part of his career in 1981 as a State Trooper in a rural part of the Texas Panhandle. During the nearly 13 years Brian was at DPS he was promoted to the rank of Training Officer, Inspector, and Bureau Commander.

Brian earned his Bachelor of Arts degree in Criminal Justice from Stephen F. Austin State University in 1981, his Masters of Public Administration from Southwest Texas State University in 1993, and his Doctor of Philosophy in Criminal Justice from Sam Houston State University in 1999.

Dr. Withrow lives in Austin, Texas with his wife Lisa. They have four grown children and two grandchildren. Brian is an Eagle Scout and continues to remain active in the Boy Scouts of America. Currently he serves as the Commissioner for the Sacred Springs District.

PART 1

Getting Started

CHAPTER 1

The Research Practice

So here you are in a research methods class. Hopefully, the email at the start of the book convinced you that this course will be valuable to you as a criminal justice practitioner or even just an everyday consumer of information. But what are research methods exactly? **Research methods** are basically the tools, techniques, and procedures that researchers use to ask and answer questions. In this book, we will focus on questions that relate to criminal justice. Some of these questions are routine:

- *How many police officers are there in the United States?*

- *How much do we spend annually on prisons?*

Other questions are more complicated:

- *What causes a person to become a serial murderer?*

- *Can a violent offender be rehabilitated?*

In Chapter 2, you will learn how these questions are asked and answered. For now, we will spend some time learning about the practice of research in general. What exactly do we mean by 'research'? And why is it so important?

Getting to the Point 1.1 – Research methods are the tools, techniques, and procedures that researchers use to ask and answer questions.

WHAT IS RESEARCH?

What do people mean when they say, "I did a little research, and …" or "The research indicates …"? The term **research** actually has two meanings. First, research is a verb. To research means to follow a logical process that uses concepts, principles, and techniques to produce knowledge. We do research every day to inform important decisions. For example, when looking to buy a new car, you may want to research the car's safety record, gas mileage, resale value, and so on. By carefully finding and evaluating this information, you can make an informed buying decision.

In the field of criminal justice, research is often more complicated. For example, a study analyzing the effectiveness of various offender rehabilitation programs might require more forethought and rigor. What do we mean by 'rehabilitation'? Do we mean that offenders do not re-offend or that they are rehabilitated in some other way? What types of offenders are we talking about? Are we talking about sex offenders or armed burglars? How will we know if the rehabilitation program actually works? Should it be considered effective if 50 percent of the offenders are rehabilitated? Or should we measure effectiveness in some other way? These are all questions we would have to consider before we even started to research this issue.

Research is also a noun. In this case, research refers to a collection of information that represents what we know about a particular topic. Research that informs everyday decisions can be found in newspapers and magazines, on the television, and through other forms of media like the Internet. A segment on NBC *Today*, for example, might feature an expert talking about a new study on effective parenting techniques. This information can be supplemented with information from books and magazines to form a body of information that a person draws upon when making decisions about how to raise his or her children. Academic research is usually found in academic journals, academic books, and formal reports. Information in these sources is usually more technical and may involve contributions from multiple academic disciplines. Research on domestic violence, for example, spans many disciplines (e.g. law, psychology, criminology, sociology, etc.) and constitutes an enormous literature.

Getting to the Point 1.2 – As a verb, 'research' means to follow a logical process that uses concepts, principles, and techniques to produce knowledge. As a noun, 'research' is a collection of information that represents what we know about a particular topic.

Whether used as a verb or noun, the critical element of research is the method or process by which the researcher collects and analyzes information. The research method is especially important in the social sciences because social science topics are often difficult to study. Chemists follow a fairly consistent research process because the standards of measurement are generally agreed upon. Social scientists are not so fortunate; there might be many different ways to measure concepts related to social relations and structure. For example, the popular website e-Harmony.com provides matchmaking services that are based on the potential compatibility between two people. But how should we measure compatibility? Should compatibility be based on hobbies and leisure interests? Political beliefs and core values? Level of education and occupation? There may be many ways of measuring compatibility and thus many ways of interpreting the success of a match between two people. As a result, we need to know how social scientists came to their conclusions. How did they measure their concepts, collect their data, and analyze the results? In the social sciences, *how* you know is as important as *what* you know.

> **Getting to the Point 1.3** – Research in the social sciences is more challenging than in the physical sciences because the concepts that social scientists study are more difficult to measure and the findings that social scientists produce are more difficult to interpret.

WHY DO RESEARCH?

Conducting good research is tedious and time consuming. It is not uncommon for a research project to take months, years, or even decades to complete. Often there are no guarantees that a research project will even produce the information the researcher is seeking. So why bother with research? Certainly, there are other ways of gathering information, which I will discuss below. But as I will suggest, these methods are not as good at producing quality information as the tried and true methods of conducting research.

One of the common alternatives to research methods is to rely on authority. There are a lot of smart and well-informed people in the world, such as parents and professors. We could simply rely on them to tell us the truth. The problem here is that parents and, yes, even professors can be wrong. Science, and therefore knowledge, changes constantly. For example, we used to think that criminal suspects who fled in vehicles were best apprehended by large numbers of police officers in fast cars equipped with bright flashing lights and loud sirens. Eventually, we learned that the only thing worse than one car traveling through a city at high speed is multiple cars traveling at high speed. High-speed chases often result in death, serious injury, and/or property damage. So researchers devised safer, more effective ways to apprehend fleeing criminal suspects.

Instead of doing research, we could also rely on tradition or custom. Most of what we do every day is based on tradition or habit. We hold open doors for people behind us. We eat lunch at noon. We put people in jail because we think the threat of jail will keep people from committing crime. To be sure, some traditions are good. But over-reliance on traditions can be harmful. In 1896, the United States Supreme Court established the 'separate but equal doctrine' in *Plessy v. Ferguson* (163 US 537, 1896), which held that individuals could be segregated by race. For years, this doctrine upheld a tradition of separate facilities for African American and White individuals, including separate seating areas in restaurants, separate school systems, and even separate drinking fountains. At the time, the Court believed that mixing the races in social situations would cause social friction and public conflict. Fifty-eight years later, a unanimous Supreme Court reversed itself and ruled in *Brown v. The Board of Education* (347 US 483, 1954) that separate could not be equal.

In delivering the opinion of the Court, Chief Justice Earl Warren cited the research of psychologists and sociologists that showed that racial segregation causes harm to children. In this case, social science research instigated a substantial change in American legal and social tradition.

A third option in lieu of research is to just rely on common sense. Common sense is information that we have learned from our experiences or through our interactions with others. It is what we believe to be true. One of my father's favorite expressions was, "That guy is educated well beyond his level of intelligence." He meant that the person lacked common sense. Common sense can be valuable, but sometimes it does not serve us well. During the 1700s, for example, England faced a substantial increase in crime. In response, the government increased criminal penalties such that even minor criminals, like pickpockets, were executed. The English government was responding to the common-sense notion that increased penalties would deter would be criminals. Did it work? Not really. Crime continued to increase and, in an infamous diary from the time, a pickpocket instructed new pickpockets to focus on victims in public crowds who were paying attention to something else, like the hanging of a convicted pickpocket (Anderson, 2002). So much for common sense.

Finally, we can rely on the media – television, radio, newspapers, and the Internet – to tell us information. Unfortunately, some media sources are biased and/or get the story wrong. And a good portion of media sources do not provide sufficient context. For example, the media has reported that from 2003 to 2009, there were 4,688 American and Allied casualties in the Iraq War. But these sources do not put this figure in context. During the Civil War (1861–1865), 618,000 Americans died. And, on a single day during World War II (D-Day, June 6, 1944), approximately 10,249 American and Allied soldiers died. These comparisons are not intended to diminish the death toll from the Iraq War. But they do suggest that context matters and that the media often miss this point. More often than not, competition between media outlets to 'get the story first' ignores the importance of 'getting the story right.' Below is an example.

Making Research Real 1.1 – The Katrina Crime Wave That Wasn't

In August 2005, a powerful hurricane (Katrina) ravaged the Gulf Coast and all but destroyed large sections of New Orleans, Louisiana. Thousands of people found themselves homeless. Many were provided shelter in mobile homes provided by the U.S. Federal Emergency Management Administration. Even more were displaced to cities, large and small, throughout the nation.

During the evacuation period, Houston, Texas saw its population rise 7 percent as it welcomed nearly a quarter of a million former residents of New Orleans. Almost immediately, Houston police and criminal justice officials began reporting sharp increases in crime, particularly homicides, robberies, and automobile theft. Most of these increases were blamed on individuals displaced by Katrina. The perception that the Katrina evacuees were causing an increase in crime became pervasive in the community, in large part due to extensive media coverage.

In 2010, five researchers decided to investigate these media claims. They evaluated official crime statistics from three cities (Houston, San Antonio, and Phoenix), all of which had received large numbers of Katrina evacuees. For each city, they examined pre- and post-Katrina crime trends in six offense categories: murder, robbery, aggravated assault, rape, burglary, and auto theft. The evidence suggested that crime rates for each of the offenses were more or less the same in each city before and after the relocation of Katrina evacuees (Verano et al., 2010). Only in Houston was there a modest increase in murder and robbery after Katrina evacuees arrived.

In the end, we have good reasons for conducting research. Research involves the systematic process of testing our claims and evaluating our knowledge. When those claims or that knowledge is not supported by evidence, they are discarded and new ideas emerge. Research ensures that the policies and procedures we use to address crime and other social problems are effective. In short, there is just no substitute for good research (see Table 1.1).

Table 1.1 Limitations of the Alternatives to Research

ALTERNATIVES	LIMITATIONS
Authority	Sometimes experts are wrong. Research enables us to be critical of expert opinions and to seek answers for ourselves.
Tradition or custom	Societies change and so do their traditions and customs. Research encourages us to question what we do and why we do it.
Common sense	What makes sense to one person or social group may not make sense to another. Research teaches us to reconsider our assumptions and to reach a consensus on the truth.
Media	Information distributed through the mass media may not be objective, valid, or sensitive to context. Research enables us to identify bias, correct false information, and provide context.

Getting to the Point 1.4 – Relying on authority, tradition or custom, common sense, and the media for accurate knowledge is risky. There is no substitute for good research in the pursuit of reliable knowledge.

WHO DOES RESEARCH?

Everybody does research, not just university professors and lab scientists. If you listen to the morning traffic report before you leave for school to be sure you will not get stuck in traffic, you are doing research. If you decide which movie to see based on the reviews from the newspaper, you are doing research. If you look a professor up using RateMyProfessors.com, you are doing research. We all do research every day. We just do not call it research.

Some people dedicate their professional life to research. In other words, some people get paid to do research! For example, in addition to their teaching and service responsibilities, university professors conduct a great deal of research. Most have a specific research agenda, or a research topic or question that they are interested in learning more about. And they use their research to inform their teaching, such that their students are exposed to current ideas and findings. A few might even use their research to advance an issue that they are passionate about. Most, however, conduct research to maintain their professional status. A university professor's work performance is evaluated, in part, on the basis of how many research papers he or she publishes in scholarly journals.

Other researchers are independent and do research to produce marketable knowledge. For example, many private companies hire researchers, often referred to as consultants, to conduct research and make recommendations. Marketing researchers use focus groups and surveys to test consumer products. Political pollsters measure the public's attitudes about political candidates and issues. Other pollsters conduct public opinion polls on various social issues. The Gallup Organization, for example, has been doing public opinion polls for decades. Organizations like this may work for corporate clients, political candidates, and/or news organizations. Finally, there are numerous think tanks that conduct research, usually to influence legislation or public policy. For example, the RAND (Research ANd Development) Corporation was created by the Douglas Aircraft Company to provide research and analysis for the United States Armed Forces. Over the years, researchers from the RAND Corporation have done research in many other areas, including criminal justice.

By far, the most prolific sponsor of research is the United States Government. Through various research agencies, the federal government provides grants and contracts to researchers to conduct research that informs public policy. Most grants in criminal justice are awarded through the Bureau of Justice Statistics or the Bureau of Justice Assistance, both part of the U.S. Department of Justice. Other government organizations (e.g., the National Science Foundation) provide research grants for thousands of research projects each year. In most cases, researchers are required to produce a final report outlining the results of their research and a copy of the data they collect. These data are cataloged and provided to other researchers interested in similar topics. In addition to funding outside researchers, the United States Government conducts its own research. For example, every 10 years the Bureau of the Census conducts a census of the nation. These data are used to make many important decisions about federal funding and congressional representation. And the Government Accountability Office analyzes how the government spends taxpayer dollars and provides objective, nonpartisan information to Congress.

Getting to the Point 1.5 – All sorts of people conduct research. Some people and organizations conduct research for a living. Anyone who follows a methodological process to produce knowledge is conducting research.

WHAT ARE THE DIFFERENT TYPES OF RESEARCH?

Most research projects can be classified into one of three categories. It is also common for a research project to progress from one category to another over time.

- **Exploratory research** is often necessary when we know very little about a new social trend. In exploratory research, the objective is to find out what is happening. For example, there appears to be an emerging crime trend called human trafficking. Exploratory researchers might ask, "What is human trafficking?" They may devise a working definition of this emerging trend, such as: "Human trafficking is the illegal trade of human beings for the purposes of reproductive slavery, commercial sexual exploitation, forced labor, or a modern-day form of slavery."

- **Descriptive research** documents social conditions or trends. In short, it describes social phenomena. There is little attempt to explain what causes the phenomena. Descriptive research is only interested in what is happening now or what happened in the past. Using the previous example, a descriptive researcher might conduct a survey of women who are victims of human trafficking. In doing so, the researcher might want to know who these women are and how they became victims of this crime. The descriptive researcher might also want to learn where these women are from or when they were placed in captivity.

- **Explanatory research** attempts to find a cause for social trends and phenomena. It goes beyond mere description to pinpoint a cause and effect. Using the previous example, explanatory research might attempt to determine the risk factors associated with becoming a victim of human trafficking. A researcher might ask, "What factors predict whether someone will become a victim of human trafficking?" In answering this question, we might be able to prevent this crime or, at the very least, educate potential victims about it.

In a way, researchers are like journalists. Both professionals gather information in an attempt to arrive at the truth and then report what they have found to a larger audience. Journalists learn that each story should contain the answers to six basic questions – who, what, when, where, why, and how. Researchers ask the same questions, but they seldom answer them in a single research project. Exploratory research always asks *what* but seldom asks *why*. Descriptive research always asks *who*, *when*, *where*, and *how*, but seldom asks *why*. Explanatory research asks *why* but seldom asks *what* because this question has usually been answered previously by researchers (see Table 1.2). Again, these are not hard and fast rules. Variation exists and it is not uncommon to encounter a research project that fits into more than one category.

Table 1.2   Questions Asked by Different Types of Research

PURPOSE	WHO?	WHAT?	WHEN?	WHERE?	WHY?	HOW?
Exploratory	Occasionally	Always	Occasionally	Occasionally	Seldom	Occasionally
Descriptive	Always	Occasionally	Always	Always	Seldom	Always
Explanatory	Occasionally	Seldom	Occasionally	Occasionally	Always	Occasionally

Getting to the Point 1.6 – Research can be classified into three different categories. Exploratory research is often necessary in order to learn about social trends and phenomena that we know very little about. Descriptive research describes social trends and phenomena. Explanatory research attempts to explain or find a cause for social trends and phenomena. Sometimes a research project can have more than one purpose.

Research can also be defined in terms of how the researcher intends for the research to be used. University professors conduct research primarily to expand the body of knowledge about a particular subject or to develop theories about social behavior. Typically, this research is published in scholarly journals and read by other scholars interested in the same topics. We generally refer to this type of research as **pure research**. The purpose of pure research is primarily to expand knowledge of a topic.

Other researchers, like practitioners, consultants, and even some academics conduct research to address and solve a particular social problem. This research is often done for a client, who intends to use the knowledge gained from the research to address a specific issue. Typically, this research is published in reports consumed internally within organizations. We generally refer to this type of research as **applied research**. Although applied researchers often produce knowledge, their primary intent is to address a specific issue or solve a current problem. We'll discuss applied research in more detail in a later chapter.

Some researchers also distinguish between applied research and **action research**. Action research is similar to applied research in that it is focused on problem solving. But action research is distinct in that it involves practitioners (e.g., the police) in research design, implementation, and evaluation. And its purpose is to improve some aspect of practice (e.g., combating gang violence). In action research, a problem is diagnosed; an intervention or strategy is devised; and data is collected to fine tune the intervention strategy.

Note that these are not mutually exclusive categories. The knowledge gained from pure research can later be used to solve a social problem. Likewise, the knowledge gained from applied or action research can later be used to develop new theories. The following hypothetical examples illustrate this point.

Making Research Real 1.2 – The 'Application' of Pure Research

Dr. Joe Smith from Central State University is one of the nation's leading experts on robbery. One afternoon, he hears that a convenience store near his home has been robbed for the fourth time this year. He wonders why that particular convenience store is frequently robbed while another store less than a mile away never seems to have any problems at all. To answer his question, he goes to the state prison and gets permission from the warden to interview convicted convenience store robbers. His research reveals a list of factors that convicted convenience store robbers consider when deciding which stores to rob. This list includes things like store lighting, advertisements on front windows that obscure the view into the store, and the visible presence of security cameras. He publishes his findings in a respected academic journal in an article titled "Factors Affecting the Decision to Rob."

Several years later, the owner of a chain of convenience stores happens to be surfing on the Internet and comes across a copy of Dr. Smith's article. He reads it and sends a copy to the vice president in charge of store security. The vice president thinks the findings have merit and contacts Dr. Smith for further information. Using this pure research, which was originally intended for the academic community, the vice president develops a comprehensive program to protect his convenience stores from being robbed.

Making Research Real 1.3 – The 'Purification' of Applied Research

Captain Ann James was assigned to the Research and Planning Unit of the Metropolitan Police Department. One afternoon, one of the police officers was injured during a high-speed vehicle pursuit. The chief asked Captain James to evaluate the department's vehicle pursuit policy to see if it needed to be revised. As part of her research, Captain James decided to interview the person that was being chased. During the interview, she asked the person why he ran from the police and why he eventually decided to stop. The driver told her that he ran because he knew a warrant had been issued for his arrest on another matter. He told her that he stopped only because he thought he had gotten away. When she asked the driver why he thought he had gotten away, the driver said "Because I didn't see any police cars or hear any sirens."

Captain James wondered whether this comment could be the basis of a new low-speed pursuit policy. She conducted additional interviews with other drivers who had run from the police and got essentially the same answers. Eventually, these findings became the focus of considerable attention among policing scholars who study vehicular pursuits. One of these scholars used Captain James' research to develop a theory he called "The Calculus of the Decision to Run from the Police."

Getting to the Point 1.7 – Research may also be classified in terms of how the researcher intends to use the research. Pure research is conducted primarily to advance theory and to expand the body of knowledge. Applied or action research is conducted primarily to address a specific issue or solve a particular problem. These forms of research are not mutually exclusive. Findings from pure research can be used to solve problems; findings from applied or action research can be used to advance theory.

WHERE IS RESEARCH FOUND?

When you conduct research, you look for information in various places. For example, most of you probably use the Internet and get a lot of information online through sources like Google, Yahoo!News, or Wikipedia. Other popular sources of information include the television, newspapers, and family and friends. Scientists are a little more selective about where they get their information. Academic or **scholarly journals** are probably the most prominent sources of information in the sciences. Journals are used as publishing outlets by university professors and other scholars to communicate their research findings to other researchers. Most are published quarterly or semi-annually. Nearly every academic discipline has its own journal and most have several. Journals like *Criminology*, *Justice Quarterly*, and the *Journal of Criminal Justice* publish research articles on a broad range of criminal justice and criminology issues. Some journals are a bit more specialized. For example, *Police Quarterly* publishes research on policing issues; *Corrections Today* publishes research on correctional issues; and *The Journal of Criminal Justice Education* publishes articles on teaching methods for criminal justice professors.

Most of the articles in scholarly journals are between 20 and 40 pages long and almost all undergo a process known as **peer review**. In the peer review process, research findings are reviewed by experts prior to their publication. Researchers first submit potential articles to a journal's editor. If the subject of the research is consistent with the journal's focus, the editor will send the manuscript to two to five scholars who are knowledgeable about the subject. After one to two months, the reviewers will return the manuscript to the editor with their comments and recommendations. The reviewers are not aware of the author's identity; and the author is not aware of the reviewers' identities. This double blind evaluation process is intended to produce frank comments from reviewers. Based on these comments, the editor will reject the manuscript outright, ask the author to revise and resubmit the article, or accept the article for publication as is. If the manuscript is rejected outright, the author must go through the same process again with another journal. Or, he or she may simply decide not to publish the research. If the author revises and resubmits the manuscript, the original reviewers will have another opportunity to review the revised manuscript. This can take another two months. The process, from original submission to actual publication, can take up to a year or more! Although onerous and time-consuming, the peer review process improves the quality of research and ensures that only good research makes it into the body of knowledge.

Getting to the Point 1.8 – Peer review is a collaborative process whereby researchers who are knowledgeable about a particular subject are asked to review and comment on another researcher's work and recommend whether it should be published.

Research on broader topics may be presented in a research **monograph**, or book. Research monographs are often published by academic publishing companies. Many universities maintain academic publishing programs to provide scholars a means to distribute their research in a longer format than would be allowed by an academic journal. Like scholarly articles, monographs report research findings from a single research project and are subjected to a peer review process. You may have been assigned to read a research monograph for one of your classes. Or you may have seen them in your school's library. Government agencies also publish monographs on research they sponsor through grants and contracts. Monographs published by government agencies, like the U.S. Department of Justice, may be presented in paper bound booklet form. These are typically found in the government documents section of the library. Textbooks are also an excellent source of research, particularly for individuals who know very little about a topic.

Publishing in scholarly venues is essential to the careers of research scholars and university professors. 'Publish or perish' means to publish research in peer-reviewed journals and monographs or risk being denied tenure or promotion; more on that later. Scholarly venues have the most rigorous review process and are generally regarded as the gold standard of scientific research. But scholarly journals and monographs are not widely read. Indeed, the readership for most scholarly journals is generally quite small. For researchers who want to share findings with a wider audience, newspapers, magazines, and trade publications may offer a better publishing outlet. Here is an example from my own personal experience.

Making Research Real 1.4 – Meeting George Kelling

On a regular basis, the College of Criminal Justice at Sam Houston State University invites prominent criminologists to campus to participate in the Beto Lecture Series. This lecture series is named for the late George Beto, who was the Director of the Texas Department of Corrections and a former Dean of the College. While on campus, invited scholars deliver formal and informal lectures and conduct symposia with students and faculty.

The logistics of getting a scholar to the Sam Houston campus in Huntsville, Texas (90 miles north of Houston) are a bit tricky. The closest airport of any size is George H.W. Bush Intercontinental Airport in Houston. Often the Dean will ask one of the Ph.D. students to be scholars' drivers throughout the three days of their campus visit. This includes picking them up at the airport, driving them to the many events on their agenda, and then returning them to Bush International at the appropriate time. As one of those Ph.D. students I always was quick to volunteer because I recognized this as an excellent way to have several hours of uninterrupted time with some of the most important criminal justice scholars. After all, these were the people I had spent many years reading about and I was anxious to put a name with a face.

In April of 1994, the College invited George Kelling. At the time, Dr. Kelling was a Research Fellow at Harvard University. His article, "Broken Windows," which he co-authored with James Q. Wilson, was groundbreaking in criminal justice research. The article suggested that police should focus on small incivilities in order to deter major crime. Given my interest in his work and his prominence, I volunteered to be his driver for the lecture series. On the way back to the airport, I asked Dr. Kelling why he and his co-author chose to publish their article in *The Atlantic*, a magazine, rather than an academic journal. I'll never forget Dr. Kelling's response. "Because at this point in my career I could [care less] about publishing an article in a journal that is read by less than a thousand people. James and I wanted to start a national conversation and share our ideas about policing with a broad audience," he explained.

Dr. Kelling's comment had a major impact on my own publishing outlets. Over the years since, I have looked for opportunities to publish research in magazines, trade publications, and newsletters that are regularly read by policing practitioners. Sometimes I will publish an article in a scholarly journal and then rewrite it for a practitioner audience. The difference in response is remarkable. Sometimes it can take years for another scholar to respond to the version of the research that is published in a scholarly journal. The practitioners respond almost immediately through emails and telephone calls. The greater impact from publishing in more popular sources is clear.

Private corporations also publish research information. Some of this is intended for members of the corporation, but some of it may be widely disseminated. When reading this information, it is important to remember that corporations have a vested interest in the outcome of their research. Corporations are not likely to disseminate a research report that casts the goods it produces or the services it provides in a negative way. Likewise, corporations are quick to disseminate information that makes their products or services look good. Hence, research sponsored by private corporations should be evaluated carefully.

Finally, research can reside hidden away in legislative actions and policy decisions. For example, in 2005, the Kansas Legislature passed a law requiring individuals who are convicted of animal abuse to submit a blood sample to the state's repository of DNA information. Research suggests that many adult serial offenders have a history of animal abuse. Supporters of the law argued that gathering DNA information on animal abusers might help the police identify adult serial murderers or rapists in the future. Criminologists, psychologists, and other scholars familiar with the developmental histories of adult serial offenders testified before Kansas Legislature in support of this bill. Their testimony, documented in the form of written transcripts, can be considered a valuable source of information on research.

In the 'old days,' researchers had to visit libraries, comb through dusty volumes that indexed articles, or leaf through card catalogs to find the information they needed. Not so today, when a quick search through an academic database on the Internet can produce a copy of the article on your computer screen within seconds! One of the most popular websites for criminal justice research is the National Criminal Justice Reference Service, or NCJRS (https://www.ncjrs.gov/). This website is administered by the Department of Justice through its Office of Justice Programs. It is essentially a database of criminal justice research and a great place to begin a literature review. The research contained in the NCJRS tends to be more applied and includes a lot of studies conducted by practitioners and criminal justice agencies. Criminal Justice Abstracts (http://www.ebscohost.com/academic/criminal-justice-abstracts) is another great source of information. Like the NCJRS, it is a database of criminal justice research. But most of the studies in this database are published in academic or scholarly journals. Both databases offer links to full text articles that are likely free through your university's library. Table 1.3 summarizes these common sources of information on criminal justice research.

Table 1.3   Where to Find Research

SOURCE	COMMENT
Academic and scholarly journals	Research is reported in 20–40-page articles. Because research is peer reviewed, other researchers can be reasonably sure that the findings have been rigorously evaluated by experts.
Research monographs	Research is reported in the form of a short book. Often the research is peer reviewed and published by a university publishing house.
Textbooks	Research is presented to a broad audience that does not know a great deal about a particular topic. The research topic is given broad coverage.
Newspapers and magazines	Research is provided in short articles written for a broad audience. Information is up to date and timely, but coverage is typically not in depth due to space limitations. Research is not subjected to peer review.
Trade publications	Research is reported in articles in newsletters and magazines read by criminal justice practitioners. Articles focus on emerging trends in crime and criminal justice practice. Articles are not peer reviewed.
Corporate research reports	Research is presented in reports intended for internal use in the corporation. Information usually pertains to research on new products and services. Typically only research that sheds a positive light on the corporation and its products and services are shared with the public.
Legislative actions and policy decisions	Research is presented in the form of comments and testimony made by policy makers, experts, and the public. This information can be difficult to find, but can provide insight into particular topics.
Databases	Individual research studies are indexed and referenced in online databases. Researchers use search terms to look for research on particular topics using these databases. Searches provide a list of citations, abstracts, and/or full-text articles.

Getting to the Point 1.9 – Research can be found in academic journals, books, newspapers, magazines, legislative actions, policy decisions, and databases. Some of this information is more objective and accurate than others.

HOW IS RESEARCH USED?

Our goal as researchers is to constantly contribute to a body of knowledge that evolves over time. So one of the primary uses of research is to understand and contribute to the body of knowledge. The existing body of knowledge is often described in a literature review, which is basically a summary of what is known about a particular research topic. Researchers write literature reviews to review the work of previous researchers, develop an understanding of a topic, and identify opportunities for further study. Ideally, they will add findings from their own research to this 'conversation' or body of knowledge. Again, research that is conducted to contribute to the body of knowledge is known as pure research.

When it takes the form of pure research, research helps to establish a scholar's professional credentials. Newly hired assistant professors typically have four to six years to establish their teaching qualifications, perform service to the university and publish their research in peer-reviewed journals and books. At the end of this time, their work is reviewed by a tenure and promotion committee, which evaluates the professor's work and decides whether he or she should be granted tenure and/or promoted to the rank of associate professor. If the professor is granted tenure, he or she can be reasonably assured of continued employment at the university. If not, the professor is given one year to find another job and leave the university. If promoted to associate professor, professors spend the next four to five years establishing more teaching, service, and research credentials to be promoted to full professor. In these tenure and promotion evaluations, research is considered a central factor in a professor's professional credentials. Even researchers who are employed by consulting firms will use research to establish their professional stature and as a basis for promotion.

Research is also conducted to decide particular court cases, inform policy decisions, or address social problems. Again, this type of research is generally referred to as applied research. For example, in 1994, State Superior Court Judge Robert Francis (New Jersey) asked Dr. John Lamberth, formerly of Temple University, to conduct a study on traffic stops by the New Jersey State Police. The state police had been accused of racial profiling by a group of African American and Hispanic drivers. Dr. Lamberth's research convinced the court that the state police had in fact targeted African American and Hispanic drivers for stops in an effort to identify drug couriers traveling on Interstate Highway 95. Eventually, the case was settled (*State of New Jersey v. Pedro Soto*, 734 A.2d 350, 1996) and the judge ordered that the routine operations of the New Jersey State Police be supervised by the court for a decade (Lamberth, 1996). Lamberth's study was the first full-scale racial profiling study ever conducted.

Finally, research is often used by organizations to develop new products or services, advance a social or political agenda, and/or to improve some aspect of professional practice. Criminal justice agencies, for example, change their policies and practices in accordance with new research findings. In one such instance, the Texas

Department of Public Safety (DPS) issued revolvers to its troopers until the mid-1980s since revolvers were more durable and more reliable than automatic pistols. But when technological improvements in automatic pistols were made, the DPS conducted a study of the relative functionality of revolvers versus automatic pistols. Researchers within the DPS interviewed hundreds of troopers and the manufacturers, conducted numerous functionality and durability tests, evaluated the training requirements for both types of weapons, and completed a cost/benefit analysis. In the end, they recommended that the DPS replace its current .357 revolver with a 9mm, 10mm or .45 caliber automatic pistol manufactured by Sig Sauer (Link, McNelly, and Withrow, 1989). Again, when using evidence to develop a set of 'best practices' for use in a criminal justice setting, practitioners and researchers are engaging in a type of research known as action research.

> **Getting to the Point 1.10** – Researchers conduct research to expand the body of knowledge, establish professional credentials, inform legal and policy decisions, address social problems, develop new products or services, advance social or political agendas, and improve professional practice.

WHEN IS RESEARCH IMPORTANT?

If you ask a university professor, "When is research important?" he or she will likely tell you that research is always important. To a university professor, research is the foundation upon which we create additional knowledge. Without this foundation, we would be forced to recreate the same knowledge over and over and we would never expand the body of knowledge. There are, however, times when research becomes *critically* important. For example, during the 1990s, methamphetamine use spread throughout the American West and Midwest. Rural areas with limited policing resources and unfettered access to the chemicals needed for methamphetamine production encouraged this trend. Police departments began to meet and confer regularly to share their experience and knowledge about this growing trend. They developed specialized units to detect and seize clandestine meth labs and they encouraged many states to pass legislation restricting the sale of over-the-counter drugs used in methamphetamine production. In this case, police officers and policing leaders were researchers; they recognized a new trend, shared information about the problem, and developed effective strategies in response.

Research is also critically important when resources are few and demands are many. Policy makers have limited funding for social and economic programs and they want to be sure to get the most out of every dollar they have available. The most effective way to make use of limited resources is to conduct research and make sure those resources are being put to good use. For example, what is the most effective strategy for reducing drunk driving? Should we spend more money on sobriety checkpoints, treatment programs, or educational campaigns? Each program is effective in its own way, but which of these is the *most* effective? Only a competent research project can determine this. Collecting evidence and conducting cost–benefit analyses can help determine which strategies and programs actually work.

Finally, research is critical during times of political instability and conflict. Ideally, policy decisions should not be swayed by political interests or ideologies. Unfortunately, in criminal justice, they often are. Research can cut through the political ideologies and help policy makers make informed decisions. For example, the trend in politics is to 'get tough on crime.' Political candidates who appear tough on crime win political points and boost their ratings. But how effective are 'tough' crime measures? For example, do three strikes laws really reduce crime or do they just fill up prisons? During times of intense political pressure, responsible criminal justice administrators rely on independent research to temper political debate and make decisions without the distracting burdens of political grandstanding.

Getting to the Point 1.11 – Research is the foundation upon which we expand the body of knowledge. Research is also important when we want to respond to critical social problems, allocate limited resources wisely, and base policy decisions on evidence rather than ideology.

FINAL THOUGHTS

You might think that after more than a century of research, we would know why people commit crime and what to do about it. For sure, we know more now than we have ever known. But there are still far more questions than answers. As a criminal justice professional with a Bachelor's degree, you may find yourself in a position to answer some of these questions using the skills and concepts introduced in this book. Thirty years ago, I was in your shoes, reading about crime in the abstract. And suddenly, there I was, in a professional policing career, being asked to evaluate policing programs and to explain how I intended to reduce crime more effectively.

There is for you, more so than there was for me, another reason to learn about research methods. When I started out as a criminal justice practitioner, there were very few computers. Information gathering was arduous and time consuming. If you wanted to know a suspect's criminal history, you had to request it, via teletype, from another person at a central repository. There were no cell phones, websites, fax machines, or emails. A lot has changed. You have access to a mind-numbing amount of information. Some of this information is useful and accurate, some of it is not. The purpose of this book and this class is to help you develop the skills to do good research, to sift through all that information at your fingertips, and to distinguish the good information from the bad.

GETTING TO THE POINT/CHAPTER SUMMARY

- Research methods are the tools, techniques, and procedures that researchers use to ask and answer questions.

- As a verb, 'research' means to follow a logical process that uses concepts, principles, and techniques to produce knowledge. As a noun, 'research' is a collection of information that represents what we know about a particular topic.

- Research in the social sciences is more challenging than in the physical sciences because the concepts that social scientists study are more difficult to measure and the findings that social scientists produce are more difficult to interpret.

- Relying on authority, tradition or custom, common sense, and the media for accurate knowledge is risky. There is no substitute for good research in the pursuit of reliable knowledge.

- All sorts of people conduct research. Some people and organizations conduct research for a living. Anyone who follows a methodological process to produce knowledge is conducting research.

- Research can be classified into three different categories. Exploratory research is often necessary in order to learn about social trends and phenomena that we know very little about. Descriptive research describes social trends and phenomena. Explanatory research attempts to explain or find a cause for social trends and phenomena. Sometimes a research project can have more than one purpose.

- Research may also be classified in terms of how the researcher intends to use the research. Pure research is conducted primarily to advance theory and to expand the body of knowledge. Applied or action research is conducted primarily to address a specific issue or solve a particular problem. These forms of research are not mutually exclusive. Findings from pure research can be used to solve problems; findings from applied or action research can be used to advance theory.

- Peer review is a collaborative process whereby researchers who are knowledgeable about a particular subject are asked to review and comment on another researcher's work and recommend whether it should be published.

- Research can be found in academic journals, books, newspapers, magazines, legislative actions, policy decisions, and databases. Some of this information is more objective and accurate than others.

- Researchers conduct research to expand the body of knowledge, establish professional credentials, inform legal and policy decisions, address social problems, develop new products or services, advance social or political agendas, and improve professional practice.

- Research is the foundation upon which we expand the body of knowledge. Research is also important when we want to respond to critical social problems, allocate limited resources wisely, and base policy decisions on evidence rather than ideology.

CHAPTER EXERCISES

The following chapter exercises are organized into two parts. The first part consists of questions that can be answered using the information from this chapter. This section will test your understanding of the chapter material. The second part consists of research application exercises. These exercises require you to apply what you have learned thus far.

CHAPTER REVIEW QUESTIONS

Respond to each of the following questions using the information from this chapter.

1. During a recent meeting of the command staff at a mid-sized police department, the chief asks the patrol captain for his recommendation for new flashlights. The captain responds, "I did a little research and I recommend that we purchase the DryLight, Model X flashlight." The patrol captain's research consisted of "asking a few of the officers" what they thought would be a good flashlight. Did the patrol captain actually conduct research? Why or why not?

2. Respond to the following statement in three to five sentences:

    Conducting research in the social sciences and in criminal justice in particular is easier than in other sciences because the things we measure are so vague that nobody really cares if we get it right or not.

3. Read the following scenarios and identify which of the following alternative sources of information is being used:
    a.   Authority
    b.   Tradition or custom
    c.   Common sense
    d.   Media

Scenario	Source of information
The City of Bigton is having a problem with graffiti. The Mayor decides that the only way to reduce graffiti is to increase the penalty. The City Council agrees and increases the penalty. However, incidents of graffiti continue to increase.	
A state senator is making a speech before the legislature and declares, "Racial profiling is an epidemic throughout our state." When asked to provide proof of this statement, the senator points to a large folder full of newspaper and magazine articles on racial profiling.	
Frustrated with the new intake process, a probation officer complains to her boss. "It just doesn't make sense." The supervisor encourages the	

probation officer to "give the new system a chance" because "after all, it was designed by the leading expert on juvenile probation in the nation."	
A recent proposal by the Bigton Police Department is to not dispatch officers to take stolen vehicle reports. Instead the vehicle owner would enter the appropriate information into an online system and get the case number needed to file an insurance claim. The City Manager rejects the proposal, arguing, "The good people of Bigton deserve a living and breathing police officer when they call one."	

4. Classify the following research proposals into one of the following research categories:
   a. Exploratory
   b. Descriptive
   c. Explanatory

Research proposal	Purpose
The Chief Probation Officer has asked one of his assistants to conduct an analysis of the probationers under the supervision of the Probation Department. The Chief wants to know basic information about the probationers, such as age, gender, criminal history, and length of probation.	
Recently, a dozen correctional officers were dismissed for participating in a drug and contraband smuggling conspiracy. The warden has asked a consultant to conduct research that would provide insight into why these officers were led to participate in this conspiracy.	
The Captain of the Narcotics Unit in a large metropolitan police department hears that prescription drug abuse is growing among juveniles in her city. She asks one of her lieutenants to conduct research to determine the extent of this new trend.	

5. A researcher conducts research for the initial purpose of explaining the linkages between illegal drug use and risky sexual behaviors among adolescents. This researcher is merely interested in this topic and hopes to publish this research report in an academic journal. What type of research is this? Explain your answer.
   a. Pure research
   b. Applied research

6. A program at a local high school is designed to reduce illegal drug use among adolescents. The school board has asked a researcher to evaluate the effectiveness of the program. What type of research is this? Explain your answer.
   a. Pure research
   b. Applied research

7. Your professor has assigned a research paper. The references for this paper must come from "peer-reviewed" research articles. Where would you find these articles?

8. You have been asked to make a presentation on a subject that you know very little about. What source(s) would you consult to obtain a general overview of the subject? Explain your answer.

RESEARCH APPLICATION EXERCISES

Access to the following articles will be provided by your instructor.

> Chappell, A.T., Monk-Turner, E. and Payne, B.K. (2011). Broken windows or window breaker: The influence of physical and social disorder on quality of life. *Justice Quarterly, 28*(3), 522–540.
>
> Reisig, M.D. and Parks, R.B. (2000). Experience, quality of life, and neighborhood context: A hierarchical analysis of satisfaction with police. *Justice Quarterly, 17*(3), 607–620.

9. Read both articles and write a critique of the research. Your critique should respond to the questions below.
   a. What was the researchers' objective in conducting this research? In other words, what did they hope to learn?
   b. Would you classify this research as exploratory, descriptive, or explanatory? Would you classify it as pure or applied? Explain your answers.
   c. To what extent has this topic been studied by previous researchers?
   d. How did the researchers gather their data for this article?
   e. What kind of data did the researchers gather for this study?
   f. What are the researchers' findings?
   g. Did the researchers achieve their research objective(s)? Why or why not?
   h. How did these researchers add to the body of knowledge on this subject?
   i. How might this research affect the practice of criminal justice?
   j. How would you improve this research and/or conduct additional research to further expand the body of knowledge on this subject?

10. After completing your research critique, attach a cover page with your name on it and turn it in to your professor. Do not include your name anywhere else on the paper. Your professor will remove the cover page and assign a unique number to your paper so that your identity will be protected. Then, they will ask one of your classmates to review it. As part of this exercise, you

will also review the research critique of one of your classmates. Write a brief peer review of your classmate's critique that responds to the questions below.

a. Does the critique address all the questions in the exercise?

b. Does the author of the critique respond accurately to each question? If not, which questions did he or she not answer accurately and why?

c. Did the author of the critique omit any important information? If so, what information did he or she omit?

d. Is the author's critique well argued? If not, what could he or she have done better?

e. Overall, do you believe the author does an adequate job of critiquing the research article?

CHAPTER 2

The Research Process

Sometimes, during my office hours, one of my students will point to the badge displayed on the wall and ask, "Do you ever miss being a cop?" I have a standard answer: "I miss the camaraderie among police officers. But I don't miss witnessing the tragedy of crime. In many ways, being a professor isn't all that different from being a police officer. Conducting research is just like conducting a criminal investigation. And I like to think that my research, like my job as a police officer, makes us safer." The similarities underlying research and policing are apparent in the true story below.

Making Research Real 2.1 – The Closest Thing to Sherlock Holmes

Pierce Brooks joined the Los Angeles Police Department (LAPD) in 1948. Brooks is famous for leading the investigation that eventually became the story line for James Wambaugh's *The Onion Field*, a book and later a film about the kidnapping of two plainclothes LAPD officers and the subsequent murder of Officer Ian James Campbell. But Brooks' contributions to American policing go far beyond his work in the LAPD.

As a homicide detective, Brooks was assigned a case that at first seemed routine. But something about the case led Brooks to believe that the offender had killed before. Shortly thereafter, he was assigned an unrelated case that struck him the same way. He decided to see if he could connect other homicides to these cases. He spent countless hours reading newspaper articles in the Los Angeles Public Library and traveled to other libraries looking for similar cases. This was before the Internet, so his task was difficult. Eventually, he found a connection between one of his cases and another murder. He matched fingerprints from both crime scenes and eventually identified a suspect (Crime Library, 2012).

Roy Hazelwood, who later became a famous criminal profiler, recognized the value of Brooks' investigative technique and suggested the creation of a central repository for unsolved serial crimes. Congressional hearings were conducted wherein experts testified that if local agencies had shared information, lives could have been saved. One of the experts, true crime writer Ann Rule, estimated that a central repository might have saved as many as 15 of the 30 women Ted Bundy murdered in seven states from 1974 to 1978 (Crime Library, 2012).

Eventually, the Federal Bureau of Investigation created a program called the Violent Criminal Apprehension Program (VICAP), which encourages local police agencies to share information about unsolved violent crimes. Brooks was its first director. When a local agency submits a case, the VICAP staff compares features of the case with other violent crimes. If they find similar modus operandi or evidence, they contact the interested departments and encourage them to share investigative information. Today, the staff at VICAP uses the latest computer technology and data mining software to do, in minutes, what it took Brooks months to do when he was a homicide investigator. Brooks passed away in 1998. Dan Browser, a retired LAPD detective who had been Pierce's partner for nearly 20 years said of him, "He was the closest thing I ever saw to Sherlock Holmes" (*San Francisco Chronicle*, 1998).

What is the actual process by which investigators like Brooks and professors like me research particular issues and topics? This chapter provides an overview. Later chapters will provide more information about each step in the research process. Here, I just provide a brief description. Before reviewing each step of the research process, we will discuss the objectives and characteristics of the research process.

OBJECTIVES OF THE RESEARCH PROCESS

The **research process** is a set of specific steps that, when done correctly, produce data. Researchers use data to produce information, what we call findings, to share with other researchers and criminal justice practitioners and policy makers. The research process has four overall objectives. The first is to answer a research question or set of research questions. A research question can be as simple as deciding what restaurant to visit. A simple check of a restaurant's published reviews on the internet provides the information (data) necessary to make this decision. In academic research, research questions tend to be a little more complicated, such as determining the cause of criminal behavior.

The second objective of the research process is to resolve disagreements among researchers. Equally competent researchers may look at the same set of facts and reach very different conclusions. Likewise, equally qualified researchers may measure social phenomena differently. Subsequent researchers may attempt to resolve these differences through additional research. The aim of subsequent researchers is not necessarily to determine who is right. Instead, they attempt to clarify how the differences came about and get us closer to the truth.

The research process also has the objective of filling gaps within the body of knowledge. No single research project produces all the answers. For example, the findings from one research project may shed light on the motivations of adult male serial killers, but not adult female serial killers. Therefore, subsequent research might want to fill this gap by focusing on the motivations of adult female serial killers. Each research project builds off previous research by targeting a different population or a different aspect of the problem.

The fourth and final objective of research is to produce more research questions. This may sound strange. Presumably, the point of research is to answer questions, not ask them. But we cannot hope to explain everything through one

study alone. We can only hope to explain bits of things. We rely on other researchers to do the same, such that we all contribute to the body of knowledge. Part of the
research process is asking additional questions such that subsequent researchers can
help put the pieces of a larger puzzle into place.

Getting to the Point 2.1 – The objectives of research are to answer research questions, to resolve disagreements among researchers, to fill gaps within the body of knowledge, and to produce more research
questions.

STEPS OF THE RESEARCH PROCESS

Figure 2.1 depicts the research process as a set of ten steps. As depicted here, it is
generally linear. By this, I mean that the steps are usually completed in a certain
order. The research process always starts when a researcher asks a research question. Then, the researcher goes to the literature to find out what we already know
about the subject. The next five steps culminate in the design of the method used
to answer the research question.

Between the literature review (step 2) and the method design (step 6), the
research process is internally cyclical. By this, I mean that the steps may be revis-
ited as researchers experiment with different ideas. For example, after the creating
measures (step 5), a researcher may determine that the measures do not adequately
capture the essence of the researcher's conceptual definitions. In this case, the
researcher may need to redefine his or her concepts (step 4) or go all the way back
to the literature review (step 2) for guidance.

The research process is also externally cyclical. By this, I mean that the research
process is on-going. A particular project may end when the findings are communicated (step 10), but begins again as researchers ask new questions. Good research
always produces additional questions and the need for additional research. For
example, during the 1930s, Clifford Shaw and Henry McKay conducted sociological
studies of Chicago (Shaw and McKay, 1942). Among other things, they identified
distinctive zones within the city. One zone was where the factories were located.
Another zone was where the men and women that worked in the factories lived.
The most important zone to their research was what they called the zone of transition. This zone was where most crime and other social problems existed. Their work
led to the creation of a new criminological theory called social disorganization. Following the work of Shaw and McKay, the automobile became more affordable and
the interstate highway system expanded. As such, factory workers could live far-
ther away from where they worked. This resulted in a change in how Chicago was
socially organized, compelling subsequent researchers to reevaluate the social disorganization theory (Bursik, 1988). Today, we commonly find that crime patterns
happen along major traffic thoroughfares rather than within transition zones.

Getting to the Point 2.2 – The research process is characteristically linear in that the steps must be completed in a certain order. However, the process is also internally cyclical, because researchers often have to revisit previous steps, and externally cyclical, because good research leads to additional research questions.

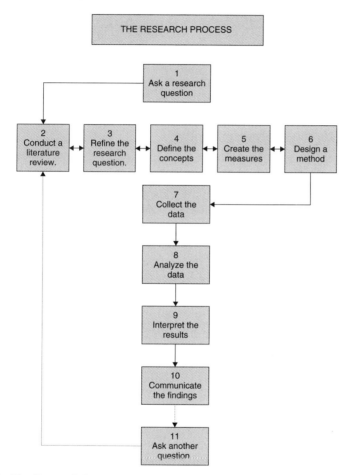

Figure 2.1 The Research Process

Step 1: Ask a Research Question

The research process begins with a question, but not just any question. **Research questions** are interrogative. This means that they are actual questions that can be answered, not statements that make some claim. For example, the statement, *"The best way to combat crime is to lock up criminals and throw away the key!"* is not a question. It is a claim about the best way to combat crime. A better research question might be: *"Do longer prison terms deter people from committing crimes?"*

Research questions often begin with casual observations or mere curiosities. For example, a researcher may observe that most of the individuals that are booked into the county jail are male. From this observation, the researcher may become curious about why males are arrested more frequently than females. Do males commit more crime than females? Are police officers more likely to arrest males than females? Do males commit the kinds of crimes that are most likely to be observed by the police? All of these questions came from a single observation.

Getting to the Point 2.3 – Research questions should be actual questions that can be answered rather than statements that make some claim.

Step 2: Conduct a Literature Review

In social science, we *search* for answers. But we do so through a process of *re*-search. The prefix 're-' in the word 'research' communicates the natural repetitiveness of the research process. Finding out what we already know and do not know about a particular research topic is an essential task of the researcher. Hence, the second step of the research process is conducting the **literature review**, which involves locating and understanding what previous researchers have learned about a topic. The literature review reveals gaps in the body of knowledge, areas of disagreement among researchers, and remaining questions that need to be answered. It can also provide tips on effective methods for conducting research. In general, the literature review helps fine tune our research question by ensuring that we are not asking a question that has already been asked and answered.

Generally speaking, there are five sources of information that researchers draw upon during the literature review process. Each source has advantages and disadvantages. Books are great sources if you are unfamiliar with a topic. But because they take years to produce, the information might be outdated. Scholarly articles are timelier, but because editors limit them to 30 or 40 pages, authors do not always have enough room to fully discuss the topic. Newspapers and magazines provide even timelier information, but they often do not contain enough details about how the information was gathered. As such, we cannot assume that the information is objective or reliable. The Internet provides probably the timeliest information, but it is often difficult to determine a website's objectivity and accuracy. Finally, experts are a great source for information, but some experts may have a professional bias. For example, you may see a seemingly objective report on the Internet written by a former chief of police claiming that a particular anti-theft device is "the only effective way to be sure you car does not get stolen." It may appear legitimate but you might also learn that this former chief of police actually works as a paid spokesman for the company that makes these devices. Table 2.1 summarizes the advantages and disadvantages of these commonly used sources. Scholars and practitioners generally draw on a combination of all five sources of information when conducting a literature review.

Table 2.1 Advantages and Disadvantages of Commonly Used Literature Review Sources

SOURCES	ADVANTAGES	DISADVANTAGES
Books	Books provide good background information on a topic for researchers who are unfamiliar with a topic.	Even newly published books may contain information that is several years old.
Scholarly journals	Scholarly journals provide objective, reliable, and more current information than books.	Topic coverage is narrower and limited due to space constraints.
Newspapers and magazines	Newspapers and magazines provide timely and accessible information.	Information on methodology is often missing. Hence the information may not be objective or reliable.
Internet sources	Internet sources provide timely and accessible information.	Information may not be objective or accurate.
Experts	Experts provide practical and timely information.	Experts may be biased.

Pyramiding is an effective technique for locating research and determining when you have enough information. Here is how it works. Say you go to the library and find four good articles or books that are relevant to your topic. You take copies of these sources home with you and glean from them the information you want to include in your literature review. This information may be in the form of quotes, findings, statistics, definitions, or anything else you want to borrow and cite. Then, you look at the bibliographies, reference pages, or footnotes included in your four sources. Chances are you will locate additional sources cited here that are relevant to your research. Even if you only find one additional source in each of the original four articles or books, you have doubled your sources. You may then go back to the library or Internet to locate these new sources and consider including them in your literature review. Then, the process begins again by looking at the references cited in this second set of sources. Ethics demand that you actually procure a copy of each source, read it, and attribute it accurately. It is not acceptable to simply use another researcher's interpretation of or reference to another person's research. So take the time to hunt down each source and review it for inclusion in your literature review.

The literature review process can take weeks, even months, to complete. Indeed, locating, collecting, reading, and incorporating previously published research into your own literature review is tedious and time consuming. So how do you know when you are done? If a particular article or book is repeatedly cited by others, it is a good sign that it is critical to the literature and that it should be included in your literature review. For example, researchers interested in TASERs might find that Geoffrey Alpert and Howard Williams have written a lot on this topic (see, for example, Alpert et al., 2011 and Williams, 2008). In fact, both of these researchers are cited frequently by nearly all other researchers. Incorporating the research by these authors in your own literature review provides some assurance that you have located the most important studies in your literature review. Once you stop seeing new repeatedly cited works, you will know your literature review is relatively complete.

Note that sometimes the literature review process provides the necessary information to answer your research questions. For example, a police officer assigned to develop a new policy on high-speed vehicular pursuits may find enough guidance in the literature review to inform his or her department's policy on this issue. If so, then it makes little sense to conduct additional research. The existing research must meet the following criteria to be useful in this regard:

- it must be credible;
- it must be timely;
- it must have been conducted in a similar context; and
- it must use an acceptable research method.

If there is little to no credible research that already exists on your topic, you would be well served to go out and conduct research yourself. Research credibility is best determined by the objectivity of the researcher and the use of a peer review process. Research that is done by a person disinterested in its outcome is far more credible than research done by a researcher interested in advocating for a particular perspective. In addition, research that is submitted to a rigorous peer review process is usually considered credible. The peer review process has a way of either eliminating or improving poorly done and biased research.

Outdated research is another good reason to go out and conduct your own research. For example, over the past two decades we have seen dramatic changes in how police officers work. Hence, research on police procedures conducted 20 years ago is not timely. This is not to say that older research is completely irrelevant. James Q. Wilson's *Varieties of Police Behavior* was originally published in 1968, but it continues to influence policing today because of the way it describes how police officers approach their duties. But if most of the research is outdated, you have every reason to suspect that circumstances have changed enough to warrant a fresh look at the phenomenon.

Another good reason to move beyond the literature review stage and conduct your own research is if the existing research focuses on a context that is unique or substantially different from the one you are interested in studying. Research on a high-speed vehicular pursuit policy for a rural police department might not be relevant to an urban police department. If the research was limited to a particular locality, region, or country and you have reason to suspect that this location is fundamentally different from the location in which you are interested, further research is warranted.

Finally, before accepting research as valid and useful, it is important to evaluate the researcher's methodology. Was the sample collected randomly? Did the previous researcher define and measure the variables appropriately? Does the interpretation of the results make sense? Again, if there are methodological problems, your best bet might be to conduct your own study. But if the information is credible and gathered reliably, you can stop at the literature review. There is no real need for further investigation.

> **Getting to the Point 2.4** – The literature review involves locating and understanding what previous researchers have learned about a topic. Researchers rely on several sources in this regard, including books, scholarly journals, newspapers and magazines, Internet sources, and experts. If the existing literature is credible, timely, context appropriate, and methodologically sound, there is no need to move past the literature review stage; the research question may be answered through the literature review alone.

Step 3: Refine the Research Question

As researchers conduct a literature review and learn what other researchers have discovered about a particular topic, they may refine their research question and begin to develop possible answers. For example, we may begin with the research question *"Does the availability of afterschool programs reduce juvenile delinquency?"* We find that many good studies on this exact same question have been conducted. But we also find that almost all the research has been conducted in urban areas. So we could refine the question and ask, *"Does the availability of afterschool programs reduce juvenile delinquency in suburban areas?"* or *"Is the relationship between afterschool programs and juvenile delinquency in suburban areas the same as the relationship found in urban areas?"* Our literature review helps us identify gaps and inconsistencies in the body of knowledge and this, in turn, helps us refine our research question.

Once we have settled on our research question, we need to develop some expectations about what the data might reveal regarding this question. In other words, we need to propose some possible answers to the question. Rather than merely guess what those answers might be, we look for theories that might give us possible answers. A **theory** is a statement, or set of statements, that attempts to explain the social world. Once we have our theory, we can develop a **hypothesis**, or a statement that predicts the answer to our research question. Consider the hypothetical example below.

Making Research Real 2.2 – Becoming a Cop

Subcultures exist in many professions. Physicians, lawyers, and professors, for example, tend to behave similarly and conform to the same standards of conduct within their professions. To the extent that police officers do the same thing, we can speak of a police subculture. Police officers, by and large, tend to act a certain way. And this may be due to the demands of the profession or to the personality types of individuals who are attracted to the policing profession. Either way, there is a process by which individuals new to the profession internalize the social norms of the policing profession. A researcher interested in this process may develop the following theory:

Understanding and adopting the norms of the policing subculture is related to long-term success in the policing profession.

To test this theory, the researcher may want to conduct interviews with newly hired police officers during the first years of their employment. The objective of this research would be to measure the extent to which these officers assimilate into the policing subculture. During the process of designing this research project, the researcher might develop the following hypothesis:

Individuals new to the policing profession who successfully adopt the norms of the policing subculture will be more likely to experience long-term professional success.

During the research process, the researcher will gather data to test the accuracy of this hypothesis. If the data supports this prediction, the theory will be confirmed.

Getting to the Point 2.5 – The literature review process helps researchers refine their research question, identify a theory related to their research question, and propose a hypothesis that predicts the answer to their research question.

Step 4: Define the Concepts

So we have our research question and we have formulated our research hypothesis. Now we need to figure out a way to test this hypothesis. Consider the research hypothesis that impoverished neighborhoods will have higher crime rates. How can we actually test this? To begin, we need to define what we mean by 'impoverished neighborhood' and 'crime rate.' These definitions will eventually determine how we measure impoverishment and crime at the neighborhood level. The first stage of this process is called conceptualization. **Conceptualization** is a process by which researchers define the concepts in their hypotheses.

Conceptualization can be quite difficult in social science research. A physicist has the luxury of precise measurement. A pound of force is a pound of force. Social scientists are not so fortunate. Though it may be relatively easy to measure something like level of education, it is much more difficult to measure something like neighborhood satisfaction. Different social scientists will define these concepts in different ways. And that is acceptable. The key is to be as precise as possible and to communicate our definitions at the outset of our study. Here is a hypothetical example.

Making Research Real 2.3 – Conceptualizing Juvenile Crime

A researcher wants to study juvenile crime. At some point, early in the process, she must define the concept of 'juvenile crime.' In a sense, there are two concepts to define: 'juvenile' and 'crime.' Developing a conceptual definition for 'juvenile' is relatively easy. The researcher may define a juvenile as any person who is less than 18 years of age. Because most states do not charge children less than eight years of age with a crime, the researcher may want to be even more precise, defining a juvenile as any person who is between 8 and 17 years of age.

Defining 'crime' is more difficult. Does the researcher mean reported crime? What about crimes that were committed but undetected? Does the researcher include status offenses, which are behaviors that are only illegal when committed by a juvenile, such as a curfew violation? Should violations of school rules count as 'crimes'? The researcher must settle on some definition before moving forward with the research. In this case, she uses the following definition for 'juvenile crime':

Any behavior committed by an individual between the ages of 8 and 17 years old resulting in a conviction for a criminal offense punishable by a fine, a sentence to jail, or term of imprisonment in a juvenile detention facility.

You may disagree with this researcher's conceptual definition. And, indeed, researchers often disagree with one another's conceptual definitions. But as long as researchers clearly define their concepts and do not overreach their conclusions, the conceptual definition is what the researcher says it is. The conceptualization stage is one of the few times when a researcher gets to be the decider.

Getting to the Point 2.6 – Conceptualization is a process by which researchers define the concepts in their hypotheses. These definitions are important because they determine how researchers actually measure the concepts they use in their research.

Step 5: Create the Measures

Once the conceptual definitions have been developed, the researcher must decide on the best way to actually measure the concepts. We call this process **operationalization**. Here is an example of operationalization.

Making Research Real 2.4 – How Religious Are You?

A researcher wants to measure how religious people are. He refers to this variable as 'religiosity' and conceptually defines it as "the extent to which an individual's behavior is affected by the practices and precepts of his or her religious tradition." Many religions require regular attendance at worship services, so the frequency of attending worship services would measure one part of this concept. Some religions have dietary restrictions, so the extent to which a person desists from eating certain types of foods or eating any food at all during fasting periods would measure another dimension of this concept. Some religions require their members to dress a certain way, not work on certain days, avoid alcoholic beverages, and not cut their hair. The extent to which a person follows each of these practices would help us measure various dimensions of religiosity.

You can see how complicated measuring religiosity might become. It is likely that the researcher will have to ask several questions in order to fully measure this concept. Furthermore, in order to completely measure an individual's adherence to his or her religious traditions, the researcher must know a great deal about the precepts of various religions.

Getting to the Point 2.7 – Operationalization is the process by which researchers decide on how they are going to measure their concepts as they have defined them. Often it is necessary to measure concepts along multiple dimensions.

Step 6: Design a Method

Remember that research is both a process and a product. As a process, research is about creating a method by which data can be collected and analyzed to respond to a question. Detailed information on the commonly used research methods in the social sciences is included in Chapters 9 through 13. Surveys, for example, are a common social research method. You have likely received a survey in your mail. Surveys can also be delivered over the telephone, on the Internet, and through person-to-person interviews. Experiments are another possible research method. They allow a researcher to control all factors that might influence an outcome and therefore isolate the effect of a single factor. In some types of research, researchers observe people and organizations in their natural environment. The list goes on and on.

There is no 'best way' to conduct research. The best method for one research project may fail miserably in another. Researchers generally pick a method that will answer their research question, work well in their research setting, and prove feasible and realistic given time and money constraints. Once the decision has been made as to which research method to use, it is the responsibility of the researcher to design it to meet his or her specific needs. The chapters in Part Three of this textbook outline in detail the processes by which many of the commonly used social research methods are developed.

Things can go wrong in research and it is nearly impossible to predict the problems that might arise. Therefore, before an actual research method is used for collecting data, many researchers pre-test their methods. For example, a researcher who has decided to use a survey to collect data may find that some questions do not work well. Maybe it is the researcher's choice of words or maybe it is the instructions, but the questions may not produce the information that is needed. Pre-testing surveys on a small group of people will help researchers discover these problems before the actual survey is distributed. The following hypothetical vignette illustrates this point.

Making Research Real 2.5 – When it All Fell Down for Professor Brown

Professor Brown is interested in the correlation between learning disabilities and delinquency among juveniles. He hypothesizes that juveniles who are diagnosed with attention deficit disorder, hyperactivity, dyslexia, and other learning disabilities are more likely to become delinquent. He observes that children with learning disabilities tend to have lower grades in reading and arithmetic. So he uses the students' grades on the latest state standardized test as a proxy for having a learning disability. In other words, instead of determining if a student has a learning disability, Professor Brown defines students with low standardized test scores as learning disabled. He then assesses whether students have committed a delinquent act in the past year and uses this as his measure of delinquency. He finds no correlation between learning disabilities and delinquency.

Where did Professor Brown go wrong? Well, for starters, his measure was not consistent with his conceptual definition. What Professor Brown did not know was that students diagnosed with learning disabilities are allowed numerous testing accommodations, such as extra time for standardized tests. So, a student with a learning disability could have performed well on the standardized test despite a disability. In the end, all the data that Professor Brown collected could not and did not answer his research question. Had he pre-tested his questionnaire on a small group of students, he might have identified these problems and fixed them before it was too late.

Getting to the Point 2.8 – Researchers should pre-test their method to be sure that the research method(s) they use will produce the data necessary to actually answer their research question(s).

Step 7: Collect the Data

At this stage, you want to implement the research method you have selected and follow through on collecting your data. The type of data collection you do depends on the actual method you have selected. Some methods are relatively straightforward. For example, after a survey is developed and pre-tested, the researcher will spend time producing copies, addressing envelopes, affixing postage, and otherwise preparing to distribute the survey. Once the survey is sent out, the researcher will distribute follow-up letters to encourage responses or prepare for the data entry phase. Other methods are a bit more complicated. For example, field researchers may confront various challenges when observing behavior in a natural setting.

What happens if it rains? What if a field worker gets sick? How should a dangerous situation be handled? These and many more questions should be asked and answered prior to the data collection phase.

Although it is important to follow the research process and schedule as originally developed, it may become necessary to make changes during this phase of the research process. Surveys with bad addresses get returned by the post office. Research subjects do not show up for scheduled interviews. Field researchers forget supplies or become fearful of their surroundings. Such mishaps are managed best by a **contingency plan**. A contingency plan is essentially a 'Plan B,' or an alternative plan of action for when problems arise. Here is an example from my own experience.

Making Research Real 2.6 – Professor Come Get Me!

In 2003, several of my graduate students approached me with a research proposal. They wanted to determine how much of a patrol officer's time is uncommitted to enforcement duties like answering calls for service, writing reports, conducting surveillances, making arrests, and conducting traffic stops. If a substantial amount of a patrol officer's time is 'free,' it is possible that they could be redirected to more proactive crime prevention duties. I agreed to supervise the research and submitted their proposal to the local police department for permission and to our university's Office of Research Administration for a human subjects review.

The only way to measure a patrol officer's use of time accurately is to ride along with officers and record the amount of time they spend doing various activities. We developed definitions for 'committed' and 'uncommitted' time, purchased stopwatches and clipboards for recording time, designed reporting forms, and selected a sample of officers to observe. Further, we pre-tested the process just to be sure it would work. We found a number of 'kinks' but those were easily resolved.

Being a former police officer, I knew that 'ride-alongs' could be dangerous. Indeed, all of the students had to sign a form releasing the local police department from any liability should the students be injured, or worse, during the ride-along. I also created a contingency plan. According to this plan, the police officers were to terminate the ride-along and to leave the student in a safe place, like a convenience store, when it appeared that they might be placed in a dangerous situation. For example, if the officer were to be dispatched to a robbery in progress or a domestic violence incident, he or she was to drop the student off at a safe place before responding to the call. I also gave each student an envelope containing $20 and a card with my cell number printed on it. I instructed them to call me or to use the cash for cab fare if they needed a ride home. The students performed dozens of field observations and called me on four occasions to ask for a ride home. All four calls were in the middle of the night. Although I lost a little sleep, I kept my students safe.

Getting to the Point 2.9 – The process by which researchers collect data depends on their research methodology. Things can and do go wrong in the process of data collection. Researchers should develop contingency plans in case problems arise.

Step 8: Analyze the Data

A plan for data analysis should be developed early in the research process. If a researcher waits until the data are in before preparing for analysis, he or she risks not having the kind of data necessary to answer the research question. For example, a researcher wanting to measure the relationship between age and the frequency of criminal behavior would need to collect the ages and number of arrests for each of the research subjects. These two numbers would be used to produce a statistic called a correlation coefficient, which would indicate whether these two factors were related. If, on the other hand, the researcher asked the subjects to "Check the box beside the age range you fit in" and provided them four categories (15–25 years of age, 26–40 years of age, 41–55 years of age, and 56 years of age or older), he or she would not be able to calculate the correlation coefficient and answer the research question.

One of the most important decisions a researcher must make while preparing to analyze data is called an **a priori assumption**. A priori means before the fact. An a priori assumption is a statement, written in the form of a rule or guideline, about what the data must reveal for the researcher to confirm his or her hypothesis. If the research is quantitative in nature, the a priori assumption is basically a finding of statistical significance. If the research is qualitative in nature, the researcher must decide, a priori, how much evidence will be necessary to answer his or her research question. This is discussed more completely in Chapter 14. For now, here are two hypothetical examples.

Making Research Real 2.7 – School Fight Experiment

Two high school principals are concerned about the number of physical fights among students in their schools. Both schools have similar student populations in terms of size and demographic make up. One principal wants to hire security guards to deter potential fights. The other wants to hire a social worker to help students find more effective conflict resolution skills. The superintendent, unconvinced of either strategy, agrees to let them do what they want, but insists that they record the number of fights to determine which strategy is the most effective.

Prior to analyzing the results of the research at the end of the year, the researcher in charge of the project establishes a rule for deciding which of the two strategies is most effective. She decides that the school that has a statistically significantly lower number of fights compared to the other school and compared to the same school during the previous year will be the school whose strategy is most effective.

Making Research Real 2.8 – Perceptions of School Safety

A superintendent of an urban school district reads a story in the local paper in which a real estate agent is quoted as saying, "Fewer people want to live in the city because the schools there are so unsafe." This statement makes the superintendent downright angry. According to the most recent crime statistics, suburban schools have just as many fights as urban schools per capita. But whoever said that perceptions are always based on facts? The superintendent decides to conduct a study on how parents in the school district perceive the safety of their children's schools.

The superintendent plans a series of town meetings during which she intends to discuss school safety and ascertain parents' perceptions of school safety. These are essentially focus groups, a qualitative research method often used in product marketing. The superintendent thinks that these community meetings will reveal the most common factors that parents consider when developing perceptions of school safety. These factors might include graffiti and poorly maintained school properties. She intends to use the information from this study to develop a plan for improving the perception of school safety in her district. She knows that she cannot address every issue so she decides to focus on the most pressing issues. But how will she know which issues are most pressing? She decides a priori that an issue is pressing if more than one fourth of the parents at any one meeting identify it as a factor that influences their perceptions of school safety. Issues meeting this criterion will be the ones that the superintendent will focus her attention on improving.

So how do researchers actually go about analyzing data? Typically, when quantitative data arrive in the researcher's office, it is first entered into a computer program. To ensure that the individuals responsible for inputting the data are consistent, a set of **coding rules** should be established. For example, a survey may ask:

When you go out at night, how safe do you feel? (Check only one of the following boxes)
- ☐ *I am never afraid when I go out at night.*$_1$
- ☐ *I am occasionally afraid when I go out at night.*$_2$
- ☐ *I am frequently afraid when I go out at night.*$_3$
- ☐ *I am always afraid when I go out at night.*$_4$
- ☐ *I am so afraid that I never go out at night.*$_5$

Did you notice the subscript numerals at the end of each response? Entering a number is easier than entering the respondent's actual response. It also makes analysis easier. You may have noticed that the numbers (1–5) increase in value as the respondent's level of fear increases – the higher the value, the higher the level of fear. When researchers code data, they assign a number to different responses for the purpose of data entry. All individuals responsible for data entry must use these codes when entering individual responses for each question.

Once the data are coded and entered, researchers evaluate the completeness and accuracy of the data set. This is often called 'cleaning the data.' Incomplete and inaccurate records can be corrected or eliminated altogether. The actual data analysis is usually done with a statistical software program. Basically, the researcher will run statistical tests to determine if and how variables are related. Qualitative data analysis is a little more complex and usually involves organizing the results into various themes. The results of either form of data analysis are called 'findings.'

Getting to the Point 2.10 – A plan for data analysis is developed early in the research process. A priori assumptions establish what the data must reveal for a researcher to confirm his or her hypothesis. Researchers code, enter, and clean the data before running statistical tests or performing other types of data analysis.

Step 9: Interpret the Results

Completing a statistical analysis or organizing the results from a qualitative analysis is the easy part. Figuring out the meaning and practical significance of these findings is more art than science. Say we distribute a survey, collect and analyze the data, and find a relationship between neighborhood poverty and property-based crime. Why are these two variables related and what is the significance of this relationship for theory and policy? The interpretation of findings is often the most interesting part of research, but it is also the most difficult.

Findings are only meaningful in the context in which they arise and they are only as useful as the quality of the data. When findings are interpreted to mean more than they actually do, we say the researcher has 'overreached' his or her findings. For example, a researcher may find that 20 percent of the stops made by police officers involve African American drivers, while only 10 percent of the community's residents are African American. This researcher may conclude that the officers are guilty of racial profiling. This interpretation, however, would overreach the findings of this research. It could be that there is a higher percentage of African Americans in the driving population than in the residential population. It could also be that more African Americans reside in high-crime areas where more police officers are assigned to work and are therefore more likely to be observed and stopped. Finally, it could be that African American drivers commit more traffic violations and, hence, are stopped more often. All possible explanations or interpretations should be explored before reaching a conclusion.

Getting to the Point 2.11 – Research findings should be interpreted in the context in which they arise and are subject to the limitations of the available data. When findings are interpreted to mean more than they actually do, the researcher has overreached his or her findings.

Step 10: Communicate the Findings

Once the analysis has been completed and the findings interpreted, the researcher turns his or her attention to writing the research report or otherwise communicating his or her findings. How a researcher goes about actually writing up a final research report depends on where it will be published, who is providing the funding, and how the research will be used. Most university professors submit their research to scholarly journals, which require a relatively standard format for reporting research results. Table 2.2 describes the sections that are commonly found in articles appearing in scholarly journals.

Table 2.2   Common Sections in Scholarly Journal Articles

SECTION	DESCRIPTION
Abstract	A summary of the research, usually about 150 words or less, that describes what the researcher did and learned.
Introduction	An overview of the research that describes the purpose of the research, the research question and hypothesis, and how the article is organized.
Literature review	A review of what is known about a particular topic and a description of areas of agreement and disagreement among researchers on the topic.
Methodology	A description of the methods used by the researcher, including the sampling procedure, the measurement of variables, the data collection method, and the analytic techniques.
Findings	A summary of what the analysis revealed, including descriptive statistics.
Discussion	An interpretation of the research findings and a consideration of alternative explanations.
Conclusion	A summary of the research project, an evaluation of the strengths and weakness of the research, and/or a set of recommendations for policy changes or questions for future research.
References	A list, organized by author's last name, of the sources that were used by the researcher. This can also be referred to as a bibliography.

Research reports published by government agencies or research organizations often include the same sections as those of a scholarly journal article. The most prominent difference is in the abstract section. An abstract in a research report is sometimes called an Executive Summary. Both are very brief summaries of the research report. Research reports appearing in magazines and newspapers are not as formally presented. In fact, it can sometimes be difficult to find information on a researcher's methodology or analytical strategy in articles appearing in these types of publications. Scholarly articles and research reports are often written at a higher level of precision than articles written for publication in magazines or newspapers.

When academic researchers submit their findings for publication in scholarly journals, they must go through a double-blind peer review process supervised by a journal's editor. This process was previously discussed in Chapter 1. Research reports written for criminal justice organizations, government agencies, or private clients often are submitted in draft format. This allows the agency or client to evaluate the report before it becomes public. The purpose of the review is still the same: to improve the quality of the research report. It is better to find and correct mistakes in the privacy of the peer review process than in the public arena.

Because the traditional publishing process can take a long time, researchers often present their findings at conferences or meetings of likeminded scholars and practitioners. These conferences are typically organized into different sessions wherein scholars and practitioners interested in similar topics share and discuss their latest research. Most criminal justice scholars attend the annual meetings of the Academy of Criminal Justice Sciences or the American Society of Criminology.

Practitioners may attend any number of meetings such as meetings sponsored by the International Association of Chiefs of Police or the American Correctional Association. There are also numerous regional, state, and local organizations that hold regular meetings wherein research is shared.

Part of the process of presenting research findings is evaluating and communicating a research project's limitations. This is difficult for many researchers. Most researchers would prefer not to point out their mistakes or their project's limitations. It is important to remember, though, that all research has weaknesses and limitations. There is no such thing as a perfect research project. Identifying, even highlighting, a research project's weakness and limitations is an important part of the research process because it sets the stage for developing new research questions. It also helps other researchers assess the strength of a research project's findings. From a practical perspective, it is better to admit your own mistakes than to have somebody else point them out for you. Identifying the weaknesses and limitations of your research is the sign of a mature and competent researcher.

Remember that when communicating research findings, '*A picture is worth a thousand words.*' Most people are visual learners. This means that they learn best when they see things, as opposed to when they hear things. Pictures, including graphs and charts, are enormously helpful to anyone wanting to communicate ideas. Consider the comparison in Figure 2.2.

The following sentence appears in the written version of a research report. It uses words to describe what the researchers learned from their research.

Overall, it appears that education has a positive effect on income. The more education one has, the higher his or her income will likely be.

Now, here is the same information presented visually.

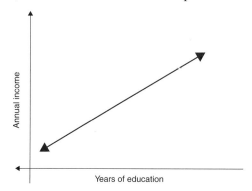

Both the words and the graph communicate the same information. Which of these are you likely to remember?

Figure 2.2   Which Message Would You Remember?

Getting to the Point 2.12 – The actual format of the research report depends on where it is published. Scholarly articles follow a standard organizational format that includes a literature review, information on methodology, a section on findings, and a discussion. Identifying the weaknesses and limitations of the research is critical when presenting research findings in publications or at conferences.

FINAL THOUGHTS

Researchers typically complete the ten steps of the research process in a particular order (see Figure 2.1). But it is also the case that researchers will revisit previous steps when they realize that something is not working or when they are not getting the data they need. The key to success in research is thinking through the entire research process before committing to a particular method. But it is also important to be flexible, to admit when something is not working, and to adjust your methods accordingly. This is what we mean by the research process being internally cyclical.

What about the 11th step, *Ask Another Question*? And you thought I forgot! The 11th step illustrates the externally cyclical nature of the research process. As mentioned previously, no research answers all our questions on a particular topic. In fact, good research raises more questions than it answers. And even good research has weaknesses and limitations. This produces gaps in the body of knowledge and the need for more research. At first this may seem frustrating, like the process never ends. But, it is also quite exhilarating to learn that there are endless opportunities to expand the body of knowledge. Above all else, stay curious, because curiosity is what expands our knowledge and makes us better at the things we do.

GETTING TO THE POINT/CHAPTER SUMMARY

- The objectives of research are to answer research questions, to resolve disagreements among researchers, to fill gaps within the body of knowledge, and to produce more research questions.

- The research process is characteristically linear in that the steps must be completed in a certain order. However, the process is also internally cyclical, because researchers often have to revisit previous steps, and externally cyclical, because good research leads to additional research questions.

- Research questions should be actual questions that can be answered rather than statements that make some claim.

- The literature review involves locating and understanding what previous researchers have learned about a topic. Researchers rely on several sources in this regard, including books, scholarly journals, newspapers and magazines, Internet sources, and experts. If the existing literature is credible, timely, context appropriate, and methodologically sound, there is no need to move past the literature review stage; the research question may be answered through the literature review alone.

- The literature review process helps researchers refine their research question, identify a theory related to their research question, and propose a hypothesis that predicts the answer to their research question.

- Conceptualization is a process by which researchers define the concepts in their hypotheses. These definitions are important because they determine how researchers actually measure the concepts they use in their research.

- Operationalization is the process by which researchers decide on how they are going to measure their concepts as they have defined them. Often it is necessary to measure concepts along multiple dimensions.

- Researchers should pre-test their method to be sure that the research method(s) they use will produce the data necessary to actually answer their research question(s).

- The process by which researchers collect data depends on their research methodology. Things can and do go wrong in the process of data collection. Researchers should develop contingency plans in case problems arise.

- A plan for data analysis is developed early in the research process. A priori assumptions establish what the data must reveal for a researcher to confirm his or her hypothesis. Researchers code, enter, and clean the data before running statistical tests or performing other types of data analysis.

- Research findings should be interpreted in the context in which they arise and are subject to the limitations of the available data. When findings are interpreted to mean more than they actually do, the researcher has overreached his or her findings.

- The actual format of the research report depends on where it is published. Scholarly articles follow a standard organizational format that includes a literature review, information on methodology, a section on findings, and a discussion. Identifying the weaknesses and limitations of the research is critical when presenting research findings in publications or at conferences.

CHAPTER EXERCISES

The following chapter exercises are organized into two parts. The first part consists of questions that can be answered using the information from the preceding chapter. Use this section to test your understanding of the chapter material. The second part consists of research application exercises. These exercises require you to apply what you have learned thus far.

CHAPTER REVIEW QUESTIONS

Respond to each of the following questions using the information from this chapter.

1. Read each of the following statements made by researchers and classify them into one of the following research objectives:
    a.   To answer research questions
    b.   To reveal inconsistencies among researchers
    c.   To fill gaps in the body of knowledge
    d.   To produce more research questions

Statement	Objective
Sutherland (1974) proposed the theory of differential association, which suggests that criminal behavior is learned through interactions with other criminals. Burgess and Akers (1966) expanded on Sutherland's theory by suggesting that other factors could combine with differential association to produce criminal behavior.	
The observations of Burgess and Akers produced the first real insight into the process by which juveniles become members of criminal gangs.	
Despite its contribution to our understanding of juvenile delinquency, the research of Burgess and Akers could not explain what motivates juveniles to join criminal gangs in the first place.	
The manner in which individuals learn criminal behavior is well documented. However, it is not clear from the research so far how access to the Internet affects this learning process.	

2. Fill in the blank: The research process is _____ in that steps are usually completed in a certain order.

3. Fill in the blank: The research process has been described as _____ cyclical because it has a tendency to produce additional questions for future researchers.

4. Read the following statements. Place a check mark '✔' next to the statements that you consider to be good research questions and an '×' beside the statements that are not good research questions.

Statement	✔ or ×
Children with undiagnosed and untreated learning disabilities are more likely to become delinquents.	
Increased patrols will result in decreased vehicular burglaries.	
Sex offenders should never be allowed to see the light of day outside of an institution.	
Prolonged periods of solitary confinement may result in psychological damage among inmates.	
The death penalty reflects our value system of 'an eye for an eye.'	

5. For the statements that you marked with an '×' above, explain why they would not make good research questions.

6. The following statements describe challenges a researcher might encounter during the literature review process. For each statement, determine where the researcher should look for information. Refer to Table 2.1 for guidance.

Research challenge	Source of information
"I need information about current research on this topic."	
"I am really unfamiliar with this topic. I need some background information and maybe a little history about it."	
"I need some information about this topic in a hurry!"	
"There is not a lot of published information about this topic. I need some kind of insight into it."	
"What is the general public likely to know about this topic?"	

7. A researcher conducting research on the relationship between alcohol use and domestic violence develops the following conceptual definition for domestic violence:

    A potentially severe and reoccurring form of physical assault wherein the victim is an intimate domestic partner.

    Use the following table to list the strengths and weaknesses of this conceptual definition. A strength might be that the definition includes the reoccurring nature of this behavior; a weakness might be that the definition does not include psychological abuse.

Research challenge	Source of information

8. The researcher in the previous question decides to measure (i.e., operationalize) domestic violence using arrests for domestic violence. Discuss the problems with this measure. Would the researcher overlook any important dimensions or aspects of the concept domestic violence using only arrests as the measure? If so, what dimensions or aspects? What other measures for domestic violence might the researcher use?

9. A researcher intends to interview 25 individuals who had previously fled from the police in a high-speed pursuit. The researcher's objectives are to determine why these individuals ran from the police and why they eventually stopped. The research has the potential to inform the local police department as it develops a new policy governing high-speed vehicular pursuits. Write five interview questions that this researcher might use to get at the information they need.

10. Develop a graph, table, or other visual representation that communicates the following research finding:

   Before they are caught and convicted for their first offense, 60 percent of all sex offenders commit five or more offenses; 20 percent commit from three to five offenses; 15 percent commit two offenses; and 5 percent commit only one offense.

RESEARCH APPLICATION EXERCISES

Access to the following articles will be provided by your instructor.

Bush, D.M. (1985). Victimization and school attitudes toward violence among early adolescents. *Sociological Spectrum,* 5(1–2), 173–190.

Williams, C. (1993). Vulnerable victims? A current awareness of the victimisation of people with learning disabilities. *Disability & Society,* 8(2), 161–172.

---

11. Read the Bush (1985) article and respond to the following questions.
    a. What was the objective of this research?
    b. How does the author describe or characterize the previous research on this topic?
    c. According to the author, what was the "flaw" in the prior research on this topic?
    d. How does the author respond to this flaw?
    e. How does this research contribute to our overall understanding of this issue?

12. Read the Williams (1993) article and respond to the following questions.
    a. What was the objective of this research?
    b. How does the author describe or characterize the previous research on this topic?
    c. According to the author, what contribution does this research make to research on this topic?
    d. How does the author contribute to the body of knowledge on this topic?

CHAPTER 3

The Ethical Principles That Guide Researchers

Not so long ago, research methods textbooks were silent on the question of research **ethics**. Eventually, authors began to include information on ethics in the final chapters of their textbooks or in their appendices. This placement suggested that ethical considerations were mere afterthoughts and not worthy of a researcher's attention. More recently, however, we have realized that a solid understanding of ethical behavior is essential for the researcher. So before we delve into technical questions about social research, we need to discuss research ethics.

Ethics is more than doing the right thing. Although there are ethical standards to which all researchers must adhere, 'doing the right thing' may change from one research situation to the next. The following hypothetical situation illustrates this point.

Making Research Real 3.1 – Please Help Our Son!

In a joint research project, a psychiatrist and a criminologist are testing a newly available psychotropic drug on violent juvenile delinquents. Like all psychotropic drugs, this medication is designed to treat psychiatric disorders, in this case extreme aggression. The researchers believe this drug will reduce aggressive behavior among violent juvenile offenders. If it works, the drug could become part of the routine treatment of some of the most difficult offenders in the criminal justice system.

The researchers receive approval from their university's Office of Research Administration and the Committee for the Protection of Human Subjects. In addition, the drug has been determined to be safe and effective by the United States Food and Drug Administration. The research design is a classic experimental design involving 50 convicted violent juvenile offenders with a history of aggressive behavior. Consistent with this design, the researchers randomly divide the research subjects into two groups. One group, the experimental group, will receive a daily dosage of the new drug. The other group, the control group, will receive a daily placebo that appears to be the same drug. None of the research subjects will know which medication they are taking. The researchers will monitor the research subjects throughout the year and then evaluate the drug's effectiveness using a series of psychological tests.

Because the research subjects are juveniles, the researchers must obtain the voluntary and informed consent of the parents or guardians of their research subjects. Following a meeting with the parents and

---

guardians, wherein the researchers explain the experiment, one of the parents approaches the researchers with a request. "Please put my son Alex in the experimental group," she asks. "We are at the end of our rope and we think he will harm somebody or himself if he doesn't get help." The researchers understand this mother's concern but politely explain to her that the decision on who actually receives the drug or its placebo will be based on random assignment. Otherwise, they explain, the validity of the research results will be affected.

Was it the 'right thing' to deny Alex a drug that might prevent his aggressive behavior, even if taking this drug could protect Alex and others from harm? In this case, the answer is yes. Because no experimental research had been done on the drug, there was no guarantee that the medication would work for him. Indeed, the purpose of the experiment was to determine if the medication was effective in reducing aggressive behavior. Without the use of random assignment, the researchers would not have been able to say whether it was the drug or some other variable that caused a decrease in aggressive behavior. Thus, doing the 'right thing' in this case meant not giving Alex or his mother any assurance that Alex would receive the medication.

The purpose of this chapter is not to provide you with a simple list of strict ethical guidelines. No such list exists. Instead, this chapter challenges you to think about and apply ethical principles to real world research situations. Researchers never know exactly what to do in every research situation. But ethical researchers do know that they must try their best to protect research subjects and enhance their quality of life.

Getting to the Point 3.1 – Social science researchers should be concerned about ethics because ultimately their obligation is to improve the human condition through research. What constitutes ethical behavior often depends on the particular circumstances of individual research projects.

PRINCIPLES OF ETHICAL RESEARCH PRACTICE

Almost all researchers in the medical, physical, and social sciences follow the basic ethical precept of doing no harm. This is a pretty obvious one. But there are other ethical principles that you might not have considered, such as protecting the safety of researchers and ensuring the privacy of research participants. In this section, we will take a look at seven important principles of ethical research practice. These principles are summarized at the end of this section in Table 3.2.

Principle 1: Do No Harm

The principle '**do no harm**' merely means that during the research process, the researcher should never do anything that will hurt another person or put any person in danger, including the researcher. This principle is easy to understand when a pharmaceutical researcher is testing a drug that might have harmful side effects or when a psychiatrist is placing research subjects under extreme stress to measure their response. Though it is obvious in these cases what could harm a research participant, it is not so obvious in other cases. What exactly do we mean by *harm*?

It is possible that nearly any research process could cause harm to a human being at some level. If research subjects spend an hour filling out a survey instead of working, they risk being disciplined by their boss. If an interviewer asks sexual assault victims to describe their experience, they risk reliving the psychological pain of their victimization. If a criminologist studying post-prison reintegration randomly assigns a research subject to a control group, his or her chances for successful reintegration may be diminished. In these contexts, how do we weigh the risks against the overall benefits of the research? In general, researchers should be attuned to the three forms of potential harm in research: physical harm, psychological harm, and legal harm (see Table 3.1).

Table 3.1   Types of Potential Harm Caused by the Research Process

TYPE OF HARM	DESCRIPTION
Physical	Occurs when research subjects are exposed to situations and elements in the research process that could cause them physical injury or death.
Psychological	Occurs when research subjects are exposed to situations and elements in the research process that could cause them severe psychological pain or exacerbate a mental illness.
Legal	Occurs when research subjects are exposed to situations and elements in the research process that could expose them to serious legal harm including criminal or civil prosecution.

When we think of a research experiment doing physical harm to people, we often recall the Tuskegee Syphilis Experiment. This clinical study, conducted from 1932 to 1972 in Tuskegee, Alabama, involved 600 impoverished African Americans, 399 of whom were infected with syphilis. The experiment was supervised by the United States Public Health Service. It was designed to study what happens naturally if syphilis is left untreated. The experimenters could have provided the research subjects with an effective cure, since penicillin became available in the 1940s, but they did not. They even failed to inform the research subjects that they were infected with the disease (Chadwick, 2002). This ethical violation caused immeasurable suffering and led to the creation of federal laws governing the use of human beings as research subjects. One of these laws requires that if there is a known effective treatment, it cannot be withheld from research subjects even if this results in the termination of the research (Belmont Report, 1979).

Research subjects can be physically harmed even in social science research. In 1971, Professor Philip Zimbardo of Stanford University conducted an experiment on the psychological effects of becoming a prisoner or prison guard. Twenty-four students were selected to participate in the study, which involved a mock prison in the basement of the Psychology Building at Stanford. Students were assigned to be either 'prisoners' or 'guards.' In both cases, student participants adapted quickly to their assigned roles. Unfortunately, some of the students adapted too well. Some of the 'guards' became abusive and the conflict between the 'guards' and 'prisoners' became intense, even dangerous. To his credit, Professor Zimbardo, who actively supervised the research, recognized the potential physical harm involved and terminated the experiment early (Quiet Rage, 1992). If you are interested, there is a website (http://www.prisonexp.org) devoted to this study where you can see a slide show of what actually happened.

Sometimes a research project can cause psychological harm. In the late 1960s, a school teacher named Jane Elliot decided to teach her elementary students about racism and prejudice. The now famous experiment, called Blue Eyes/Brown Eyes, involved separating her students into two groups based on their eye color. The blue-eyed children were allowed to sit at the front of the class and have classroom privileges that the brown-eyed children were denied. During the first day of the experiment, she also ignored the brown-eyed children and instructed the blue-eyed children to do the same. The next day, she reversed the roles and focused her attention on the brown-eyed children at the expense of the blue-eyed children. This experiment expanded our knowledge of the psychological effects of racism and prejudice. But it was also quite controversial (Bloom, 2005). Decades later, the children, now adults, remember the psychological pain they experienced. I had the opportunity to attend one of Ms. Elliot's presentations wherein she discussed her long career in diversity education. One of the children, now an adult, attended the presentation and was asked about her experience. The woman tearfully recalled the pain she experienced as a child in that classroom decades earlier. It would not be fair to suggest that Ms. Elliot's exercise caused this person long-term psychological harm, but it is clear that it did have a lasting emotional effect.

Finally, a research project should never put a research subject in legal harm. No research is important enough to cause somebody to be arrested or convicted of a crime. Similarly, a research project should not cause a person to fear civil or legal liability. In 1970, Laud Humphreys published his Ph.D. dissertation, which later became a book called *Tearoom Trade* (Humphreys, 1975). This research was an ethnographic study of anonymous male homosexual encounters in public toilets. Humphreys observed these homosexual contacts as a voyeur and then identified some of the men from their vehicle license plate numbers. He later tracked them down in their homes and interviewed them and/or their wives posing as a census taker or pollster. About half of the men were outwardly heterosexual and had unsuspecting families at home. Humphreys was interested in how these men negotiated their public and private lives. To fully understand the ethical problem associated with this study, we need to remember that during the 1970s, homosexuality and homosexual activities were illegal in most states. And it was not at all uncommon for homosexual men to be victimized. Had the information about these men been discovered, many of them would have been physically threatened, socially ostracized, fired from their jobs, and/or sued for divorce. Luckily, this information was never revealed. But Humphreys is still criticized for not disclosing his research intentions and for not securing his subjects' voluntary and informed consent to participate in the research.

The procedure by which a researcher ensures that he or she will cause no harm begins with an honest assessment of the potential harm research can cause. The simple rule is, if you can think of a potential harm, it can (and may indeed) happen. Here is an example from my own experience.

Making Research Real 3.2 – Who Knew?

Several years ago, one of my students wanted to conduct a study of the effects of divorce on children after they become adults. She hypothesized that the children of divorced parents experienced more diffi-culty maintaining relationships when they were adults than children whose parents had never divorced.

Over the next several months, the student conducted a literature review and developed a survey to administer to adult children of divorce. The survey was approved by the Office of Research Administra-tion, but only on the condition that the consent forms include the telephone number of the on-campus counseling center. The office contended that answering the survey questions might cause students to recall long-suppressed feelings that might require counseling. We agreed and the consent form was changed to include this information.

To my knowledge, none of the students that took the survey actually requested counseling because of it. But it was important to have this information just in case a student was psychologically impacted by their participation in the survey.

As the above example suggests, researchers should consider changing the research plan to avoid or reduce the potential for harm. This could be as simple as revising a survey question or as dramatic as abandoning the research project altogether. Researchers should always be prepared to amend their research question if necessary to avoid inflicting harm upon their research subjects. The final step is to build contingencies into the research plan to prevent or mitigate potential harm. Ultimately, the research subjects should be well informed of the risks associ-ated with their participation in a research project *and* be allowed to opt out of the research at any point without penalty, ridicule, or risk.

Getting to the Point 3.2 – The principle of doing no harm means that researchers should never subject research participants to physical danger, cause them psychological harm, or expose them to legal liability. Researchers should build contingencies into the research plan to prevent or mitigate potential harm. In extreme cases, they should abandon the research project altogether.

Principle 2: Ensure Privacy

Privacy is the right to be left alone. Closely associated with this right is the right to prohibit others from knowing things about you that you do not want them to know. Researchers have an obligation to protect the privacy of their research subjects. This means that the researcher must not disclose private information about a research subject without that person's permission. Disclosure of information by a researcher that causes a research subject to be unduly harmed, or even inconvenienced, is a serious breach of ethical standards. Say, for example, that you have asked a group of sexual assault victims to tell you details about their victimization. To encourage them to be frank, you have assured them that you will neither ask for their identity nor attempt to associate the information you gather from them with their personal identity. In other words, you have assured them privacy. Unfortunately, in the process of reporting your results, you inadvertently provide information that could be used to identify one or more of the research subjects. This may happen when you report specific details about a case that is well known to the public or include information specific to a particular victim. This disclosure could be embarrassing to the research subject, cause problems within the victim's family, and/or jeopardize a legal proceeding.

Protecting the privacy of subjects in research extends to organizations. In the course of research, organizations may be willing to provide a researcher access to people and information so long as the researcher agrees not to publish damaging information about the organization. Normally, this is achieved by referring to the organization in a generic sense or with a pseudonym. For example, instead of identifying a police agency by name, the researcher may refer to it as "a medium-sized police agency in the northeastern United States."

Researchers who gather information from human subjects must decide early in the research process whether the subjects will participate confidentially or anonymously. **Confidentiality** means that the researcher can connect specific research information to a research subject, but he or she can not divulge the subject's identity to outsiders. Knowing the research subjects' identities might be essential to a researcher if he or she wants to either verify information or conduct a follow-up interview. But the promise not to divulge these identities to outsiders is essential in that research subjects are more likely to express their feelings if they are assured that no one else will know that they are responsible for their statements. Imagine a study involving interviews with inmates about the correctional officers who supervise them. What inmate would want his or her opinion about a correctional officer made known? Without an assurance of confidentiality, inmates would not likely participate in the research for fear of retaliation.

Some researchers go further and grant anonymity to their research subjects. **Anonymity** means that nobody, not even the researcher, can connect the information that a subject provides to that particular research subject. Research subjects are even more likely to be candid or provide accurate information if they are assured of anonymity. Anonymity is best achieved by not requiring the research subjects to divulge their identities in the first place. For example, many surveys are conducted anonymously and sometimes research subjects are specifically instructed not to write or sign their names on the survey instrument. Sometimes researchers want to ensure anonymity but also maintain access to their research subjects over time. For example, a researcher may want to ask the same research questions to the same research subjects over several months. Political pollsters do this all the time to measure the effectiveness of campaign strategies on certain types of voters. In this case, it would be necessary to establish some way of identifying the research subjects without using their name. This can be achieved by issuing them personal identification numbers or alias names and instructing them to use these numbers or aliases every time they fill out their survey.

Getting to the Point 3.3 – Privacy means the right to be left alone and free from public scrutiny. There are two types of privacy in research. Confidentiality means that the researcher knows who the research subjects are, but does not disclose their identity to others. Anonymity means that nobody, not even the researcher, knows the identity of the research subjects.

Principle 3: Obtain Voluntary and Informed Consent

Imagine that you have been assigned to write a research paper on burglary. You decide to interview your uncle, who served time in prison for burglary decades ago. Casually, you ask your uncle to describe how he chose houses to burglarize, how he gained entry, and how he fenced the stolen goods. Unbeknownst to your uncle, you use this information for your research paper. In doing so, you have violated a core ethical principle, namely to get your uncle's **voluntary and informed consent** to use the information.

In most research situations, it is essential to obtain consent from research subjects prior to the actual collection of information. It does not matter whether the research involves participation in an experimental drug trial or answering a short survey; consent is required. Consent has two important dimensions. First, consent must be voluntary, meaning that the research subject agrees to participate in the research without influence, pressure, or force. This also means that the research subject is free to decide not to participate without fear of reprisal. The research subject must be given the option of revoking his or her consent at anytime during the research process. Say, for example, that after your uncle tells you about his criminal past, you ask if you can use the information for your research paper and he declines. You must accept his decision and not pressure him to do otherwise.

Consent must also be informed, meaning that the research subject is fully aware of what he or she is expected to do during the research project and how the information will be used. This may be as simple as explaining to research subjects that they will answer a few questions on a particular topic or as complex as telling them the potential side effects of an experimental drug. A critical part of informed consent is informing research subjects about the risks involved in the research. In our example, you would have to inform your uncle that the information will be used in your research paper but that his name will not be used. Hence, there will be minimal risks involved.

In a way, obtaining voluntary and informed consent is analogous to the process by which criminal investigators obtain a legal confession. Under the *Miranda* rule, a confession must be voluntary, meaning that the suspect must not be coerced into making the confession. In addition, the suspect must be informed of his or her rights under the law. This is normally done when an investigator informs a suspect of his or her *Miranda* rights prior to an interrogation. Both elements are required for the confession to be admissible in court. Likewise, both elements are required for ethical research involving human subjects.

> **Getting to the Point 3.4** – Researchers must obtain consent from research subjects prior to collecting information from them. This consent must be given voluntarily, meaning that the research subjects must be completely free to participate or not participate without threat. In addition, the consent must be informed, meaning that the researcher must inform the research subjects about the research and any risks associated with participation in the research.

Principle 4: Get Permission

In general, researchers are not required to seek permission to study the general population. For example, you do not have to get permission from the city council to send a survey to the residents of your community. Accessing some populations, however, requires special permission. These are often referred to as special or vulnerable populations. A **vulnerable population** is a group of research subjects who, by virtue of their age, physical or mental condition, legal status, or life situation, have a diminished capacity to negotiate their affairs or protect themselves from harm. Vulnerable populations include children, the mentally ill, the infirm, the elderly, and even prisoners. Researchers interested in studying individuals in vulnerable populations must get special permission and accept higher levels of scrutiny. For example, a researcher wanting to conduct research involving children would be required to get the parents' or guardians' permission.

Special populations are vulnerable for several reasons. First, they have limited capacity to protect themselves from harm. This is more than a lack of physical stature to defend oneself from physical harm. It is more that members of this population are less able to understand and weigh the risks associated with their participation in the research project. Second, individuals in special populations may have a diminished capacity to give consent. Some, like children and some mentally ill persons, do not have the legal authority to give consent. Others may not have the mental capacity to understand that they have the right *not* to give their consent. Finally, individuals may experience extreme forms of emotional or psychological stress that render them vulnerable. For example, women in domestic violence shelters would be considered a special population because of the psychological trauma they have endured or are enduring.

It is easy for us to think of children, the mentally ill, the infirm, and the elderly as vulnerable. But why might prisoners constitute a special population? Prisoners, like members of other special populations, are totally dependent upon others for their survival. For security reasons, they cannot correspond directly with researchers and therefore cannot evaluate the risks associated with the research, verify the researcher's credentials, or even get a copy of the final research report. Incarcerated individuals may also feel more pressure to participate in research projects. For example, they may perceive that their decision not to participate would reduce their opportunity for special privileges or a favorable decision from a future parole board.

Even when not working with special populations, it may be a good idea to ask permission to access certain populations. For example, if a researcher wants to conduct a survey on correctional officers, they would be well advised to inform the prison's administration of the survey. Although permission may not be legally required, it is good practice.

Getting to the Point 3.5 – Researchers must seek and obtain permission to work with individuals who are considered vulnerable by virtue of their diminished capacity to direct their own affairs. Vulnerable populations include children, the mentally ill, the infirm, the elderly, and prisoners.

Principle 5: Avoid Sponsorship Bias and Suppression

A lot of research is sponsored by private organizations and companies. In many cases, these organizations want to learn more about the effectiveness or the safety of the goods and services they provide. It is their right to do so and, indeed, may be their obligation to do so. **Sponsorship bias**, however, may occur if the sponsor of a research project attempts to influence the study design and/or interpretation of the data. Sponsors may also be guilty of **suppression**, which occurs when a research sponsor fails to disclose findings that do not benefit the organization. For example, before *oleoresin capsicum*, commonly known as pepper spray, was allowed to be sold it had to undergo years of testing to be sure it was safe and effective for its intended use. In this case the private companies that intended to sell this substance had a financial interest in the outcome of the research and could have attempted to influence the findings. However, there is no evidence that such sponsorship bias occurred in this case. Here is an example of a case in which the sponsoring company attempted to suppress research findings.

Making Research Real 3.3 – Daring D.A.R.E.

Since its inception in 1983, Drug Abuse Resistance Education (D.A.R.E.) programs have been credited with preventing millions of children from experimenting with and using illicit drugs. The programs are delivered by police officers through schools. Nearly 70 percent of all schools in America have some form of D.A.R.E. programming. To create a D.A.R.E. program, a local police agency must purchase materials from a company called D.A.R.E. America, Inc.

Several years ago, D.A.R.E America, Inc. commissioned a study on the effectiveness of its programs. The study revealed that participation in a D.A.R.E. program did not reduce a juvenile's drug use. At first, D.A.R.E. America, Inc. chose not to publish the results of the study, since doing so would reduce demand for the agency's materials and, hence, cause a decline in the agency's profits. Eventually, the results were made public and the decision to suppress the study findings caused considerable controversy (Hanson, 2007). The results and the controversy, however, did not appreciably affect D.A.R.E. America, Inc.'s sales.

Organizations may also restrict a researcher's access to information in an effort to avoid an unfavorable evaluation, as the example below suggests.

Making Research Real 3.4 – Liar, Liar, Pants on Fire

Many years ago, a colleague of mine supervised a Master's student's thesis on the effectiveness of a drug and alcohol program for juvenile offenders. We will call the student Michael. The drug and alcohol program was operated in a southern U.S. county and the provider of the service was a for-profit corporation that offered similar programs to correctional systems throughout the country. It turns out that Michael was actually an employee of this company. And the company agreed to allow Michael to analyze the effectiveness of the program and provided him with data from their files. Michael analyzed the data and concluded that the program was effective.

During the process of reviewing the thesis, my colleague noticed a substantial difference in the number of juveniles that the company provided data on and the number of juveniles they reported to have served in the county. He asked Michael to determine the cause of this difference. A few days later, Michael returned with a more complete data set that had been given to him by his immediate supervisor. Michael's subsequent analysis led to very different results. This time, he found that the program was not effective. In fact, it appeared that juveniles who participated in this program were more likely to use alcohol and drugs.

You can imagine how Michael reacted to this. Not only was his Master's thesis (and degree) in jeopardy, but the publication of his results might cost him his job. My colleague informed Michael that despite the protections afforded him through state and federal 'Whistle Blower' statutes, the publication of his thesis might result in his termination. Michael's choice was to publish the thesis with the accurate results and risk being fired, or to complete a different thesis. To my colleague's surprise, Michael chose to publish his thesis, which he did.

After a few weeks, both Michael and his supervisor were fired. The corporation attempted to suppress Michael's thesis by requesting that it be removed from the university library and by deleting references to it appearing in indexes. Thanks to the university's attorney, the corporation was unsuccessful. A few months later, the county chose not to renew the provider's contract, based in large part on Michael's findings. Eventually, several other counties heard about the research and cancelled their contracts with the corporation, as well.

This story does have a happy ending. Within a month of his graduation, Michael was offered a full-time position as a contract analyst with the county. His new job required him to evaluate the effectiveness of various county programs. His salary was nearly double what he had been making with his former employer.

Bias and suppression are not limited to private corporations. Government agencies have also been guilty of this ethical violation. Political leaders and government institutions can attempt to influence the outcome of a research project in order to serve their own interests. This normally occurs when a political leader wants to further his or her political career or when a government agency wants to increase its funding. In all of these cases, the key to avoiding bias and suppression is to ensure that the data you are provided is accurate and complete and that your access to information and people within the organization is unfettered.

Getting to the Point 3.6 – Sponsorship bias occurs when the sponsor of a research project attempts to influence the study design or interpretation of data for its own benefit. Suppression occurs when a research sponsor fails to disclose findings that shed an unfavorable light on the sponsor's products or services.

Principle 6: Prevent Misrepresentation

Misrepresentation is essentially lying. It can involve lying about the data, the results, and even authorship. In conducting research, researchers can be motivated by many interests besides the pursuit of scientific knowledge. Some researchers are overly interested in furthering their careers, which may lead them to falsify their findings or claim the ideas of others as their own. Others may be interested in earning more money, which may make them susceptible to legitimizing questionable research in return for payment. All of these interests can lead research down an unethical path.

Research fraud is an extreme form of misrepresentation. It involves lying about or fabricating research findings. Although researchers usually seek approval for their research projects, the actual data collection and analysis are done without much supervision. So there is really nothing to keep researchers from merely making up their data and/or results to enhance their professional reputation. Research fraud is not the same as making a mistake. Researchers make measurement, calculation, and interpretive errors all the time. Research fraud is an *intentional* attempt to present false information as genuine research findings. Unfortunately, there are cases of this happening and the results can be profound. Here is an example.

Making Research Real 3.5 – The MMR Vaccine/Autism Connection

In 1998, Andrew Wakefield, a British surgeon and medical researcher, published an article in a prestigious medical journal called *The Lancet*. In the article, Wakefield presented evidence of a causal link between autism and the measles, mumps, and rubella (MMR) vaccine (Wakefield et al., 1998). For decades, physicians have administered the MMR vaccine to infants and children in an effort to reduce the incidence of these childhood diseases.

Wakefield's findings came at a time when diagnoses for autism were increasing exponentially worldwide. As you might imagine, news like this had a profound effect on vaccination rates. Throughout England, and the world, parents began rejecting vaccinations for their children. Predictably, the incidence of measles, mumps, and rubella increased. In addition, lawsuits were filed by the parents of autistic children against the physicians who prescribed these immunizations and the pharmaceutical companies who manufactured them.

In 2004, with the controversy raging, a journalist named Brian Deer published the first in a series of articles in London's *Sunday Times* alleging that Dr. Wakefield had manipulated his evidence, failed to disclose conflicts of interest, and violated numerous other ethical principles. Later that year, *The Lancet* retracted parts of the article. In 2010, after considering additional information, *The Lancet* retracted the entire article. And just one year later, an article appearing in the *British Medical Journal* declared Wakefield's study fraudulent. Wakefield was convicted of professional misconduct and lost his medical license.

Meanwhile, some of the most prestigious medical research organizations in the world investigated Wakefield's 1998 claims. These included the Centers for Disease Control and Prevention, the American Academy of Pediatrics, the Institute of Medicine of the U.S. National Academy of Sciences, and, in England, the National Health Service. None of these organizations found any evidence in support of Wakefield's claims.

Not only did Wakefield falsify his results, but, in doing so, he caused immeasurable harm to countless families. Lawsuits based on his research cost millions of dollars. Thousands of children contracted measles, mumps, and rubella needlessly. And the parents of autistic children were left with the hollow feeling that they were no closer to solving the riddle of what caused, or what might cure, their children's disability.

The peer review process is the most effective means by which mistakes and fraudulent research are discovered. During the peer review process, researchers submit their data to independent and anonymous reviewers. These reviewers are often notable experts in a particular area who are quite familiar with the literature. If the findings from studies are radically different from what these experts know to be true, the peer review process becomes more intense and may even involve the submission or reevaluation of the author's original data. But sometimes, fraudulent research can slip past the peer review process.

Plagiarism is another form of research misrepresentation. It is presenting the work of others as your own. When a researcher borrows a statement, an idea, or any form of intellectual property from another person and fails to give proper credit to the original researcher, he or she is considered guilty of plagiarism. Typically, researchers give one another credit by citing the work of the original researcher and/or discussing the work of the researcher in depth. A researcher's work is actually strengthened by the liberal use and citation of previous research. It is a way that we show collective interest in a particular research topic and a foundation for our own research on that topic. By citing previous work, we show that we are contributing to the body of knowledge, thereby making our own research scientifically relevant.

In recent years, the problem of plagiarism has intensified. The ability to easily access information electronically may encourage some researchers to overlook the fact that they are using the intellectual property of another person. Word processing programs that allow researchers to cut and paste large amounts of information from an original source into a research report may also provide an easy mechanism for researchers to commit plagiarism. In response to what appears to be a growing problem, many colleges and universities, along with some publishers, have begun to use electronic programs that identify potentially plagiarized material. The career of a researcher who plagiarizes may be permanently derailed.

A final form of research misrepresentation is **deception**, which occurs when a researcher inappropriately lends his or her name and reputation to an unscrupulously produced research project. Occasionally, a dishonest research sponsor will approach a highly regarded researcher with a request and an offer of money to 'evaluate' the results of its research project. In these cases, the research is already complete and usually the results are favorable to the sponsor's interest. These sponsors do not really want the researcher's objective analysis. They merely want to associate their report with the researcher's perceived objectivity or reputation. In other words, they want the researcher's name, reputation, and implicit sanction of a research project to legitimize their often biased research findings. The research sponsor might be a for-profit company that has a financial interest in the outcome of the research. It might also be a government agency, a non-profit organization, or a political lobbying group. Below is a hypothetical example.

Making Research Real 3.6 – It's Really Not Safe in That Neighborhood

The owner of a very large apartment complex located in a high-crime area of town conducted a study of neighborhood crime rates. He found that the reported crime rate within his apartment complex was substantially lower than in the surrounding neighborhood. This was likely due to the fact that the apartment manager had hired a private security company to handle emergency calls, thereby reducing the number of crimes that were reported to the police department. Furthermore, the owner used the maximum occupancy of the complex as the baseline population of the apartment community, even though fewer than half of the units were occupied. Had the owner used the actual number of residents, the crime rate within the apartment complex would have been much higher than in the surrounding neighborhood.

The apartment complex owner wanted to use his dubious finding to market his apartments as a safer alternative to the housing in the surrounding neighborhood. As part of his marketing efforts, he approached a local university professor and offered him $5,000 to "look over the results and confirm their validity." The professor reviewed the report, checked the calculations, and concluded that the report's findings were legitimate. The owner included copies of the professor's evaluation in the report, produced numerous copies, and routinely distributed them to prospective renters.

Several months later, the local police department conducted audits of crime rates in apartment complexes throughout the community as part of a 'hot spot' analysis. This audit revealed a very different picture of crime in the apartment community. In fact, the actual crime rate in this apartment complex was among the highest in the city. The department listed the crime rates of apartment complexes on its website. The owner complained and produced a copy of the 'independent' analysis of the professor. An analyst from the police department contacted the professor, who was forced to admit that he had not analyzed the data carefully.

A researcher should never agree to be part of research deception. Unless the sponsor is willing to grant full access to the original data, documentation of the research methodology, and complete authority to reanalyze the data, a researcher should politely refuse to put his or her stamp of approval on any research findings.

Getting to the Point 3.7 – Research misrepresentation involves lying about data, results, and authorship in research. It may include research fraud, which is fabricating research data or results; plagiarism, which is presenting the intellectual property of another as one's own; or deception, which is lending one's name and/or reputation to a research project that one does not know much about.

Principle 7: Ensure the Safety of Researchers

The first ethical principle discussed in this section was to do no harm. The principle of doing no harm focuses on the safety of the research subjects. But this principle extends to the safety of researchers, as well. Many social science researchers collect information in the field. This can put them in unsafe situations and in close proximity to dangerous people. For example, criminal justice researchers may meet with criminals in the process of conducting research. This exposes researchers to potential physical harm. And it is not unheard of for researchers to be sued or served with a subpoena demanding that they provide their research data, thereby exposing them to potential legal harm. So, it is important for us as researchers to be equally concerned about our own safety. Here is an example from the experience of a friend of mine.

Making Research Real 3.7 – Harrowing Homelessness

An anthropologist friend of mine, we will call him Lloyd, spent many years studying homelessness. He had done some interesting research, but mostly on a theoretical level. One year, he decided that the only way to advance his research agenda was to actually live as a homeless person. So he decided that for one month during his summer break he would do just that.

Lloyd knew that homeless people are often victimized, but he was unprepared for the physical and psychological ruggedness of this lifestyle. He witnessed, first hand, the effects of sickness, addiction, untreated mental illness, hunger, exposure to the elements, conflict, and, as he put it, "the intense volume of loneliness." He was never able to relax, not even for a minute. He took copious notes only to have them, along with his other worldly possessions, stolen from a grocery cart he had 'borrowed' from a local grocery store. He was physically threatened almost daily. He lived in fear most of the time.

Lloyd had intended to spend a month on the streets, but after only a week he decided that his health would not hold. At the time, Lloyd was in his late forties and in good physical condition. I saw a photograph of him shortly after he returned from the 'field' and frankly I would not have recognized him had we met on the street. To this day, Lloyd has occasional nightmares about the experience. To be sure, the experience advanced his research agenda, and even took it in a direction that he never dreamed possible. But the physical and psychological effects of the experience will live with him forever.

Another problem that can happen to researchers in the field is that they become aware of criminal activities. Most of these criminal activities are minor, but sometimes they can be serious. The question is whether a researcher is obliged to share this information with the authorities and/or to assist in a crime investigation. Under many state laws, a failure to act constitutes an *actus reus* (criminal act). For example, many states require school teachers and medical personnel to report suspected cases of child abuse. There is no law, however, that requires researchers to report criminal activities that they encounter in the field. Though they may not be legally bound to share crime information, researchers may be ethically bound to do so. Many professional organizations, for example, have established codes of ethics that require researchers to report criminal activities.

In the end, researchers need to weigh these ethical standards and use their own best judgment when deciding whether to share criminal information. For example, it would seem appropriate to overlook minor violations committed by a research subject, like defacing public property or disturbing the peace. On the other hand, behaviors that can reasonably cause death, serious bodily injury, or substantial property damage should be addressed appropriately by the researcher. In between these two extremes are dozens of other behaviors that are better left to the judgment of a responsible and ethical researcher to decide whether to divulge or not. Below is an example from my own experience.

Making Research Real 3.8 – How About NO!

In 2001, the Wichita (Kansas) Police Department (WPD) approached me and asked me to analyze the traffic stop data that they were collecting to assess whether racial profiling was occurring in the department. I agreed, but only on the condition that we had a formal written agreement that prohibited me from distributing the results of the analysis without their permission. I was the one that requested this agreement. My concern was that if instances of racial profiling were found, I would expose individual police officers (my research subjects) to legal harm by sharing this information. At the time, the racial profiling controversy was raging. Nearly every police department in America had been accused of racial profiling. Lawsuits were emerging and the potential for litigation in Wichita was evident. This agreement allowed me to prevent legal harm to myself and research subjects.

At the end of my study, I reported my findings that the data did not support an allegation of racial profiling and participated in numerous press conferences and community meetings. Shortly thereafter, a reporter from the local newspaper and a community advocacy group asked for a copy of the data, ostensibly to verify that I was telling the truth. I informed them that the data contained personal information about the officers that conducted the stops and that Kansas law prohibited me, or anyone else, from disclosing the information without their permission. I also explained that I had assured the officers that I would not divulge information about them or the stops they made on an individual basis. Indeed, the written agreement between me and the WPD forbade me from doing so. The WPD was the sole owner of the data and only they could distribute it.

The newspaper reporter understood my reasoning and secured a copy of the original data directly from the WPD. The reporter's analysis confirmed my findings. The advocacy group was not so agreeable. They wanted the officers' personal information. Eventually, our attorneys talked to their attorneys and I was informed that the data in its original format was the property of the WPD, but once I received it and prepared it for analysis, it was my personal intellectual property. I could do with it what I chose, and I chose to keep it to myself. I told them that I had made a promise to the officers and I would not violate that promise.

In the end, nothing happened. Because the newspaper reporter's analysis was consistent with my findings, the advocacy group moved on to another issue. As for me, I continued to assist the department with subsequent follow-up studies, thereby establishing a rather fruitful research agenda that continues to this day.

Getting to the Point 3.8 – The principle of doing no harm extends to the safety of researchers. Research supervisors should ensure the physical and psychological safety of researchers, who may find themselves in potentially dangerous situations. They should also ensure that researchers are protected from legal harm. Consistent with this principle, researchers have an ethical obligation to report criminal activity that could cause harm to themselves or others.

The ethical principles discussed in the preceding pages are summarized in Table 3.2.

Table 3.2 Principles of Ethical Research Practice

PRINCIPLE	DESCRIPTION	APPLICATION
Do no harm	The research process should never cause physical, psychological, or legal harm to research subjects.	Researchers should be aware of all the potential harm that research subjects may be exposed to during a research project. They should prevent, mitigate, and inform participants of these potential harms.
Ensure privacy	Researchers should respect an individual's right to be left alone and ensure that the personal information of research subjects will not be inappropriately divulged.	When personal information about research subjects is collected confidentially, the researcher should be the only person that can attribute the information to a particular research subject. When personal information is collected anonymously, nobody, not even the researcher, should be able to attribute it to a particular research subject.
Obtain voluntary and informed consent	Researchers should secure consent from research subjects before they participate in a research project.	Consent must be given voluntarily, without threat or duress. Researchers must disclose, up front, what the research subjects will be asked to do and whether there are any risks involved.
Get permission	Researchers should get special permission to study members of vulnerable populations.	Certain populations, like children, the elderly, the mentally ill, and prisoners, are particularly vulnerable to abuse. Researchers must use special care and receive special permission to study these populations.
Avoid sponsorship bias and suppression	Researchers should avoid relationships that may lead to sponsorship bias and/or suppression.	Some research sponsors may attempt to control the research process so that it results in findings favorable to their financial, political, or personal interests. Researchers should never agree to participate in research if there is a chance that their objectivity or intellectual freedom will be limited.
Prevent misrepresentation	Researchers should not lie about or fabricate their research findings (research fraud), represent another person's work as their own (plagiarism), or sanction another person's work without conducting a careful analysis (deception).	To avoid the potential for misrepresentation, researchers must subject their work to rigorous and well-informed peer review. They must be honest about their methodology and their findings. And, when necessary, they must permit another party to independently evaluate their data and analysis.
Ensure the safety of researchers	The research process should never cause physical, psychological, or legal harm to researchers or their assistants.	Researchers have an obligation to know the potential harms that they, their colleagues, and their assistants may be exposed to during a research project. These potential harms must be mitigated and researchers must accept their responsibility to intervene if necessary, even if it means terminating the project.

MINIMIZING ETHICAL DILEMMAS

Most of the ethical principles discussed in the previous section have been codified into statutes, regulations, and procedures by governments, research institutions, and universities. In this section, we will take a look at some of the rules and procedures that have been put into place to make sure researchers adhere to minimum standards for ethical research practice. Compliance with these rules, however, is not always enough. Just because a researcher complies with the letter of the law does not mean that no harm will come to the research subjects or the researchers. Therefore, the rules discussed in this section should be considered a *minimum* ethical standard.

Legislation and Policy Oversight

In response to ethical misbehavior among errant researchers, numerous governing bodies have implemented ethical guidelines to ensure the safety of human research subjects. Among the most prominent at the international level are:

- The Nuremberg Code (1947) – This code was created following the Nuremberg Trial of Nazi doctors who conducted cruel experiments on human beings during World War II. It consists of ten points defining legitimate research on human subjects and includes such principles as informed consent and avoidance of potential harm to subjects.

- The Declaration of Helsinki (1964) – This declaration was developed by the 18th World Medical Assembly to provide ethical guidelines in human experimentation. It includes 12 principles to guide physicians on ethical issues relating to biomedical research and puts forth the idea that the needs of the research subject should come before research.

- The Belmont Report (1979) – This report was created by the National Commission for the Protection of Human Subjects of Biomedical and Behavioral Research. It establishes three principles for ethical conduct in research, including respect for persons, beneficence, and justice.

In the United States, there are also numerous federal and state statutes governing the treatment of human research subjects. At the federal level, the Common Rule (45 CFR Part 46) requires that each research institution with federally sponsored research involving human subjects have an Assurance with the Office of Human Research Protections on file. In addition to this statute, every federal agency (e.g., National Institutes of Health, National Science Foundation, Department of Justice) must have policies governing the behavior of researchers who involve human subjects in sponsored research. Most states, state agencies, and universities have similar statutes and regulations.

Institutional Review Boards

Nearly every university, research organization, or government agency that conducts research has policies and procedures governing the protection of human subjects. These policies and procedures extend to students who conduct research using human subjects. And, these regulations are in addition to the aforementioned federal statutes. Consistent with these policies and procedures, researchers must seek written approval from a review board prior to conducting their research. These review boards are typically referred to as **Institutional Review Boards**, or IRBs for short. IRBs usually consist of other researchers in the organization.

The level of scrutiny that a research project undergoes during the review process largely depends on the research project's potential for harm or controversy. No organization will sponsor research that could potentially harm its research subjects without requiring substantial safeguards. Generally, there are two levels of review. An **expedited review** is conducted on research projects that will have a minimal effect on research subjects. An anonymous survey on a relatively noncontroversial topic might fit into this category. For example, a researcher who wants to know in general how the people in a community feel about the services provided to them by the local police department might be eligible for an expedited review if the information requested through the survey is collected anonymously. The only potential 'harm' suffered by the respondents is the small amount of time they must devote to completing and returning the survey.

Full reviews are conducted on research projects that have more potential for harm. For example, if a researcher wants to interview individuals who have been arrested by the police and to collect personal information from them, a higher level of scrutiny might be warranted. In this case, the respondents might be fearful that their frank comments may cause police scrutiny and lead to criminal convictions. Such a research project would require a more in-depth review.

Codes of Ethics

Codes of ethics are normally statements of principles that guide professional behavior or practice. Most codes of ethics are created by industry organizations or professional associations. For example, many criminologists are members of the Academy of Criminal Justice Sciences (ACJS). The ACJS has a code of ethics that deals with various aspects of professional practice. By far the largest section within the ACJS code of ethics deals with research. Look at the following portion of the ACJS code of ethics to see if you can identify any of the ethical principles we have covered in this chapter.

Making Research Real 3.9 – Academy of Criminal Justice Sciences' Code of Ethics

Objectivity and Integrity in the Conduct of Criminal Justice Research

1. Members of the Academy should adhere to the highest possible technical standards in their research.

2. Since individual members of the Academy vary in their research modes, skills, and experience, they should acknowledge the limitations that may affect the validity of their findings.

3. In presenting their work, members of the Academy are obliged to fully report their findings. They should not misrepresent the findings of their research or omit significant data. Any and all omitted data should be noted and the reason(s) for exclusion stated clearly as part of the methodology. Details of their theories, methods, and research designs that might bear upon interpretations of research findings should be reported.

4. Members of the Academy should fully report all sources of financial support and other sponsorship of the research.

5. Members of the Academy should not make any commitments to respondents, individuals, groups, or organizations unless there is full intention and ability to honor them.

6. Consistent with the spirit of full disclosure of method and analysis, members of the Academy, after they have completed their own analyses, should cooperate in efforts to make raw data and pertinent documentation available to other social scientists, at reasonable costs, except in cases where confidentiality, the client's rights to proprietary information and privacy, or the claims of a field worker to the privacy of personal notes necessarily would be violated. The timeliness of this cooperation is especially critical.

7. Members of the Academy should provide adequate information, documentation, and citations concerning scales and other measures used in their research.

8. Members of the Academy should not accept grants, contracts, or research assignments that appear likely to violate the principles enunciated in this Code, and should disassociate themselves from research when they discover a violation and are unable to correct it.

9. When financial support for a project has been accepted, members of the Academy should make every reasonable effort to complete the proposed work on schedule.

10. When a member of the Academy is involved in a project with others, including students, there should be mutually accepted explicit agreements at the outset with respect to division of work, compensation, access to data, rights of authorship, and other rights and responsibilities. These agreements should not be exploitative or arrived at through any form of coercion or intimidation. Such agreements may need to be modified as the project evolves and such modifications should be clearly stated among all participants. Students should normally be the principal author of any work that is derived directly from their thesis or dissertation.

11. Members of the Academy have the right to disseminate research findings, except those likely to cause harm to clients, collaborators, and participants, those which violate formal or implied promises of confidentially, or those which are proprietary under a formal or informal agreement.

Disclosure and Respect of the Rights of Research Populations by Members of the Academy

12. Members of the Academy should not misuse their positions as professionals for fraudulent purposes or as a pretext for gathering information for any individual, group, organization, or government.

13. Human subjects have the right to full disclosure of the purposes of the research as early as it is appropriate to the research process, and they have the right to an opportunity to have their questions answered about the purpose and usage of the research. Members should inform research participants about aspects of the research that might affect their willingness to participate, such as physical risks, discomfort, and/or unpleasant emotional experiences.

14. Subjects of research are entitled to rights of personal confidentiality unless they are waived.

15. Information about subjects obtained from records that are open to public scrutiny cannot be protected by guarantees of privacy or confidentiality.

16. The process of conducting criminal justice research must not expose respondents to more than minimal risk of personal harm, and members of the Academy should make every effort to ensure the safety and security of respondents and project staff. Informed consent should be obtained when the risks of research are greater than the risks of everyday life.

17. Members of the Academy should take culturally appropriate steps to secure informed consent and to avoid invasions of privacy. In addition, special actions will be necessary where the individuals studied are illiterate, under correctional supervision, minors, have low social status, are under judicial supervision, have diminished capacity, are unfamiliar with social research or otherwise occupy a position of unequal power with the researcher.

18. Members of the Academy should seek to anticipate potential threats to confidentiality. Techniques such as the removal of direct identifiers, the use of randomized responses, and other statistical solutions to problems of privacy should be used where appropriate. Care should be taken to ensure secure storage, maintenance, and/or destruction of sensitive records.

19. Confidential information provided by research participants should be treated as such by members of the Academy, even when this information enjoys no legal protection or privilege and legal force is applied. The obligation to respect confidentiality also applies to members of research organizations (interviewers, coders, clerical staff, etc.) who have access to the information. It is the responsibility of administrators and chief investigators to instruct staff members on this point and to make every effort to ensure that access to confidential information is restricted.

20. While generally adhering to the norm of acknowledging the contributions of all collaborators, members of the Academy should be sensitive to harm that may arise from disclosure and respect a collaborator's need for anonymity.

21. All research should meet the human subjects requirements imposed by educational institutions and funding sources. Study design and information gathering techniques should conform to regulations protecting the rights of human subjects, regardless of funding.

22. Members of the Academy should comply with appropriate federal and institutional requirements pertaining to the conduct of their research. These requirements might include, but are not necessarily limited to, obtaining proper review and approval for research that involves human subjects and accommodating recommendations made by responsible committees concerning research subjects, materials, and procedures.

(Academy of Criminal Justice Sciences, 2012)

Instances of ethical violations that might result in formal punishment are rare, especially when one considers how much research the members of the Academy do each year and how few ethical violations are brought to the organization's attention. Even so, the Academy does have a procedure that provides for sanctions such as the termination of a researcher's membership. In most cases, ethical violations are handled by the researcher's sponsoring agency.

It is likely that you, as a university student, are also governed by a code of ethics. Most universities publish student codes of conduct. For example, at the university where I work, students, faculty, and staff are required to adhere to an Honor Code, which spells out the expectations for students, faculty, and staff, as well as the procedures that will result if the code is violated. After you graduate and begin working as a criminal justice practitioner, you will likely also be governed by a code of ethics. One of the most popular is the Law Enforcement Code of Ethics, which has been used for decades by police departments throughout the nation. Similarly, the American Correctional Association offers a code of ethics to guide correctional officers' behavior. Many other organizations have adopted their own organizational codes of ethics. These codes are designed to provide general guidance to the members of these organizations as they perform their duties.

Getting to the Point 3.11 – Many professional organizations and most universities publish formally written codes of ethics. These codes are intended to provide guidance to professionals and members of organizations on how to behave ethically.

FINAL THOUGHTS

Social science researchers rely upon human beings as sources of data and information. Without human involvement in the research process, there is no social science.

But studying human beings demands accountability and responsibility toward our research subjects. To be ethical means to protect our research subjects from harm and to improve their welfare in some way. Both require us to be proactive. We cannot simply wait for ethical challenges to present themselves; we must think of all the possible ethical problems that might arise and develop plans to prevent and/or address these problems during the research planning phase.

One way to identify the potential ethical problems that a research project may encounter is to put ourselves in the research subject's position. We should ask, *"How would I feel if somebody asked me to do what I am asking these research subjects to do?"* Or better yet, *"If I were in the same situation that my research subjects are in, how would I feel about what I am being asked to do?"* These questions and others like them have the added benefit of discovering potential problems in methodology. In other words, *ethical* research makes for *good* research.

GETTING TO THE POINT/CHAPTER SUMMARY

- Social science researchers should be concerned about ethics because ultimately their obligation is to improve the human condition through research. What constitutes ethical behavior often depends on the particular circumstances of individual research projects.

- The principle of doing no harm means that researchers should never subject research participants to physical danger, cause them psychological harm, or expose them to legal liability. Researchers should build contingencies into the research plan to prevent or mitigate potential harm. In extreme cases, they should abandon the research project altogether.

- Privacy means the right to be left alone and free from public scrutiny. There are two types of privacy in research. Confidentiality means that the researcher knows who the research subjects are, but does not disclose their identity to others. Anonymity means that nobody, not even the researcher, knows the identity of the research subjects.

- Researchers must obtain consent from research subjects prior to collecting information from them. This consent must be given voluntarily, meaning that the research subjects must be completely free to participate or not participate without threat. In addition, the consent must be informed, meaning that the researcher must inform the research subjects about the research and any risks associated with participation in the research.

- Researchers must seek and obtain permission to work with individuals who are considered vulnerable by virtue of their diminished capacity to direct their own affairs. Vulnerable populations include children, the mentally ill, the infirm, the elderly, and prisoners.

- Sponsorship bias occurs when the sponsor of a research project attempts to influence the study design or interpretation of data for its own benefit. Suppression occurs when a research sponsor fails to disclose findings that shed an unfavorable light on the sponsor's products or services.

- Research misrepresentation involves lying about data, results, and authorship in research. It may include research fraud, which is fabricating research data or results; plagiarism, which is presenting the intellectual property of another as your own; or deception, which is lending one's name and/or reputation to a research project that one does not know much about.

- The principle of doing no harm extends to the safety of researchers. Research supervisors should ensure the physical and psychological safety of researchers, who may find themselves in potentially dangerous situations. They should also ensure that researchers are protected from legal harm. Consistent with this principle, researchers have an ethical obligation to report criminal activity that could cause harm to themselves or others.

- Researchers are subject to numerous international treaties, federal and state laws, and institutional regulations that are designed to protect human research subjects.

- Nearly every university and many research organizations maintain Institutional Review Boards (IRBs) and require researchers to seek approval from these boards prior to doing research on human subjects. Research projects that pose minimal risk to human subjects undergo an expedited review; research projects that pose considerable risk to human subjects undergo a full review. The level of scrutiny depends on the potential for human harm.

- Many professional organizations and most universities publish formally written codes of ethics. These codes are intended to provide guidance to professionals and members of organizations on how to behave ethically.

CHAPTER EXERCISES

The following chapter exercises are organized into two parts. The first part consists of questions that can be answered using the information from the preceding chapter. Use this section to test your understanding of the chapter material. The second part consists of research application exercises. These exercises require you to apply what you have learned thus far.

CHAPTER REVIEW QUESTIONS

Respond to each of the following questions using the information from this chapter.

1. Classify each of the following ethical violations into one of the following ethical principles:
    a. Do no harm
    b. Ensure privacy
    c. Obtain voluntary and informed consent
    d. Get permission
    e. Avoid sponsorship bias and suppression
    f. Prevent misrepresentation
    g. Ensure the safety of researchers

Ethical violation	Principle
A criminologist conducts a study on the effectiveness of a new violent offender rehabilitation program at the request of the program developer, a for-profit company. She determines that the program is largely ineffective. A few weeks later, she reads in the paper that the state prison authorities have adopted this program because it "has been evaluated by a competent criminologist and has been found to be effective."	
A tribal police department has asked you to evaluate an alcohol dependency program being offered on a Native American reservation. You immediately travel to the reservation and begin interviewing patients, all alcoholics, in the treatment facility. You presume that since the tribal police department invited you to evaluate the program, you can get started right away.	
Two graduate students have been assigned to conduct field observations of juveniles who 'hang out' on street corners. The research site is a known high-crime area. When one of the students expresses concern about their safety, the research director says, "Don't worry about it. What could possibly happen?"	

You have been asked to determine the extent to which the local police department enforces marijuana laws. You hire ten students and ask them to openly smoke marijuana in various public places. You want to see if the police confront them.	
After conducting a case study of a child who had been the victim of bullying in school, you realize that others might be able to determine the identity of the research subject (the child). You decide to publish the results anyway because you have the guardian's permission and you doubt that anyone will read your article.	
At the request of the local police chief, you are conducting research on the work habits of police officers. You tell the officers about the nature of the study and the information you are going to collect in interviews with them. You also suggest that their failure to participate in the 'department approved' research project will be reported to the chief.	
After analyzing the data from a study you are conducting on a drug use prevention program, you find that your results are not as definitive as you had predicted. You suspect that some of the data may have been coded wrongly so you change some of the data. This changes the results dramatically and 'proves' that you were right.	

2. For each research scenario below, indicate the type of harm with which a researcher should be concerned:
    a. Physical harm
    b. Psychological harm
    c. Legal harm

Research scenario	Type of harm
A criminal justice researcher interviews violent criminal offenders in their homes.	
A researcher asks respondents to disclose their names, addresses, and information on their criminal behavior.	
An interviewer asks young sexual assault victims to recount the details of their victimization.	

3. When it is not possible for anybody, including the researcher, to determine the identities of the research subjects using the information they provide on a survey, we say that research subjects have been granted:

    a.   Anonymity

    b.   Confidentiality

    c.   Privacy

4.   When a researcher knows but agrees not to disclose her research subjects' identities she has likely assured them of:

    a.   Privacy

    b.   Anonymity

    c.   Confidentiality

5.   Researchers should secure consent from research subjects prior to gathering information from them. This consent must be both:

    a.   Voluntary and written

    b.   Voluntary and informed

    c.   Informed and written

    d.   None of the above

6.   If a researcher threatens to tell a research subject's boss that the subject has refused to participate in the research study, the subject's consent is considered:

    a.   Contrived

    b.   Involuntary

    c.   Reliable

    d.   Uninformed

7.   Which of the following groups of research subjects would be considered a vulnerable population, requiring a more detailed review by an Institutional Review Board?

    a.   School children

    b.   Incarcerated offenders

    c.   Nursing home residents

    d.   All of the above

8.   When should a research report on the safety and effectiveness of a new non-lethal weapon used by police officers be reviewed more critically?

    a.   If the research report was published by a government agency that tests consumer products for safety

    b.   If the research report was written by a researcher for a peer-reviewed scholarly journal

    c.   If the research were conducted by a private research firm that tests products for the insurance industry

    d.   If the research were sponsored by the same company that manufactures the new weapon

9.   A researcher is hired to evaluate the effectiveness of a substance abuse rehabilitation program for incarcerated offenders. After reviewing the data provided by the organization administering the program, the researcher notices that a large amount of information is missing. The researcher should do which of the following?

   a.   Not worry about it because criminal justice data is notoriously incomplete

   b.   Proceed with the analysis and report that data are missing

   c.   Refuse to conduct the analysis until the data set is complete

10. A researcher uses information from an open source website similar to Wikipedia. Because this information is readily available to anyone who wants it and does not include the name of the person who provided the information, the researcher decides not to attribute the information to the website from which it came. This researcher is guilty of:

   a.   Deception

   b.   Lying

   c.   Nothing

   d.   Plagiarism

11. Researchers who intend to gather information from human subjects should seek approval for their research from an Institutional Review Board:

   a.   Every time human subjects are involved in the data collection

   b.   In cases where research subjects are considered a vulnerable population

   c.   Only if they think their data collection will expose the research subjects to harm

   d.   When the research plan involves some kind of medical intervention

12. Which of the following research projects would likely require a full review, as opposed to an expedited review, by an Institutional Review Board?

   a.   A focus group involving airline passengers who travel frequently

   b.   A series of interviews of parents whose children have been murdered

   c.   A survey of the general population on how they intend to vote in an election

   d.   An unobtrusive observational study of people in a shopping mall

RESEARCH APPLICATION EXERCISES

Access to the following articles will be provided by your instructor.

> Hochstetler, A., Copes, H. and Williams, J.P. (2010). "That's not who I am": How offenders commit violent acts and reject authentically violent selves. *Justice Quarterly, 27*(4), 492–516.
>
> Sexton, L., Jenness, V. and Sumner J.M. (2010). Where the margins meet: A demographic assessment of transgender inmates in men's prisons. *Justice Quarterly, 27*(6), 835–866.
>
> Stogner, J.M., Miller, B.L. and Marcum, C.D. (2012). Learning to e-cheat: A criminological test of internet facilitated academic cheating. *Justice Quarterly* (online version).

13. Read the article by Hochstetler, Copes, and Williams (2010) and respond to the following questions.

   a.   What was the purpose of this research?

   b.   How and from whom did these researchers gather the data they needed for their research?

    c.   Did these researchers anticipate or encounter any ethical problems during this research project?

    d.   What steps did these researchers take to ensure their research subjects were not subjected to legal harm following the publication of the research?

14. Read the article by Sexton, Jenness, and Sumner (2010) and respond to the following questions.

    a.   What was the purpose of this research?

    b.   How and from whom did these researchers gather the data they needed for their research?

    c.   Did these researchers anticipate or encounter any ethical problems during this research project?

    d.   Why did these researchers consider their research subjects to be a vulnerable population?

15. Read the article by Stogner, Miller, and Marcum (2012) and respond to the following questions.

    a.   What was the purpose of this research?

    b.   How and from whom did these researchers gather the data they needed for their research?

    c.   Did these researchers anticipate or encounter any ethical problems during this research project?

    d.   How did these researchers ensure the privacy of their research subjects?

PART 2

Learning Research
Design Basics

CHAPTER 4

Classifying Research

Research is often classified into categories. For the most part, these categories provide us a way to organize research so we can access it more efficiently. For example, a criminologist might wonder whether there is any research on the process by which a police officer becomes socialized into the police subculture. Using an index of published research (e.g. Criminal Justice Abstracts), the criminologist may use the search term 'police subculture' to locate the relevant research. This may produce hundreds, maybe thousands, of articles. To narrow the search, he may add the terms 'explanatory' and 'longitudinal' to the search browser. This search would produce information on research that might *explain* (explanatory) how police officers become socialized into the police subculture *over time* (longitudinal).

Research classifications also enable researchers to evaluate research and in some cases identify logical errors. Say, for example, that a researcher surveys a group of correctional officers. They learn that, as a group, these officers tend to be politically conservative. Later, they meet a correctional officer at a community meeting and assume that this correctional officer is politically conservative. In making this assumption, the researcher is committing a logical error. This type of error, which we will discuss toward the end of this chapter, happens when a person uses information collected at the group level of analysis to predict the behavior of an individual who is part of that group. Knowing the unit of analysis in a research study, among other things, helps us detect these logical errors and understand the limitations and contributions of the research study.

The information in this chapter is meant to give you a sense of the different types of research, not to suggest a hierarchy of research approaches. Unfortunately, some researchers consider some forms of research to be less 'scientific' than others. You should avoid making this assumption. It is important to regard all forms of research as potentially valuable. The following classification strategies are the most commonly used among researchers and are the major classification schemes explored in this chapter (see Table 4.1).

Table 4.1 Common Classification Schemes for Research

CLASSIFICATION SCHEME	DESCRIPTION	CATEGORIES OF RESEARCH
Paradigms of research	Describes the general organizing framework for social theory and empirical research	Positivist Interpretive Critical
Purpose of research	Describes what the research hopes to achieve	Exploratory Descriptive Explanatory
Time dimension of research	Describes the time frame in which data collection takes place	Cross-sectional Longitudinal
Nature of data	Describes the type of data collected and, in some cases, the type of research method used	Quantitative Qualitative
Method of reasoning	Describes the method of reasoning used by the researcher	Deductive Inductive
Unit of analysis	Describes from whom or what the researcher collects information	Individual Group Community Nation

Getting to the Point 4.1 – Research is often organized by different classification methods in order to help researchers access it more efficiently and evaluate its strengths and limitations.

PARADIGMS OF RESEARCH

When we develop research questions, we generally draw from a particular paradigm of the social world. A **paradigm**, or **paradigm of research**, is a general organizing framework for social theory and empirical research. More succinctly, a paradigm is a lens through which a person views social phenomena. It reflects a researcher's assumptions about reality. There are three common paradigms in social science research. Each makes its own contribution to the body of knowledge.

- **Positivist** social science inquiry is most like research in the natural sciences. A positivist relies on empirical observations and may attempt to establish a causal relationship between variables. For example, a positivist may hypothesize that poverty is a cause of crime. To test this hypothesis, she may develop quantitative measures for poverty (e.g. annual income) and crime (e.g. number of arrests). She may then calculate the relationship between these two variables within a sample of individuals. If poorer people tend to have a higher number of arrests, the researcher may be in a better position to allege that poverty causes crime.

- **Interpretive** social science inquiry is based on the notion that social science research is fundamentally different from research in the natural sciences. Rather than simply measure human behavior from the 'outside,' interpretive social scientists attempt to get 'inside' to understand the meaning behind human behavior. This involves interpretation rather than simple observation. For example, an interpretive social scientist might live as an impoverished person for a time so he can understand the experience of poverty. He may find that poverty is experienced as a lack of social security and, in many cases, leads to social aggression. This aggressive behavior may manifest itself in behaviors that we, as a society, define as criminal.

- **Critical** social science inquiry is based on the assumption that research is not value free and that every researcher brings his or her own particular biases into the research process. Critical researchers do not attempt to be unbiased and instead believe that they should use their research skills to affect social change. Critical criminologists tend to focus on the structure of race, class, and gender inequalities and the relationships between these inequalities and crime and punishment. A critical criminologist may find in her research that poor people get harsher sentences because they cannot afford competent legal representation. She may use this research to argue for an increase in funding for public defenders. Indeed, a critical criminologist might have even decided to conduct this research for the sole purpose of improving poor people's access to legal representation.

None of these paradigms is considered 'the best way.' They are merely beginning assumptions that guide researchers through the research process. Each of these approaches makes an important contribution to the body of knowledge.

Getting to the Point 4.2 – Researchers often approach research questions from a particular paradigm or perception of social reality. These perceptions affect how the researcher conducts the research and, in many cases, the outcome of the research findings. The positivist, interpretive, and critical paradigms all contribute to our understanding of social phenomena.

THE PURPOSE OF RESEARCH

In Chapter 1, you were introduced to the three primary **purposes of research**: exploratory, descriptive, and explanatory. To review, the purpose of **exploratory research** is to learn something about a new or emerging social phenomenon. The purpose of **descriptive research** is to describe social behavior or phenomena. And, the purpose of **explanatory research** is to explain why individuals or groups behave the way they do. Seldom is a research project exclusively exploratory, descriptive, or explanatory. For example, we may conduct exploratory research to learn something about how terrorist groups use the Internet to communicate or plan terroristic events. This research may include a description, in the form of a case study, of how a terrorist organization planned a specific event. This single research project might even provide some insight into why these groups decide to engage in terrorism. In this case, our research would be some combination of exploratory, descriptive, and explanatory research.

Research agendas often progress from exploratory to descriptive to explanatory research. For example, in 1990, the term 'racial profiling' was relatively new. Some researchers began to conduct exploratory research into this alleged policing practice by analyzing the stories told by individuals who accused police officers of racial profiling. Eventually, researchers began to collect data on traffic stops. These data sets provided opportunities to describe the patterns and practices of police departments with respect to who they stopped, searched, and arrested. Finally, researchers turned their attention to developing theories to explain why police officers might engage in this practice.

Getting to the Point 4.3 – Research is often conducted for a specific purpose. Exploratory research provides initial insight into new or emerging social phenomena or behavior. Descriptive research describes existing social phenomena or behavior. Explanatory research explains why individuals or groups behave the way they do. It is not uncommon for a single research project to serve more than one purpose. It is also not uncommon for a research agenda to move from exploratory to descriptive to explanatory research.

THE TIME DIMENSION OF RESEARCH

The **time dimension of research** describes the time frame in which the data collection takes place. Most research in Criminology and Criminal Justice is cross-sectional. By **cross-sectional**, we mean that the research findings are based on data collected at one point in time. Even though it may take days, weeks, or even months to collect the data, once they are analyzed and reported by the researcher, it is considered cross-sectional. Cross-sectional research is sometimes referred to as a 'snapshot' because the research findings are based on what is happening at a particular time.

A single annual Uniform Crime Report published by the Federal Bureau of Investigation (FBI) is an example of cross-sectional research. Since the 1930s, the FBI has been a central repository of information about crimes reported to the police, the arrests that result from these crimes and other police department information. The information is compiled each year into what is known as the Uniform Crime Report, or UCR. Nearly all city, county, state, tribal, university, and other police agencies report this information to the FBI. It takes a year for all of the participating departments to compile this information. The results are often not available until well into the following year. Using this information, the UCR calculates the annual crime rate, or the number of crimes per 100,000 residents. Though it takes a bit of time to collect these data, the results from a single year's UCR are used to measure crime during that specific year. Hence, it is cross-sectional.

Research based on cross-sectional data does not measure social phenomena prior to or after the data were collected. In other words, cross-sectional data cannot document change over time. For example, a **cross-sectional survey** gathers information from respondents at a single point in time. A respondent to a cross-sectional survey might indicate that she opposes the death penalty on a survey. There is no way for the researcher to know whether she opposed the death penalty last year or might continue to oppose the death penalty in the future. Despite this limitation, research based on cross-sectional data can be highly useful. For example, a correctional administrator may conduct an analysis of the inmates at her prison facility. She may learn that a majority of the inmates have a history of violent behavior. This cross-sectional data may justify an increase in the number of anger management programs available to the inmates at the facility. Sometime in the future, the correctional administrator may reanalyze the inmates at her prison facility and find that fewer have a history of violent behavior. At this point in time, she may decide to decrease the number of anger management programs. At each point in time, cross-sectional data can provide a snapshot of particular populations and issues. Below is an actual example of a cross-sectional research project.

Making Research Real 4.1 – What Makes Police Officers Happy?

In the late 1990s Jihong Zao, Quint Thurman, and Ni He conducted a survey of the police officers in the Spokane (Washington) Police Department. The purpose of this survey was to identify the factors that influence job satisfaction among police officers. Job satisfaction (the dependent variable) was measured in relation to the officers' work, their relationships with supervisors, and their relationships with co-workers. The factors they considered important to determining job satisfaction (the independent variables) included the officers' ethnicity, gender, educational attainment, years of service, rank, and the work itself (e.g. skill required, level of autonomy, and feedback provided).

The researchers found that job satisfaction was closely associated with the work itself. Officers that performed repetitive and monotonous work tended to be less satisfied than officers who were allowed to perform their duties with a higher degree of autonomy.

These findings seem might seem rather obvious. After all, few people like mundane work and a lot of people like to work with a high degree of autonomy. But, this research was done at a time when American policing was experiencing a philosophical shift. Policing leaders were only beginning to accept the notion that police officers were capable of solving their own problems and completing their job tasks without supervisors watching their every move. Previously, American policing was characterized by strict rules and tended to value consistency and discipline. This research demonstrated that a new generation of police officers wanted to be set free from the limitations of their predecessors and to use their skills to solve the crime problems facing their particular patrol districts. In some ways, research like this encouraged police leaders to adopt a problem-oriented policing philosophy.

(Zhao, Thurman and He, 1999)

Zhao, Thurman, and He's research took a snapshot of the police officers that were working in the Spokane Police Department in the late 1990s. Although this research makes a contribution to the literature, it cannot explain what happened when these police officers left and were replaced by a new generation of police officers. The new officers might conform to the behaviors and motivations of their predecessors, but they might not. There is some evidence that the individuals entering the policing service today are very different from their predecessors. In fact, employers in nearly all industries are only now learning how to address the particular needs of the new 'Net Generation.' This cohort of workers is the first generation of individuals raised and educated with the benefit of the internet, cable television, and social media. As a group, they think and behave very differently from their predecessors (Tapscott, 2008). So, would it be useful to replicate Zhao, Thurman, and He's research to find out what factors influence the job satisfaction of this new generation of employees?

Getting to the Point 4.4 – Cross-sectional research involves data collection at one point in time. The findings from this research cannot be used to draw conclusions about change over time. But they can provide a snapshot of a social condition or population at that point in time.

Some criminological and criminal justice research is based on longitudinal data. By **longitudinal**, we mean that the data are collected at multiple points over an extended period of time. Researchers often compare the data from two or more collection periods, or waves, to document change over time. As I explained earlier, one annual Uniform Crime Report would represent cross-sectional research because that report is only using data from one particular year. Taken as a whole, however, all the Uniform Crime Reports present us with longitudinal data because they have been compiled every year since the mid-1930s. As such, we could compare the annual crime rate for a community from one year to the next and identify trends in crime.

One important limitation to longitudinal research is the amount of time it takes to collect data. A researcher must collect and recollect data over multiple periods, often waiting to report their results for many years. Sometimes the gaps between data collection waves are substantial. For example, data for the United States Census are collected every ten years. The UCR attempts to mitigate this problem by issuing quarterly crime reports throughout the year. For example, the quarterly crime reports for the months January through March might be issued the following May so criminal justice administrators can get a sense of emerging crime trends a bit earlier.

Another limitation to a longitudinal design is that the data collection procedures must remain consistent throughout each data collection wave or else the data will be useless for comparison purposes. What exactly do we mean by this? In general, we have to ask the same questions in the same exact way using the same data collection procedures if we want to compare answers from different data collection waves. The U.S. Census, for example, collects a large amount of descriptive data on the U.S. population every ten years. One piece of information it has consistently collected is information on the race of each person residing in the United States at the time of the census. The census, however, has not asked the race question in the same way and it has not collected the data in the same way, making it difficult to track racial trends over time. The original census, taken in 1790, differentiated only between slave, free White persons and other free persons. One hundred years later, in 1890, the census designated the following racial categories: White, Black, Mulatto, Quadroon, Octoroon, Chinese, Japanese, and Indian. By 1990, a somewhat different set of racial categories was used: White, Black, American Indian and Alaskan Native, Asian, Native Hawaiian and Pacific Islander, and Some Other Race. Complicating things even further, beginning with the 2000 census, individuals could select more than one racial category. These changes render analyses of change in the U.S. racial populations over time quite difficult (Anderson and Feinberg, 2000; Winker, 2004).

When done well, though, longitudinal studies can provide important insight into how populations and social phenomena change over time. In fact, some of the most important criminological studies are based on longitudinal designs. Beginning in the 1920s, for example, Sheldon and Eleanor Glueck conducted a detailed longitudinal study of juvenile delinquency. They followed a sample of 500 delinquent boys over decades with follow-up surveys and interviews. This research revealed complicated, and previously unknown, processes that lead juveniles to delinquent behavior and, eventually, to adult criminality (Glueck and Glueck, 1950).

In 1972, the Gluecks donated their data and personal papers to the Harvard University Library. Decades later, Robert Sampson and John Laub rediscovered this data in the basement of the library. After resolving numerous technological challenges and ethical issues, they followed up on the Gluecks' sample of delinquent boys. Their research demonstrated that during certain times, which they called "turning points," individuals are either more or less vulnerable to deviant behavior. Informal social controls like school, family, marriage, and employment affect individual behavior throughout the life course (Sampson and Laub, 1995). Table 4.2 summarizes the advantages and disadvantages of cross-sectional and longitudinal research.

Table 4.2 The Time Dimension of Research

TIME DIMENSION	DESCRIPTION	ADVANTAGES	DISADVANTAGES
Cross-sectional	Research based on data collected at one point in time.	Provides quicker insight into the status of a social situation or phenomenon.	Does not measure how social situations and phenomena change over time.
Longitudinal	Research based on data collected at multiple points over an extended period.	Provides insight into how social situations and phenomena change over time.	Cannot provide quick insight into the status of a social situation or phenomenon.

There are three types of longitudinal designs. **Trend studies** collect the same data at different times from different samples of the same population. Trend studies are also known as repeated cross-sectional studies, because researchers are basically conducting the same cross-sectional study at different points in time. The Gallup polls are a good example of trend studies. Each year, the Gallup organization conducts telephone surveys of a random sample of U.S. adults to determine changing public attitudes in the United States. The organization asks the same questions over a period of time. For example, it first asked about support for the death penalty in 1936, at which time 59 percent of Americans supported it. Support has varied over the years, reaching an all-time high of 80 percent in 1994. Since then, support has declined and was around 61 percent in 2011.

Panel studies collect data from the same individuals – the panel – over multiple points in time. The difference between a panel study and a trend study, then, is that a panel study follows the same sample of individuals. The Gluecks' study is an example of a panel study. In another example, Niles Langstrom (2002) studied 126 young sex offenders in Sweden over 15 years (1980–1995). The purpose of this study was to determine how risk factors influenced when, or if, sex offenders reoffend. He found that after six or seven years, young sex offenders were less likely to be reconvicted of sexual offenses. However, their potential for non-sexual and violent convictions remained unchanged. This panel study provides us some insight into the effectiveness of post-release rehabilitation programs.

The third type of longitudinal design is called a **cohort study**. In a cohort study, the panel consists of a group of individuals that share a common characteristic or experience within a defined period of time. For example, people born between 1946 and 1964 are known as the 'Baby Boomers'; they constitute a cohort of people born around the same time who experience historical events at similar points in their lives.

Getting to the Point 4.5 – Longitudinal research utilizes data that are collected over a period of time. The findings from this research indicate how a social condition or particular population changes over time. There are three types of longitudinal research designs. Trend studies collect the same data over time from different samples of the same population. Panel studies collect the same data over time from the same sample. Cohort studies collect data over time from samples of individuals who share common characteristics.

THE NATURE OF DATA

The **nature of the data** collected in the course of research is another dimension by which we can classify research. **Quantitative research** measures variables numerically, hence the name *quantitative*. It assumes that the social world can be understood objectively and measured accordingly. For example, a quantitative researcher might measure education in terms of the number of years a person was involved in an organized learning environment, like a school. He might assume that a person with 12 years of education might have a high school diploma and a person with 16 years of education might have a Bachelor's degree. **Qualitative research** examines variables in a natural social setting and probes the qualitative meaning of these variables. Qualitative research is less about measurement and more about meaning. It assumes that the social world is best understood subjectively, or from the perspective of research subjects. For example, a qualitative researcher might ask a person to describe her education in her own words and/or to interpret the underlying purpose of the school system.

Of all the classification schemes, the quantitative–qualitative scheme is the most controversial. Researchers tend to be primarily quantitative or qualitative, and only a few actually publish research within both traditions. Some social science disciplines tend to be overly influenced by either quantitative research (e.g. Economics) or qualitative research (e.g. Cultural Anthropology). And some researchers tend to be critical of researchers from the other camp. For example, some quantitative researchers do not regard qualitative research as scientific because this type of research typically does not produce findings that can be generalized to other social settings. Likewise, some qualitative researchers regard quantitative researchers as overly scientific, arguing that the social world is too complex to understand through numbers alone. Researchers should avoid these rigid perspectives. Research is research and it is inappropriate to regard one tradition of research as more or less valuable. The objective of any researcher should be to use whichever research tool is appropriate – quantitative or qualitative – to respond to a research question.

> **Getting to the Point 4.6** – Quantitative research measures variables numerically and assumes that the social world can be understood objectively. Qualitative research probes the meaning of variables and assumes that the social world is best understood subjectively, often from the perspective of the research subject.

METHOD OF REASONING

We may also classify research in terms of the **method of reasoning** used by the researcher. Some researchers start with a theory, develop hypotheses based on that theory, and then collect information (or data) that either supports or falsifies the theory. This method of reasoning is called deduction or **deductive reasoning**. Here is a hypothetical example.

Making Research Real 4.2 – Deductive Reasoning

Rational choice theory proposes that potential offenders weigh the risks associated with getting caught with the benefits of committing the crime. If the benefits outweigh the risks, the potential offender is more likely to commit the crime. Conversely, this theory holds, if we increase the risk associated with certain behaviors, fewer potential offenders will commit crimes because the risks will outweigh the benefits. Using this theory a researcher may develop the following research expectation:

If the penalty for driving while intoxicated were increased, drunk driving arrests would decrease.

Having developed this hypothesis, the researcher might gather information about the incidence of drunken driving arrests before and after a law requiring jail time for all individuals convicted of drunk driving goes into effect. If, after the law passes, the number of drunken driving arrests decreases, the hypothesis will be supported.

In the absence of a theory that might explain a social behavior or phenomenon, a researcher may use another method of reasoning. In this case, he would observe the behavior or phenomenon over a period of time until he has enough information to propose a theory for the behavior or phenomenon. This method of reasoning is called induction or **inductive reasoning**. Here is another hypothetical example.

Making Research Real 4.3 – Inductive Reasoning

After evaluating the data from a city-wide vehicle stop study, a researcher observes that White drivers appear to be more at risk of being stopped in patrol beats that are principally populated by Black residents. Conversely, in patrol beats that are principally populated by White residents, Black drivers appear to be more at risk of being stopped. From these observations, the researcher proposes a theory that he calls the theory of contextual attentiveness. The theory is as follows:

Police officers develop ideas about what is usual, customary, or expected within a particular context. They become attentive to individuals or behaviors that appear inconsistent with their idea of what is usual, customary, or expected within a particular context.

Once an individual or behavior is defined by the police officer as inconsistent with what they understand to be usual, customary, or expected within a particular context, the police officer may seek a pretext to justify an official encounter.

(see Withrow, 2004)

Either of these approaches is a perfectly legitimate method of reasoning. It just depends on whether a theory already exists to explain the behavior or phenomenon. Typically, researchers that do exploratory and descriptive research follow a deductive process; researchers that do explanatory research follow an inductive process. But these are only general guidelines. Figure 4.1 illustrates these two methods of reasoning.

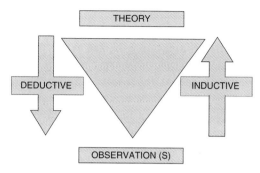

Figure 4.1   Deductive and Inductive Reasoning

Getting to the Point 4.7 – Deductive reasoning begins with a theory that explains social behavior and uses observations to test the theory. Inductive reasoning begins with observations of social behavior and uses those observations to develop a theory that explains the behavior.

UNIT OF ANALYSIS

The **unit of analysis** is the 'what' or 'whom' that we are studying during the course of a research project. For example, we might be doing an in-depth study of the professional lives of police officers. In this case, we are studying police officers, or people. So our unit of analysis, or the object of our study, is an individual. A unit of analysis can be an individual, a group, a community, a state, or even an entire nation. For example, if you were to compare crime rates across various countries, your unit of analysis would be a nation. Or you might compare the history and organizational structure of two street gangs. In this case, you would be studying gangs and your unit of analysis would be a group. Most social research projects have an individual unit of analysis, meaning that the researcher gathers information from individual respondents.

Getting to the Point 4.8 – The unit of analysis is the 'what' or 'whom' about which researchers gather information during a research project. A unit of analysis can be an individual, a group, a community, a state, or even an entire nation.

An understanding of a research project's unit of analysis is important in order to avoid making one of two errors of logic. These errors have rather heavy names, but the idea behind them is actually quite simple. One error is called an **ecological fallacy**. It occurs when a researcher makes a prediction about individual behavior based solely on observations that were gathered at the group level. Here, the unit of analysis is a group and the researcher may use this data to make predictions on how this group or a similar group might behave now or in the future. What the researcher cannot do is use information collected at this group level to predict how an individual within that group might behave.

Consider this example. Say that your local police department reports a very low 'clearance rate' for vehicular burglaries. By this, we mean that the department *as a whole* does not have a good record of identifying and arresting individuals who burglarize cars. Upon entering your car one morning, you notice that your stereo system and extensive CD collection is missing. You call the police to report the burglary. The police officer fills out a report and assures you that they will investigate the crime. When you get to work, you tell your colleague about your experience. Your colleague responds: "Well, don't get your hopes up that the officer will find the guy. They seldom do." Your colleague has committed an ecological fallacy. He assumed that because the department as a whole (a group unit of analysis) has a bad record for arresting vehicle burglars, the officer assigned to your case (an individual level of analysis) will also be unsuccessful. Now, it may be true that the individual officer assigned to your case will be unsuccessful. After all, the department overall has a bad record of catching car burglars because a lot of individual officers are unsuccessful at identifying and arresting these culprits. But logically speaking, you cannot infer that the officer assigned to your case will be unsuccessful because the department as a whole is unsuccessful.

Reductionism is the other logical error. It is the mirror image of an ecological fallacy. Reductionism occurs when a researcher reaches a conclusion about group behavior based solely on observations gathered at the individual level. For example, during a public meeting of juvenile rehabilitation service providers, an area probation officer might declare: "Our job is to ride these kids until we convince them the error of their ways. If that means locking them up for a technical violation, even as minor as being five minutes late to an appointment, then fine by me!" After the meeting, your supervisor instructs you, "Let's try not to refer anybody to that guy's probation office. I don't think our clients would do well in that environment." Your supervisor is assuming that all of the probation officers in that office have the same philosophy expressed by the individual probation officer. A prediction about the probation officers assigned to that office (group level of analysis) cannot be made based on a single probation officer's (individual level of analysis) comments. Again, the logical error occurs regardless of whether the conclusion turns out to be correct. Table 4.3 summarizes these two errors.

Getting to the Point 4.9 – An ecological fallacy occurs when a researcher makes a prediction about how an individual might behave based on data collected at the group level of analysis. Reductionism occurs when a researcher makes a prediction about how a group might behave based on data collected at the individual level of analysis.

Table 4.3   Logical Thinking Errors

LOGICAL ERROR	DESCRIPTION	EXAMPLE
Ecological fallacy	When a researcher makes a prediction about how an individual might behave based on data collected at the group level of analysis.	A high school guidance counselor reads a study about adolescent skateboarders and learns that, as a group, they tend to be risk-takers. One day while counseling a student who identifies herself as a 'skate rat,' he asks the student to participate in a cognitive intervention program designed to reduce risk-taking behaviors among adolescents. This counselor has falsely assumed that this individual student is a risk-taker based solely on a research finding that skateboarders, as a group, are risk-takers.
Reductionism	When a researcher makes a prediction about how a group might behave based on data collected at the individual level of analysis.	During an individual counseling session with a high school student who happens to be a member of the Skate Boarding Club, a guidance counselor classifies the student as a risk-taker. Because risk-takers are more likely to engage in illegal drug use and unprotected sex, he asks all members of the Skate Boarding Club to participate in a group therapy session designed to reduce their tendencies to take risk. This guidance counselor has made a prediction about the group as a whole based on his evaluation of this one individual.

FINAL THOUGHTS

For the most part, classification systems are conveniences and should not be thought of as a way to distinguish 'good' from 'bad' research. All types of research make a contribution to the body of knowledge. As such, all types of research are important to our understanding of social phenomena. For example, two researchers might be interested in the patterns of offenses committed by sexual offenders. One researcher might study the criminal histories of these offenders and measure the severity of their crimes using a numerical scale. This same researcher may learn that serial sexual offenders begin with relatively minor sex crimes (e.g. public lewdness) and progress to more serious forms of sexual misbehavior (e.g. aggravated sexual assault). The other researcher, primarily a qualitative researcher, might conduct interviews with these offenders and ask them questions about how they select victims, progress from minor crimes to more serious offenses, and how they feel before and after a criminal event.

Each of these researchers will make a contribution to the body of knowledge about serial sexual offending. Taken together, they improve what we know about this serious type of criminal offending. Thus, researchers should never dismiss a researcher's paradigm, purpose, time dimension, data, method of reasoning, or unit of analysis merely because they do not appreciate or feel comfortable with it. Social phenomena are almost always multi-faceted and thus better studied from multiple perspectives.

GETTING TO THE POINT/CHAPTER SUMMARY

- Research is often organized by different classification methods in order to help researchers access it more efficiently and evaluate its strengths and limitations.

- Researchers often approach research questions from a particular paradigm or perception of social reality. These perceptions affect how the researcher conducts the research and, in many cases, the outcome of the research findings. The positivist, interpretive, and critical paradigms all contribute to our understanding of social phenomena.

- Research is often conducted for a specific purpose. Exploratory research provides initial insight into new or emerging social phenomena or behavior. Descriptive research describes existing social phenomena or behavior. Explanatory research explains why individuals or groups behave the way they do. It is not uncommon for a single research project to serve more than one purpose. It is also not uncommon for a research agenda to move from exploratory to descriptive to explanatory research.

- Cross-sectional research involves data collection at one point in time. The findings from this research cannot be used to draw conclusions about change over time. But they can provide a snapshot of a social condition or population at that point in time.

- Longitudinal research utilizes data that are collected over a period of time. The findings from this research indicate how a social condition or particular population changes over time. There are three types of longitudinal research designs. Trend studies collect the same data over time from different samples of the same population. Panel studies collect the same data over time from the same sample. Cohort studies collect data over time from samples of individuals who share common characteristics.

- Quantitative research measures variables numerically and assumes that the social world can be understood objectively. Qualitative research probes the meaning of variables and assumes that the social world is best understood subjectively, often from the perspective of the research subject.

- Deductive reasoning begins with a theory that explains social behavior and uses observations to test the theory. Inductive reasoning begins with observations of social behavior and uses those observations to develop a theory that explains the behavior.

- The unit of analysis is the 'what' or 'whom' about which researchers gather information during a research project. A unit of analysis can be an individual, a group, a community, a state, or even an entire nation.

- An ecological fallacy occurs when a researcher makes a prediction about how an individual might behave based on data collected at the group level of analysis. Reductionism occurs when a researcher makes a prediction about how a group might behave based on data collected at the individual level of analysis.

CHAPTER EXERCISES

The following chapter exercises are organized into two parts. The first part consists of questions that can be answered using the information from this chapter. This section will test your understanding of the chapter material. The second part consists of research application exercises. These exercises require you to apply what you have learned thus far.

CHAPTER REVIEW QUESTIONS

Respond to each of the following questions using the information from this chapter.

1. Read each of the following statements and determine the paradigm (positivist, interpretive, or critical) that the researcher followed.

Research statement	Paradigm
A criminologist hypothesizes that illegal drug use is a cause of poor school performance. He measures school performance by grades and drug use by the number of times the respondent uses illegal drugs per month.	
A criminal justice professor does a lot of research on the effect of poverty on juvenile delinquency. She hopes to use her research findings to provide information on how to structure poverty reduction programs.	
After completing research on crimes committed by girls, a researcher concludes that "when girls commit crimes, they do not consider their behavior criminal. Instead they consider their behavior a normal response to social inequality."	

2. Read each of the following research findings and determine the most likely purpose (exploratory, descriptive or explanatory) of the research project.

Research finding	Purpose
The majority of individuals who are arrested for driving while intoxicated are males between the ages of 22 and 35.	
The data reveal that an increasing number of teens involved in traffic accidents report that they were texting at the time.	
The analysis reveals that the pressure to 'fit into the group' is the most likely cause of corruption among police officers.	

3. Read the following research proposals and determine the time dimension (cross-sectional, trend or panel) that the researcher will use.

Research proposal	Time dimension
To understand the changing demographic characteristics of juvenile offenders, the researcher will survey a random sample of 1,000 juvenile offenders every five years over the next 15 years.	
The researcher will conduct a survey of 100 women who are victims of domestic abuse to determine the circumstances surrounding their decision to call the police for help.	
To evaluate the effect of a drug prevention program delivered to junior high school students, the researcher will conduct follow-up surveys of the students each year until 12th grade.	

4. Read each of the following research findings and determine the nature of the data (quantitative or qualitative) that the researcher collected.

Research finding	Nature of data
The research revealed that feelings of guilt were expressed by adult offenders who grew up in a religious household.	
The research revealed that 80 percent of all adult offenders did not receive religious instruction as children.	

5. Read each of the following research findings and determine which method of reasoning (deductive or inductive) the researcher used.

Research finding	Method of reasoning
After observing their behavior for several months, the researcher theorized that correctional officers become personally detached from inmates as a means of reducing the stress associated with their professional responsibilities.	
The researcher theorized that correctional officers become personally detached from inmates as a means of reducing the stress associated with their professional responsibilities. Subsequent observations of correctional officers supported this theory.	

6. Circle the unit of analysis in the following research proposals.
    a. Interviews with police officers are proposed to study how they cope with the everyday stresses associated with their jobs.
    b. A survey of state prisons is designed to determine how much time it takes officials to process newly admitted inmates into the prison system.
    c. A comparative analysis is proposed to see how the rate of sexual assaults compares between European nations.
    d. A secondary analysis of census data is suggested to understand how different counties in one state compare with respect to rates of poverty.

7. Read each of the following statements and determine which type of logical error (ecological fallacy or reductionism) the researcher has committed.

Statement	Statement
Because the research suggests that police officers are more likely as a group to experience alcoholism, the chief of police concluded that Officer Smith's recent illness was likely caused by his excessive drinking	
A psychologist who recently treated a correctional officer for a stress-related illness concludes that "most correctional officers experience debilitating stress associated with their jobs."	

8. Fill in the blank: One type of longitudinal research design is called a panel study. Another type of longitudinal design is called a_____study, also known as a repeated cross-sectional study.

9. Fill in the blanks: When a researcher commits an ecological fallacy, he or she uses data collected at the _____level to predict behavior at the _____level.

10. Fill in the blank: If a researcher were to collect data on police departments around the country to understand how they were responding to human trafficking violations, their unit of analysis would be a _____.

RESEARCH APPLICATION EXERCISES

Access to the following articles will be provided by your instructor.

Visher, C.A., Debus-Sherrill, S.A. and Yahner, J. (2011). Employment after prison: A longitudinal study of former prisoners. *Justice Quarterly, 28*(5), 698–718.

Weisburd, D. and Green, L. (1995). Policing drug hotspots: The Jersey City drug market analysis experiment. *Justice Quarterly, 12*(4), 711–735.

11. Read each article listed on the previous page and classify each using the classification schemes discussed in this chapter. You may use the following table.

Classification scheme	Description	Categories of research	Visher et al. (2011)	Weisburd and Green (1995)
Paradigms of research	Describes the general organizing framework for social theory and empirical research	Positivist Interpretive Critical		
Purpose of research	Describes what the research hopes to achieve	Exploratory Descriptive Explanatory		
Time dimension of research	Describes the time frame in which data collection takes place	Cross-sectional Longitudinal		
Nature of data	Describes the type of data collected and, in some cases, the type of research method used	Quantitative Qualitative		
Method of reasoning	Describes the method of reasoning used by the researcher	Deductive Inductive		
Unit of analysis	Describes about whom or what the researcher collects information	Individual Group Community Nation		

12. Write a brief essay discussing the time dimension of the study by Visher et al. (2012). At a minimum, your essay should answer the following questions:
    a. What type of longitudinal design did they use: trend, panel, or cohort?
    b. What were the advantages and disadvantages of this particular time dimension?
    c. How would their results have been different had they used a cross-sectional research design?

13. Write a brief essay discussing the article by Weisburd and Green (1995). Your essay should answer the following questions:
    a. Would you classify this research as exploratory, descriptive, or explanatory? Explain your answer.

b. Would you describe the data collected in this study as quantitative or qualitative? Explain your answer.
c. Would you describe the method of reasoning used by these researchers as deductive or inductive? Explain your answer.
d. What is the unit of analysis in this study?

CHAPTER 5

Causality

Criminal justice researchers and practitioners want to know the cause of everything. What is the cause of crime? What causes a person to become a serial murderer? Who caused this accident? The list goes on and on, and we never seem to find an answer that satisfies all of us. Here is a true story that demonstrates one of my student's frustrations with finding the cause of crime. Maybe you have felt the same way.

Making Research Real 5.1 – What Exactly Is the Cause of Crime?

I had just stepped out of a statistics class for a break when I encountered Eddie, a mid-career police lieutenant who was also on a break from his graduate criminological theory class. The look on Eddie's face was unmistakable: he was frustrated.

"What's the matter, Eddie?" I asked. "Oh, sorry, Doc. I'm just frustrated with my theory class. I took this class because I thought it would teach me why people commit crime. And I figured that if I knew that, I could do a better job of preventing it. The first week, we talked about biological causes. Then we discussed psychological causes. Now we're talking about sociological causes. I'm beginning to think nobody actually knows the cause of crime," he said.

I felt his pain. Many years ago, I was a mid-career policing professional who went back to graduate school. I recall being equally frustrated with the theory class I was required to take. "Listen, Eddie, don't worry about it. There is no one single cause of crime and no single theory can explain all types of crime. Some theories are better at explaining some crimes but fall flat on their face when they attempt to explain other crimes," I explained. I couldn't cure his frustration. But I could counsel him on what to expect from his theory class: a discussion, but no resolution, to what exactly is the cause of crime.

One of the toughest things to do in social research, *maybe the toughest*, is to prove a causal relationship between two variables. How exactly can we *prove* that poverty causes crime, or that crime causes poverty? Maybe you know somebody who is poor but would never think of committing a crime, whereas your rich friend regularly violates the law, or vice versa. If poverty is a cause of crime, then why did crime rates go down during the Great Depression? If poverty and crime are not related, then why is it that most inmates currently in prison are poor? The purpose of this chapter is to go into some detail about how researchers establish the cause of phenomena like crime. We cannot always do this, but we need to be clear on how we might be able to. In particular this chapter sets the stage for a later discussion on the experimental design, which is the preferred method among social researchers for establishing causal relationships.

Over the years, social researchers have developed a set of rules for establishing **causality** or causal relationships between variables. Generally referred to as **causal rules**, these requirements constitute the standard for establishing whether a causal relationship exists between two variables. Each of these requirements must be met in order to confidently conclude that one variable (e.g. poverty) causes another (e.g. crime). Table 5.1 outlines these rules, which we will explore in this chapter.

Table 5.1   Causal Rules

CAUSAL RULE	EXPLANATION
Temporal order	The cause (independent variable) must happen prior to the effect (dependent variable). In other words, the cause must happen first, then the effect.
Correlation	A change in the cause (independent variable) must result in a change in the effect (dependent variable). In other words, there must be a relationship between the two variables.
Lack of plausible alternative explanations	All other reasonable explanations (other independent variables) must be considered and eliminated. In other words, we have to rule out other potential causes.

Getting to the Point 5.1 – Researchers use three causal rules to determine whether a causal relationship exists between two variables. Each of these three rules must be met before a researcher can prove that one variable is the cause of another.

TEMPORAL ORDER

The first causal rule is **temporal order**, which simply states that the cause must precede the effect. This is pretty logical, right? If X is the cause of Y, then X must have happened first. If we think crime is caused by the strain associated with economic inequality, then we must prove that strain from economic inequality happened prior to crime. Unfortunately, some researchers sidestep this crucial requirement. Here is a hypothetical example of a researcher who forgot this rule.

Making Research Real 5.2 – But Is it Racial Profiling?

Following a controversial and highly publicized traffic stop involving three African American teenagers, the city council directed the police chief to conduct a racial profiling study. The department collected data on the race and ethnicity of the motorists they stopped. A researcher from the local university used the residential population to estimate the racial and ethnic proportions of drivers in the city.

The results indicated that African American drivers were over-represented in police stops by nearly a 2 to 1 ratio. Based on the residential population, only 11 percent of the driving population was estimated to be African American. Yet 20 percent of the stops involved African American drivers. The researcher concluded that African American drivers were victims of racial profiling.

The president of the local police officers association questioned the researcher's conclusion. Legally speaking, to be guilty of racial profiling, a police officer must know the driver's race before he or she initiates the stop, and must stop the driver based on a predisposition (i.e. prejudice) that a person of that race is more likely to be guilty of committing a more serious violation (e.g. drug trafficking). This would mean that the police officer would have to know the race of the driver prior to the stop.

Based on his street experience, the association president proposed that the police seldom knew the race of the driver before they made the decision to stop. In fact, the race of the driver was recorded by the police officer on the form used to gather the research data only after the stop had been concluded. The president argued, "Unless you are able to determine that the officer knew the race of the driver before he or she made the decision to stop, then you cannot legitimately accuse the officer of racial profiling." Thus, in this case, the researcher did not establish temporal order.

The issue in the above scenario is whether the officers knew, or could have known, the driver's race or ethnicity *prior* to initiating the stop. Luckily, we have at least some insight into this particular issue based on previous research.

Making Research Real 5.3 – What (and When) Do Officers Know?

In 2007, Geoffrey P. Alpert, Roger G. Dunham, and Michael R. Smith published a study that, in part, tested whether police officers could accurately determine a driver's race or ethnicity prior to initiating a traffic stop. This research question was part of a comprehensive racial profiling study conducted in Miami-Dade County, Florida.

The researchers placed research assistants in patrol cars to observe the police officers. When a police officer initiated a traffic stop, the observers asked them to identify the race of the driver. Then, during the stop, the observers looked at the drivers to determine whether the officers were correct. They seldom were correct. In fact, overall, the officers were correct only 29 percent of the time.

Although the study above was limited and involved only 168 observations, it is the only study available that at least attempts to determine whether a police officer can accurately know the race or ethnicity of a driver prior to initiating a traffic stop. And this is crucial to establishing temporal order in studies of racial profiling.

CORRELATION

The second causal rule is that of **correlation**. Another word for correlation is association. When two variables are correlated, they are related. If X causes Y, then X and Y must be related to or associated with one another. Again, this is pretty logical. You cannot have a causal relationship if there is no relationship whatsoever between the variables! For example, illegal drug use is associated with criminal behavior. As illegal drug use increases, so does criminal behavior. Age and crime are also correlated, but in a different direction. As age increases, criminal behavior decreases.

When an increase in one variable is associated with an increase in another variable, we refer to this as a **positive correlation**. When a decrease in one variable is associated with a decrease in another variable, this is also a positive correlation. What makes a correlation positive is that the variables change at the same time and in the same direction. For example, education is positively correlated with income. The more education a person has, the higher his or her lifetime earnings will be. Likewise, the less education a person has, the lower his or her lifetime earnings will be. Figure 5.1 is a visual representation of a positive relationship.

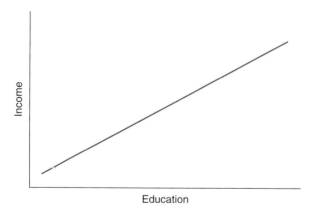

Figure 5.1   Visual Representation of a Positive Correlation

When an increase in one variable is associated with a decrease in another variable, we refer to this as a **negative correlation**. When a decrease in one variable is associated with an increase in another variable, this is also a negative correlation. What makes a correlation negative is that the variables change at the same time but in different directions. For example, education and violent crime are negatively correlated. The more education a person has, the less likely that person will commit a violent crime. Likewise, the less education a person has, the more likely that person will commit a violent crime. Figure 5.2 is a visual representation of a negative relationship.

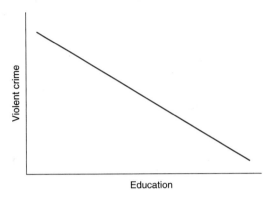

Figure 5.2   Visual Representation of a Negative Correlation

The slopes of the lines in Figures 5.1 and 5.2 illustrate the strength of the relationships between the variables. When two variables are highly correlated, the slope is very steep. As the strength of the relationship (correlation) lessens, the slope of the line becomes flatter. For example, there is likely very little correlation between education and number of traffic violations. A well-educated person probably gets as many (or as few) traffic tickets as a poorly educated person. Figure 5.3 is a visual representation of no correlation between two variables.

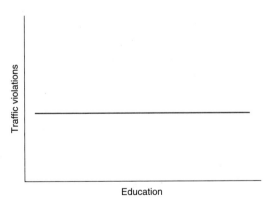

Figure 5.3   Visual Representation of No Correlation

Table 5.2 provides a summary of the differences between the types of correlations.

Table 5.2 Differences Between Types of Correlations

TYPE OF CORRELATION	DEFINITION	EXAMPLE
Positive Correlations		
Increase in x → *Increase in* y	When an increase in the independent variable (cause, or *x*) is associated with an increase in the dependent variable (effect, or *y*).	An increase in illicit drug use (the independent variable) is associated with an increase in promiscuous sexual behaviors (the dependent variable).
Decrease in x → *Decrease in* y	When a decrease in the independent variable (cause, or *x*) is associated with a decrease in the dependent variable (effect, or *y*).	A decrease in associations with other juvenile delinquents (the independent variable) is related to a decrease in school-related misbehavior (the dependent variable).
Negative Correlations		
Increase in x → *Decrease in* y	When an increase in the independent variable (cause, or *x*) is associated with a decrease in the dependent variable (effect, or *y*).	An increase in alcohol consumption (the dependent variable) is associated with a decrease in academic performance (the dependent variable).
Decrease in x → *Increase in* y	When a decrease in the independent variable (cause, or *x*) is associated with an increase in the dependent variable (effect, or *y*).	A decrease in school attendance (the independent variable) is associated with an increase in associations with juvenile delinquents (the dependent variable).

Correlation is measured statistically using one of several methods, depending on how the variables are measured. The **Pearson *r*** is the most commonly used statistic for measuring correlation. Numerically, this statistic ranges from –1 to 0 or from 0 to +1. Perfect correlations, which are exceedingly rare, are either +1 (in the case of positive correlations) or –1 (in the case of negative correlations). The closer the Pearson *r* gets to 0, the less the two variables are correlated. The Pearson *r* for the relationship represented in Figure 5.3 would be 0 because, in this case, there is no relationship between the variables.

In a statistics course, you will learn how to actually calculate these statistics. But for now it is only important that you know how to interpret these when you are reading the research. Consider, for example, the following sentence in a research report: *"The analysis reveals a Pearson r correlation of –.80 between the level of education (measured in years of formal schooling) and criminal behavior (measured by the number of arrest as an adult)."* This one statistic tells you two things. First, the relationship between these two variables (education and criminal behavior) is relatively strong. Negative .80 is very close to –1.00, the highest Pearson *r* score available. Second, the relationship is negative. This means that an increase in education leads to a decrease in criminal behavior, or a decrease in education leads to an increase in criminal behavior. Chapter 14 includes a more detailed discussion of these two important statistical techniques.

Getting to the Point 5.3 – The second causal rule, correlation, requires that the variables in a causal relationship be related to one another, or change together. A change in one variable must be associated with a change in another variable. Correlations can be positive or negative.

LACK OF PLAUSIBLE ALTERNATIVE EXPLANATIONS

The final causal requirement is often the most difficult to meet. The **lack of plausible alternative explanations** requires the researcher to eliminate all of the other reasonable causes for the change in the **dependent variable**, leaving only the variable that the researcher alleges to be the cause. To establish that the **independent variable** is the cause, all other possible causes (i.e. independent variables) have to be ruled out. (For a fuller explanation of dependent and independent variables, see Types of Variables on page 139.) This is easier said than done. Consider the hypothetical example below.

Making Research Real 5.4 – What Is the Cause of Truancy?

A school resource officer wants to determine the cause of truancy. After interviewing a sample of truants, the officer comes to the conclusion that academic performance, or more specifically poor academic performance, is the cause of truancy. He determines that nearly all truants have a history of poor academic performance prior to becoming truant. This would establish the temporal order between the cause (poor academic performance) and the effect (truancy). The officer also learns that the relationship between academic performance and truancy is negative. A decrease in academic performance is associated with an increase in truancy violations.

Though the officer met two of the causal requirements, he failed to eliminate any plausible alternative explanations for truancy. For example, truancy might also be caused by a lack of attachment to the school. This would mean that students who are not involved in extracurricular activities (e.g. sports, clubs, etc.) feel less attached to the school and thus are more likely to skip. What about students who are victims of chronic bullying? Would they be more likely to skip school because they are fearful of being victimized? What effect does the lack of parental involvement or supervision have on truancy?

These plausible alternative explanations (lack of attachment, bullying, lack of parental involvement or supervision) weaken the alleged causal relationship between academic performance and truancy. To strengthen his case that poor academic performance causes truancy, the school resource officer must eliminate these alternative explanations.

What do we mean by *plausible* alternative explanations? The dictionary defines plausible as reasonable, persuasive, or worthy of belief. This is where research methods get a little subjective. Most researchers rely on their own professional judgment to determine the plausibility of an alternative explanation. I suppose it is possible that an increase in robberies might be caused by a change in the moon phase, solar storms, or gamma rays from distant planets, but it is not plausible.

As a criminal justice or criminology student, you are probably familiar with the terms 'reasonable doubt,' 'probable cause,' and 'reasonable suspicion.' These terms describe various levels of proof that must be reached prior to making a criminal justice decision. For example, in a criminal case, the state must prove the defendant's guilt beyond a reasonable doubt. I would say that the jury must be 99.9 percent sure that the defendant did it before returning a guilty verdict, assuming of course that there is no such thing as absolute proof. Before issuing a search warrant, a magistrate will require a police officer to establish probable cause. If I were a judge, I would ask the officers to be a little more than half sure that the subject of their investigation is guilty, or about 51 percent sure. When a police officer has a reasonable suspicion that an individual has violated the law, the officer is allowed to initiate an enforcement action, such as a traffic stop. I would define reasonable suspicion as a little less than half sure, or about 49 percent sure. As a researcher, I tend to use the reasonable doubt standard (99.9 percent). This is a pretty tough standard and, from time to time, I find it nearly impossible to meet; but I try.

Finding the evidence to eliminate plausible alternative explanations can be difficult. In some cases, researchers may find this evidence in the data they used for their research. For example, if I am doing a survey to measure public attitudes about the death penalty, I would want to make sure that I ask the respondents for all the information that could possibly explain an individual's attitude toward this type of punishment. My survey might include questions on gender, age, religious preference, criminal history, victimization, and other factors because I know from my review of the literature that these factors influence a person's attitude toward the death penalty. When I analyze the survey data, I can use statistical techniques to control for these variables, such that I isolate the cause that I am interested in investigating.

Another way of identifying plausible alternative explanations is to submit the research to peer review. Well informed peer researchers often have the experience necessary to identify plausible alternative explanations. For example, a few years ago I came across some data demonstrating that children who are involved in extracurricular activities (e.g. sports) are less likely to engage in juvenile delinquent acts. From this, I concluded that juvenile delinquency was caused, at least in part, by a lack of involvement in extracurricular activities. A peer reviewer, who is more knowledgeable of this subject than I am, suggested that the relationship between these two variables may not be causal. "Involvement in extracurricular activities such as sports and band," he argued, "may be more indicative of parental support (e.g. providing transportation) and socio-economic status (e.g. having the disposable income to participate in the activity), and either of these could be plausible alternative explanations for a reduction of juvenile delinquent acts." He was right.

Finally, researchers should rely on the work of previous researchers to identify plausible alternative explanations. It is likely that previous researchers have evaluated, and maybe reevaluated, alternative explanations. You can use these in your own research as evidence to support your elimination of plausible alternative explanations. Below, I return to the racial profiling example we discussed earlier to illustrate.

Making Research Real 5.5 – Using Prior Research to Eliminate Plausible Alternative Explanations

The overall goal of racial profiling research is to determine to what extent, if any, a driver's race or ethnicity influences a police officer's decision to initiate a traffic stop. The overall allegation is that the driver's race or ethnicity, rather than the actual driving performance, is the cause of the officer's decision to initiate a traffic stop.

During our study, we are able to determine that police officers are able to accurately determine the driver's race or ethnicity prior to the stop in 95 percent of the cases. This would satisfy our temporal order rule. We then estimate the racial and ethnic proportions of the driving population. Looking at the traffic stop data, we find that African American and Hispanic drivers are stopped at higher proportions than they are represented in the driving population (see the data below). This would satisfy our second rule of causality – correlation, because it appears that African American and Hispanic drivers are more likely to be stopped than White, Asian, Native American, or Other race drivers.

RACE OR ETHNICITY	PERCENT OF DRIVERS	PERCENT OF STOPS
Caucasian or White	75%	60%
African American or Black	12%	21%
Hispanic	8%	15%
Asian	3%	3%
Native American	1%	1%
Other race	1%	1%
Totals	**100%**	**100%**

Is this sufficient proof of racial profiling? No, because we have another causal rule to satisfy, namely the lack of plausible alternative explanations. Other than racism, what are the plausible alternative explanations for an over-representation of African American and Hispanic drivers in police stops? First, it is possible that these drivers violate the law more often than drivers from other racial or ethnic categories. In 2001, Lange, Blackman, and Johnson (2001) observed drivers on the New Jersey Turnpike to determine if African American and Hispanic drivers were more likely to speed. They used digital cameras and RADAR to record images of the drivers and the speeds they travelled and found that African American and Hispanic drivers were more likely to speed, particularly in higher speed zones. Their findings contradicted an earlier study by John Lamberth (1994), who found that African American and Hispanic drivers were no more likely to speed than drivers of other races. Therefore, I would characterize these findings as inconclusive. But, based on this evidence, I might consider this a plausible alternative explanation for the over-representation of African American and Hispanic drivers in police stops.

Another plausible alternative explanation is that, by virtue of living in higher crime areas, African American and Hispanic drivers are exposed to higher levels of police supervision. As such, they are more likely to be stopped by the police. Crime is not evenly distributed across a community. It tends to concentrate in particular neighborhoods and these neighborhoods tend to have larger populations of racial and ethnic minorities. It is likely that the police will assign more patrol resources to high crime areas because that is where the demand for their services is most needed. These two factors taken together might suggest that the people who live in high crime areas are exposed to higher levels of police supervision. Even if the predisposition to commit crime is equal across racial and ethnic groups, those who are exposed to higher levels of police observation are more likely to be stopped. These were the findings from a study I did in 2004 in Wichita, Kansas (Withrow, 2004).

Getting to the Point 5.4 – The third causal rule, lack of plausible alternative explanations, requires the researcher to eliminate all other reasonable causes before concluding that one variable causes another.

THE QUESTION OF SPURIOUSNESS

When a researcher falsely proposes a causal relationship, we say that the relationship is **spurious**. Spurious just means false. So when a finding is spurious, it is a false finding. More often than not, researchers commit this error because they have failed to confirm one or more of the three causal rules. Remember, all three must be confirmed before a causal relationship can be proposed. Here is a hypothetical example of a spurious finding.

Making Research Real 5.6 – Can it Really Be Too Hot to Swim?

Several years ago, the police chief at a popular resort community noticed an increase in drowning incidents at one of the public beaches. He set out to determine the cause of this increase. He learned that the number of drowning incidents increased shortly after the water temperature increased. In this case, he established temporal order. The water got hotter before the drowning increased.

He then looked at the relationship (correlation) between water temperature and drowning incidents. As the water temperature increased, the number of drowning incidents also increased. Thus, he established a positive correlation. Assuming he had solved the problem, he concluded that an increase in water temperature caused an increase in drowning incidents. Thus, he suggested a policy to close the public beaches on the hottest days of the year, since the hotter the water, the higher the number of drowning incidents.

As you might imagine, the mayor was not too keen on this idea. She called the chief and asked, "Couldn't the increase in drowning incidents be caused by more people being on the beach and in the water on hot days?" Of course it could. Had the police chief considered alternative explanations, he might have found that the number of swimmers at the beach was also positively correlated with the water temperature, and hence drowning incidents. After all who goes swimming during the winter when the water is cold?

Getting to the Point 5.5 – Spuriousness refers to a false causal finding. It occurs when a researcher alleges a causal relationship between two variables but fails to confirm at least one of the three causal rules.

FINAL THOUGHTS

In criminal justice and criminological research, there is seldom a single cause of anything. For example, poverty is consistently associated with juvenile delinquency, but so are a lack of education, single parent households, and many other factors. So which of these is the *cause* of juvenile delinquency? Is it possible that multiple causes combine to produce juvenile delinquency? Do some factors have more of an influence than others? What about the impoverished and poorly educated children who never engage in juvenile delinquency? How do we account for the different paths that their lives took? These are the kinds of questions that drive researchers in the field of criminal justice and criminology.

More than a century of criminological research has yet to produce a single factor or theory that explains all forms of crime. In all likelihood, crime and other complicated social phenomena have multiple causes. Furthermore, when we consider the unpredictable nature of social interactions and the effects of dynamic situations on individual and group behavior, identifying causes becomes nearly impossible. All we can do is to try to pinpoint causes, wrap our heads around complex problems, and accept that there are not always simple answers or simple solutions.

GETTING TO THE POINT/CHAPTER SUMMARY

- Researchers use three causal rules to determine whether a causal relationship exists between two variables. Each of these three rules must be met before a researcher can prove that one variable is the cause of another.

- The first causal rule, temporal order, requires that the cause must precede the effect. In other words, the variable that is alleged to be the cause of another variable must happen first.

- The second causal rule, correlation, requires that the variables in a causal relationship be related to one another, or change together. A change in one variable must be associated with a change in another variable. Correlations can be positive or negative.

- The third causal rule, lack of plausible alternative explanations, requires the researcher to eliminate all other reasonable causes before concluding that one variable causes another.

- Spuriousness refers to a false causal finding. It occurs when a researcher alleges a causal relationship between two variables but fails to confirm at least one of the three causal rules.

CHAPTER EXERCISES

The following chapter exercises are organized into two parts. The first part consists of questions that can be answered using the information from this chapter. This section will test your understanding of the chapter material. The second part consists of research application exercises. These exercises require you to apply what you have learned thus far.

CHAPTER REVIEW QUESTIONS

Respond to each of the following questions using the information from this chapter.

1. A study of juvenile delinquency reveals a strong correlation between illegal drug use and delinquent acts. The researcher concludes that illegal drug use is the cause of delinquent acts. Looking at the same data, another researcher comes to the conclusion that delinquent acts lead to illegal drug use. Which causal rule are both researchers forgetting here?
    a. Temporal order
    b. Correlation
    c. Lack of plausible alternative explanations

2. A recent analysis of aggravated assaults in a northern city reveals that aggravated assaults tend to increase during the warmest months of the year and decrease during the coldest months of the year. In this case, we would say which of the following about the correlation between temperature and aggravated assaults:
    a. The correlation is positive.
    b. The correlation is negative.
    c. There is no correlation.

3. A recent analysis of domestic violence in a northern city reveals that domestic violence incidents tend to increase during the coldest months of the year (i.e. winter) and decrease during the warmest months of the year (i.e. summer). In this case, we would say which of the following about the correlation between temperature and domestic violence:
    a. The correlation is positive.
    b. The correlation is negative.
    c. There is no correlation.

4. A recent analysis of vehicular burglaries in a northern city reveals that, on average, there are 25 vehicular burglaries throughout the city each month. About as many occur during the winter months as do during the summer months. In this case, we would say which of the following about the correlation between temperature and vehicular burglaries:
    a. The correlation is positive.
    b. The correlation is negative.
    c. There is no correlation.

5. Look at the following graphs and determine the type of correlation (positive, negative or none) that occurs between the two variables x and y.

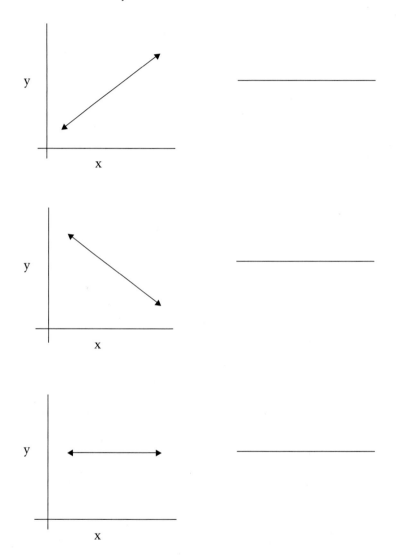

6. A state legislature wants to outlaw promotional events (e.g. happy hours, ladies night, etc.) that are sponsored by bars and other drinking establishments. She argues that "there is a strong and positive correlation between these sorts of promotional events and DWI fatalities." You are a lobbyist for the Association of Distillers and Brewers. Offer an alternative explanation for the alleged causal linkage between these promotional events and DWI-related traffic fatalities.

7. Your patrol captain is convinced that moon phases are a cause of street crime. Specifically, he argues that "violent crimes increase as the moon gets full." You think your captain is crazy. Describe how you would disprove this hypothesis using the three causal rules outlined in this chapter.

8. You have completed your study on the causal relationship between the moon phase and street crime. You have determined that there is no correlation between the fullness of the moon and the rate of reported street crimes. As such, you plan to inform your patrol captain that the causal relationship between the moon phase and street crime is:
   a. A product of reductionism
   b. A spurious relationship
   c. An ecological fallacy

9. Fill in the blank: When a researcher alleges a causal relationship between two variables, but fails to confirm even one of the three causal rules, we say that their research finding is_____.

10. Fill in the blanks: According to the rule of temporal order, a change in the_____ variable must happen prior to a change in the _____ variable.

RESEARCH APPLICATION EXERCISES

Access to the following articles will be provided by your instructor.

Higgins, G.E. Vito, G.F. and Walsh, W.F. (2008). Searches: An understudied area of racial profiling. *Journal of Ethnicity in Criminal Justice, 6*(1), 23–39.

Paternoster, R. (1987). The deterrent effect of the perceived certainty and severity of punishment: A review of the evidence and issues. *Justice Quarterly, 4*(2), 173–217.

11. Read the Higgins et al. (2008) article and write a brief essay that answers the following questions.
    a. To what extent were these researchers able to establish a causal link between a driver's race and the probability of being searched during a traffic stop?
    b. What alternative explanations, if any, do the researchers offer?
    c. Develop three alternative explanations for the increased probability that racial and ethnic minorities will be searched.

12. Read the Paternoster (1987) article and write a brief essay that answers the following questions.
    a. To what extent was Paternoster able to establish that the threat of certain punishment deters crime?

b. To what extent was Paternoster able to establish that the severity of punishment deters crime?

c. Based on your understanding of Paternoster's research, is there a causal linkage between deterrence and crime? Explain your answer.

CHAPTER 6

Measurement

My father taught me how to drive. We spent hours driving the family car around our small town until he determined I was ready to take the drivers' license test. I passed, but just barely. One of the lessons he taught me was how to park the car in the garage. He showed me how to line up the car in the driveway before entering the garage and how to tell when I was far enough inside to ensure the garage door would close. "Just a *tad* more," he said as I crept into the garage during my first lesson. "Okay, that's far enough. Stop!" In my nervousness, I tapped the accelerator rather than the brake to stop, crashing into the wall of the garage and leaving a gaping hole. In my attempt to deflect my father's anger, I jokingly asked, "Exactly how far *is a tad*?" My father was not, and is still not, amused.

In research, we want to be a little more precise than "a tad." In other words, we want our measures to be exact. This is hard to achieve in the social sciences. In the physical sciences, measurement is well established and incredibly precise. To a chemist, for example, a gram is a gram. We have no such measurement standards in the social sciences. The social phenomena we measure are much more complex. For example, how should we measure compatibility? This is a term that has various meanings and can conceivably be measured in numerous ways. In the end, there is really no 'best way' to measure compatibility, or any other social phenomena. The best we can do is to develop an acceptable measure and to be forthcoming about its limitations. We begin here with an interesting measurement challenge.

Making Research Real 6.1 – I Can't Measure It, But That Don't Mean It Ain't Real

Measuring the perception of safety is an important part of policing research. If the residents of a community do not feel safe, they do not venture from their homes and/or interact with others. This reduces the number of capable guardians whose presence in a community can prevent crime and who can provide important information to the police when crime occurs.

A feeling of safety, of course, is difficult to measure. It is really a combination of feelings associated with discomfort, maybe even danger. The perception of safety may even vary from person to person or from situation to situation. For example, I am very comfortable in the woods. I have spent weeks in the mountains backpacking with friends very far from civilization. I feel very safe in the woods because I know the dangers and can prepare for them adequately. Several years ago, a colleague of mine, Bob, who grew up in inner-city Chicago, joined me on a backpacking trip to the Rocky Mountains. He was frightened from the first step out of base camp. "I just can't sleep, it's too quiet and there aren't any street lights or traffic noises," he said one evening around the campfire. "That's the point, ain't it?" one of my friends responded. "Maybe so, but this place scares the bejeebers out of me," said Bob.

A few months later, I found myself on a business trip in Chicago. Bob invited me to his house for supper. While I was there, his wife sent us to the grocery store for a few things. On the walk to the grocery store, about six blocks away, I was probably the most frightened I have ever been in my life. There were hundreds of people hanging out on the corners with seemingly no place to go and nothing to do but yell at each other. About halfway to the store, a very large man in a silver body suit approached us and asked, "Have you been saved by Jesus?" I nearly turned and ran. "How can you live like this? I would be scared all of the time," I exclaimed.

A feeling of safety is exceedingly difficult for us to measure, at least quantitatively. We can ask people in a survey if they feel safe. We can even ask people what makes them feel safe. But in the end, the perception of safety is just that, a perception. Even so, perceptions are real.

The purpose of this chapter is to introduce you to the practice of **measurement**, or the process by which social science researchers determine how to assess the social phenomena they study. We will begin with a detailed discussion of conceptualization and operationalization. You may recall that these are two of the steps in the research process discussed in Chapter 2. After discussing the levels of measurement, we will turn our attention to validity and reliability, two very important research methods concepts. Validity and reliability refer to the accuracy and consistency of our measurements, respectively. Next, we will talk about indexes, scales, and typologies, which refer to different measurement strategies. The final section of this chapter compares quantitative and qualitative measurement strategies.

Getting to the Point 6.1 – Measurement is a process by which social science researchers determine how to assess the social phenomena they study.

CONCEPTUALIZATION AND OPERATIONALIZATION

If it happens, you can measure it. And if you can measure it, you can analyze it. This is the basic idea of measurement in social research. If crime happens, you can record it. And if you can record it, you can evaluate its frequency, severity, and duration. But the question is *how* do you record it? How, exactly, do you measure crime?

Measurement begins with **conceptualization**. You may recall from Chapter 2 that conceptualization is the process by which researchers develop precise definitions for vague concepts. A researcher cannot measure crime, for example, unless he or she first defines what 'crime' is. How to define crime might seem obvious, but it is not. One researcher may not define an individual's behavior as a crime unless the person is apprehended and convicted of an actual criminal violation. Another researcher might have a less rigorous standard and define an individual's behavior as a crime if the individual is arrested for some criminal violation. And a third researcher may define crime as any behavior that is defined as criminal by the penal code regardless of whether the person committing the crime is caught. Each of these definitions is valid and each has limitations.

Below is another example of the challenges of conceptualization. In criminal justice, it is important to know when a person legally becomes an adult, since adults and juveniles are processed differently in criminal justice. To police officers in most states, adulthood begins at a person's 18th birthday. But researchers may define adulthood differently.

Making Research Real 6.2 – What Is an Adult?

How would a criminologist differentiate between a juvenile and an adult? The easiest way would be to simply use a person's chronological age. In this case, an adult might be a person who is 18 years of age or older. Eighteen-year-olds can get married without permission, vote, and serve in the military, though they cannot legally possess or consume alcohol.

Chronological age provides some indication of adulthood, but it does not necessarily equate to maturity. So another strategy might be to establish conditions that define adulthood regardless of chronological age. For example, we might designate a person as an adult if he or she has completed their schooling, left the home of their parents, and become financially independent. These markers of adulthood make some sense. But recent research indicates that less than one third of 30-year-olds in the United States fit this definition. If we added marriage and parenthood to this definition, the percentage would fall even further (Leake, 2004).

Which of these conceptual definitions of adulthood is better? Well, they are both just fine. Ultimately, the decision to go with one or the other depends on the research at hand. A criminologist interested in how the criminal justice system responds differently to adult and juvenile crime might use the chronological age definition because that is how the system differentiates between adult and juvenile offenders. Another criminologist doing research on the relationship between maturity and criminal behavior may find the second definition more useful. The point is to think through and explain your choices.

Getting to the Point 6.2 – Conceptualization is the process by which researchers develop precise definitions for vague concepts.

Once we have our conceptual definitions, we need to move on to the next step, which is **operationalization**. You may recall from Chapter 2 that operationalization is the process by which a researcher decides how to actually measure the variables as they are defined conceptually. Below is a discussion of how we might operationalize our definitions of adulthood.

Making Research Real 6.3 – Operationalizing Our Definitions of Adulthood

Operationalizing our first definition of adulthood, based on chronological age, is easy. We would need only to determine how old a research subject is. To do this we might ask:

How old are you in years? _____

    If a research subject responded with a number equal to or more than 18, we would classify him or her as an adult.

    Operationalizing our second definition of adulthood, based on maturity, is a bit more difficult. We would have to ask more questions. We might ask the research subjects:

Have you completed the formal schooling or training required by your profession? Yes or No

Do you live apart from your parents? Yes or No

Are you financially independent from your parents? Yes or No

Are you married or living with another person in a committed relationship? Yes or No

Are you a parent? Yes or No

    From here, the researcher must decide how many 'Yeses' are necessary to label a person as an adult. Would three 'Yeses' be enough for a person to be classified as an adult? Or, are some of these life experiences more important than others?

    Another approach might be to ask at what age the research subject achieved these life experiences. That would provide us even more insight into when adulthood (based on our second conceptual definition) happened for each of the research subjects.

Have you completed the formal schooling or training required by your profession? Yes or No

If you answered "Yes" to the above question, how old were you when this happened? _____

Do you live apart from your parents? Yes or No

If you answered "Yes" to the above question, how old were you when you moved out of your parents' home? _____

Are you financially independent from your parents? Yes or No

If you answered "Yes" to the above question, how old were you when you became financially independent? _____

Are you married or living with another person in a committed relationship? Yes or No

If you answered "Yes" to the above question, how old were you when you married or formalized this relationship? _____

Are you a parent? Yes or No

If you answered "Yes" to the above question, how old were you when you had your first (or only) child? _____

> **Getting to the Point 6.3** – Operationalization is the process by which researchers decide how to measure the variables as they are defined conceptually.

LEVELS OF MEASUREMENT

Before discussing the levels of measurement it is important to learn a few new definitions. A **variable** is anything that varies. For example, age, height, weight, gender, and income are all variables because they vary from person to person or from time to time within the same person. The variations within a variable are called **attributes**. So, there are two attributes for the variable gender – male and female. Theoretically, there are an infinite number of attributes for the variable income because a person's income is unlimited. We will discuss variables and attributes in more detail in the next chapter. For now it is important to understand that all variables (things that vary) have attributes (the variations within the variable).

The level at which a variable is measured, the variable's **level of measurement**, has important implications. Generally speaking, higher levels of measurement provide more detailed information. For example, if I describe myself as 'middle aged,' you really would not know how old I am. I could be from 35 to 55 years old. On the other hand, if I tell you I am 55 years old, you would know more about me. In addition to knowing exactly how long I have lived, you would know the year I was born and, hence, something about the historical period in which I was raised. When I was born in 1957 there were only 48 states. When I was six years old President John F. Kennedy was assassinated. I was nearly 12 when Neil Armstrong became the first man to land on the Moon. My value system and world view were affected by the space race, the Civil Rights movement, and the Vietnam War. So, how might my attitudes be different from yours? All this you deduced from a single number – my age.

The level at which we measure things also determines how we analyze the data that we collect during our research. We have fewer analytical techniques available to us at lower levels of measurement. For example, if you asked 100 professors to describe their age as 'young,' 'middle aged,' or 'elderly,' about the best you could do is report the percentages of each age category within your sample. On the other hand, when we use higher levels of measurement, we can use more precise statistical techniques. If you asked the professors in your sample to tell you their ages in years, for example, you could calculate the average age of the professors in your sample and whether or not they are mostly young, middle aged, or elderly. You could also calculate their range of ages and how much their ages vary. With this information, you might even be able to predict when the professors in your sample are likely to retire and how many teaching positions will be available in the future. We will spend more time on how to analyze data in Chapter 14. For now let's introduce the levels of measurement.

Getting to the Point 6.4 – The level at which a variable is measured has important implications. Generally speaking, higher levels of measurement provide more detailed information and allow for more precise analytical techniques.

The lowest level of measurement is called **nominal**. Nominal variables are merely names or labels. They are simply things we can categorize, such as ethnicity, religion, and gender. The attributes (i.e. the categories) of nominally measured variables cannot be arranged in any logical order or sequence. For example, a researcher might organize a sample of adult offenders by their race. He might use categories like *Caucasian* or *White*, *African American* or *Black*, *Latino*, *Asian*, *Native American*, *Multiracial*, and so on. The order in which the researcher presents these categories does not matter because the attributes of this variable (i.e. the racial categories) cannot be arranged in any logical order or sequence.

The next level of measurement is called **ordinal**. Ordinal variables are also categories, but their attributes can be rank ordered. For example, a warden might be asked to rank order juvenile offenders into these categories: *most likely to reoffend, likely to reoffend, not likely to reoffend*, and *least likely to reoffend*. These categories have a rank order, from highest to lowest likelihood for reoffending. However, these categories are not precise. In other words, we cannot really say how much more likely an offender is to reoffend if he or she is in the *least likely to reoffend* category versus the *not likely to reoffend* category.

The next level of measurement is called **interval**. Interval variables are also categories like nominal level variables and can also be arranged in a logical order like ordinal level variables. But interval variables have one additional feature that makes them more precise: they have equal differences between their attributes. Consider, for example, the variable education, which is often used in studies of criminal behavior. Education, measured in years, is an example of an interval level measure. The difference between a person who has 11 years of education and a person who has 12 years of education is one year. Likewise the difference between a person who has 15 years of education and a person who has 16 years of education is also one year. One year separates each of the attributes of this variable. Interval level measures have one limitation: they do not have an absolute zero. Though it is possible for a person to have no education at all, it is not very likely.

The highest and most precise level of measurement is called **ratio**. Ratio level variables have all of the features of nominal, ordinal, and interval variables plus the added benefit of an absolute zero. Income is a good example. Income, like education, is often used in criminological research since it is associated with criminal behavior. Income, measured in dollars, can be zero. Table 6.1 is a summary of the levels of measurement.

Getting to the Point 6.5 – In the social sciences there are four levels of measurement: nominal, ordinal, interval, and ratio. Nominal variables are merely names or categories. The attributes of nominally measured variables cannot be arranged in any logical order or sequence. Ordinal variables are also names, but their attributes can be ordered in a logical sequence. The attributes of interval variables can also be arranged in a logical order. But interval level variables have equal differences between their attributes. Ratio level variables are the same as interval level variables except that their attributes include an absolute zero.

Table 6.1   Levels of Measurement

LEVELS/ CHARACTERISTICS	NAME ONLY	RANK ORDER	EQUAL DISTANCE	ABSOLUTE ZERO	EXAMPLES
Nominal	Yes	No	No	No	The races or ethnicities of adult offenders
Ordinal	Yes	Yes	No	No	Categories for the likelihood of reoffending
Interval	Yes	Yes	Yes	No	The number of years of formal education
Ratio	Yes	Yes	Yes	Yes	The number of dollars a person earns in one year

It is possible to convert a variable measured at a higher level of measurement into a variable measured at a lower level of measurement. However, it is not possible to convert a variable measured at a lower level of measurement into a variable measured at a higher level of measurement. Below are two examples of how this conversion would, or would not, work.

Making Research Real 6.4 – Converting From a Higher to a Lower Level of Measurement

On a survey, a researcher asks the following question:

What is your annual household income in dollars? _____

Theoretically, this variable would be measured at the ratio level because it is possible for a person to report that they earn no income. More practically, this variable would be measured at the interval level because few respondents would report absolutely no income.

The researcher could then organize the responses to this question into one of three categories he or she calls 'poor,' 'middle class,' and 'wealthy.' Note that these categories can be organized into a logical order from less income to more income, but that the internal ranges (dollar values) within these categories are different. For example, the 'poor' category has an income range of $20,000 ($0–$20,000), whereas the 'middle class' category has an income range of a little under $25,000 ($20,001–$45,000). Thus, the income variable in this case would be measured (or in this case converted into) an ordinal level of measurement.

INCOME LEVEL	CATEGORY
$0–$20,000	Poor
$20,001–$45,000	Middle class
$45,001 and above	Wealthy

Using the same data that was collected at the ratio or interval level, the researcher could even organize the responses into nominal categories. For example, the researcher may want to designate whether a household is eligible for financial assistance based on its income. The attributes for the financial assistance eligibility variable would be 'eligible for financial assistance' and 'not eligible for financial assistance.' At this level of measurement, the cases cannot be rank ordered; they would just be categorized into one of these groups.

INCOME LEVEL	CATEGORY
$0–$20,000	Eligible for financial assistance
$20,001 and above	Not eligible for financial assistance

Making Research Real 6.5 – Trying to Convert From a Lower to a Higher Level of Measurement

Assume that you ask a question about household income like this:

Place a check in the box next to the range of incomes that includes your annual household income.

INCOME RANGE
$0–$20,000
$20,001–$45,000
$45,001–$75,000
$75,001 and above

In this example, the income variable is measured at the ordinal level. These income categories can be rank-ordered from highest to lowest or lowest to highest, but they are not equidistant from one another. If a researcher were to collect information on income in this way, it would not be possible for him or her to convert this into a higher level of measurement (e.g. interval or ratio). Neither would they be able to calculate an average (mean) income for this sample of survey respondents.

The examples above demonstrate the importance of collecting data at the highest level of measurement possible. Of course some variables, by their very nature, cannot be collected at higher levels of measurement. For example, race, ethnicity, and gender are inherently nominally measured variables. But, when possible, variables should be collected at the highest level of measurement available. Not only does this increase the level of measurement precision, but it also provides the researcher with much more analytical flexibility.

> **Getting to the Point 6.6** – It is possible to convert a variable measured at a higher level of measurement into a variable measured at a lower level of measurement. However, it is not possible to convert a variable measured at a lower level of measurement into a variable measured at a higher level of measurement.

For analytical purposes, interval and ratio level variables are the same. This means that the statistical techniques used to analyze interval level measures are the same as those used for ratio level variables. Because of this, many researchers use the terms interval or scale when referring to either interval or ratio level variables.

There is another commonly used method for classifying the levels of measurement that bears mentioning. Some researchers define variables as either discrete or continuous. **Discrete variables** are similar to nominal or ordinal variables. These variables have a fixed number of attributes. For example, gender is a discrete variable because it only has two attributes – male or female. **Continuous variables** are similar to interval or ratio variables. These variables have an almost unlimited number of values. For example, the number of arrests is a continuous variable. A person can have no arrests or dozens of arrests. Theoretically, there is no limit to the number of times a person can be arrested.

VALIDITY AND RELIABILITY

In our everyday language, valid means legitimate, official, or sound. Reliable means dependable, consistent, or trustworthy. In research methods, these terms take on slightly different meanings. As mentioned in previous chapters, social science research does not have the advantages of measurement precision. In the physical sciences, scientists meet and confer regularly to create standard measures for the things they study. In chemistry, for example, a *mole* of a pure substance is the mass of the material in grams that is numerically equal to the molecular mass in atomic mass units. Carbon has an atomic mass of exactly 12.0 atomic mass units. Therefore a mole of carbon is 12 grams. (And you thought a mole was a burrowing mammal!) Social scientists do not use precise and agreed upon measures for the things they study. For example, how would you measure school misbehavior? You would probably get three different answers to this question if you asked three different criminologists.

Because social science does not have generally agreed upon and precise measurements, we spend a lot of time evaluating, and sometimes arguing about, how to measure things. Though we do not always agree on how to measure variables, we do agree on how to evaluate the quality of our measurements. These quality standards are what we call validity and reliability.

Key Point 6.7 – Social scientists rely on the concepts of validity and reliability in order to improve the quality of their measures.

In research, **validity** refers to the ability of a measure to *accurately* measure the concept it claims to measure. Let's again use income as an example. Income may be a valid measure of how much a person earns, but would income be a valid measure of wealth? Usually, a high-income earner is also a wealthy person. But high-income earners may not have a lot of personal wealth or they may have a lot of debt. Likewise, many low-income earners may have a lot of assets. There are millions of people, such as retirees, who earn very little actual income but who would be considered wealthy because they own their homes and have substantial savings. In these cases, income would not be an accurate measure of wealth. Here is another example.

Making Research Real 6.6 – Are Searches an Accurate Measure of Racial Bias?

In recent years, a great deal of attention has been given to the searches police officers conduct during their routine enforcement duties. In some cases, searches are considered an indicator (i.e. a measure) of potential racial bias. An analysis of police searches in a community may reveal that African American and Hispanic drivers are more likely than White drivers to have their cars searched after being pulled over by the police. Before we decide whether this is an indication of racial bias, however, we need to know more about why police conduct vehicle searches.

But are searches, per se, a valid measure of racism? To interpret this enforcement activity properly we need to understand more about searches. In many cases, police officers use their discretion when deciding to conduct a search. In consent searches, for example, a police officer can conduct a search for any reason, or for no reason at all, if they obtain the consent of the driver. The officer need only ask, "Do you mind if I search your car?" If the motorist waives his or her Fourth Amendment rights, the officer may conduct the search and use any evidence found against the driver. In cases of discretionary searches, racial bias may play some role.

But not all searches are discretionary. Some searches, such as inventory searches and searches incident to an arrest, are required by policy. If a police officer impounds a vehicle or arrests an individual, he or she is required to conduct a search. In these cases, racial bias cannot play a role since the police officer has no discretion in the matter. So if we use search data as a measure of potential racial bias, we should only consider those searches wherein the officer is allowed to exercise discretion. This would be a more valid indicator of potential racial bias.

There are several types of validity. **Face validity** refers to whether a measure appears to be valid, or whether it makes sense. For example, if we measure a person's lifetime level of criminal behavior using only his or her adult criminal convictions, our measure would not have face validity because it excludes juvenile criminal convictions. It just does not make sense to exclude juvenile convictions if we want to measure criminal behavior over someone's lifetime.

Criterion or **predictive validity** refers to the extent to which a measure relates to another, more direct measure of the same concept. For example, we might ask someone whether she has been arrested for a crime and test the criterion validity of this measure by comparing her answers to official arrest records. If the two reports are more or less the same, we can say that our self-report measure of arrests has criterion validity.

Construct validity refers to the extent to which a measure corresponds to other variables that are related to the underlying variable we are interested in studying. For example, there appears to be a relationship between creditworthiness and certain types of behavior. Individuals with poor credit histories tend to be involved in more automobile accidents, have lower self-esteem and are generally less able to maintain long-term relationships. All of these factors, in turn, are strongly correlated with criminal behavior. So, one might ask if a credit score has construct validity with regard to various forms of criminal behavior.

Content validity refers to the degree to which a measure includes every dimension of the concept. For example, we know that individuals with strong social bonds are less likely to commit crime. But what are social bonds? Marriage, parenthood, and friendship are social bonds. Academic and work performance is an indicator that a person is 'bonded' to or controlled by school teachers and supervisors. So, if we wanted to ensure that our measure of social bonds has content validity, we would have to include all of these dimensions, and maybe more. Table 6.2 summarizes the common types of validity.

Table 6.2 Common Types of Validity

TYPE	DEFINITION	EXAMPLE
Face	The extent to which a measure makes sense	A researcher wants a measure for an adolescent's propensity to become a delinquent. He uses the number of delinquent peers as his measure. A peer reviewer argues that the measure has face validity because it makes sense as a measure of adolescent propensity to become delinquent.
Criterion/ predictive	The extent to which a measure relates to another, more direct measure of the same concept	The Ames Pro-Social Inventory is intended to measure an adolescent's ability to make pro-social (i.e. non-delinquent) decisions. To verify the criterion validity of this measure, a researcher might evaluate whether delinquents score lower on this inventory than non-delinquents.
Construct	The extent to which a measure corresponds to other variables that are related to the underlying construct	Researchers at the state parole commission develop the Parole Success Indicator (PSI) to measure a parolee's potential post-release success. They find that years married, years of steady employment, and number of children are positively related to post-release success. The PSI score would have construct validity if it was related to these three variables.
Content	The extent to which a measure includes all the dimensions of the concept	A psychologist believes that risky sexual behaviors are related to delinquency among juveniles. He designs a survey wherein he asks high school students about their sexual behavior. The researcher spends a lot of time creating questions that get at all aspects of risky sexual behavior so as to ensure that the measure has content validity.

There are statistical tests (e.g. Pearson *r*) that can be used to determine the level of criterion/predictive or construct validity. These statistical tests are discussed in detail in Chapter 14. Establishing face and content validity is less clear cut; we use our logic and common sense to determine whether a variable has face and/or content validity.

Getting to the Point 6.8 – Validity refers to the ability of a measure to *accurately* measure the concept it claims to measure. There are four types of validity – face validity, criterion or predictive validity, construct validity, and content validity.

In research methods, **reliability** refers to the ability of a measure to *consistently* measure the concept it claims to measure. A measure is reliable if it produces relatively similar results every time we measure our concept. To illustrate, let's use the example of a test commonly used to evaluate the personality traits of police officer applicants.

Researchers use four methods for assessing the reliability of a measure. The **test–retest reliability** method requires a researcher to administer a measure twice to the same group to see if the results are similar. The measure is considered reliable if the results from each test administration are similar. Here is an example of how the reliability of a measure can be evaluated using the test–retest method.

Making Research Real 6.7 – Testing the Personalities of Police Officer Applicants

Many states require police departments to conduct psychological tests on police officer applicants. The idea behind this is to identify individuals who, because of a personality problem or psychological disorder, should not become police officers. We invest a great deal of authority in police officers, so we want to be sure they have a personality that is conducive to good decision making.

The most commonly used exam for this purpose is called the Minnesota Multiphasic Personality Inventory, or MMPI. If you apply for a job as a police officer, you will probably be required to take the MMPI or some other similar type of test during the application process. Originally developed in 1939, the test has produced decades' worth of data that we can use to evaluate its reliability. At issue here is whether or not the test can consistently measure a person's personality structure. In other words, is it a reliable measure of personality structure and psychopathology?

Let's say an individual applies to be a police officer at the Bigton Police Department. As part of the employment process, and in accordance with state law, this applicant takes the MMPI. The psychiatrist who is hired by the department to evaluate the results reports that the applicant is a psychopathic deviate, meaning that he has serious problems with conflict, anger management and respect for social rules. Based on this, the Bigton Police Department decides to reject the applicant.

Undaunted, our applicant decides to apply for employment at the Middleton Police Department. This department also uses the MMPI. Here again, the psychiatrist who administers the test on behalf of the department determines that this applicant has serious problems with conflict, anger management, and respect for social rules. Likewise, the Middleton Police Department decides to reject the applicant.

In this situation we would consider the MMPI to be a reliable measure of personality structure and psychopathology. It tested the same person twice and the results were interpreted independently by two different psychiatrists. The results were the same in both instances. Had the results been different, we would consider this measure unreliable. Generally speaking, the MMPI is considered a reliable measure of personality structure and psychopathology.

Another way to evaluate the reliability is called the **inter-rater reliability** method. Using this method a researcher would ask two or more researchers to observe and measure the same thing. Then the researcher would compare the results to see if they generally have the same impression of what they observed. For example, a group of field researchers might be attempting to measure incidents of gang activity based on visible public graffiti. Gang graffiti is not easy to 'read.' One researcher may classify a symbol painted on a trash dumpster as a gang 'tag' while another would classify it as an innocuous symbol. So, to improve the reliability of this measurement process, we might want to send teams of three field researchers to observe public graffiti. The observers would each classify the graffiti they observe independently and then compare their decisions at the end of the day. If all three agreed that the graffiti is 'gang related,' then we would consider this (i.e. observation) to be a more reliable measure.

The **split half reliability method** requires a researcher to split a measure in half and administer each half to two similar groups. The measure is considered reliable if the results from each half are similar. For example, a researcher may want to evaluate whether a new drug rehabilitation program gets clients to recognize the potential bad effects of illegal drug use. There is some evidence that drug addicts are not able to assess the possible bad outcomes of their behavior. The researcher's paper and pencil test includes 100 questions. Each question is asked twice on the test but in slightly different ways. So the researcher may split the test into two halves with 50 questions each, making sure that one version of each question is on each test. Then, he or she might administer one 50-question test to one group of clients and the other 50-question test to another group of clients. If these two groups score similarly, then the measure is reliable.

Some researchers assess the reliability of their measures based on **benchmarks** and **baselines** that are established by previous researchers. For example, an educational administrator at a juvenile detention facility may use a commercially available reading inventory to assess the educational needs of the delinquents housed at her facility. Commercially available inventories like this cost money, and sometimes a lot of money. So, to save a little money for the state, the administrator may develop a reading test of her own. To test the reliability of this new test, the administrator might give the test to a sample of the juvenile delinquents that have previously taken the commercially available inventory. The administrator's new test would be reliable if its results were essentially the same as those on the commercially available test. Some researchers call this **concurrent reliability**. This simply means that the results from one measure *concur* with the results from another. In other words, the results are consistent. Table 6.3 summarizes these different methods for assessing the reliability of a measure.

Table 6.3 Common Methods for Assessing Reliability

METHODS	DESCRIPTIONS	EXAMPLES
Test–Retest	The researcher administers the measure twice to the same group to see if the results are similar.	A researcher has developed a 50-question test to measure a juvenile's propensity to experiment with drugs. The researcher may administer this test to a sample of 50 juveniles. To evaluate the reliability of the test, the researcher may reorder the questions and re-administer the reordered test to the same group juveniles a week later. If the results are similar, then the measure is reliable.
Inter-rater	Multiple researchers independently measure the same thing and compare their results.	A team of three researchers observe cars at a busy intersection to determine the race or ethnicity of the drivers. At the end of the day they compare their results to see they perceived and classified the drivers' races or ethnicities similarly.
Split half	The researcher splits a measure in half and administers each half to two similar groups.	A probation department develops a test to measure an offender's potential for success during probation. The test measures 15 dimensions of the potential for success. Each dimension is measured by two questions for a total of 30 questions. To assess the reliability of the test, the researcher splits the test in half, ensuring that each of the 15 dimensions is included in each half. She administers one half to a sample of probationers and the other half to a similar sample of probationers. If the results are similar between the two groups, the measure is considered reliable.
Concurrent reliability (benchmarks and baselines)	The researcher uses previous research or generally agreed upon standards to test the reliability of a new measure.	Dissatisfied with the cost of the commercially available intelligence tests, a prison education program develops its own test. It administers the old and new test on the next group of inmates and compares the results. If the results are similar (i.e., intelligence levels are similar for each inmate on both exams), the new test is considered a reliable indicator of intelligence.

Getting to the Point 6.9 – Reliability refers to the ability of a measure to *consistently* measure the concept it claims to measure. There are four methods for determining the reliability of a measure: test–retest, inter-rater, split half, and benchmarks (concurrent reliability).

INDEXES, SCALES, AND TYPOLOGIES

Indexes, scales, and typologies enable researchers to collect detailed information about complicated social phenomena within a single measure. In other words, these measurement devices are a great way of summarizing a lot of information into a single number.

An **index** is a single number that represents a compilation of other measures. The most common index used in criminal justice is calculated by the Federal Bureau of Investigation through its Uniform Crime Reporting Program. Every year the FBI compiles data on many types of crimes that are reported to police agencies. Seven of these crimes, commonly called Part I crimes, are considered the most valid and reli- ›able measure of crime because they are more likely to be reported to the police. Part I crimes include the following: aggravated assault, forcible rape, murder, robbery, arson, burglary, larceny-theft, and motor vehicle theft. The FBI totals the number of these crimes that are reported to the police and calculates a rate per 100,000 resi- ›dents to create the Crime Index for each community, state, region, and the nation. Here is how this works in more detail.

Making Research Real 6.8 – How Crime-Ridden Is Your City?

Let's say you live in a community with a population of 2,500,000 people. Last year, there were 10,000 Part I offenses reported to the police. This is the total number of aggravated assaults, forcible rapes, murders, robberies, arsons, burglaries, larceny-thefts, and motor vehicle thefts that were reported to the police last year. To calculate your community's crime index you would first divide your community's population by 100,000. This would tell you how many 100,000 population 'units' exist in your community.

2,500,000/100,000 = 25

Then, you would divide the total number of Part I offenses (10,000) by the number of 100,000 units within your community's population (25).

10,000/25 = 400

This means that there were 400 Part I crimes per 100,000 residents in your community last year. Of course, using the same process you could calculate crime rates for each type of crime. This would give you a more detailed picture of crime rates. But the value of the overall index lies in the way it summarizes a broad range of crimes into a single number. Regardless of whether your community's population changes, each year you will have an index to determine quickly whether crime is going up or down each year.

Getting to the Point 6.10 – An index is a measurement device that compiles various measures into a single number.

A **scale** is a method for quantitatively measuring a single phenomenon or variable using some type of rating system. Scales are typically found on surveys. The following is an example of a scale:

Using the scale provided, how concerned are you about being a victim of crime?

Very Concerned								Not at all concerned
10 9	8	7	6	5	4	3	2	1

In the example above, the scale measures a single dimension – fear of criminal victimization. Respondents are asked to rate their fear on a scale from 1 to 10. The most common types of scales are **Likert scales**. These five-point scales were originally developed by a psychologist named Rensis Likert (pronounced 'lick-urt' with a short *i*). Likert's scales, developed as he was completing his Ph.D. in 1932, consist of five points:

1. Strongly disagree

2. Disagree

3. Neither agree nor disagree

4. Agree

5. Strongly agree.

Over the years, many researchers have created countless variations of Likert's original five-point scale. The most controversial adaptations involve the removal of the neutral category (i.e., neither agree nor disagree). Removing the neutral category requires that the respondent actually take a position on a particular issue.

Getting to the Point 6.11 – A scale is a method for quantitatively measuring a single phenomenon or variable using a rating system.

Finally, a **typology** is a method for classifying observations, people, or situations into nominal categories. Typologies are often used in qualitative research. For example, a researcher may develop categories (i.e. types) in a research project on juvenile gang membership – active gang member, wannabe gang member, and no gang membership. This researcher would develop conceptual definitions for each of these categories. Then, the researcher might observe students in a local high school and sort them into one of the categories based on how they are dressed. Below is another hypothetical example.

Making Research Real 6.9 – Sorting Inmates by Behavioral Categories

Over the past year, a state prison has experienced an increase in physical confrontations between the inmates and staff. In response, the warden decides to classify the inmates based on their potential for assaultive behavior. Once this typology is completed, the warden intends to segregate inmates based on this classification. He will place the inmates with the highest risk of assaultive behaviors into a separate part of the prison facility and staff that part of the prison with more correctional officers. Using the variables that his experience teaches him to be the most useful for predicting violence (age, substance abuse, violent criminal history, and gang affiliation), the warden places each inmate into one of the following categories, or types:

- **High risk of violence** (younger inmates, heavy or long-term drug use, frequent violent criminal history, active gang affiliation)

- **Medium risk of violence** (middle-aged inmates, occasional or recreational drug use, some violent criminal history, former gang affiliation)

- **Low risk of violence** (old or elderly inmates, no history of drug abuse, little or no violent criminal history, no gang affiliation)

Admittedly, the classification of inmates into this typology is a bit subjective. But it provides the warden with some guidance on how to reduce violence within his prison.

Getting to the Point 6.12 – A typology is a method for classifying observations, people, or situations into nominal categories.

QUANTITATIVE VERSUS QUALITATIVE MEASURES

Although quantitative measures represent a great deal of the criminological research, there is a large and growing body of research that is qualitative in nature. Many students, and a few professors, erroneously assume that qualitative measures are less precise than quantitative measures. This is probably because qualitative measures do not involve numbers. But it is possible that the opposite is true. Because they do not rely on numbers, qualitative measures are more difficult to operationalize. This often forces qualitative researchers to be more precise and develop a deeper understanding of the phenomenon. Here is an example.

Making Research Real 6.10 – A Framework for Understanding Poverty

Quantitative researchers often define poverty in terms of income (in dollars). They assume that if a family's combined income is less than the designated poverty level, the family must be impoverished. In reality, however, poverty is much more complicated. For example, educator Ruby Payne (2003) argues that poverty manifests itself in various dimensions; it's not just a question of how much money a person has. Personally, I think her conceptualization of poverty would be helpful in criminological research and quantitative research more generally. She defines poverty using the following framework.

Financial – having the money to buy goods and services

Emotional – being able to control emotional responses to negative situations

Mental – having the mental abilities and acquired skills to deal with daily life

Spiritual – believing in divine purpose and guidance

Physical – having a basic level of health and mobility

Support systems – having friends, family, and resources in times of need

Relationships – having access to adults who are nurturing and do not engage in self-destructive behavior

Knowledge of hidden rules – knowing the unspoken cues and habits of a group

Some of the measures in Dr. Payne's qualitative definition might lend themselves to quantitative measures. A simple question, "How much money do you earn?," for example, could help determine if a person has sufficient money to buy goods and services. But it would be more difficult to estimate or quantify some of the dimensions of poverty that she identifies. For example, how might a researcher measure whether a person knows the unspoken cues and habits of a group? This would be much more difficult to measure quantitatively. This is where qualitative measurement would come in handy. Certain phenomena cannot be captured by numbers and must be described in detail.

Getting to the Point 6.13 – Quantitative measures rely on numbers and qualitative measures rely on descriptions to measure social phenomena. Often both are necessary to fully understand a concept.

FINAL THOUGHTS

If you have absolutely nothing to do this afternoon, go to the library and skim over some of the articles in a scholarly journal published for the physical sciences. Any of the scholarly journals in biology, chemistry, or physics will work. As you flip through a few articles, notice the amount of space devoted to descriptions of the measures and the methodologies used by the authors while conducting their research. You do not have to understand these descriptions, just notice how *long* these sections are in each article. Now go to the section of the library where the social sciences journals are shelved and skim over a few of these articles. Any of the scholarly journals in criminal justice, criminology, or sociology will work. As you flip through a few articles, you might notice that the space devoted to a description of the measures and methodologies is much larger. Why is this?

Measurement in social science research is much less precise and often much more subjective than in physical science research. A biological researcher has the luxury of standard measures like grams, milliliters, and parts per million. And every other biologist will know what he or she is talking about when he or she refers to these measures. Social scientists are not so fortunate. The concepts we measure – poverty, trust, cohesion, and so on – are much more difficult to define. As a result, social scientists find it necessary to explain our conceptual definitions and how we operationalize our variables in much greater detail.

GETTING TO THE POINT/CHAPTER SUMMARY

- Measurement is a process by which social science researchers determine how to assess the social phenomena they study.

- Conceptualization is the process by which researchers develop precise definitions for vague concepts.

- Operationalization is the process by which researchers decide how to measure the variables as they are defined conceptually.

- The level at which a variable is measured has important implications. Generally speaking, higher levels of measurement provide more detailed information and allow for more precise analytical techniques.

- In the social sciences there are four levels of measurement: nominal, ordinal, interval, and ratio. Nominal variables are merely names or categories. The attributes of nominally measured variables cannot be arranged in any logical order or sequence. Ordinal variables are also names, but their attributes can be ordered in a logical sequence. The attributes of interval variables can also be arranged in a logical order. But interval level variables have equal differences between their attributes. Ratio level variables are the same as interval level variables except that their attributes include an absolute zero.

- It is possible to convert a variable measured at a higher level of measurement into a variable measured at a lower level of measurement. However, it is not possible to convert a variable measured at a lower level of measurement into a variable measured at a higher level of measurement.

- Social scientists rely on the concepts of validity and reliability in order to improve the quality of their measures.

- Validity refers to the ability of a measure to *accurately* measure the concept it claims to measure. There are four types of validity – face validity, criterion or predictive validity, construct validity, and content validity.

- Reliability refers to the ability of a measure to *consistently* measure the concept it claims to measure. There are four methods for determining the reliability of a measure: test–retest, inter-rater, split half, and benchmarks (concurrent reliability).

- An index is a measurement device that compiles various measures into a single number.

- A scale is a method for quantitatively measuring a single phenomenon or variable using a rating system.

- A typology is a method for classifying observations, people, or situations into nominal categories.

- Quantitative measures rely on numbers and qualitative measures rely on descriptions to measure social phenomena. Often both are necessary to fully understand a concept.

CHAPTER EXERCISES

The following chapter exercises are organized into two parts. The first part consists of questions that can be answered using the information from this chapter. This section will test your understanding of the chapter material. The second part consists of research application exercises. These exercises require you to apply what you have learned thus far.

CHAPTER REVIEW QUESTIONS

Respond to each of the following questions using the information from this chapter.

1. Identify the level of measurement (nominal, ordinal, interval, and ratio) of the following variables and their attributes.

Variable	Level of measurement
Income (*in dollars*)	
Education (*High school diploma or equivalent, Bachelor's degree, Masters degree or higher*)	
Gender (*Male, Female*)	
Age (*in years*)	

2. Which of the following levels of measurement would be the most precise?
    a. Nominal
    b. Ordinal
    c. Interval
    d. Ratio

3. The extent to which a measure accurately measures what it purports to measure is referred to as the measure's:
    a. Capacity
    b. Reliability
    c. Validity
    d. Accuracy

4. The extent to which a measure consistently measures a social phenomenon is referred to as the measure's:
    a. Capacity
    b. Reliability
    c. Validity
    d. Accuracy

5. Read the following excerpts from a researcher's report. Identify the type of validity (face, criterion/predictive, construct, or content) that the researcher has established in each case.

Statement	Type of validity
Researchers use intermittent school attendance to predict traffic accident involvement among juvenile drivers. They reason that since intermittent school attendance is related to poor academic performance, itself a well-known predictor of juvenile traffic accident involvement, this is a valid measure.	
To determine whether a new self-evaluation measure of an inmate's likelihood of success on parole is accurate, researchers compare the results of the self-evaluation with the results of an evaluation administered by a trained professional.	
Researchers are examining the relationship between education and violent crime among inmates at a state prison. They decide to measure education as the number of years the inmate has spent in a formal educational setting.	
A researcher studying the physical fitness of police officers must decide on a measure for physical fitness. She decides to assess the police officers' strength, flexibility, and cardiovascular capacity, reasoning that these are the three basic dimensions of physical fitness.	

6. Read the following excerpts from a researcher's report. Identify the method (test–retest, interrater, split half, or benchmark/concurrent) this researcher used to test the reliability of the measures that were used in the research.

Explanation	Reliability method used
"We considered a parolee 'unsuccessful' if he was re-arrested for a new criminal offense within three years of his release from prison. This three-year time frame has been used consistently by criminological researchers for decades."	
"The researchers administered the new test to a sample of 100 female juvenile offenders. Then, to test the reliability of this measure, the researchers re-administered the test to the same sample of 100 female juvenile offenders."	
"The inventory included ten questions, each asked two different ways for a total of 20 questions to determine a domestic violence victim's tendency to experience subsequent victimization. In order to test the reliability of this inventory, we divided the questions into two equivalent ten-question inventories. Then, we divided our sample into two equal groups and administered one version of the inventory to each group."	

A researcher is interested in bullying but learns it is difficult to differentiate between actual bullying and normal playful interactions between third-graders during recess. After developing her definition of bullying she asks her three graduate students to observe behavior at an elementary school during recess and identify bullying incidents. At the end of the day the researcher compares the independent results of the three researchers.

7. A criminologist develops a measure she calls the 'Public Safety Indicator.' This measure ranges from 0 to 10. A community that scores lower on the measure has a lower probability of experiencing violent crimes. The Public Safety Indicator includes numerous factors, such as the number of police officers per 1,000 residents, the number of convicted felons per 10,000 residents, and the number of non-rainy days. This measure is best described as a:
   a. Scale
   b. Inventory
   c. Index
   d. Typology

8. A police officer develops a way to classify her colleagues in terms of their professionalism on the job. The categories are *career officer*, *work-a-day officer*, and *slacker officer*. This measure is best described as a:
   a. Scale
   b. Inventory
   c. Index
   d. Typology

9. A criminal justice professor is attempting to measure the level of public support for the death penalty. He develops a survey that includes six statements that deal with the death penalty. Respondents must indicate whether they agree or disagree with the statements. An example of one of the statements is: "*The death penalty should be used when the victim is a child or old person.*" To measure support for the death penalty, the number of 'agrees' are added up. A respondent with more 'agrees' is considered to have greater support for the death penalty. This measure is best described as a:
   a. Scale
   b. Inventory
   c. Index
   d. Typology

10. A researcher who reports that "the average Body Mass Index of police officers in the Bigton Police Department is 27.8" is using what type of measure?
   a. Quantitative
   b. Qualitative
   c. Neither
   d. Both

RESEARCH APPLICATION EXERCISES

Access to the following articles will be provided by your instructor.

> Krohn, M.D., Lizotte, A.J., Phillips, M.D. Thornberry, T.P. and Bell, K.A. (2011). Explaining systematic bias in self-reported measures: Factors that affect the under- and over-reporting of self-reported arrests. *Justice Quarterly, 30*(3), 501–528.
>
> Van Voorhis, P. (1994). Measuring prison disciplinary problems: A multiple indicators approach to understanding prison adjustment. *Justice Quarterly, 11*(4), 679–709.

11. Read the Krohn et al. (2011) article. Write a brief essay on the article responding to the following questions:
    a. What was the researchers' purpose for conducting this research?
    b. Why did the researchers question the validity and/or reliability of self-report crime measures?
    c. How did the researchers evaluate the validity and/or reliability of self-report measures of criminal activity?
    d. What did the researchers conclude about the validity and/or reliability of self-report measures of crime?

12. Read the van Voorhis (1994) article. Write a brief essay on the article that responds to the following questions:
    a. What was the researcher's purpose for conducting this research?
    b. What was the concept that the researcher was attempting to measure?
    c. How did the researcher define the concept?
    d. How did the researcher operationalize (i.e. measure) this concept?
    e. Why did the researcher use several measures of this concept?
    f. What were the researcher's conclusions about the reliability of the measures used?

CHAPTER 7

Variables and the Structure of Research

In social science, we use variables to describe the different characteristics of individuals, groups, organizations, and social phenomena. The manner in which we describe things can sometimes help us understand a problem or phenomenon more precisely. Here is a hypothetical example of a police chief who, by necessity, defined a problem more precisely and, in doing so, increased the probability of finding a solution.

Making Research Real 7.1 – Aggravated Assaults in the Midwest

The chief of police in a Midwest farming community had a problem. Aggravated assaults were increasing. After reviewing the case reports of aggravated assaults, he noticed that most of the victims and suspects were Hispanic. This community had always had a large population of Hispanic residents. Many of them were migrant workers employed by the agribusiness industry. However, the Hispanic population seldom caused any crime problems. They tended to work hard and keep to themselves. So what was causing this increase in aggravated assaults among Hispanics?

To better understand the problem, he paid a visit to the local Catholic priest. Father Joe had been at St. Catherine's Parish for decades. He was a respected member of the community and actively served the migrant workers who lived in the community. "Father," the chief began, "I just don't understand what's causing the increase in aggravated assaults within the Hispanic community." The old priest thought for a while and then responded. "I think your problem, chief, is that you think of the Hispanic community as a homogenous group of people. The fact is that there are considerable differences within the Hispanic community. Sometimes these differences cause conflict," the priest explained. "How so?" the chief asked. "Well, and I'm just guessing here, for decades, the Hispanics in this community came from Mexico. More recently, we've seen an increase in residents from Guatemala, El Salvador, and Nicaragua. I've noticed that the Mexican members of my parish don't interact with these newer immigrant groups from Central America. And I've heard rumors of conflicts between them. Maybe this is the cause of your crime wave," the priest suggested.

After returning to his office, the chief pulled a small sample of cases and went to the jail to interview the suspects. What he learned seemed to validate Father Joe's suspicion. When asked, most of the suspects told him that the person they assaulted, although Hispanic, was from a different Central American

---

country than them. At this point, the chief knew that he did not have enough evidence to definitively say that national differences within the Hispanic community was an adequate explanation for the increase in aggravated assaults. But, the chief did have enough evidence to warrant a change in how the officers recorded information about the suspects and victims of aggravated assaults. Instead of merely checking the box next to 'Hispanic,' the chief asked the officers to indicate the nationality of the individuals involved in the aggravated assaults.

Although this change would not, by itself, solve the aggravated assault problem, at least the chief would learn more about the ethnicities and nationalities of the suspects and victims. In essence, by measuring the variable 'ethnicity' more precisely, he might understand the problem more completely.

A **variable** is any characteristic of an individual, group, organization, or social phenomenon that changes. Income, age, weight, and gender are all examples of variables. Variables change from one person to another and even within the same person. My wife and I, for example, vary with respect to the variable 'age' in that I am nearly a year older than she is. Individually, I vary with respect to the variable 'weight' in that my weight fluctuates depending on how closely I adhere to my diet.

Getting to the Point 7.1 – A variable is any characteristic of an individual, group, organization, or social phenomenon that changes.

Variables are the basic building blocks of research. They help researchers articulate research questions and hypotheses. As we learned in Chapter 2, all research starts with a research question. A research question is simply a question about some social phenomenon or issue. What is causing the increase in aggravated assaults in a small farming community? How are age and criminal activity related? Which kids are prone to bullying behavior? All these questions consist of variables, such as aggravated assaults, criminal activity, and bullying behavior. When a research question is re-worded as a predictive statement about how a change in one variable will affect a change in another variable, it becomes a **hypothesis**. In this chapter, we will explore the different types of variables and how to construct research questions and hypotheses using variables.

Getting to the Point 7.2 – A hypothesis is a statement that predicts how a change in one or more variables will cause a change in another variable.

TYPES OF VARIABLES

Generally speaking, there are three types of variables. Each functions a bit differently within a causal relationship. **Independent variables** are causal variables. These are the variables that we hypothesize will cause a change in another variable. For example, a researcher may predict that a lack of education causes poverty. In this case, education is the independent variable, or the potential cause of poverty. Another researcher may hypothesize that poverty causes a lack of education. In this case, poverty is the independent variable, or the potential cause of a lack of education.

> **Getting to the Point 7.3** – An independent variable is the causal variable, or the variable that a researcher predicts will be the cause of a change in another variable.

Dependent variables are the variables that change as a result of a change in an independent variable. They are, in essence, the effects. For example, a researcher may hypothesize that poverty causes crime. In this case, crime is the effect, or dependent variable. Another researcher may hypothesize that crime causes poverty. After all, inmates do not earn a lot of money in prison and ex-felons have an extremely hard time finding work after leaving prison. In this case, poverty is the dependent variable.

> **Getting to the Point 7.4** – A dependent variable is the effect, or the variable that a researcher predicts will change as a result of a change in another variable or set of variables.

An easy way to distinguish between the independent and dependent variables is to ask which happens first and which happens second. The independent variable always happens first. It has to. You may recall that temporal order is one of the three rules of causality. This rule says that the cause must happen before the effect. So the independent variable must happen before the dependent variable. Figure 7.1 illustrates a causal relationship between an independent and dependent variable. The illustration shows that a change in the independent variable must come first to cause a change in the dependent variable.

    Intervening variables occur between independent and dependent variables and change the nature of the causal relationship. In other words, they *intervene* in the relationship. For example, a researcher may hypothesize that the experience of poverty may cause a person to commit crime, but this effect is lessened if the person is raised in a two-parent household. This hypothesis suggests that living in a two-parent household (the intervening variable) reduces the effect of poverty (the independent

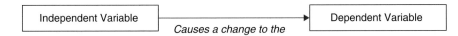

Figure 7.1 Causal Relationship Between an Independent and Dependent Variable

variable) on crime (the dependent variable). Intervening variables can also strengthen the relationship between independent and dependent variables. For example, a researcher may hypothesize that an impoverished child may be more likely to commit a crime if he or she is an active member of a juvenile gang. In this case, active gang membership (the intervening variable) is believed to increase the likelihood that poverty (the independent variable) will lead to crime (the dependent variable).

Figure 7.2 illustrates how an intervening variable might affect the causal relationship between an independent and dependent variable. The illustration suggests that the intervening variable might result in a different effect on the dependent variable. Note the dashed line leading from the independent variable to the intervening variable, which suggests that the variable may or may not intervene in the relationship.

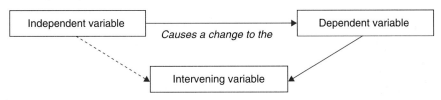

Figure 7.2 A Causal Relationship Between an Independent, Dependent, and Intervening Variable

Getting to the Point 7.5 – An intervening variable is any variable that occurs between the independent and dependent variables, changing how, or even if, the independent variable affects a dependent variable.

Below is a hypothetical example of how a causal relationship between an independent and dependent variable might be affected by the introduction of an intervening variable.

Making Research Real 7.2 – An Intervention to Reduce Traffic Fatalities Caused by Intoxicated Drivers

Last year, at the urging of restaurant and bar owners, the city council approved a change to the ordinance regulating the number of hours that alcoholic beverages could be sold. The restaurant and bar owners were successful at convincing the city council that allowing them to remain open until 2:00 am on Friday and Saturday nights would increase their revenues, and in turn increase sales tax revenues. Previously, drinking establishments were required to close at midnight.

In her argument against the ordinance change, the chief of police predicted that an increase in serving hours would result in an increase in traffic accident fatalities caused by intoxicated drivers. In research methods terms, the chief was alleging that an increase in alcoholic beverage drinking hours (the independent variable) would cause an increase in traffic fatalities caused by intoxicated drivers (the dependent variable). We could illustrate this as follows.

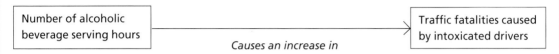

It turns out, the chief's prediction was correct. The community experienced a 20 percent increase in traffic fatalities following the increase of alcoholic beverage serving hours. Furthermore, most of these new fatalities occurred on Friday and Saturday nights. The city manager met with the chief of police. "Chief, you have to do something to reduce traffic fatalities caused by intoxicated drivers. The council is not willing to reduce serving hours. Isn't there something we can do to reduce these fatalities short of reducing serving hours?" the manager asked. The chief asked for a few days to come up with an idea.

After meeting with her command staff, the chief recommended a new program called "Get a Ride – Save a Life." This program, staffed by trained volunteers using existing city vehicles, would provide free rides home to intoxicated drivers. Restaurant and bar owners were trained on how to recognize intoxicated patrons. They were also strongly encouraged to call the Get a Ride – Save a Life service when an intoxicated patron intended to leave. The effect of this program was nearly immediate. Traffic fatalities caused by intoxicated drivers began to decrease. After six months, the number of traffic fatalities caused by intoxicated drivers decreased to below what it was prior to the increase in serving hours. In short, the Get a Ride – Save a Life program was a success.

The Get a Ride – Save a Life program acted as an intervening variable. Specifically, it changed the causal relationship between the independent variable (number of alcoholic beverage serving hours) and the dependent variable (traffic fatalities caused by intoxicated drivers). An illustration of the effect is provided below. Again, notice the dashed line leading from the independent variable (number of alcoholic beverage serving hours) and the intervening variable (number of patrons who use the Get a Ride – Save a Life program). This dashed line means that the intervention of the Get a Ride – Save a Life program may or may not happen. If it does not happen, the causal effect between alcoholic beverage serving hours and traffic fatalities caused by intoxicated drivers will remain the same.

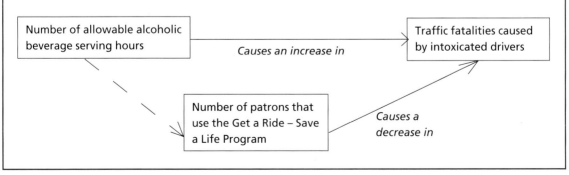

VARIABLE ATTRIBUTES

The variations of any one variable are known as the variable's **attributes**. A variable's attributes are the different characteristics or values within the variable. As we learned in the previous chapter, some variables have a limited number of attributes. For example, nominally measured variables, such as *gender*, have only two attributes – *male* and *female*. Other variables have an unlimited number of levels. *Income*, for example, is measured at the ratio level. Theoretically, there is no limit to how much income a person can earn.

A variable's attributes depend on how we define and measure our concepts. If we define *education* as the number of years that a person has spent in a formal educational setting, the number of attributes might range from 0 (for a person who has not yet started school) to 25 (for a person who has earned a doctorate degree), and maybe even higher. If, on the other hand, we define *education* as the type of academic credential a person has earned, we might have just six attributes: *High school degree or GED, Associate's degree, Bachelor's degree, Technical or professional degree, Master's degree,* or *Doctorate degree.*

Getting to the Point 7.6 – Attributes are the different characteristics or values that a variable can take on.

A variable's attributes must be both exhaustive and mutually exclusive. What do we mean by this? **Exhaustiveness** refers to the completeness of the list of attributes. All of the possible attributes for each variable must be included. For example, if you send out a survey that asks the respondents their religious preference, you must list all of the possible religious preferences. This is harder that it seems! Consider this survey question on religious preference:

Check the box beside the religion that best describes your preference.

- *Roman Catholic*

- *Baptist*

- *Presbyterian*

- *Episcopalian*

- *Hindu*

- *Jewish*

- *Muslim*

Methodist, Mormon, and Buddhist are just some of the religions not found on this list. Which box, then, would a Methodist, Mormon, or Buddhist check? There is no box for them. This list is not exhaustive. Of course, it is difficult to list *all* of the possible religions in the world. Even if we could create such a list, it would be too long to include in a survey. As a practical rule, each attribute that likely constitutes at least 5 percent of the population or sample that is being surveyed should be included on the list. The rest can be collapsed into an 'Other' category to ensure that the list is exhaustive. Had we added an 'Other' box to the question above, the Methodist, Mormon, or Buddhist would have had a box to check.

> **Getting to the Point 7.7** – Exhaustiveness refers to the completeness of the list of a variable's attributes.

When we say that attributes must be **mutually exclusive**, we mean that each attribute must be distinctive, such that a respondent can pick one, *and only one*, option. Let's use another survey question on religious preference:

Check the box beside the religion that best describes your preference.

- *Roman Catholic*
- *Protestant*
- *Christian*
- *Hindu*
- *Jewish*
- *Muslim*

Here, again, we have failed to account for every world religion. So our list is not exhaustive. But, we have also failed to make each attribute mutually exclusive. Specifically, we have boxes for Roman Catholics, Protestants, and Christians. A Christian is defined as anyone professing a belief in Jesus Christ or following a religion based on the teachings of Jesus Christ. This would include Roman Catholics and Protestants. A Roman Catholic respondent, therefore, would be torn between two options: Roman Catholic and Christian. A Protestant respondent would also have two options: Protestant and Christian. When we consider a variable's attributes, we have to make sure that there is not any overlap between them.

> **Getting to the Point 7.8** – Mutual exclusivity refers to the capacity for a list of attributes to provide one, *and only one*, option for each respondent.

Some readers may be thinking, *"How would I know whether my list of attributes is exhaustive and mutually exclusive? For example, I don't know anything about religion. To do this right, I would have to learn something about religious preferences."* Yes, that is exactly what I am saying. This does not mean that you have to go to a seminary and become an expert on the world's religions. It just means that you have to understand the meanings of your variables and the differences between the variables' attributes. Here is how a researcher, unfamiliar with how to measure religious preference, might approach this challenge.

Making Research Real 7.3 – Learning About Religious Preferences, With a Little Help From Our Friends

In her first assignment as an analyst for the Bigton Police Department, Amy Weaver was asked to develop a community survey about citizens' attitudes toward the police department. After reviewing a draft of the survey, the chief called Amy and asked her to include religious preference among the list of questions. "Why? Do you think that would make a difference in people's attitudes about the police department?" Amy asked. "Because of the new Islamic Center in the south part of town, we might have a higher percentage of Muslim residents. We've worked pretty hard to improve our relationship with the Islamic community. I just want to know how we're doing," the chief explained.

The chief's request worried Amy. She was not raised in a religious tradition. Her parents never went to church. "I don't know the difference between a Baptist and a Methodist," she thought. She went to the local library and checked out a book called *The World's Religions*. After perusing the text, she was even more confused about which religions to include in her question. But then she had an idea. "I'm probably not the first person who ever asked this question. Surely, other researchers have come up with good questions on religious preference," she thought.

It turns out, Amy was correct. Religious preference is a commonly asked question in surveys. The Gallup Organization, one of the leading polling organizations in the world, conducts several surveys each year about religion. Amy learned from their website (http://www.gallup.com/home.aspx) that the most common religious preferences in America are:

Protestant/Other Christian (52.5%)

- Catholic (23.9%)

- Mormon (1.9%)

- Jewish (1.6%)

- Muslim (0.5%)

- Other non-Christian religion (2.4%)

She also learned that about 15 percent of the American population describes their religious preference as None/Atheist/Agnostic. Using this and other information for guidance, Amy included the following question on her survey:

Which of the following best describes your religious preference? (Check only one box.)

- Protestant
- Roman Catholic
- Mormon
- Jewish
- Muslim
- Other non-Christian religion, specify _____
- None/Atheist/Agnostic

The attributes that Amy used for the variable religious preference are mutually exclusive. It is likely that a respondent will only be able to select one attribute. The attributes are also exhaustive. It is likely that every respondent will be able to have a choice. This includes individuals who have no religious preference. And, if for some reason a large group of Wiccans or Buddhists happened to have moved to Bigton, they would be able to check the Other non-Christian religion box.

ELEMENTS OF A GOOD RESEARCH QUESTION

Once you have identified the variables and their attributes in your research, you are poised to construct a good **research question**. Research questions may come from mere curiosities about social phenomena or from a casual observation of some behavior. But in all cases, a research question is an interrogative statement. This simply means that research questions are actual questions, as opposed to statements. In some cases, research questions arise from prior research. For example, after reading a research report done by another researcher, you may recognize a limitation or gap in the research. This may encourage you to improve or expand the body of knowledge by conducting your own research.

One of the most common mistakes researchers make when developing research questions is that they are not specific enough. Overly broad research questions become problematic during the literature review and data collection portions of the research process. For example, say you are interested in juvenile delinquency. If you type 'juvenile delinquency' into a search engine, you are likely to get thousands of articles and books on this topic. Working through all of these would be a formidable task. Narrowing the research question into a manageable topic that can reasonably be done within the time frame allotted is essential. For example, you might narrow your topic on juvenile delinquency to the relationship between juvenile delinquency and adult criminal behavior. Another thing to keep in mind when developing a good research question is to ask about something you are genuinely interested in. Research takes time and it is worth your while to find a topic that is either meaningful to you or beneficial to society in some way. Here is an example from a recent experience of a student of mine.

Making Research Real 7.4 – Measuring Jesus

A former student of mine, we will call him Angelo, came to the university to party and have a good time. After a semester of bad grades placed him on academic probation, he decided to buckle down. During the course of getting serious about school, he experienced a religious conversion. In his words, "I found Jesus." As far as I could tell, the conversion was both sincere and complete. He developed a habit of evangelizing to other students and delivering sermons during class discussions. To Angelo, every problem in criminal justice had a biblical solution. For the most part, we all just smiled and encouraged him to be a bit more scientific in his reasoning.

In the first semester of his senior year, Angelo was assigned to write a research paper. This exercise required him to conduct an extensive literature review and develop a plan for answering a research question. He chose to write about the contribution that religion can make in the rehabilitation of ex-offenders. "Do you have a research question or hypothesis yet?" I asked. "Yes, sir, I do. Are criminals more likely to be rehabilitated when Jesus enters their heart?" he replied. I thought for a little bit before responding. I could tell he was excited about this topic and suspected that he really wanted to use this research to merge his religious convictions with his academic studies.

"How would you measure the variables in your research question?" I finally asked. "Well, a criminal is defined as any person who is incarcerated for a crime. And I'll measure rehabilitation as having no new arrest during the three years following release from prison," he responded. "What about the independent variable? How are you going to measure whether Jesus is in the heart of an ex-offender?" I asked. "Oh that's the easy part. All a person has to do is ask Jesus to enter into their heart as their Lord and Savior." "Does it have to be Jesus? Can it be Muhammad or Buddha?" I asked. "What do you mean?" Angelo asked. "Well, the behavioral requirements of many of the world's religion are rather consistent. So, if an ex-offender becomes a devout Muslim or Buddhist while incarcerated, wouldn't this have the same effect as becoming a Christian?" I asked. "Well, no. Jesus is the one true Son of God. It is only through Jesus that we reach the Kingdom of Heaven," Angelo responded.

Angelo struggled on that day to come up with a workable research question. His research question was certainly a question. And it was meaningful to him and significant to society. But it took him some time to find a way to relate his question to the body of knowledge and not rely totally on his legitimate faith. He decided to measure an ex-offender's religious conviction based on three elements – a public statement of belief, regular participation in religious worship, and adherence to a behavioral code consistent with a stated belief system. Ultimately, he was successful. He completed his research paper, graduated, and became a counselor in a state prison.

If you are responsible for coming up with a good research question like Angelo, you might keep a few tips in mind. First, research questions should be measurable. In other words, you should be able to measure the variables in the research question. For example, the question *"Are Fords better than Chevrolets for patrol use?"* is not a good research question. How would you measure *"better"*? A more appropriate research question would be *"Which of the two vehicles (Ford of Chevrolet) currently under consideration for patrol use by our department has a lower operating cost per mile?"* You can measure the "operating costs" of the two vehicles and make a decision.

Research questions should also be unanswered. Most questions in the social sciences have been asked and answered by another researcher. This does not mean that we cannot ask them again or in different ways. Societies change constantly and sometimes dramatically. Thus, old research needs to be replicated, lingering questions from past research need to be explored, and new techniques need to be applied. There is always more to do. For example, as computers become more prevalent in everyday commerce, identity theft is increasing. There is nothing new about impersonation or theft. These crimes have been well known for centuries. But does identity theft happen in the same way as regular theft? This is a question we have yet to answer.

Third, research questions should be doable. Money and time are always finite. So researchers need to ask whether a particular research project is practical or feasible. For example, a researcher may want to conduct a survey on the physical health of federal inmates. Such a study is easily done by enlisting (or maybe paying) the physicians who work in federal correctional facilities to fill out health assessment forms during annual health assessments for inmates. But how long would that take? And how much would it cost? These are central questions to ask before posing a formal research question.

Finally, research questions should be disinteresting to the researcher. When we say that a research question is 'disinteresting,' we mean that it should be indifferent to the outcome. Researchers should never try to 'prove' anything. Researchers, like criminal investigators, should be prepared for any answer, even if the answer turns out to be different from what they suspected, or hoped, it would be. For example, a researcher who personally believes that predatory sex offenders should be incarcerated for life should be prepared to accept a research finding that offenders who undergo rigorous psychological counseling are less likely to reoffend. There is nothing wrong with wanting a research project to reveal a truth that is consistent with your personal beliefs. Just be prepared to accept the answer if it is not.

> **Getting to the Point 7.9** – Good research questions should be measurable, unanswered, feasible, and disinteresting.

HYPOTHESES IN SOCIAL RESEARCH

A **hypothesis** is a predictive statement that alleges a plausible connection between two or more variables. By 'predictive' I mean that the hypothesis makes a specific prediction about how two or more variables are connected. By 'plausible connection' I mean that the hypothesis must describe the nature of the connection between the variables. For example, does an increase in the independent variable cause an increase in the dependent variable? Or, does an increase in the independent variable cause a decrease in the dependent variable?

A hypothesis must contain at least two variables. One of these must be an independent variable and the other must be a dependent variable. Here is an example of a hypothesis with one dependent and one independent variable:

Adults who were victims of abuse as children are more likely to abuse their own children.

This hypothesis predicts that the independent variable (*experience of abuse as a child*) is related to the dependent variable (*abusive behavior as an adult*). Notice that the hypothesis alleges exactly how the independent variable will affect the dependent variable. The researcher predicts that being a victim of abuse *increases* the likelihood that a person will abuse his or her own children. Describing exactly how the independent variable affects the dependent variable is an essential characteristic of a hypothesis.

Sometimes hypotheses contain more than two variables. For example a hypothesis might contain one dependent variable and two or more independent variables:

Men who were victims of abuse as children are more likely to abuse their own children.

Though it may not be obvious, there are two independent variables in this hypothesis: *gender* and *experience of abuse as a child*. It is possible to add other independent variables to this hypothesis. But in doing so, researchers might overly complicate their analysis. As such, many researchers create separate hypotheses for each independent variable.

Some hypotheses also contain intervening variables. As you may recall, intervening variables step in and change the nature of the causal relationship between an independent and dependent variable. Here is an example:

Men who were victims of abuse as children are more likely to abuse their own children unless they undergo extensive psychological counseling.

This hypothesis has two independent variables (*gender* and *experience of abuse as a child*), one dependent variable (*abusive behavior as an adult*), and one intervening variable (*psychological counseling*). In this hypothesis, the researcher predicts that extensive counseling will lessen the effect of the independent variables on the dependent variable.

Hypotheses developed by scholars often include complex language and statistical jargon. As such, it may take a few readings of a hypothesis to understand what the researcher is getting at. Hypotheses, however, do not have to be difficult to understand. In fact, it is likely that you 'create' hypotheses every day. Have you ever stepped on your bathroom scale and thought, "Oh my! I need to watch what I eat"? If so, then you have created a hypothesis. You have suggested a causal link

between what you eat and how much you weigh. As a criminal justice practitioner,
you will likely make many hypotheses. For example, a correctional officer might
advise "Don't house the new inmate in Tier A because his gang membership might
result in a physical confrontation with the inmates already housed there." Below
is a hypothetical example of how a researcher and a practitioner develop separate
hypotheses that make the same prediction.

Making Research Real 7.5 – Can't We Just Agree on the Question?

The chief of police and her command staff are anxiously awaiting the results of a study on the effect of
a new program designed to reduce robberies in their community. Last year, the city experienced a 50
percent increase in robberies. The most common victims of these robberies were convenience stores and
gasoline stations. In an effort to reduce robberies, a lieutenant had proposed a comprehensive enforcement strategy that he called Operation Target Hardening. This enforcement strategy involved the following elements:

*   meetings with store owners to enlist their assistance;
*   inspections of stores to identify potential structural changes that would reduce the likelihood of a
    robbery (e.g. better lighting);
*   a training program for cashiers designed to teach them how to prevent a robbery (e.g. making eye
    contact with customers as they enter the store) and how to respond in the event of a robbery;
*   strategically placed policing resources (e.g. patrol cars) and/or private security officers in and around
    the stores.

The lieutenant believed that these four strategies would reduce robberies throughout the community.
The chief agreed and approved the plan. She also hired a criminal justice professor from an area university
to conduct an evaluation of the plan.

When the professor had completed his analysis of Operation Target Hardening, he presented his
findings at a staff meeting. "The training and environmental features of Operation Target Hardening in
conjunction with the increased physical presence of police and security personnel combine to produce
specific and general deterrence at the individual and macro-sociological levels, resulting in a statistically
significant decrease of the targeted criminal behavior." The chief of police raised her hand to interrupt,
"I'm confused. Did the program work or didn't it? "The professor responded, "Well, yes it did. Isn't that
what I just said?"

Both the professor and the chief of police had the same question and hypothesis. They just asked
them in different ways. The professor, bound by scholarly norms and standards, used very precise language to assess the relationship between four independent variables and one dependent variable. The
chief of police, compelled by her need to know for practical purposes, just wanted to know if robberies
went down after Operation Target Hardening had been implemented.

In making hypotheses, researchers distinguish between alternative and null hypotheses. An **alternative hypothesis** is what the researcher hopes to prove as true during
the research. But before a researcher can prove an alternative hypothesis, he or she

must first disprove a competing hypothesis. We refer to these competing hypotheses as null hypotheses. A **null hypothesis** is a statement that alleges no plausible connection between two or more variables. Here is an example:

Alternative hypothesis (Ha): Poor academic performance in the early elementary school years is positively related to juvenile delinquency in the adolescent years.

Null hypothesis (Ho): Poor academic performance in the early elementary school years is not related to juvenile delinquency in the adolescent years.

In this case, the researcher is alleging that if a child performs poorly during his or her early elementary years, he or she will be more likely to be a juvenile delinquent as an adolescent. Notice that the null hypothesis alleges that poor academic performance in the early elementary school years (the independent variable) is not *at all* related to juvenile delinquency in the adolescent years (the dependent variable). The null hypothesis is not a prediction of the opposite relationship (e.g. poor academic performance will *reduce* the likelihood of juvenile delinquency). The null hypothesis is a prediction that there is *no* relationship.

Getting to the Point 7.10 – An alternative hypothesis is a predictive statement that alleges a plausible connection between two or more variables. A null hypothesis is a statement that alleges no plausible connection between two or more variables.

In order to 'prove' the alternative hypothesis, the researcher must first collect and analyze data. These data will reveal which of these two hypotheses (the null or alternative) is a correct statement. We always start with the null hypothesis. If, after analyzing the data, the researcher finds no relationship between early academic performance and adolescent juvenile delinquency, he or she would accept the null hypothesis and, in doing so, reject the alternative hypothesis. If, on the other hand, the researcher discovers that poor early academic performance results in a higher incidence of adolescent juvenile delinquency, he or she would reject the null hypothesis and, in doing so, accept the alternative hypothesis.

Why not just ignore the null hypothesis altogether and just try to prove the alternative hypothesis? I admit that this would make the research process less cumbersome. But just as a police officer must presume innocence, so, too, must a researcher presume no relationship between the variables in a research project. Here is a story that illustrates this point.

Making Research Real 7.6 – Sherlock the Researcher

The phone rang on Detective Joe Sherlock's desk. It was the captain with a late Friday afternoon assignment. "Joe, get over to 920 Elm Street and see a lady about a burglary," the captain ordered. Joe threw his jacket on and went to the woman's home to investigate. After collecting some evidence and taking some photographs, Joe learned that the only thing that was missing was the woman's television. Joe asked, "Any idea who might have done this?" The woman told Joe that while she was out of town, she asked one of the neighborhood kids to look after her cat. "He had a key to the front door," she told Joe.

Joe walked over to the neighbor's house. As he approached the front door, he saw a young man walking out the side door with a large television set that fit the description of the one the woman said had been stolen from her house. Joe ordered him to put the television down and arrested him on suspicion of burglary. Joe had enough evidence to initiate the arrest. Putting this in research methods terms, Joe's alternative hypothesis was as follows:

Ha: *The young man burglarized the woman's house while she was out of town.*

The young man's case now went to the District Attorney, who would make the final decision about whether to prosecute the young man. At this point, consistent with our system of justice and our rules of research, the hypothesis changed. Because the young man is presumed innocent, the District Attorney and the detective investigating the case must first consider the null hypothesis:

Ho: *The young man did not burglarize the woman's house while she was out of town.*

Joe visited the jail to interrogate the young man. "Did you steal that woman's television?" he asked. "No sir, I did not. I was only borrowing it while she was away. Plus I had her permission" the young man responded. "Do you have any evidence that she gave you permission?" Joe asked. "Yeah I do. In the wallet they took from me I have a note from her," the young man replied. Joe went to the property room and sure enough there was a note addressed to the young man and signed by the woman. The note said:

It is fine with me if you want to borrow my television for your party. Just be sure it's back in my house and hooked up before I get back on Saturday night. Thanks for looking after the cat.

Joe drove to the woman's house. "If he actually had permission to use the television, then no burglary occurred," he reasoned. "I'm sorry to bother you again, ma'am, but there has been a development in your case," Joe began. He showed her the note. "Did you write this note?" Joe asked. "Oh officer," the woman gasped. "I'm so sorry. I completely forgot that I had given him permission to use my television for his party. And I did come back a day early. He was probably just bringing the television back when you caught him. I'm so embarrassed." The young man was released later that afternoon and the case was closed.

What Detective Joe Sherlock did in his investigation was precisely what any credible social science researcher would do. He began with a hunch that the young man stole the television. A researcher would call this an alternative hypothesis. But our system of justice requires the presumption of innocence. So Joe had to begin the investigation with the assumption that the young man was innocent. A researcher would call this a null hypothesis. To investigate, Joe gathered additional evidence, just as a social science research might collect data. After analyzing the evidence, Joe accepted the null hypothesis and released the young man from jail. Similarly, after evaluating data, a researcher might accept the null hypothesis and reject the alternative hypothesis.

Separate from the distinction between the null and alternative hypotheses, a hypothesis can also be categorized into one of two types. The first type is association. **Hypotheses of association** allege a constant and predictable correlation, or relationship, between independent and dependent variables. In other words, the independent and dependent variables vary together. Here is an example.

Ha: *Regular exercise during a police officer's career is associated with a longer life expectancy.*

This hypothesis alleges a positive association between exercise and longevity among police officers. It also suggests that police officers who do not exercise regularly during their careers live fewer years.

Getting to the Point 7.11 – A hypothesis of association alleges that a change in the independent variable(s) is associated with a change in the dependent variable. As one increases/decreases, the other increases/decreases.

The second type is difference. **Hypotheses of difference** allege that the independent variable(s) makes groups different in some respect. Here is an example.

Ha: *Police officers who participate in the Department's wellness program will have a lower incidence of cardiovascular disease than police officers who do not participate in the Department's wellness program.*

This hypothesis alleges that active participation in the Department's wellness program (the independent variable) changes the police officers' level of cardiovascular disease (the dependent variable). In other words, the officers who participate in the Department's wellness program become different from the officers who do not participate.

Getting to the Point 7.12 – A hypothesis of difference alleges that the independent variable(s) makes groups different with respect to the dependent variable.

The distinction between a hypothesis of association and a hypothesis of difference is sometimes difficult to see. This may be due to the fact that, with a little work, a researcher can turn a hypothesis of association into a hypothesis of difference, and vice versa. Consider the following hypothesis of difference:

Ha: *Police officers who have a Bachelor's degree will score higher on the Department's promotional examinations than police officers who do not have a Bachelor's degree.*

With a little work, we can reformat this hypothesis into a hypothesis of association:

Ha: *A police officer's level of education is positively associated with performance on the promotional examination.*

Whereas the previous hypothesis of difference predicted that police officers with a Bachelor's degree would score higher on the promotional exam, the hypothesis of association predicts that as level of education increases, performance on the promotional exam will also increase.

One way of differentiating between a hypothesis of association and a hypothesis of difference is to consider your independent variable. If your independent variable is ordinal, interval, or ratio, your hypothesis will be one of association, because you are alleging that as the independent variable increases or decreases, so too will the dependent variable increase or decrease. If your independent variable is nominal, your hypothesis will be one of difference, because you are alleging that two or more groups will differ with respect to the dependent variable. Note, too, that this distinction affects how the data can be presented. The data used to test a hypothesis of association can be illustrated in a linear graph (see Figure 7.3).

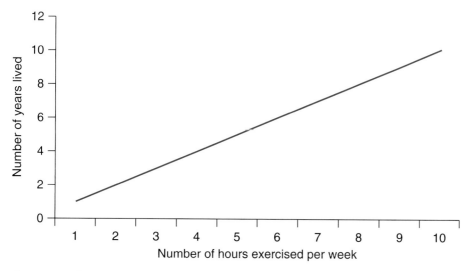

Figure 7.3 Illustrating the Data in a Hypothesis of Association

In Figure 7.3, the number of hours exercised each week is measured on the horizontal axis. The number of years lived is measured on the vertical axis. These data suggest a positive relationship between the frequency of exercise and the number of years lived.

The data used in a hypothesis of difference can be illustrated in a bar graph (see Figure 7.4).

As Figure 7.4 suggests, officers who participate in the wellness program have, on average, a lower resting heart rate, suggesting that they are less likely to develop cardiovascular disease. This evidence suggests that the officers who participate become different from the officers who do not participate.

Getting to the Point 7.13 – If the independent variable is ordinal, interval, or ratio, the hypothesis will be one of association. Hence, the data used to test a hypothesis of association can be illustrated in a linear graph. If the independent variable is nominal, the hypothesis will be one of difference. Hence, the data used to test a hypothesis of difference can be illustrated in a bar graph.

FINAL THOUGHTS

Sometimes it seems as if the research process is set up so that scientists fail. In other words, it is set up to favor the null hypothesis and to reject the alternative hypothesis, which is the hypothesis we want to prove! But this is what makes science so rigorous. It is not about stating opinions and arguing in favor of them; it is about making hypotheses and testing them. Scientists do not want to be right so much as they want to know. And this requires that the standards be set high for proving or disproving hypotheses.

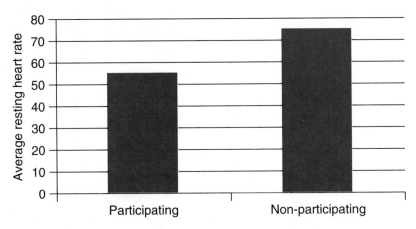

Figure 7.4   Illustrating the Data in a Hypothesis of Difference

In a previous chapter, you were introduced to the peer review process. If there is a venue through which scientists hold one another to these lofty standards, this is it. Sometimes this process can be brutal. But it has to be because the findings from our research can have far-reaching implications. Right now, as I write this textbook, criminologists are debating how best to deter criminals. These are not just philosophical debates; these are practical questions with real-world consequences. If we can make educated guesses about how to stop crime and if we can collect data that lend weight to these guesses, we can develop laws and programs that work. Yes, science is hard, but we are all the better for it.

GETTING TO THE POINT/CHAPTER SUMMARY

- A variable is any characteristic of an individual, group, organization, or social phenomenon that changes.

- A hypothesis is a statement that predicts how a change in one or more variables will cause a change in another variable.

- An independent variable is the causal variable, or the variable that a researcher predicts will be the cause of a change in another variable.

- A dependent variable is the effect, or the variable that a researcher predicts will change as a result of a change in another variable or set of variables.

- An intervening variable is any variable that occurs between the independent and dependent variables, changing how, or even if, the independent variable affects a dependent variable.

- Attributes are the different characteristics or values that a variable can take on.

- Exhaustiveness refers to the completeness of the list of a variable's attributes.

- Mutual exclusivity refers to the capacity for a list of attributes to provide one, *and only one*, option for each respondent.

- Good research questions should be measurable, unanswered, feasible, and disinteresting.

- An alternative hypothesis is a predictive statement that alleges a plausible connection between two or more variables. A null hypothesis is a statement that alleges no plausible connection between two or more variables.

- A hypothesis of association alleges that a change in the independent variable(s) is associated with a change in the dependent variable. As one increases/decreases, the other increases/decreases.

- A hypothesis of difference alleges that the independent variable(s) makes groups different with respect to the dependent variable.

- If the independent variable is ordinal, interval, or ratio, the hypothesis will be one of association. Hence, the data used to test a hypothesis of association can be illustrated in a linear graph. If the independent variable is nominal, the hypothesis will be one of difference. Hence, the data used to test a hypothesis of difference can be illustrated in a bar graph.

CHAPTER EXERCISES

The following chapter exercises are organized into two parts. The first part consists of questions that can be answered using the information from this chapter. This section will test your understanding of the chapter material. The second part consists of research application exercises. These exercises require you to apply what you have learned thus far.

CHAPTER REVIEW QUESTIONS

Respond to each of the following questions using the information from this chapter.

1. Which of the following is a variable?
   a. Gender
   b. Annual income
   c. Hair color
   d. All of the above

2. A formal statement that predicts how a change in one or more variables might cause a change in another variable is called a(n):
   a. Alternative hypothesis
   b. Educated guess
   c. Informed prediction
   d. Scientific proposition

3. Read each of the following hypotheses. Indicate the independent, dependent, and intervening variable. If the hypothesis does not have an intervening variable, write 'none.'

Hypothesis	Independent variable(s)	Dependent variable	Intervening variable
Police officers who pursue hobbies unrelated to their profession are less likely to develop cardiovascular disease.			
Young, male African American motorists are more likely to be searched by a police officer during a traffic stop.			
Inmates who successfully complete a degree in prison are less likely to recidivate, unless they are released to the same social environment where they lived prior to their incarceration.			

Correctional officers with prior military service are less likely to approach their job from a therapeutic perspective.			
Unless they later become wealthy, individuals who are raised in poverty are less likely to be dishonest on their federal income taxes.			

4. A(n) _____ variable is also known as a causal variable.
    a. Continuous
    b. Dependent
    c. Independent
    d. Intervening

5. A set of attributes that allows for one and only one response is said to be:
    a. Clearly independent
    b. Fully measurable
    c. Mutually exclusive
    d. Totally exhaustive

6. Develop an exhaustive and mutually exclusive list of attributes for each of the following variables.

Variable	Attributes
Gender	
Hair color	
Race	
Level of education	

7. Which of the following lists of attributes for the variable 'age' would be both mutually exclusive and exhaustive?
    a. 0–18; 18–25; 25–40; 40–55; 55 and older
    b. 0–18; 19–25; 26–40; 41–55; 56 and older
    c. 0–18; 19–25; 26–40; 41–55; 56–64
    d. 15–18; 19–25; 26–40; 41–55; 56 and older

8. Read the following research questions and indicate which element of a good research question is missing (i.e., measurable, unanswered, feasible, or disinteresting). Some questions may be missing more than one element.

Research question	Element(s) missing
Will teenagers who use drugs be more likely to commit crimes for the rest of their lives?	
Do men commit more crimes than women?	
Are inmates who accept Jesus as their Lord and Savior less likely to recidivate?	
Why are juvenile delinquents so difficult to deal with?	
Why do human beings murder other human beings?	

9. The following table contains either an alternative or a null hypothesis. Using the available hypothesis, complete the table by writing the other corresponding hypothesis.

Null hypothesis	Alternative hypothesis
There is no correlation between regular church attendance and juvenile delinquency.	
	Mandatory exercise programs reduce the incidence of cardiovascular disease among career police officers.
	Cognitive intervention programs reduce recidivism among parolees.
Educational achievement is not related to drug experimentation among adolescents.	
	Children of alcoholics are more likely to become alcoholics themselves in adulthood.
Gender does not influence the decision to engage in unprotected sexual behavior.	

10. Classify each of the following statements as either a hypothesis of difference or a hypothesis of association.

Hypothesis	Association or difference
Female police officers are less likely than male police officers to conduct searches at night.	
A police officer's ability to catch criminals increases as he or she becomes more experienced.	
African American motorists are more likely to be searched than Caucasian motorists when stopped for routine traffic violations.	
The more impaired an offender is with respect to drug and alcohol consumption, the more violent their crime.	

RESEARCH APPLICATION EXERCISES

Access to the following articles will be provided by your instructor.

Morris, R.G. and Piquero, A.R. (2011). For whom do sanctions deter and label? *Justice Quarterly.* http://www.tandfonline.com. DOI: 10.1080/07418825.2011.633543.

Wilcox, P., May, D.C. and Roberts, S.D. (2006). Student weapon possession and the "Fear and Victimization Hypothesis": Unraveling the temporal order. *Justice Quarterly, 23*(4), 502–529.

Respond to the following questions for each of the articles cited above.

11. What variables did the researchers use in their research?

12. What were the attributes for each of the variables used?

13. Were the attributes both exhaustive and mutually exclusive? If not, why not?

14. What were the researchers' null and alternative hypotheses (either presented or implied)?

15. Would you classify the alternative hypothesis as a hypothesis of association or a hypothesis of difference?

16. Which of the hypotheses (null or alternative) did the researchers accept after analyzing the results?

CHAPTER 8

Sampling

Turn on any television in October of an even-numbered year and you will hear political pundits attempting to predict the outcome of the next election. Listen closely to the political polls they use. Their predictions about how millions of Americans will vote are based on the responses of a relatively small sample group of individuals. Sometimes these groups are less than 1,000 'registered' or 'likely' voters. How is it possible to predict how a large group of people will act based on a small group of individuals? The answer is sampling.

Sampling is a scientific technique that allows a researcher to learn something about a population by studying a few members, or a sample, of that population. There are numerous types of sampling. Some sampling techniques allow researchers to predict, with some degree of accuracy, something about a population based on what is learned from a representative sample of that population. Other sampling techniques merely provide researchers insight into a population. Here is an example of how a county sheriff used sampling to identify a problem with his employees.

Making Research Real 8.1 – Low Morale at the Jail

The sheriff of an urban community received an anonymous letter from a jail employee. The employee wrote, "Sheriff, morale is so low among the jailers that I would not be surprised to see them walk out one day and leave the jail unattended. You have to do something about this."

Alarmed about the possibility of a serious labor or security problem, the sheriff called an emergency staff meeting. "Any of you heard of any serious morale problems at the jail?" The sheriff asked. They all shook their heads no and a few suggested that it might just be an isolated disgruntled employee.

Later that evening, the Sheriff re-read the letter. There was something about what the anonymous writer said that seemed both legitimate and serious. By the next morning, he decided to personally conduct interviews with the jailers and ask them about their morale. He soon realized that doing so would be nearly impossible. There were 235 employees assigned to the jail. Interviewing each of them, even briefly, would take weeks. So the sheriff decided to interview only a sample of them.

He secured a list of jailers by shift (day, evening, and night) and randomly selected ten jailers from each list. With the help of his administrative assistant, he made appointments with each of these

---

employees over the course of a two-week time frame. Before the sheriff was halfway through the interviews, he had found the problem. Recent administrative changes had inadvertently reduced the chances that a jailer could promote within the department or even compete for merit salary increases.

With this information, the sheriff made administrative changes, which he announced at the next staff meeting. Eventually, morale improved among the jailers and one of the jailers even promoted to the rank of captain.

Sampling allows researchers to learn a great deal about a population without having to solicit information from every member of that population. Without sampling, researchers would not have the time or money to study and learn about large populations. In this chapter, we will discuss the rationale behind sampling and the different types of sampling techniques. Table 8.1 is a summary of the sampling techniques that are discussed in this chapter.

Table 8.1 Summary of Commonly Used Probability and Non-Probability Sampling Techniques

PROBABILITY SAMPLING	
Simple or systematic random sampling	Cases are randomly selected from a complete list of the entire population.
Cluster sampling	The sample is collected randomly in a series of stages or from randomly selected natural clusters wherein the cases are more readily accessible.
Stratified random sampling	Cases are selected from well defined strata within the overall population to further enhance the representativeness of the overall sample.
NON-PROBABILITY SAMPLING	
Convenience sampling	The sample consists of individuals that are either convenient or readily available to the researcher.
Snowball sampling	The sample consists of individuals who are referred to the researcher individually by previous research subjects.
Typical or extreme case sampling	Individuals or situations are selected to be studied because in the researcher's judgment they are either typical or extreme examples.

Getting to the Point 8.1 – Sampling is a scientific technique that allows a researcher to learn something about a population by studying only a few members of the population.

SAMPLING BASICS

Scientifically, sampling is based on a concept called the **central limit theorem**. This theorem proposes that if we want to measure something in a population (e.g., years of education), and we record this measure from a large enough sample of the population, the average will always be around the same. In technical terms, the averages will be **normally distributed**, or will hover around the middle. Say, for example, that we want to learn how many times juvenile delinquents engage in physical confrontations. We go to a juvenile probation office that supervises 500 delinquents and randomly pick 50 of these delinquents to survey. We ask each of them *"How many fights have you had in the last month?"* From this, we learn that the average (mean) number of fights per month is 2.0. We are not sure if this is a good measure of the average numbers of physical confrontations for the entire population of 500 juvenile delinquents. So we do the exact same thing again. We take the 500 juvenile delinquents, randomly pick 50 to survey, and ask each of them *"How many fights have you had in the last month?"* This time we find that the average number of fights is 1.75. We repeat this process over and over, each time randomly picking 50 delinquents to ask and each time calculating the average. Eventually, we will begin to see a pattern emerge. Most of the averages cluster around the same number. If we were to plot these averages on a graph, it would look something like Figure 8.1, wherein most of the averages cluster around the middle with fewer and fewer averages taping off on either end. This is what a 'normal distribution' looks like. Normal distributions often take the shape of a bell, which is why you will often hear this distribution described as a bell curve. The central limit theorem gives us confidence that if we draw a large enough sample and do so randomly, the members within it will always be representative of the larger population.

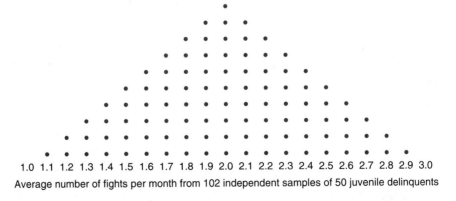

Average number of fights per month from 102 independent samples of 50 juvenile delinquents

Figure 8.1   An Illustration of Normally Distributed Data

Sampling is incredibly popular in social science research. The primary reason is that the time and cost associated with studying everyone or everything in a population are prohibitive. Sampling is more feasible and, when done well, fairly accurate. As such, most social science research uses some form of sampling. Note that you can sample just about anything. If you were interested in studying juvenile delinquents, as we were in the example above, you could randomly pick a sample of juvenile delinquents from a larger population. But if you were interested in studying state prisons, you could randomly pick a sample of state prisons to study from a larger population of state prisons. Note, too, that if the goal of your research is to generalize to the larger population, it is essential that these samples be representative. We will discuss how to obtain a representative sample later in this chapter.

Getting to the Point 8.2 – Sampling is based on a concept called the central limit theorem. The central limit theorem gives us confidence that if we collect a large enough sample, the sample will be representative of the larger population.

Before getting further into the details of the sampling process, it might be useful to introduce some basic terms. A **population** is the entire set of individuals or groups that is relevant to a research project. Say, for example, we wanted to study county jails in the United States. Our population would be every county jail in the United States. There are probably more than 3,000 such jails currently in operation. A **sample** is a subset of a population that is measured or studied to provide insight into the overall population. Again, if we wanted to study county jails, we could randomly select 100 county jails to study in order to gain insight about all county jails in the U.S.

When we collect information on every member of a population, we are conducting a **census** rather than observing a sample. A census is a study of an entire population. In the example above, we would gather information about every single county jail in operation in the United States. Again, it is usually too time-consuming and costly to conduct such a study. One of the few censuses regularly conducted in the United States is the decennial United States Census. The 2010 Census cost nearly $11 billion. And the preliminary results were not available until well into 2011. Indeed, it usually takes a full two years before all of the data are analyzed and distributed. Few researchers have that much time and money. So sampling is more efficient than a census and makes more sense in most social science research studies. For less money and time, we can learn enough from a sample to understand a larger population with a reasonable degree of accuracy.

Getting to the Point 8.3 – A population is the entire set of individuals or groups that is relevant to a research project. A census collects information from an entire population. A sample collects information from a group within that population. Samples are typically less expensive and time-consuming than censuses.

When we want to describe the individual components of a population or sample, we use the terms **members**, **cases**, or **elements**. These terms are often used interchangeably. For example, in a sample of 1,500 juvenile offenders, one individual juvenile offender would be referred to as a member, case, or element of the sample. In a sample of 200 federal prisons, an individual federal prison would also be referred to as a member, case, or element of the sample.

Researchers often begin the sampling process with a list of all the members of elements of a population. This is known as a **sampling frame**. For example, say we want to study participants in a particular drug treatment program. The organization administering the program may have a list of all past and present participants. Using this list, or sampling frame, we can select a subset of these participants for our sample. The exact process we use to select that subset is called a **sampling plan**. A sampling plan is a procedure or set of instructions that helps a researcher decide which cases to select into the sample.

Now that we have defined these terms, we will take a look at the factors to consider when actually drawing a sample.

Getting to the Point 8.4 – The terms 'members,' 'cases,' and 'elements' are used interchangeably to describe the individual components of a population or sample. A list of the individual components of a population is referred to as a sampling frame. This list enables researchers to select a subset of the population for their sample. The exact process used to select the sample is called a sampling plan.

SAMPLE BIAS AND PRECISION

When we choose a sample, we want to go about our selection process in a systematic way so that the sample truly represents the larger population. If we do not go about this process systematically, we will have the problem of bias. **Bias** is a condition that causes a sample to be unrepresentative of the population from which it came. There are several causes of bias. First, bias may be caused by random sampling error. **Random sampling error** is simply the difference between the results the researcher gets from the sample and the results the researcher might have gotten had he or she actually polled the entire population. For example, say you want to measure community support for the police department. You select a sample of 1,000 residents and ask them questions about how they feel about the services provided by the police department. Prior research indicates that race, age, and socio-economic class affect attitudes about the police. So, you want your sample to be representative of the community with respect to race, age, and socio-economic class. Unfortunately, the random selection process may not produce a sample that truly reflects the overall community with respect to these factors. As a result, the findings from the sample may be quite different than they would be if you polled the entire community.

Often it is impossible to know exactly how much random sampling error exists. Using a statistical process, however, researchers can estimate sampling error. Samples from highly diverse populations tend to have more sampling error because samples from these populations are less able to capture the full range of diversity within the population. In these cases, a researcher might choose to collect a larger sample to be sure the sample represents the diversity of the population. Similarly, when researchers are interested in studying things that happen rarely, they must collect larger samples in order to be sure they have a sufficient number of cases in the sample. Here is an example of when this might happen.

Making Research Real 8.2 – How Safe Is Your Hamburger?

The United States Food and Drug Administration (USDA) is, among other things, responsible for the safety of the food that we consume. For example, employees of the Food Safety Inspection Service (FSIS), which is part of the USDA, inspect and monitor food producers to be sure their products are safe for human consumption.

Several years ago, the FSIS noticed that although investigators at the FSIS were testing appropriate samples, an unexpectedly high percentage of meat products were being distributed to consumers that contained potentially life-threatening pathogens. Something had to be done.

An inspection of the frequency of pathogenic infection within the meat supply revealed that large cuts of meat, such as roasts, had the least and ground meats had the highest incidence of pathogenic infection. This difference was caused by the amount of human contact with the product during processing. Based on these findings, the FSIS began drawing larger samples of the larger cuts of meat and smaller samples of ground meats in order to more accurately evaluate the overall safety of meat products that are produced in a particular facility.

Getting to the Point 8.5 – Random sampling error is one form of bias. It represents the difference between the results the researcher gets from the sample and what the results might have been had the entire population been polled. Samples from highly diverse populations tend to have more sampling error.

Bias may also be caused by selection. **Selection bias** is any process that systematically increases or decreases the chances that certain members of a population will be selected into the sample. Ideally, all members or elements of a population should have an equal chance of being selected into the sample. If not, there will be selection bias and the sample will not be representative of the population. Here is an example.

Making Research Real 8.3 – It's Just a Simple Telephone Survey

The students in Professor Jackson's graduate research seminar had been assigned to conduct a study on the fear of crime in the community surrounding the university. It was not possible to contact each of the 35,000 residents that lived in the community, so the researchers chose to sample approximately 1,200.

After developing the interview questions, they decided that the best way to access the population was through the telephone. Using the printed telephone directory as a sampling frame, the researchers selected every 134th number. The calls began on a Tuesday night and, within a week, the researchers had a sample of 1,283 respondents.

The analysis of the interviews revealed some alarming findings. First, there was a very high degree of fear of victimization within the community. Nearly 80 percent of the respondents said that they were afraid, very afraid, or extremely afraid of being a victim of crime. Second, there was a high level of anxiety over traffic safety. Almost 55 percent of the respondents reported that they were fearful of being involved in a serious traffic accident in their own neighborhoods. A majority of the respondents (75 percent) reported that "roving gangs" of teenagers were another major fear.

Given these findings, Professor Jackson spent some time reviewing the research plan. Almost immediately, he recognized a bias. Professor Jackson knew from his review of the literature that older people are more fearful of crime than younger people. The students in this case had used the printed telephone directory as their sampling frame, which restricted the sample to members of the community that had published land line telephone numbers. It just so happens that people with land line telephones tend to be older, since younger people are beginning to use cellular phones instead of land line phones. As a result, older residents, who were more likely to fear crime, were more likely to be included in the sample, resulting in selection bias.

Getting to the Point 8.6 – Selection bias is another form of bias. It is caused by any process that systematically increases or decreases the chances that a member of a population will be selected into the sample.

Again, when a sample is biased, it is not representative of the larger population from which it was drawn. The measure of a sample's representativeness is referred to as its **level of precision**. For example, say we find that 52 percent of a sample of participants in a drug rehabilitation program remained drug free two years after completing the program. Based on the size of our sample and the population, among other factors, we can calculate a level of precision for this sample. In this case, we find that our level of precision is +/– 5 percentage points. Therefore, we are saying that the percentage of participants in the population that are likely to remain drug free after two years will be anywhere from 47 percent (52 percent minus 5) to 57 percent (52 percent plus 5). Here is an example.

Making Research Real 8.4 – Predicting the Outcome of the Public Safety Bond Election

The City of Bigton needed to make substantial improvements to its public safety infrastructure. After decades of budget cuts, for example, the police department was forced to keep patrol cars in service longer than their operational life. The city council decided that the best way to raise funds to improve the public safety infrastructure was through a bond election.

After a few months of active campaigning, the police chief decided to ask a political pollster to predict the likely outcome of the bond election. Despite the overwhelming need for additional equipment, there was strong opposition to raising taxes among many Bigton residents. The pollster conducted a telephone survey of 800 'likely' voters. The survey indicated that 55 percent of the residents were in favor of raising their taxes to fund public safety improvements. The chief was quite pleased with the results. But the pollster cautioned the chief not to get too excited. She explained that the sample had a +/– 10 percentage point margin of error. As such, the percentage of likely voters that supported the bond measure could range anywhere from 45 percent to 65 percent. If support came out along the lower end of this range, the bond measure would fail.

The level of precision of a sample is determined primarily by the size of the sample in relation to the size of and variability within the population. Larger populations tend to require larger samples. For example, a sample of a population of 4 million would have to be larger than a sample of a population of 100. Again, populations that are diverse also require larger samples. For example, a sample of Americans (an incredibly diverse nation) would have to be larger than a sample of Japanese (a more homogenous society). Sample precision is also determined by the frequency with which the social phenomenon of interest to the researcher occurs. If a social phenomenon occurs infrequently, the researcher must collect a larger sample to study that phenomenon. Crime is a good example. Because crime is relatively rare, a researcher would have to collect a very large sample to be sure he or she has enough cases to analyze.

Getting to the Point 8.7 – A sample's representativeness of a population is referred to as its level of precision. The level of precision is influenced by the size of the population, the amount of variability within the population, and the frequency with which relevant social phenomena occur.

Note that the cost associated with sampling is a practical consideration with which researchers must contend. Researchers must balance an acceptable level of precision with the amount of research funds available. It would be nice to draw huge samples in research to ensure a high level of precision, but this not always economically feasible. For example, a researcher conducting research on the ability of a behavioral modification program designed to reduce violence among incarcerated offenders might be able to use a relatively small sample that has a larger margin of error. To be sure, prison violence is a serious matter, but, as long as the institution is appropriately staffed with trained professionals, the occurrence of violence can be managed adequately. In other words, this researcher can afford a larger margin of error because the consequences of being wrong are not as dire. On the other hand, a researcher conducting research on the reliability of new body armor would likely want a larger sample with a smaller margin of error. Here the consequences of being wrong are severe so the additional cost associated with collecting a large sample of test data is more than justified.

PROBABILITY SAMPLING TECHNIQUES

There are two major types of sampling techniques: probability sampling and non-probability sampling. **Probability sampling** techniques rely on random selection and allow researchers to predict what is happening in the larger population from which the sample came. For example, using a probability sample, a researcher can predict, with some level of precision, overall public opinion about the expanding prison population.

Again, probability sampling relies on the random selection of members or elements from the overall population. This **random selection** is what distinguishes probability sampling from non-probability sampling. When we say that the sample has been randomly selected, we mean that all the members or elements of the population have an equal and non-zero chance of being selected into the sample. For example, if the population consists of 1,000 people, each person's probability of being selected into the population would 1/1000, or .001. I know that is small, but it is not zero. Also, each member must have an equal chance of being selected. This means that the sampling process must not favor certain members of the population in terms of the selection process. For example, say our population is 1,000 inmates from a prison. On the day we collect our sample, 200 prisoners are away at a court appearance, in administrative segregation, or in the hospital. These 200 members would not have had an equal chance of being selected into the sample and our sample would not be random.

Figure 8.2 illustrates how a researcher might collect a random sample. In this example, the population consists of 100 individuals. Half of these members are male and the other half are female. The researcher wants to draw a sample of ten members and does so using some process of random selection. The actual members selected are highlighted. The sample is represented to the right of the line. In this particular situation the sampling processes produce a sample of six males and four females.

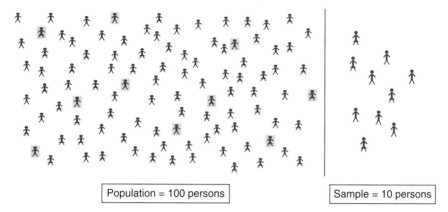

Population = 100 persons   Sample = 10 persons

Figure 8.2   Simple Random Sampling

Getting to the Point 8.8 – Probability sampling is a general type of sampling that relies on random selection. Random selection means that each member of a population has an equal and non-zero chance of being selected into the sample.

Though all probability sampling techniques rely on some form of random sampling, there are distinctive types of probability sampling techniques. The most common forms of probability sampling are simple and systematic random sampling. These are the easiest and purest forms of probability sampling. Once the researcher identifies the sampling frame, which is again a list of all members of the population, members are selected randomly from the list for inclusion into the sample. The random selection process continues until the researcher has enough cases for the desired level of precision. Say, for example, that you want to interview the police chiefs in all U.S. cities. You would begin with a sampling frame, or a list of all police chiefs in U.S. cities. Then, you would randomly select individuals from this list.

How exactly do we *randomly* select members of cases for our sample? This process could be as simple as writing the names of the population members on slips of paper and drawing them out of a hat. This would be an example of a **simple random sampling** technique. Another method used in simple random sampling is flipping a coin. If the coin lands heads up, the member or element of the population is selected into the sample; if it lands tail up, the member or element is not selected into the sample.

In some cases, the sampling process is more structured. For example, researchers may use a random number generator, which is typically a computer program that generates a random number that can be used to create a random sample. Assume we want to select 100 cases from a population of 1,000 members. We use a random number generator that gives us the number 17. We then look at our list of 1,000 members that are listed randomly to avoid bias, and select every 17th case until the 100-member sample is collected. So the 17th member on the list would be selected for the sample, as would the 34th member, the 51st member, and so on. In this particular case, we would not reach our 100th case by the time we reach the end of the 1,000 person list. The 986th member on the list would only be the 58th person in our sample. So we would have to cycle through the list, again picking every 17th member, until we reached 100 cases for our sample. Researchers generally refer to this type of random sampling as **systematic random sampling**.

Getting to the Point 8.9 – In simple random sampling, a researcher randomly selects cases into a sample directly from a population, similar to drawing names out of a hat. In systematic random sampling, a researcher uses a structured process to randomly select cases into a sample. For example, the researcher might select every 10th case from the population.

In some cases, researchers may want to break up the random selection process into two or more stages. This is generally referred to as **multi-stage sampling**. **Cluster sampling** is one type of multi-stage sampling. It typically occurs when the members of a population are more accessible in natural groups, such as churches, schools, or organizations. For example, a researcher may want to randomly select all state prisons in the first stage of the selection process, and then randomly select prison guards from each of these prisons during the second stage. Here is how this might work in an actual research situation.

Making Research Real 8.5 – A Survey of Probationers

In most states, the probation process is managed at the local level. Probation departments are attached to county and district level courts and seldom coordinated at the state level. If a researcher wanted a sample of 1,000 probationers from throughout the state, it would be unlikely that a list (i.e., a sampling frame) of all probationers in the state would be available.

To overcome this problem, the researcher might first list all of the probation departments in the state. From this list of departments, he or she might randomly select 20 departments. Then, the researcher would approach each of these departments and ask for a list of the probationers that are currently under that department's supervision. The researcher might randomly select 50 probationers from each list (20 departments × 50 members each = 1,000). Alternatively, the researcher might merge all 20 lists into a single list and then randomly select 1,000 members from this single list to create the sample.

Because the criminal justice system is often fragmented or coordinated at different levels (e.g., county, state, federal), multi-stage and cluster sampling is often the only way to access the population of interest to the researcher. It is important to note, however, that error is introduced at each stage in the sampling process. In the example above, we have two opportunities for error: once in the process of selecting probation departments and, again, in the process of selecting the actual probationers. These opportunities for error are exacerbated by the fact that clusters may be qualitatively different. For example, the probation department in a large urban area might supervise a very different type of offender than a probation department in a rural area. Thus, the first stage of the selection process in the example above might inadvertently select a higher percentage of either urban or rural departments. And this would adversely affect the sample's representativeness of the overall population of probationers in the state. To mitigate this potential problem, the researcher may want to implement another stage in the process whereby urban and rural departments are separated into two lists. The researcher might select 800 cases from the urban district lists and 200 from the rural district lists. Of course, this additional stage might introduce even more error into the process. But when balanced against the overall desire for the sample to be representative, it might be an appropriate decision.

Figure 8.3 illustrates how a researcher might collect a sample using a cluster sampling technique. In this example, the population consists of 100 members. The cases in this population are members of one of ten civic organizations in the community. To begin the process, the researcher identifies the clusters (i.e., the civic organizations) and randomly selects two of these clusters. Then, the researcher approaches the two civic organizations selected and asks for a roster of their members. Using these rosters, the researcher randomly selects five members from each organization (highlighted) to complete the sample.

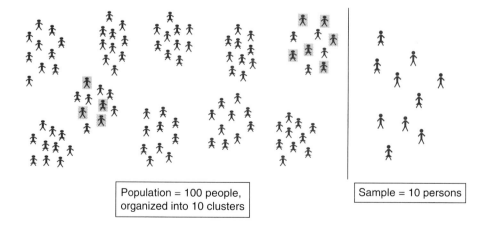

Population = 100 people, organized into 10 clusters

Sample = 10 persons

Figure 8.3 Cluster Sampling

Getting to the Point 8.10 – In cluster sampling, researchers identify natural groupings (i.e., clusters) that exist within the population. Some of these natural groupings are randomly selected in the initial stage of the sampling process. Cases are then randomly selected from the chosen clusters until an appropriate sized sample has been reached. Cluster sampling is a type of multi-stage sampling because it involves multiple stages in the random selection process.

Another multi-stage probability sampling technique is known as **stratified random sampling**. Stratified random sampling resembles cluster sampling, except that the researcher creates the groupings, or clusters, within the population. Say, for example, that we are conducting a survey of crime victimization in a community with a high percentage of Latinos. We believe that the Latino population may be at high risk of victimization due to a number of factors, such as immigration status. So we want to make sure that our sample contains the same percentage of Latinos as the larger community population. We know that Latinos make up 30 percent of the community. So if we want a sample of 100 community residents, we want to ensure that 30 members of our sample are Latino. In this case, we have defined groups in the population. These groups are referred to as strata. Once we have defined these groups, we can randomly select cases from each group until we have an appropriately sized sample from each. Here is how this might work in an actual research situation.

Making Research Real 8.6 – Measuring Binge Drinking

The Dean of Students at a large university is concerned about alcohol consumption among the students on campus. She is particularly concerned about students who consume a large amount of alcohol over a short period of time, a phenomenon commonly called binge drinking. With the assistance of a professor from the Psychology Department, the Dean decides to conduct a survey to determine the extent of the problem.

To begin, the researcher decides to organize the students into the following groups:

Lower undergraduates (freshmen and sophomores)   45%
Upper undergraduates (juniors and seniors)   35%
Graduate students (Master's and Ph.D. students)   20%

The psychology professor decides that an overall sample of 1,000 students would produce the appropriate level of precision. Then, she randomly selects students from each of these groups such that the proportion of lower undergraduate, upper undergraduate, and graduate students in the sample is the same as their proportion in the larger student population. Ultimately, her sample of 1,000 students includes: 450 lower undergraduates (45 percent), 350 upper undergraduates (35 percent), and 200 graduate students (20 percent). This process ensures that all strata within the student population are proportionally represented.

Figure 8.4 illustrates how a researcher might collect a sample using a stratified sampling technique. In this example, the population consists of 100 members and the researcher wants a sample size of ten members. In this case, the researcher suspects that gender is an important factor so he wants to be sure the sample contains an equal number of males and females. To begin the process, the researcher divides the population into two groups or strata, one consisting of males and the other consisting of females. Then, the researcher randomly selects five cases from each of these strata (highlighted). In the previous examples (see Figures 8.2 and 8.3) you may have noticed that the samples from this population consisted of six males and four females. In this particular case the sample consists of five males and five females (see Figure 8.4).

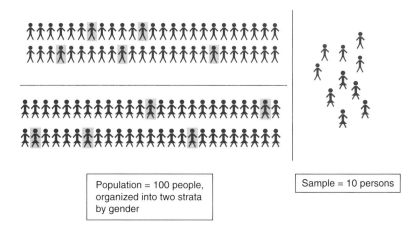

Population = 100 people, organized into two strata by gender

Sample = 10 persons

Figure 8.4 Stratified Random Sampling

Getting to the Point 8.11 – Stratified random sampling is a multi-stage probability sampling technique that involves randomly selecting cases from groups created within the population. These groups, called strata, are defined by the researcher. This form of probability sampling helps researchers ensure the sample will be representative of the overall population.

NON-PROBABILITY SAMPLING TECHNIQUES

Unlike probability sampling, **non-probability sampling** techniques do not rely on random selection and therefore do not allow a researcher to use the sample to predict what might be happening in the larger population. Not all of the members of the population from which a non-probability sample is obtained have an equal and non-zero chance of being selected into the sample. Thus, the sample is not totally representative of the population. It is legitimate to ask: if we can't use our findings from this type of sample to predict what's occurring in the larger population, why bother with this type of sampling?

You should avoid the temptation of thinking that non-probability samples are less useful than probability samples. Neither should these samples be considered a last resort. Researchers choose non-probability samples for many reasons. First, a researcher may choose to study a group of people because he or she has over time established a high level of trust with the members. This would enable the researcher to ask more penetrating or personal questions. For example, a researcher might gain entrée into an urban gang and establish relationships with some of the gang members. This connection might allow her to ask questions or make observations that would be unheard of for a researcher using a random sampling technique on the same population.

Second, a definitive list of the population, or sampling frame, from which to draw a random sample may not be available. With a little effort, we could get a list of the convicted burglars who live in a community, but that would by no means represent all burglars, only the ones who got caught. It would be far more interesting to study burglars who are capable of not getting caught, even though our sample would not be representative of all burglars.

Third, occasionally researchers may encounter a distinctive and accessible group of people who can provide insight into a subject matter, even if the group is not representative. For example, as an undergraduate, I completed an internship with the Federal Bureau of Prisons. I was assigned to the Federal Correctional Institute (FCI) at Texarkana, Texas. While I was there, the state prison facility in Albuquerque, New Mexico experienced a severe riot forcing the state to close the prison and distribute the inmates to various federal prisons. The FCI Texarkana received a large number of low-level offenders from the Albuquerque state prison. This group of prisoners experienced severe victimization during the riot. Had I had the means, I would have studied this group of prisoners, even if they were not randomly selected from the Albuquerque state prison. I could have learned a lot about prison riots studying this sample and used this information to develop theories about prison riots that could have then been tested in future research. In this and other cases, studying a non-probability sample can help us develop theories that can later be tested using probability sampling techniques.

Getting to the Point 8.12 – Non-probability sampling techniques do not rely on random selection and therefore do not allow a researcher to use the sample to predict what might be happening in the larger population. Even so, non-probability samples can provide in-depth information on a population that might not otherwise be accessible and/or information that can be used to develop theories about various phenomena.

One type of non-probability sample is a **convenience sample**, also known as an availability sample. A convenience sample is created when a researcher selects a sample from a group of people who are at hand or easily available. As the name implies, these members are *convenient* to or known by the researcher. As with all non-probability sampling techniques, convenience sampling does not lend itself to generalizing about a larger population. Even so, convenience sampling may make sense in certain contexts. Here is an example.

Making Research Real 8.7 – What Is Life Like for an Undocumented Immigrant?

The police chief of a mid-sized town in the Southwestern part of the United States knows that 30 percent of his community is made up of undocumented immigrants. Because of their immigration status, these residents are less than willing to contact the police department, either as victims or witnesses. Moreover, nearly a third of the community's residents are essentially unknown to the police department. This makes engaging this community in any form of proactive crime prevention nearly impossible.

    Because there is not a list of undocumented immigrants available, the chief decides to draw a convenience sample of this population through one of the local churches. He contacts the pastor of the church and asks him to hold a community meeting with members of this community. The pastor agrees. At the meeting, the police chief begins with a brief presentation wherein he expresses his desire to work with them in matters of crime prevention. He then sits down and listens to them explain how they manage to negotiate life as an undocumented immigrant. They discuss the difficulties they have in obtaining drivers' licenses and automobile liability insurance. They also discuss problems of theft and assault, which they are hesitant to report to the police due to fears of being deported. The meeting lasts for two hours.

    In the end, the chief learns a lot about this segment of his community. Because the chief's 'sample' was not randomly selected, he cannot assume that everything they tell him holds for all members of the undocumented immigrant population. But it is the best information he can gather given the hidden and undocumented nature of this community. Indeed, the information proves useful and provides a basis on which the chief makes several changes to department policy.

    Figure 8.5 illustrates how a researcher might collect a convenience sample. In this example, the population size is unknown. The researcher merely selects ten members of the population (highlighted) that are either in close proximity to the researcher or otherwise available to him or her.

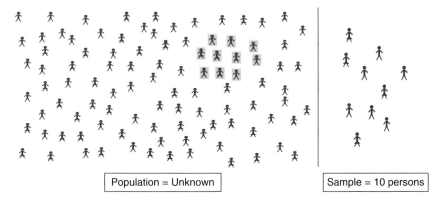

Population = Unknown   Sample = 10 persons

Figure 8.5 Convenience Sampling

Getting to the Point 8.13 – Convenience samples, also known as availability samples, are created when a researcher selects a sample from a group of people who are at hand or easily available. Normally, researchers rely upon their own experience and judgment when creating a convenience sample.

Snowball sampling is another non-probability sampling technique, which relies on the sample members themselves to increase the sample size. It works like this. After a member of the population is identified and 'measured' (usually interviewed), the researcher asks the member to identify other members of the population. The researcher then contacts these prospective members and repeats the process until he or she feels enough members have been 'measured' to produce meaningful results. As the name implies, the sample 'snowballs' in size as each contact produces more contacts. For example, a researcher might identify a low-level drug dealer and interview him about his illicit activity. After the interview, the researcher might ask him to identify other low-level drug dealers that the researcher might also interview.

Because this sampling strategy is often used to study illicit activities or organized criminal behaviors, researchers who use this technique should be mindful of the potential ethical and safety concerns associated with it. Use of this technique often places researchers in contact with dangerous people who would prefer not to be identified, even by an associate. Sometimes the research subjects are vulnerable in that their participation in a research project places them at risk of physical harm or criminal conviction. Here is an example.

Making Research Real 8.8 – The Prostitute Study

Billy Smith, a detective assigned to the vice squad, noticed an alarming trend among the women arrested for prostitution. These women appeared to be sicker than usual. A higher percentage of them were actively addicted to drugs. He suspected that they were being subjected to a new or additional form of abuse. And with the permission of the captain, the detective decided to study the issue further.

Because prostitution is illegal in Detective Smith's state, getting a complete list of individuals who provide sexual services for pay was impossible. Furthermore, many prostitutes were hesitant to provide information for fear that they would get arrested or that their pimps would harm them.

Fortunately Detective Smith had worked with this population of offenders for several years and was familiar with about a dozen prostitutes who trusted him enough to talk confidentially. To not attract the attention of pimps, Detective Smith had one of these women 'arrested' and brought to the county jail. While she was there, he shared his observations with her and asked, "What the hell is going on?"

The prostitute explained that a new pimp had recently moved to the city. He had a reputation for being overly aggressive with the women he 'supervised.' Detective Smith asked the prostitute to give him the names of a few prostitutes that worked for this man. She did. He then contacted these women, in the same way, and interviewed them. At the end of each interview, the Detective asked the prostitutes for more names. Eventually, his sample grew to about 20 prostitutes.

What Detective Smith learned from the prostitutes in his sample cannot be inferred to be true of all prostitutes in the community, much less the nation. But what he learned was useful to him because it provided additional insight into an emerging crime trend.

If a social scientist conducted research using the sampling method that Detective Smith used then he or she would be required to disclose that his or her sample was not collected randomly, so he or she could not infer that the trend affecting the prostitutes was also affecting other prostitutes. Even so the findings would be insightful. Detective Smith is not likely interested in publishing these results in a scholarly journal. But I suspect he would be interested in sharing what he learned with the District Attorney.

Figure 8.6 illustrates how a researcher might collect a snowball sample. In this example, the researcher is not aware of the size of the population. Instead the researcher knows one person in the population. The researcher contacts this member and, after gathering the necessary information, asks the member to identify another person in the population. The researcher repeats this process with every member that is recruited into the sample until he feels that a complete understanding of the social phenomenon has been obtained. In this case, the researcher stops after interviewing a sample of ten members.

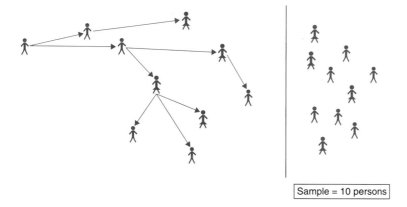

Sample = 10 persons

Figure 8.6   Snowball Sampling

Getting to the Point 8.14 – Snowball sampling is a non-probability sampling technique that relies on the sample members themselves to increase the sample size. Members recruited into the sample identify other members of the population and refer the researcher to these contacts until the sample 'snowballs' in size.

Sometimes a sample can be a single case. **Case studies** are highly detailed inquiries into or descriptions of a population or phenomenon. There are two types of case samples. A **typical case sample** exemplifies a common or typical pattern. Maybe the case is a cocaine addict or a rural community experiencing an increase in methamphetamine use. Whatever the situation, the researcher gathers enough information to produce a detailed description of the case. In doing so, the researcher hopes to convey what is usual, typical, or normal of similar cases. The case study of the cocaine addict, for example, might be used to describe how an individual becomes addicted to cocaine and copes with this addiction over several years. Of course, the researcher is unable to determine exactly how normal or typical this one case might be within the total population of cocaine addicts. Even so, typical case studies are useful research tools because they can provide insight into a population or situation.

An **extreme case sample** is atypical, uncharacteristic, or uncommon. Maybe the case is a young man who was raised in a crime family, but who took a path that was more straight and narrow. This case could provide insight into how people avoid a criminal life despite being socialized into a life of crime. The process of researching the case is more or less the same as it is for typical case samples. The researcher gathers enough information about the case to produce a detailed description. But in contrast to typical case samples, extreme case samples produce insight into what could go very wrong or right in any given situation. Here is an example of an extreme case study that a student of mine completed several years ago.

Making Research Real 8.9 – What Happened to Sally May?

Sally May (not her real name) was a nine-year-old girl who was murdered by her stepfather. She was known to the child welfare authorities in her state from the moment she was born. Her mother was a heroin addict and her father was a convicted sex offender. During the course of her short life, she was treated numerous times for injuries caused by her parents and other family members, removed from her home and placed in emergency foster care many times, and seldom sent to school. Eventually her parents divorced and her mother remarried. One afternoon, Sally May's stepfather got angry at her for spilling a glass of milk. He struck her with a hammer and she subsequently died from her injuries.

This tragedy occurred despite intensive supervision by the state's child welfare agency. Sally May's social worker visited the home frequently. The local police department was well aware of the family's abusive history. Sally May's teachers kept a close eye on her for evidence of abuse. Unfortunately, none of this supervision prevented the tragedy of Sally May's death. My student was granted substantial access to the court records and case files in this case. She conducted a detailed case study to see where the system failed for Sally May. In this case, her case sample was extreme.

My student's research revealed numerous missed opportunities for official intervention that might have saved Sally May's life. For example, certain policies prohibited the social worker from conducting a background check on Sally May's stepfather, who later turned out to be a parole absconder from another state with a history of violent behavior. The information the researcher gained from this extreme case revealed the 'cracks in the system' of child welfare. Using this information, criminal justice practitioners changed their response to children in need of care.

> **Getting to the Point 8.15** – Typical and extreme case samples consist of a single case study of a population or phenomenon. In a typical case sample, a researcher uses a case study to illustrate a common or typical pattern. In an extreme case sample, a researcher uses a case study to illustrate an uncommon or atypical pattern.

FINAL THOUGHTS

Later in Part Three of this textbook you will be introduced to some of the most common research methods used in criminological and criminal justice research. You will learn that there is no one 'best way' of conducting research. Some research questions are best answered with a survey, while others demand a classic experimental design. The same holds true for sampling. There is no 'best' sampling technique. It is wrong, for example, to think that probability samples are 'better' than non-probability samples. In fact, some of the most important things we know about crime and criminals come from non-probability samples.

The most appropriate sampling technique ultimately depends on the purpose of the research and the nature of the population. If you want to generalize to a larger population and a sampling frame is available, you should use a probability sampling technique. But if your purpose is to develop a theory that can be tested in future studies and/or there is no sampling frame for or access to the population of interest, a non-probability sample would be best. In either case, it is important to acknowledge the limitations of your sample and not to overreach your findings given these limitations. The great American humorist Mark Twain is credited with saying, "It ain't so much what we know that gets us into trouble. It's what we know that just ain't so." I think he is right and this is good advice for researchers.

GETTING TO THE POINT/CHAPTER SUMMARY

- Sampling is a scientific technique that allows a researcher to learn something about a population by studying only a few members of the population.

- Sampling is based on a concept called the central limit theorem. The central limit theorem gives us confidence that if we collect a large enough sample, the sample will be representative of the larger population.

- A population is the entire set of individuals or groups that is relevant to a research project. A census collects information from an entire population. A sample collects information from a group within that population. Samples are typically less expensive and time-consuming than censuses.

- The terms 'members,' 'cases,' and 'elements' are used interchangeably to describe the individual components of a population or sample. A list of the individual components of a population is referred to as a sampling frame. This list enables researchers to select a subset of the population for their sample. The exact process used to select the sample is called a sampling plan.

- Random sampling error is one form of bias. It represents the difference between the results the researcher gets from the sample and what the results might have been had the entire population been polled. Samples from highly diverse populations tend to have more sampling error.

- Selection bias is another form of bias. It is caused by any process that systematically increases or decreases the chances that a member of a population will be selected into the sample.

- A sample's representativeness of a population is referred to as its level of precision. The level of precision is influenced by the size of the population, the amount of variability within the population, and the frequency with which relevant social phenomena occur.

- Probability sampling is a general type of sampling that relies on random selection. Random selection means that each member of a population has an equal and non-zero chance of being selected into the sample.

- In simple random sampling, a researcher randomly selects cases into a sample directly from a population, similar to drawing names out of a hat. In systematic random sampling, a researcher uses a structured process to randomly select cases into a sample. For example, the researcher might select every tenth case from the population.

- In cluster sampling, researchers identify natural groupings (i.e., clusters) that exist within the population. Some of these natural groupings are randomly selected in the initial stage of the sampling process. Cases are then randomly selected from the chosen clusters until an appropriate sized sample has been reached. Cluster sampling is a type of multi-stage sampling because it involves multiple stages in the random selection process.

- Stratified random sampling is a multi-stage probability sampling technique that involves randomly selecting cases from groups created within the population. These groups, called strata, are defined by the researcher. This form of probability sampling helps researchers ensure the sample will be representative of the overall population.

- Non-probability sampling techniques do not rely on random selection and therefore do not allow a researcher to use the sample to predict what might be happening in the larger population. Even so, non-probability samples can provide in-depth information on a population that might not otherwise be accessible and/or information that can be used to develop theories about various phenomena.

- Convenience samples, also known as availability samples, are created when a researcher selects a sample from a group of people who are at hand or easily available. Normally, researchers rely upon their own experience and judgment when creating a convenience sample.

- Snowball sampling is a non-probability sampling technique that relies on the sample members themselves to increase the sample size. Members recruited into the sample identify other members of the population and refer the researcher to these contacts until the sample 'snowballs' in size.

- Typical and extreme case samples consist of a single case study of a population or phenomenon. In a typical case sample, a researcher uses a case study to illustrate a common or typical pattern. In an extreme case sample, a researcher uses a case study to illustrate an uncommon or atypical pattern.

CHAPTER EXERCISES

The following chapter exercises are organized into two parts. The first part consists of questions that can be answered using the information from this chapter. This section will test your understanding of the chapter material. The second part consists of research application exercises. These exercises require you to apply what you have learned thus far.

CHAPTER REVIEW QUESTIONS

Respond to each of the following questions using the information from this chapter.

1. The scientific basis that allows researchers to use samples to predict conditions within a larger population is called the _____ theorem.
   a. Central limit theorem
   b. Normal curve
   c. Probability
   d. Pythagorean

2. A researcher contacts every police department in the United States and asks them what color of uniforms their officers wear. What is the researcher doing in this case?
   a. Conducting a census
   b. Drawing a sample
   c. Inferring to a population
   d. Selecting random cases

3. The individual units of analysis in a population that constitute a sample are called the:
   a. Cases
   b. Elements
   c. Members
   d. All of the above

4. A complete list of the population from which a researcher will draw a sample is referred to as a sampling _____.
   a. Frame
   b. Plan
   c. Scheme
   d. Unit

5. Any condition that causes a sample to be less than representative of the population from which it came is referred to as:
   a. Bias
   b. Discrimination
   c. Error
   d. Prejudice

6. Read the following research descriptions and identify the type of bias (random sampling error or selection bias) that could be involved.

Research statement	Type of bias
A researcher is interested in whether participants in a drug treatment program are successful in their rehabilitation. He asks for volunteers to participate in a long-term study of post-treatment success. Twenty of the 130 participants volunteer to participate in the four-year follow-up study.	
A researcher wants to study a drug use prevention program targeted at high school freshmen in Chicago. The student population is around 200,000 and is extremely diverse with respect to race, ethnicity, and socio-economic status. The researcher makes a list of all the high school freshmen in the city and randomly draws 100 names from the list.	

7. The measure of a sample's representativeness and therefore its ability to accurately predict conditions within the population from which it was collected is referred to as its:
   a. Accuracy indicator
   b. Estimated error
   c. Level of precision
   d. Overall reliability

8. What can be said about the following statement?: Results from a non-probability sample can be inferred to the larger population from which the sample was obtained.
   a. This statement is always true.
   b. This statement is always false.
   c. This statement may be true or false.

9. Read the following descriptions of sampling plans and determine which probability sampling technique (simple random, systematic random, cluster, or stratified) is being used.

Sample plan	Probability sampling technique
A researcher draws names out of a hat to see which police officers in a particular precinct will be interviewed for a study on workplace satisfaction.	
A researcher randomly selects ten drug treatment centers in the state and then randomly selects 20 patients at each of the drug treatment centers to survey.	

A researcher divides the residents of a low-income housing project into two groups: those age 30 and under, and those over age 30. Ten people from each group are randomly selected for interviews.	
A researcher selects every 20th name from a list of probation officers in the state to create a sample for a study of officer education and training.	

10. Read the following descriptions of sampling plans and determine which non-probability sampling technique (convenience, snowball, typical case, or extreme case) is being used.

Sample plan	Non-probability sampling technique
A researcher interviews a member of a dangerous religious cult that she has been introduced to. At the end of the interview, she asks for the names of other members of the cult that she might interview.	
A researcher conducts an in-depth study of a town experiencing rapid population growth to understand the relationship between population growth and crime.	
A researcher writes a life history of a reformed repeat sex offender to see if the offender's life provides any insight into rare cases of rehabilitation among repeat sex offenders.	
A researcher wants to understand how serial killers justify their murders. He interviews convicted serial killers who are currently on death row.	

RESEARCH APPLICATION EXERCISES

Access to the following articles will be provided by your instructor.

Lieber, M.J., Nalla, M.K. and Farnworh, M. (1998). Explaining juveniles' attitudes toward the police. *Justice Quarterly, 15*(1), 151–174.

Miller, J.M. (2011). Becoming an informant. *Justice Quarterly, 28*(2), 203–220.

Respond to the following questions for each of the articles cited above.

11. Why did the researchers conduct this research? In other words, what did they hope to learn?

12. Describe the population of interest to the researchers. In other words, from what population did the researchers draw their sample?

13. What type of sampling technique did the researchers use?

14. What were the strengths and limitations of this sampling technique(s)?

15. Given the sampling technique used, were the researchers' conclusions justified by the results?

16. If you were the researcher, what type of sampling technique would you have used?

PART 3

Acquiring and Analyzing Data

CHAPTER 9

Experimental Design Research Methods

Experimental design research methods are considered one of the 'purest' forms of social science inquiry. When done correctly, results from an experimental design provide very good insight into the actual causes of social phenomena. Because of their ability to isolate and measure the effect of a single independent variable on a single dependent variable, experimental design models are especially useful in explanatory research.

Here is where I get to argue that a police detective's job is a lot like a researcher's job. Sherlock Holmes explained the science of deduction to his assistant Dr. Watson by saying, "Eliminate all other factors, and the one which remains must be the truth" (*The Sign of Four*, 1890, in Conan Doyle, 2004). This is a pretty good summation of the experimental model. Here is another example of how an experimental design can help us uncover the truth.

Making Research Real 9.1 – Would a Speed Trap Reduce Traffic Crash Fatalities?

The City of Bigton is bisected by an interstate highway that runs north and south. Within the city, the speed limit on this interstate is 60 miles per hour. After leaving the city, the speed limit increases to 70 miles per hour. Over the past year, the number of traffic crash fatalities has increased on this freeway at both the northern and southern boundaries, where the speed limit changes.

To address this problem, the mayor wants to keep the speed limit at 60 miles per hour for five miles beyond the city limits. Unfortunately, the state law does not give a city the authority to change the speed limit beyond its incorporated limits. The law does, however, allow a city to enforce speed laws within a five-mile zone beyond its incorporated limits. Thus, the chief suggests a speed trap: "Let's initiate a month-long speed trap on the northern boundary of the city. After a month, we'll compare average vehicular speeds, traffic crashes, and fatalities occurring in this area with those occurring at the southern boundary. If the speed trap works, we can initiate it as a standard enforcement protocol." The mayor agrees to the plan.

Prior to initiating the speed trap, the chief assigns officers in unmarked pick-up trucks equipped with RADARs to measure the speed of traffic at the northern and southern borders of the city. He also collects information on the number of traffic accidents and fatalities within two miles of these boundaries. Then

---

he implements a month of intense speed enforcement on the freeway at the northern border of the city. Over the next month, he repeats the covert speed survey at both the northern and southern borders of the city and, again, analyzes the traffic accident and fatality reports for the two-mile stretch of freeway at the northern and southern boundaries of the city. Prior to the initiation of the speed trap, the chief finds the following:

- At the northern boundary, the average speeds of vehicles traveling into and out of the city were 78 and 75 miles per hour, respectively.

- At the southern boundary, the average speeds of vehicles traveling into and out of the city were 79 and 74 miles per hour, respectively.

- At the northern boundary, the police department investigated 36 traffic crashes; of these, 10 included fatalities.

- At the southern boundary, the police department investigated 37 traffic crashes; of these, 9 included fatalities.

After the initiation of the speed trap, the chief finds the following:

- At the northern boundary, the average speeds of vehicles traveling into and out of the city were 69 and 58 miles per hour, respectively.

- At the southern boundary, the average speeds of vehicles traveling into and out of the city were 78 and 75 miles per hour, respectively.

- At the northern boundary, the police department investigated 15 traffic crashes; of these, none included fatalities.

- At the southern boundary, the police department investigated 35 traffic crashes; of these, 11 included fatalities.

The police chief convincingly shows that the average speeds, as well as the number of traffic accidents and fatalities were essentially equal at the northern and southern boundaries of the city prior to initiating the speed trap. Further, the average speeds and number of traffic accidents and fatalities decreased on the freeway at the northern boundary after the initiation of the speed trap. Finally, the average speeds and number of traffic accidents and fatalities remained unchanged on the freeway at the southern border of the city. The chief concludes that the speed trap is an effective enforcement strategy for reducing traffic accidents and fatalities. The mayor has to agree.

Whether he intended to or not, the police chief in the above example used an experimental design research method to determine whether a speed trap would reduce traffic fatalities. He started with two parts of town that were essentially equal in terms of vehicular speed and traffic fatalities. Then, he applied a treatment (i.e., the speed trap) to one part of town but not the other. Finally, he showed that the treatment he applied changed the vehicular speed and traffic fatalities on the "treated" portion of the freeway.

The purpose of this chapter is to introduce the basics of experimental design research methods. As part of this introduction, the chapter will use the steps of the research process outlined in Chapter 2 to discuss how researchers conduct experimental research. You will find in this chapter the now familiar "Making Research Real" and "Getting to the Point" features. But you will also find a new feature called "Developing the Method." The information presented in this feature will illustrate how actual researchers went about designing and conducting an experimental research design.

EXPERIMENTAL DESIGN RESEARCH BASICS

An **experiment** is a research method that measures how much, if any, an independent variable causes a change to a dependent variable. There are various types of experimental design models. Some are quite simple and others are very complicated. Primarily the differences between experimental design models lie in the features or processes that researchers incorporate into them. All experimental design models have three essential characteristics.

First, all experimental design models have an experimental group. The **experimental group** is a group of research subjects that is exposed to the independent variable that the researcher believes will cause change to a dependent variable. For example, a researcher may want to organize a sample of chronic sex offenders into an experimental group and ask them to take a new medication designed to reduce their sexual impulsivity (i.e. uncontrollable sexual urges). This medication, like many psychosomatic drugs, is designed to help the users change their thought processes. If this new drug works then it may become a useful treatment strategy for these recidivistic offenders. In this example the independent variable is the new medication and the dependent variable is sexual impulsivity.

Second, all experimental design models include a treatment. The **treatment** is the independent variable that the researcher alleges will be the cause of a change in the dependent variable. In our example the researcher alleges that the new medication will reduce the chronic sex offenders' sexual impulsivity.

Third, all experimental design models have a posttest. Using a **posttest** the researcher measures the dependent variable after the treatment has been administered. Using the same example, after administering the treatment the researcher would conduct a test or observation to determine whether the medication reduces sexual impulsivity among this sample of chronic sex offenders. In our example the posttest is a questionnaire that the researcher develops and administers to measure sexual impulsivity among the sex offenders in the experimental group. Let's assume that after administering the medication the researcher finds, based on the responses to the questionnaire, that the average level of sexual impulsivity among the chronic sex offenders is lower. In other words, the medication worked.

At this point you may be asking several critical questions. *How much, if any, did the new medication actually reduce sexual impulsivity? What if the chronic sex offenders are just faking it so they can get out of prison earlier?* These are very good questions. Unfortunately, experimental design models that only have an experimental group, a treatment, and a posttest cannot answer these questions. To answer these questions a researcher must include additional features into the experimental design model.

How much, if any, did the new medication actually reduce sexual impulsivity? To answer this question the researcher would need to measure the level of sexual impulsivity among the members of the experimental group *before* they take the new medication and then compare these results to the posttest results. This is a called a pretest. A **pretest** measures the dependent variable before the treatment is applied. Let's suppose in our example that the researcher measures sexual impulsivity (using the questionnaire) on a scale ranging from 0 to 100. A score of 50 is 'normal' and a score of 90 or above indicates an uncontrollable level of sexual impulsivity. Let's further suppose that the average score among the sex offenders in the experimental group is 85, pretty high. Then the researcher administers the new medication. Following this the researcher would, using the same questionnaire, measure sexual impulsivity among the members of the experimental group. Let's assume the average score among the sex offenders, after taking the new medication, is now 65. This might indicate that the new medication is effective at reducing sexual impulsivity by an average of 20 points. The researcher now knows exactly how much the new medication reduces sexual impulsivity. Case closed, right? Well, not so fast. We have another question.

What if the chronic sex offenders are just faking it so they can get out of prison earlier? To answer this question the researcher would have to add another feature to the experimental design model – a control group. A **control group** is a group of research subjects that are similar to the research subjects in the experimental group with one important exception. The members of the control group are not actually exposed to the treatment. In some experimental design models the members of the control group may also be given both a pretest and a posttest.

Researchers who use control groups might start with a larger sample of research subjects and then divide them into two groups – an experimental group and a control group. Typically, researchers use **random assignment** to place research subjects into the experimental and control groups to ensure these groups are equivalent with respect to other variables that could affect the outcome. In our example, let's suppose the researcher starts with 30 research subjects. He randomly assigns each research subject into one of the two groups so that both groups have 15 members each. It would be essential for the researcher to ensure that, with respect to the other variables that could affect the outcome of the experiment, the experimental and control groups are equivalent. For example, while conducting the literature review the researcher might have learned that age, education, and criminal history affect sexual impulsivity. So, the researcher would want to be sure that the members of the experimental and control groups are about the same ages, the same levels of education, and have the same criminal histories.

After establishing that the groups are equivalent the researcher would then administer the pretest to all of the research subjects. Let's suppose that the members of both groups have an average score of 85 on the questionnaire that our researcher is using – further substantiating the equivalency of the groups. Now, the researcher gets a little tricky. He issues the new medication to the members of both groups, but the 'medication' that the control group members receive is inert, meaning it has no medicinal value. It is a **placebo**, in this case a sugar pill that looks exactly like the medication that the members of the experimental group get. So the members of the control group do not know they are not receiving any medication. In fact, they might think they are actually receiving the medication.

Finally, after the treatment is administered the researcher conducts a posttest on both groups. Let's say that the members of the experimental group scored, on average, 65 and that the members of the control group scored 85 on the posttest. These results would further substantiate the researcher's claim that the new medication actually reduces sexual impulsivity. All things being equal, chronic sexual offenders who actually took the new medication reduced their levels of sexual impulsivity by an average of 20 points. The research subjects in the control group did not actually take the medication so we should not be surprised to learn that their posttest scores are equal to their pretest scores.

> **Getting to the Point 9.1** – An experiment is a research method that measures the effect of an independent variable on a dependent variable. All experimental design models feature an experimental group, a treatment, and a posttest. More sophisticated experimental design models also include a pretest and a control group.

TYPES OF EXPERIMENTAL DESIGN RESEARCH MODELS

As mentioned in the previous section, there are several types or variations of the experimental designs model. In this section I will introduce you to the five most commonly used experimental design models.

- The one group no pretest experimental design model
- The one group pretest/posttest experimental design model
- The two group no pretest experimental design model
- The two group pretest/posttest experimental design model
- The Solomon four group experimental design model

The most basic experimental design model is often called a **one group no pretest experimental design model**. This type of design only has the basic elements of the experimental design model – an experimental group, a treatment, and a posttest (see Figure 9.1).

	PRETEST	TREATMENT	POSTTEST
EXPERIMENTAL GROUP	NO	YES	YES

Figure 9.1   The One Group No Pretest Experimental Design Model

In a way a typical university class is like a one group no pretest experimental design model. Let's assume that rather than a researcher organizing a sample of students into an experimental group, the students self-select themselves into an experimental group by enrolling in the class. In this experiment the dependent variable is the students' knowledge of the course's subject matter. Starting on the first day of class the instructor gives the students reading assignments and exposes them to a treatment in the form of lectures. This treatment, the lectures, is the independent variable. After a few weeks of treatment the students are given an exam that measures what they know about the course's subject matter. This exam would be the posttest, or the measure of the dependent variable, which in this case is the students' knowledge of the course's subject matter. Let's assume that the average grade on the first exam is 95. It would appear that the students learned a lot about the subject matter by attending the lectures. These results are illustrated in Figure 9.2.

	PRETEST (first exam)	TREATMENT (lectures)	POSTTEST (first exam)
EXPERIMENTAL GROUP	None	Attended lectures	95

Figure 9.2   The Effect of Lectures on the Students' Knowledge of the Course's Subject Matter Using a One Group No Pretest Experimental Design Model

Or did they? Because there is no measure of what the students knew prior to the treatment, the instructor cannot be sure that the lectures actually improved the students' knowledge of the course's subject matter. They might have already known something about the course's subject matter or improved their knowledge by reading the book. Moreover, because there is no control group, the instructor cannot be sure whether the students' knowledge of the course's subject matter increased for some reason other than the lectures.

Getting to the Point 9.2 – The one group no pretest experimental design includes only the basic elements of an experimental design model – the experimental group, a treatment, and a posttest. This design does not include a pretest or a control group. Because of this the effect of the treatment cannot be accurately measured and the influence of other factors on the dependent variable cannot be identified.

The **one group pretest/posttest experimental design model** also includes the basic elements of an experimental design model – an experimental group, a treatment, and a posttest. This model does not include a control group; however, it does include a pretest that measures the dependent variable prior to administering the treatment. This allows the researcher to measure the actual effect of the treatment on the dependent variable (see Figure 9.3).

	PRETEST	TREATMENT	POSTTEST
EXPERIMENTAL GROUP	YES	YES	YES

Figure 9.3 The One Group Pretest/Posttest Experimental Design Model

In our example, the instructor could have passed out a copy of the first exam on the first day of class and asked the class to take it. Let's assume that the students averaged 30 on the first exam. The students' performance on this exam would be a good measure of their understanding of the course's subject matter before reading the textbook and being exposed to the first few weeks of lectures. A few weeks later, after the students have been exposed to the lectures the instructor could ask the students to retake the exam. If the students' performance on the posttest is better than their performance on the pretest, the instructor would have some indication of the effect of the lectures on the students' knowledge of the course's subject matter. Let's assume that the students averaged 95 on the posttest. These results are illustrated in Figure 9.4.

	PRETEST (first exam)	TREATMENT (lectures)	POSTTEST (first exam)
EXPERIMENTAL GROUP	30	Attended lectures	95

Figure 9.4 The Effect of Lectures on the Students' Knowledge of the Course's Subject Matter Using a One Group Pretest/Posttest Experimental Design Model

This design is not ideal because there is no control group. So we cannot say for certain whether some factor other than the lectures caused a change in the students' knowledge of the course's subject matter.

Getting to the Point 9.3 – The one group pretest/posttest experimental design model includes the basic elements of an experimental design model – an experimental group, a treatment, and a posttest. In addition, this model includes a pretest that allows the researcher to measure the actual effect of the treatment (independent variable) on the dependent variable. This design does not include a control group so there is really no way for the researcher to know whether something other than the treatment caused a change to the dependent variable.

The **two group no pretest experimental design model** also includes the basic elements of the experimental design model – an experimental group; a treatment, and a posttest. This design also includes a control group; however, there is no pretest that would measure the effect of the independent variable on the dependent variable (see Figure 9.5).

	PRETEST	TREATMENT	POSTTEST
EXPERIMENTAL GROUP	NO	YES	YES
CONTROL GROUP	NO	NO	YES

Figure 9.5   The Two Group No Pretest Experimental Design Model

In this case, the instructor would randomly divide the students on the first day of class into two groups – an experimental group and a control group. The instructor tells the control group to go home, read the textbook, and come back to class in three weeks. Over the next three weeks, the instructor asks the students in the experimental group to read the same textbook and attend lectures. After three weeks, both groups of students take the first exam.

Let's assume that the students in the experimental group who read the textbook and attended the lectures earned an average score of 95 percent in the first exam. The students in the control group who only read the textbook earned an average score of 30 on the first exam. These results are illustrated in Figure 9.6.

	PRETEST (first exam)	TREATMENT (lectures)	POSTTEST (first exam)
EXPERIMENTAL GROUP	None	Attended lectures	95
CONTROL GROUP	None	Did not attend lectures	30

Figure 9.6   The Effect of Lectures on the Students' Knowledge of the Course's Subject Matter Using a Two Group No Pretest Experimental Design Model

From this we can conclude that the instructor's lectures improved the students' knowledge of the course's subject matter. This of course is based on the assumption that both groups were more or less the same with respect to their knowledge of the course's subject matter prior to the treatment. We cannot know this for sure because the instructor did not administer a pretest. Therefore, there is no way to determine how much the lectures improved the students' knowledge of the course's subject matter.

Getting to the Point 9.4 – The two group no pretest experimental design model includes the basic elements of the experimental design model – an experimental group, a treatment, and a posttest. This design also includes a control group so the researcher would be able to determine that the independent variable, by itself, had some effect on the dependent variable. However, because there is no pretest the researcher cannot measure how much effect the independent variable had on the dependent variable.

The **two group pretest/posttest experimental design model** also includes the basic elements of the experimental design model – an experimental group, a treatment, and a posttest. In addition this model has both a pretest and a control group. This experimental design model is sometimes referred to as the classic experimental design model because it includes all five of the features discussed in the previous section (see Figure 9.7).

	PRETEST	TREATMENT	POSTTEST
EXPERIMENTAL GROUP	YES	YES	YES
CONTROL GROUP	YES	NO	YES

Figure 9.7   The Two Group Pretest/Posttest Experimental Design Model

Using our example, on the first day of class the instructor randomly divides the class into two groups – an experimental and a control group. That same day the instructor asks every student to take the first exam. Let's assume that both groups of students average 30 on the first exam. Upon completing the exam the instructor tells the students in the control group to go home, read the textbook, and come back to class in three weeks. Over the next three weeks, the instructor asks the students in the experimental group to read the same textbook and attend lectures. After three weeks, both groups of students retake the first exam. Let's assume that the students who read the textbook and attended the lectures scored an average of 95 on the first exam while the students that only read the textbook scored an average of 45. These results are illustrated in Figure 9.8.

	PRETEST (first exam)	TREATMENT (lectures)	POSTTEST (first exam)
EXPERIMENTAL GROUP	30	Attended lectures	95
CONTROL GROUP	30	Did not attend lectures	45

Figure 9.8   The Effect of Lectures on the Students' Knowledge of the Course's Subject Matter Using a Two Group Pretest/Posttest Experimental Design Model

We might conclude from this that the lectures had a positive effect on the students' understanding of the course's subject matter. After all, the students who read the material and attended class did much better than those who only read the textbook. Looks like the instructor did a good job. What would you conclude if the students in both groups scored the same on the posttest? What would you conclude if the students in the experimental group did worse than the students in the control group?

Notice in this case that the students in both groups did better on the posttest than they did on the pretest. Of course the students in the experimental group did much better than the students in the control group, we think because they attended lectures. But, the students in the control group improved their average by 15 points, without attending the lectures. How did this happen? Maybe the students in the control group did a little better on the posttest because they had seen the test beforehand, during the pretest.

Getting to the Point 9.5 – The two group pretest/posttest experimental design model includes the basic elements of the experimental design model – an experimental group, a treatment, and a posttest. In addition this model has both a pretest and a control group. These two features enable the researcher to measure the actual effect of the treatment on the dependent variable and to determine whether or not other factors might have caused a change in the dependent variable.

It is reasonable to expect that a student who takes same test twice would do better the second time merely because the student already knows what is on the test. In our example the students in the control group scored an average of 30 on the pretest and then 45 on the posttest. Some of this increase may be attributable to the fact that the students in the control group read the textbook. However, some of this increase may have been caused by the student's familiarity with the test.

To account for this a researcher might use a **Solomon four group experimental design model**. This model includes the basic elements of the experimental design model – an experimental group, a treatment, and a posttest. This model also contains a pretest and a control group. More significantly, this model also contains an extra experimental group and an extra control group. This results in an experimental model with four groups of research subjects:

- An experimental group that is pretested, treated, and posttested
- A control group that is pretested and posttested, but not treated
- An experimental group that is treated and postested, but not pretested
- A control group that is postested but neither pretested nor treated.

Essentially this model combines the two group pretest/posttest experimental and two group no pretest experimental design models into a single experimental design model (see Figure 9.9).

	PRETEST	TREATMENT	POSTTEST
PRETEST/POSTTEST EXPERIMENTAL GROUP	YES	YES	YES
PRETEST/POSTTEST CONTROL GROUP	YES	NO	YES
POSTTEST ONLY EXPERIMENTAL GROUP	NO	YES	YES
POSTTEST ONLY CONTROL GROUP	NO	NO	YES

Figure 9.9   The Solomon Four Group Experimental Design Model

To deploy this experimental design model in our example the instructor would need a large class. On the first day the instructor would randomly divide the students into four equivalent groups. The students in the posttest only experimental group and the posttest only control group would be asked to leave the room and wait in the hallway. While they are out of the classroom the instructor would administer the pretest to the students in the pretest/posttest experimental group and the pretest/posttest control group. Let's assume that the students in both of these groups earn an average of 30 on the first exam. Then the instructor would reconvene the entire class. After all of the students are back in the room the instructor asks:

- the students in the pretest/posttest experimental group to read the textbook and attend lectures for the next three weeks;
- the students in the pretest/posttest control group to read the textbook but not attend the lectures for the next three weeks;
- the students in the posttest only experimental group to read the textbook and attend the lectures for the next three weeks;
- the students in the posttest only control group to read the textbook but not attend the lectures for the next three weeks.

During the next three weeks the students in both of the experimental groups read the textbook and attend lectures while the students in both of the control groups stay home and watch *The Price is Right* after, of course, they read their textbooks. At the end of the first three weeks the instructor reconvenes the class and asks all of the students to retake the first exam. Let's assume the following results.

- The students in the pretest/posttest experimental group scored an average of 95 points on the posttest.
- The students in the pretest/posttest control group scored an average of 45 points on the posttest.

- The students in the posttest only experimental group scored an average of 95 points on the posttest.
- The students in the posttest only control group scored an average of 30 points on the posttest (see Figure 9.10).

	PRETEST (first exam)	TREATMENT (lectures)	POSTTEST (first exam)
PRETEST/POSTTEST EXPERIMENTAL GROUP	30	Attended lectures	95
PRETEST/POSTTEST CONTROL GROUP	30	Did not attend lectures	45
POSTTEST ONLY EXPERIMENTAL GROUP	None	Attended lectures	95
POSTTEST ONLY CONTROL GROUP	None	Did not attend lectures	30

Figure 9.10 The Effect of Lectures on the Students' Knowledge of the Course's Subject Matter Using a Solomon Four Group Experimental Design Model

These results provide the instructor with much more insight into the actual effect of the lectures on the students' knowledge of the course's subject matter. All of the students who read the textbook and attended lectures scored very well on the first exam, during the posttest. Conversely, the students who read the textbook but did not attend lectures performed much worse on the first exam, during the posttest. More interestingly, these results indicate that exposure to the pretest does have some effect on the posttest results. We learned that exposure to the pretest, by itself, resulted in a 15-point increase in scores (see the pretest/posttest control group). Contrast these results with those of the students in the posttest-only control group who took the posttest without taking the pretest and attending lectures. So, we can more confidently say that the instructor's lectures, by themselves, resulted in no less than a 50-point increase in the students' knowledge of the course's subject matter.

Getting to the Point 9.6 – The Solomon four group experimental design model includes the basic elements of the experimental design model – an experimental group, a treatment, and a posttest. This model also contains a pretest and a control group. More significantly, this model contains an extra experimental group and an extra control group. These additional features enable the researcher to determine how much, if any, the research subjects' exposure to the pretest affects their performance on the posttest.

THREATS TO INTERNAL VALIDITY IN EXPERIMENTS

You may recall that validity is the extent to which a measure actually measures the concept it purports to measure. For example, feet and inches would be valid measures for height, but not for weight. In experimental designs, the term validity is used in a slightly different sense. **Internal validity** refers to the ability of an experimental design to document the causal relationship between an independent variable and a dependent variable.

There are numerous threats to the internal validity in experimental models (Campbell and Stanley, 1963; Cook and Campbell, 1979). For example, external events unrelated to the experiment can affect research subjects, a threat we refer to as **history**. In the social sciences, research subjects are seldom sequestered when they participate in an experiment. Instead, they remain in the community and experience everyday life as anyone else would. As such, any event can occur that might cause the research subjects to change their behavior, thereby masking the effect of the treatment or stimulus. Here is an example.

Making Research Real 9.2 – So Much for Community Relations

A media consultant hired by the local police department has been evaluating the effects of a public relations campaign designed to improve the citizens' attitudes toward the police department. The dependent variable in this experiment is 'citizens' attitudes toward the police.' The public relations campaign involves the airing of public service announcements on television that communicate positive images of the police in the community. These public service announcements are the treatment, or independent variable, that the media consultant thinks will cause a change in the citizen's attitudes toward the police.

Prior to implementing the public relations campaign, a survey of citizens' attitudes toward the police revealed that only 30 percent of the citizens had a favorable opinion of the police department and police officers. The consultant thinks the campaign is having its intended effect of improving citizen's attitudes toward the police, but to be sure she decides to repeat the survey. The consultant selects another representative sample of citizens and prepares to mail them the same survey. The night before the consultant mails out the survey, the local news stations show a video of several police officers beating a suspect captured in a high-speed chase. The consultant realizes that this event will probably heighten negative attitudes toward the police. She decides to wait before mailing out the survey, lest the event negate the effect of the public service announcements.

Sometimes a threat to the internal validity of an experiment occurs naturally within the research subjects themselves. We refer to this threat as **maturation**, which occurs when natural changes within the research subjects mask the effects of the treatment. Here is an example of maturation.

Making Research Real 9.3 – Measuring the Effect of Pornography

A psychologist is interested in measuring how teenagers' exposure to sexual content in the media affects their decision to engage in risky sexual behaviors. He gathers a sample of 15-year-olds and asks them to complete a questionnaire that measures their engagement in risky sexual behaviors. Then, over the next three years, he sends each student a follow-up survey that asks them how many times they accessed a website, watched a movie, or looked at a magazine containing sexual content. The surveys also contain the same questions measuring engagement in risky sexual behaviors.

At the end of the third year, when the children are around 18 years of age, the psychologist finds that many of the children are engaged in risky sexual behaviors. But a fellow researcher points out that a person's engagement in risky sexual behaviors would increase naturally during this period in life regardless of the stimuli. Thus, the psychologist cannot conclude that risky sexual behaviors are solely the result of exposure to sexual content in the media.

A third threat to internal validity shows up frequently in longitudinal experimental designs. **Mortality** occurs when, for whatever reason, research subjects become unavailable to the researcher during an experiment. Mortality can be caused by the death of a research subject, but more commonly it happens when a research subject simply refuses to continue participating in the experiment, moves away, or becomes ineligible to continue. Here is an example.

Making Research Real 9.4 – Measuring the Effect of Video Games

A criminologist is conducting an experiment on the effect of violent video games on aggressive behavior. She hypothesizes that teenagers exposed to fewer violent video games will be less likely to exhibit violent behaviors toward others. She collects a sample of 100 teenagers and randomly divides them into two groups. Members of the experimental group are asked to desist from playing all video games for two months. Members of the control group are asked to play whatever video games they want, including the violent ones.

During the experiment, she follows up with each of the research subjects to be sure they are following the instructions. One afternoon, she learns that one of the research subjects in the experimental group 'forgot' and played a violent video game with some of his friends. Because this research subject violated an important rule, he becomes ineligible to participate in the experiment and the researcher is forced to remove him from the experiment. This happens seven more times to members of the experimental group. Finally, the criminologist realizes that there is a real threat to the internal validity of the experiment because so many research subjects are becoming ineligible to participate.

There are four other threats to internal validity that are worth mentioning. In experiments in which a pretest is administered, the test itself can change the outcome of a posttest. We discussed this threat, known as **testing**, earlier in this chapter. **Instrumentation** is another threat to internal validity and it also relates to the pretest and posttest. In this case, slight differences in the pretest and posttest (i.e., the instrumentation), change the outcome of the experiment. Finally, the results of an experiment may indicate that the treatment has a significant effect on the dependent variable, but, over time, this effect disappears. We refer to this threat as **regression**. **Selection bias** occurs when assignment to the experimental and control groups is not random and some members of the population are more or less likely to be included in the experimental group. Because the experimental and control groups are not equivalent, there is no way to isolate the effect of the treatment (independent variable) on some outcome (dependent variable). Below is an example of selection bias. Table 9.1 summarizes these common threats to the internal validity of an experiment. Researchers can mitigate these threats with a little attentiveness and planning.

Making Research Real 9.5 – Self-Esteem Among Child Abuse Victims

A researcher studying self-esteem among adults who were victims of child abuse decides to assign the research subjects into an experimental and control group on the basis of their scores on a self-esteem diagnostic test. In this case, the researcher wants to ensure that both groups have equal levels of self-esteem. He intends to see if a newly developed counseling program is effective at improving the self-esteem of these victims.

   Before the treatment is applied, the researcher learns that the experimental group has a higher proportion of female research subjects than the control group. The effect of abuse on self-esteem is affected by the victim's gender. Any findings from the experiment might be tainted because the groups are not equivalent with respect to gender. To correct this, the researcher divides the research subjects into two groups – one male and one female. Then, the researcher randomly assigns the males and then the females into the experimental and control groups. After that, the new groups are equivalent with respect to their levels of self-esteem and gender.

Table 9.1   Threats to Internal Validity in an Experiment (continued on the next page)

THREAT TO INTERNAL VALIDITY	DESCRIPTION	EXAMPLE
History	Major events happen during an experiment that affect the research subjects and thus the dependent variable.	During an experiment on the effect of an education program intended to reduce underage drinking, a popular rap star dies from alcohol poisoning. Empathetic research subjects may decide to drink less as a result. This will affect the researcher's ability to measure the independent effect of the educational program.
Maturation	Natural developmental changes in the research subjects affect the outcome of the experiment.	A researcher is testing the effects of a new drug use prevention program on high school students. Because young people change within a very short time span, some of the research subjects may mature and become less likely to abuse drugs regardless of whether they participated in the program.

Table 9.1 Continued

THREAT TO INTERNAL VALIDITY	DESCRIPTION	EXAMPLE
Mortality	A loss of research subjects over the course of an experiment, affecting the outcome of the experiment.	A criminologist studies juvenile delinquents from their 15th through 30th birthdays to determine the effect of life course changes on criminal behavior. Some of these research subjects move, drop out of the experiment, or die over the 15-year study. As a result, the researcher does not have enough research subjects to ensure her results are significant.
Testing	Exposing research subjects to a pretest prior to the treatment changes the outcome of the posttest.	To evaluate the effect of a prison-based rehabilitation program, a researcher administers a pretest to members of the experimental and control groups. Following the six-week training program, in which only the subjects from the experimental group participate, the researcher administers the same test to both groups. The members of the experimental group report higher scores suggesting that the training program has its intended effect. But so does the control group. It is possible that the members of the control group 'improved' because they had taken the pretest beforehand.
Instrumentation	Differences between the pretest and posttest instruments cause a change in the dependent variable.	In order to avoid a testing effect, the researcher in the example above decides to make the pre- and posttest slightly different. The experiment indicates that the rehabilitation program had an enormous effect, so big that a peer reviewer asks to review the pre- and posttests (i.e., the instruments). The reviewer argues that the questions were so different between the two tests that the results are not comparable.
Regression	Although there may be an initial treatment effect, the effect diminishes over time, indicating that the independent variable has no long-term effect.	An educator conducts an experiment to evaluate a program similar to Head Start, whereby impoverished children are allowed to enter school at an earlier age. His results suggest that the program does improve reading and math scores in elementary school. But by the time the children enter junior high school, their reading and math scores are more or less equal to the children in the control group. In short, the independent variable has no long-term effect.
Selection Bias	Occurs when assignments to the experimental and control groups do not result in equivalent groups.	A researcher assigns research subjects into the experimental and control groups based on their scores on an intelligence test. He later learns that there is a gender bias in the test that inadvertently measures girls as more intelligent than boys.

Getting to the Point 9.7 – Internal validity refers to the ability of an experimental design to document the causal relationship between an independent variable and a dependent variable. There are seven common threats to the internal validity of an experiment: history, maturation, mortality, testing, instrumentation, regression, and selection bias.

THREATS TO EXTERNAL VALIDITY IN EXPERIMENTS

Another type of validity with which experimental researchers should be concerned is what we call external validity. **External validity** refers to the capacity of a research finding to be applicable to similar research settings. This is also known as **generalizability**. In short, the results of an experiment conducted in one setting may not be relevant to another setting (Campbell and Stanley, 1963; Cook and Campbell, 1979). For example, the findings from research conducted on juveniles during the Great Depression of the 1930s might not be applicable to juveniles today. Unless a researcher is able to control the threats to external validity, the results of the experiment may not be generalizable to other settings and situations.

There are several types of threats to external validity. One threat, called reactivity, is the most common. **Reactivity** occurs when research subjects change their behavior when they become aware that they are being watched or measured. It is human nature for us to change behavior when we know we are being evaluated. For example, when a teacher walks into a noisy classroom, the students often quiet down. Here is another example.

Making Research Real 9.6 – Watching Out for Bullies

A school security officer is interested in finding out whether bullying is occurring at her elementary school. Because bullying incidents tend to happen more frequently on the playground, she decides to observe children during recess. At the end of her observations, the officer concludes that there are no bullying incidents at the elementary school. But the officer fails to consider that her presence on the playground, in uniform, may have discouraged a bully from confronting another student.

When reminded of this threat to external validity, the officer decides to make a small, but important, change to her study. Rather than observing the children directly, she uses a set of remote cameras installed around the playground. During the first week of observations, she observes nine incidents of bullying.

The external validity of an experiment's results can also be threatened by an interaction between selection bias and the dependent variable. This threat occurs when the experimental and control groups are not equivalent. Moreover, one of these groups includes members who are differentially affected by the independent variable.

Table 9.2 summarizes the two most common threats to external validity. Again, with care, researchers can mitigate these threats.

Table 9.2   Threats to external validity in an experiment

THREAT TO EXTERNAL VALIDITY	DESCRIPTION	EXAMPLE
Reactivity	An awareness that they are being measured causes a change in the behavior of research subjects.	A psychologist conducting an experiment on the effect of a new exercise program on obese juvenile delinquents requires his research participants to report their weight on a weekly basis. Overweight participants ashamed of their weight may report lower weights, thwarting the researcher's ability to measure the effect of the exercise program.
Interaction between Selection bias and the dependent variable	There is a failure to ensure that the subjects assigned to the experimental and control groups are more or less equivalent with respect to the variables that might influence the dependent variable.	A researcher is conducting an experiment to determine the effect of frequent shift changes on police officers' cardiovascular health. She inadvertently assigns a larger proportion of older officers to the experimental group. Because age is an influential factor in cardiovascular health, age and not frequent shift changes may affect a change in the dependent variable.

Getting to the Point 9.8 – External validity refers to the generalizability of an experiment's results to other settings and situations. There are two common threats to external validity: reactivity and selection bias. Reactivity occurs when research subjects change their behavior when they become aware that they are being watched or measured. Selection bias occurs when some members of the population are more or less likely to be included in the experimental group, such that the experimental and control groups are not equivalent.

THE BENEFITS AND LIMITATIONS OF EXPERIMENTAL RESEARCH

Experimental design models are effective in isolating a cause (the independent variable) and effect (the dependent variable). In criminology and criminal justice research, this is exceedingly helpful. The outcomes in which we are interested typically have multiple causes. For example, poverty, education, age, and gender all have an effect on crime. But which of these has the greatest effect? A properly controlled experiment allows a researcher to hold multiple factors constant while isolating the effect of a single independent variable.

Experimental designs are also highly useful for measuring how much of an effect an independent variable has on a dependent variable. For example, an experimental design might reveal that in comparison with working five eight-hour shifts per week, working four ten-hour shifts decreases stress among police officers by as much as 50 percent.

Finally, the results of an experimental design are more convincing than the results from other types of research because experiments demonstrate what actually happens rather than what might happen. In survey research, for example, we cannot say definitively whether one variable causes another. We can simply show the relationships between variables and make predictions about what might happen. In experimental research, we can demonstrate causality. These benefits are summarized in Table 9.3.

Table 9.3   The Benefits of Experimental Research

- Ability to isolate the effect of an independent variable on a dependent variable
- Ability to measure how much of an effect a treatment has on an outcome
- Ability to demonstrate causality, or cause and effect

Getting to the Point 9.9 – Experimental research is effective at isolating and measuring the effect of a single independent variable on a dependent variable. Experimental research is also effective at demonstrating a causal relationship between two variables.

Like all research methods, experimental designs do have some disadvantages. First, experimental designs require a great deal of time, attention, and resources. Experimental designs require that researchers maintain full control over the conditions of research, which can be especially difficult in longitudinal research designs. In one of the examples discussed above, a researcher was unable to ensure that an experimental group of teenagers did not play violent video games. In this case, it was nearly impossible to exert full control over the research subjects outside of a clinical setting and the experiment suffered from mortality.

Second, experimental research introduces many ethical concerns into the research process. On the one hand, experiments can be invasive because researchers are literally exposing research subjects to some treatment or stimulus. Perhaps the researcher is investigating the effect of psychological stress, which requires that some negative stimulus be applied to members of an experimental group. On the other hand, experiments can deny access to treatment for research subjects in a control group. Perhaps the researcher is interested in whether a life skills course prevents recidivism. In this case, members of the control group would not be able to take advantage of the course.

Finally, experimental designs are not always feasible. For example, how might you test whether the threat of the death penalty deters a criminal from committing murder? In this case, you cannot feasibly assign potential criminals to an experimental group, in which the death penalty is a possible penalty, and a control group, in which the death penalty is not a possible threat. The best we can hope for here is a quasi-experimental model. For example, a researcher might calculate murder rates before and after the death penalty was introduced or reinstated in a country. The limitations of experimental design are summarized in Table 9.4.

Table 9.4   The limitations of experimental research

- Requirement of much time, money, and control
- Potential for serious ethical concerns
- Possible lack of feasibility

Getting to the Point 9.10 – Experimental research requires considerable resources (e.g. time and money). Often experimental research is not feasible because of the amount of control the researcher must exert over the research subjects. In experiments involving human subjects there is a potential for ethical violations.

THE EXPERIMENTAL RESEARCH PROCESS

Reading about how a research method should be conducted is important. However, learning a new research method is easier when you can see how another person applied the method in an actual research situation. In this section, we will take a look at how a researcher might implement an experimental design following the basic steps of the research process outlined in Chapter Two. At the end of each research step, you will notice a box called "Developing the Method." Within these boxes, you will read about an actual research experiment in the field of criminology. We begin with a general introduction of this study.

Developing the Method 9.1 – A Case Study in Experimental Research
(The Minneapolis Domestic Violence Experiment)

One of the most difficult questions in American policing is how to effectively respond to domestic violence incidents. Calls for service to locations experiencing domestic violence are among the most dangerous of policing activities. Strong emotions, drug and alcohol abuse, and/or severe economic problems are present in nearly every domestic violence incident. These are very personal events and the police are often viewed, even by the victims, as interlopers into a private matter. How to respond to these calls and how to handle cases of alleged domestic violence, therefore, are important to the police.

In 1984, Lawrence W. Sherman and Richard A. Berk published an article called "The Specific Deterrent Effects of Arrest for Domestic Assault" in the *American Sociological Review* (1984a). The research considered whether the threat of an arrest had a deterrent effect on perpetrators of domestic violence.

The research was conducted from 1981 to 1982 in Minneapolis, Minnesota with the cooperation of the Minneapolis Police Department and the Police Foundation. The project was funded through a National Institute of Justice grant.

The results of this research had a profound effect on the policing procedures relating to domestic assault and violence (Buzawa and Buzawa, 1990). Specifically, policing leaders throughout the nation reconsidered their long-standing policies and procedures for dealing with domestic abuse. In short, this research was a 'game changer' in criminal justice practice.

Ask a Research Question

Every research process starts with asking a research question. Then, and only then, should the decision be made on which method would best produce the data necessary to answer the research question. No researcher should ask, *"What research question should I ask so that I can conduct an experiment?"* This would be like a golfer asking, *"Which golf course should I play so that I can use this particular club?"* If you ask a research question that can be answered with an experimental design, then and only then should you adopt an experimental design.

First, let us consider what types of questions do not lend themselves to experimental designs. An experimental method would not be a good method of choice to answer a question like, *"What is the average age that juveniles commit their first delinquent act?"* This particular question is descriptive in nature. Experimental designs are generally not appropriate for descriptive or exploratory research, which are best pursued using surveys and/or interviews. Experimental research is best suited for research studies in which a researcher is attempting to determine causality. Because of their ability to isolate the effect of a single variable, experimental designs are most often used for explanatory research. Here are some research questions that would justify the use of an experimental design:

- *Does participation in a court-imposed drug abuse intervention program (the independent variable) decrease the probability of relapse (the dependent variable)?*

- *What effect does a Bachelor's Degree in Criminal Justice (the independent variable) have on employment in a criminal justice agency (the dependent variable)?*

- *Does a criminal record (the independent variable) reduce an individual's probability of being hired for a job (the dependent variable)?*

Experiments can be used for both pure and applied research questions. For example, a psychologist may conduct an experiment on how stress affects memory. This would be an example of pure research if the initial purpose of the research was to develop knowledge rather than apply the findings to solve a problem. It would be an example of applied research if the criminologist wanted to see whether eyewitness testimony was reliable in a criminal proceeding.

Developing the Method 9.2 – Asking a Research Question in Experimental Research

Before the 1980s, the standard response to domestic violence in most police departments was to not get involved. Police officers were routinely trained that domestic assault was a private matter not warranting an official response, such as an arrest. In fact, in only the most egregious cases were police officers even *allowed* to arrest an individual they suspected of being guilty of domestic assault. In addition to being emotionally charged, domestic assault cases often involve individuals who pose a real safety risk to the police officers who respond to the call. Moreover, the victims of domestic violence, usually women, are often hesitant to testify against their domestic partners in court. In many cases, the alleged abuser is the principal wage earner in the family and without his or her income, the family might be destitute. Regardless of the reasons, a victim's unwillingness to testify makes it very difficult for a police officer to convince a prosecutor to file charges, especially since the officer does not witness the abuse in most cases.

Despite this standard response, many policing leaders became convinced that a more proactive approach might be warranted since police officers were repeatedly called to the same houses. The thinking was that a more preventive approach would reduce the overall number of calls for service, thereby enabling the police to focus on other criminal matters. Advocates for battered women also entered the debate and encouraged the police to take domestic assault more seriously. Some of these groups even filed lawsuits against local police departments to compel officers to arrest suspected domestic abusers.

At the height of this controversy, Sherman and Berk began the Minneapolis Domestic Violence Experiment, or MDVE. According to Sherman and Berk, the "purpose of the experiment was to address an intense debate about how police should respond to … cases of domestic violence" (1984b: 1). The researchers recognized three existing police responses to domestic violence: (1) the traditional approach of doing as little as possible, (2) active mediation or arbitration of disputes, and (3) arrest. In the researcher's words, "If the purpose of police responses to domestic violence calls is to reduce the likelihood of that violence recurring, the question is which of these approaches is more effective than the others?" (1984b: 1).

The MDVE is most appropriately classified as explanatory research in that it attempted to explain which of the three police responses deterred future domestic violence incidents. Because the researchers initially intended that the results would influence public policy, the experiment would be an example of applied research. Some might even argue that given the common policing response to domestic violence at the time, the experiment and its results could be classified as action research.

Getting to the Point 9.11 – Because of their ability to isolate the effect of a single variable on an outcome, experimental designs are most often used in explanatory research. Experiments are appropriate for both pure and applied research purposes.

Conduct a Literature Review

Pre- and posttest instruments are critical to the design of an experimental model. These instruments measure the dependent variable prior to and after the treatment is applied. Experimental researchers often use standardized tests that have proven over time to be both valid and reliable ways to measure the dependent variable.

Thus, the literature review stage should focus on testing instruments that have been used successfully to measure that outcome. Indeed, it is completely acceptable to use previous researchers' pre- and posttest instruments if they have been shown to accurately and reliably measure the dependent variable. In this case, it is important to give credit to previous researchers both in the text and in the bibliography of a research report. Occasionally, a pre- or posttest instrument may be copyrighted. In this case, researchers may be required to pay a fee for the use of another researcher's instrument.

Another piece of information that is critical to investigate in literature reviews for experimental research is the set of variables that past researchers found to be relevant to the outcome. For example, you may learn in your literature review that age, education, and socio-economic status affect your dependent variable. In this case, you would have to ensure that your experimental and control groups are more or less equivalent with respect to these variables. Most researchers use random assignment to ensure that the experimental and control groups are equivalent. But in some cases, random assignment can result in important differences in these two groups, such as a disproportionate number of men in one group and women in another. If gender has been shown to have a significant effect on the dependent variable, this situation could threaten the internal validity of your results. Previously, we defined this threat to internal validity as selection bias. In this case, the researcher might split the research subjects into two groups by gender. Then, the researcher would assign the research subjects from each list randomly into the experimental and control groups. In either case, a literature review would reveal which variables are known to affect the dependent variable and, hence, which variables should be more or less the same in the experimental and control groups.

The literature review process might also uncover previous research on a slightly different population or setting. For example, the previous researcher might have focused on adults, whereas you want to focus on juveniles. Or the previous research might have been conducted in an urban setting and you are interested in conducting the study in a suburban setting. You may even disagree with how the previous researcher measured the variables. In any of these cases, you would want to explain how your study will build on this previous research.

Developing the Method 9.3 – Conducting a Literature Review in Experimental Research

The literature review for the MDVE drew on three broad areas of research: classic research on police decision-making, research on mediation and arbitration in domestic violence prevention, and more contemporary research on police responses to domestic violence (Sherman and Berk, 1984a and 1984b).

The researchers' review of the literature confirmed that, for the most part, the police tended to respond to misdemeanor domestic violence cases rather informally. Very few departments reported a substantial number of arrests in these cases and some even had policies that prohibited the police from making arrests for misdemeanor domestic violence. With respect to mediation and arbitration, the researchers consistently found that mediation and arbitration did not reduce repeat offending in cases of domestic violence. Finally, the researchers learned that a high percentage of spousal homicides occurred in homes that the police had previously been called to on allegations of domestic assault.

In short, the literature review revealed what the researchers suspected: domestic violence has a strong potential for recidivism. Ignoring it and attempting to mediate it were doing very little to reduce repeat offending. As for whether arrests would make a difference, the existing research was not instructive. In the words of the researchers, "[I]t was impossible to determine from the data whether making more or fewer arrests would have reduced the homicide rate" (Sherman and Berk, 1984b: 2). Therefore, they decided to proceed with their own experiment.

Getting to the Point 9.12 – In preparing to conduct an experiment, researchers should review the previous literature, paying particular attention to how past researchers measured the dependent variable and what independent variables have been found to affect the dependent variable.

Refine the Research Question

Because experimental models are best suited to explanatory research, it is important for the researcher to create solid hypotheses. The hypotheses for an experimental design should be as specific as possible. For example, asking how a directed patrol strategy affects the incidence of prostitution merely alleges a relationship between a directed patrol strategy and the incidence of prostitution. It is unclear from this hypothesis *how* the independent variable actually affects the dependent variable. Does a directed patrol strategy reduce or increase the incidence of prostitution? Here is an example of a more specific alternative hypothesis:

Ha: *A directed patrol strategy is an effective method for reducing prostitution.*

This hypothesis alleges that the independent variable (use of a directed patrol strategy) will result in a *decrease* in the dependent variable (incidence of prostitution). In this particular experiment, the null hypothesis would be:

Ho: *A directed patrol strategy is not an effective method for reducing prostitution.*

If the dependent variable (the incidence of prostitution) remains unchanged or increases after the application of the independent variable (the directed patrol strategy), the researcher would accept the null hypothesis and reject the alternative hypothesis. These results would demonstrate that a directed patrol strategy would not be an effective method for reducing prostitution. If, on the other hand, prostitution decreased after implementing this patrol strategy, the researcher would reject the null hypothesis, accept the alternative hypothesis, and conclude that the directed patrol strategy is effective at reducing prostitution.

Developing the Method 9.4 – Refining the Research Question in Experimental Research

Sherman and Berk identified three possible strategies that might reduce domestic violence reoffending: (1) arrest, (2) separate (send the suspect from the scene for eight hours), and (3) mediate. The objective of the research was to determine which of these strategies would reduce the frequency and seriousness of future domestic violence incidents among the research subjects.

This research involved one independent variable – *police response*. The attributes of this independent variable were – arrest, separate, and mediate. Although most research experiments have only one dependent variable, Sherman and Berk decided to evaluate the effect of the independent variable on two outcomes: *the frequency of reoffending* and *the seriousness of future domestic violence incidents*. This resulted in six sets of alternative and null hypotheses.

Ha: *Arresting* individuals suspected of domestic violence *reduces the frequency of reoffending*.
Ho: *Arresting* individuals suspected of domestic violence *does not affect the frequency of reoffending*.

Ha: *Arresting* individuals suspected of domestic violence *reduces the seriousness of future domestic violence incidents*.
Ho: *Arresting* individuals suspected of domestic violence *does not affect the seriousness of future domestic violence incidents*.

Ha: *Separating* individuals suspected of domestic violence from their domestic partners *reduces the frequency of reoffending*.
Ho: *Separating* individuals suspected of domestic violence from their domestic partners *does not affect the frequency of reoffending*.

Ha: *Separating* individuals suspected of domestic violence from their domestic partners *reduces the seriousness of future domestic violence incidents*.
Ho: *Separating* individuals suspected of domestic violence from their domestic partners *does not affect the seriousness of future domestic violence incidents*.

Ha: *Mediating* between individuals suspected of domestic violence and their domestic partners *reduces the frequency of reoffending*.
Ho: *Mediating* between individuals suspected of domestic violence and their domestic partners *does not affect the frequency of reoffending*.

Ha: *Mediating* between individuals suspected of domestic violence and their domestic partners *reduces the seriousness of future domestic violence incidents*.
Ho: *Mediating* between individuals suspected of domestic violence and their domestic partners *does not affect the seriousness of future domestic violence incidents*.

Getting to the Point 9.13 – Because experimental models are used in explanatory research, creating specific hypotheses is an essential step in the experimental research process.

Define the Concepts and Create the Measures

Experimental researchers should be concerned about three areas of measurement. The first area concerns the variables and measures used to determine the equivalency between the experimental and control groups. For example, a literature review may reveal that the effectiveness of a rehabilitation strategy we are studying is influenced by the age, religion, and gender of the participants. Because these variables are believed to be important to the outcome of our treatment, we want to be sure that both groups are similar in each of these respects. If we can show that the groups are similar in each respect, we can establish that the experimental and control groups are more or less the same before applying the experimental treatment.

Experimental researchers should also be concerned about the conceptualization and measurement of the independent variable. Again, in experiments, the independent variable is the treatment or stimulus that is applied to the experimental group. Often, the researcher describes this treatment in great detail. This includes a discussion on the evidence supporting the researcher's hypothesis that the treatment will affect the dependent variable in some way. For example, an experimental researcher may believe that when criminal offenders are exposed to faith-based programs while in prison, they will be less likely to reoffend after they are released. Before conducting an experiment to see if this is the case, the researcher must define what they mean by 'faith-based programs.' What are these programs? How are they different from other types of rehabilitation? Then, they must describe exactly how they intend to measure an offender's exposure to these programs. Is attending church service once a week enough? Or, should an offender have successfully completed a more rigorous religious training program? Finally, the researcher must describe why these programs might work. Do faith-based programs produce attitudinal and behavioral changes that would deter an individual from engaging in criminal behavior? If so, how?

The conceptual definition and operational measurement of the dependent variable is the most critical element of an experimental design. There are two reasons for this. First, the dependent variable is often measured twice – once before the treatment (pretest) and once after (posttest). If the measure is poorly conceptualized or measured, you will have two sets of bad measurements! Second, the measurement of the dependent variable must be sophisticated enough to avoid a pretesting bias. If your professor gave you a pop quiz on a subject unfamiliar to you on Monday and then repeated the same quiz on Wednesday, it is likely that you would do better on Wednesday because you have already been exposed to the testing instrument. There are two common ways of avoiding this threat to internal validity. First, you could simply wait longer to administer the posttest. The longer you wait before administering the posttest, the more the chances decrease that the research subjects will recall taking it as a pretest. Second, you could produce two versions of the test. This is a little trickier. In this case, you could reorder the questions so that the research subjects will not recognize the test. Another way is to ask the questions in a slightly different manner. Either way, the objective is to measure the same thing twice and to do so reliably.

Developing the Method 9.5 – Conceptualization and Measurement in Experimental Research

Before embarking on their experiment, Sherman and Berk had to define their concepts and operationalize their variables. They used the term 'domestic abuse' broadly to include numerous forms of abusive behaviors including psychological, economic, and physical abuse. Drawing from a Minnesota state statute, they defined 'domestic assault' as an assault on an individual by a cohabitant or spouse (Sherman and Berk, 1984a: 263).

Sherman and Berk conceptualized the frequency of reoffending as the number of repeat offenses that occurred within a six-month period following the first domestic violence incident. They do not report how they conceptualized the 'seriousness of future domestic violence incidents' variable. They only indicate, in a footnote, that the "protocols were based heavily on instruments designed for an NIMH-funded study of spousal violence" (Sherman and Berk, 1984a: 263). The citation for this research in the bibliography is not apparent, so there is really no way for us to know how they defined this variable. Given the importance of this dependent variable, this is a rather stark omission. All we really know is that during the six-month follow-up interviews, the researchers asked the victims whether subsequent domestic abuse incidents included actual assault, threatened assault, or property damage. It does not appear that the researchers attempted to measure the seriousness of future domestic violence incidents more precisely than this.

In terms of measurement, the researchers had two important challenges. First, they had to determine which domestic assaults to include in their research. Although all domestic assaults are serious, they vary with respect to severity. Severe cases of domestic violence are relatively rare. Had the researchers included only the most severe cases, it would have reduced their sample size significantly. At the same time, the researchers did not want to include relatively minor domestic disturbance cases, such as verbal confrontations. There were so many of these cases that including them would have caused problems during the analysis phase. Instead, Sherman and Berk chose to include:

> simple (misdemeanor) domestic assaults, where both the suspect and victim were present when the police arrived. Thus, the experiment included only those cases in which police were empowered (but not required) to make an arrest under a recently liberalized Minnesota state law; the police officer must have probable cause to believe that a cohabitant or spouse had assaulted the victim within the last four hours, but the police need not have witnessed the assault.
>
> (Sherman and Berk, 1984a: 263)

In order to avoid the risk of further injury, the researchers chose to exclude domestic assaults involving "life-threatening or severe injury" (Sherman and Berk, 1984a: 263). Minnesota law defined this as felony aggravated assault. These cases were too serious to include in the experiment because someone's life was at stake and they demanded an immediate arrest. For obvious ethical reasons, these cases could not be randomly assigned into the separation, mediation, and arrest groups.

Getting to the Point 9.14 – Experimental researchers should be concerned about conceptualization and measurement of the independent and dependent variables, as well as the variables used to determine equivalency between the experimental and control groups.

Design a Method

The next step in the experimental research process is to design the actual experimental method. In a previous section, you were introduced to several types of experimental designs (see Figures 9.1–9.10). The choice of experimental design depends on a number of factors, including how confident you want to be in your results, what is feasible and ethical in a given research setting, and what you want to know about the research subjects. If you want to isolate the independent variable and test its effect on some outcome, for example, you need a design that uses a control group (i.e., two group posttest only, pretest/posttest control group, Solomon Four Group). But there are circumstances in which using a control group simply is not feasible. For example, it may be unethical to deny human subjects some treatment, as in the MDVE, in which the researchers decided to exclude cases of severe domestic abuse since it would 'deny' some victims an arrest of the suspected abuser. In cases where a control group is not feasible, a quasi-experimental design using just one group may be a researcher's only option (i.e., one group no pretest or one group pretest/posttest).

In cases where a researcher wants to know if a treatment has some effect and, if so, how much of an effect, an experimental design employing a pretest is important (i.e., one group pretest/posttest, pretest/posttest control group, Solomon Four Group). But some researchers are not concerned with the question of 'how much'; they simply want to know *if* there is an effect, in which case a simple posttest will suffice. In other cases, the threat of a pretesting effect is too high and a researcher might opt to forgo a pretest (i.e., one group no pretest or two group posttest only) or to employ a Solomon Four Group design. Again, it all depends on what you want to know, how precise you want to be, and what instruments you are using.

Once an experimental design has been chosen, a strategy for recruiting research participants must be developed. Identifying, contacting, and convincing enough suitable individuals to participate in an experiment can be a daunting task. Persuading an individual to spend a few moments filling out a survey is difficult enough. Getting a person to agree to be tested, exposed to a treatment program, and then tested again is more difficult. It is always a good idea to plan every detail of an experiment before subjects are recruited. By developing a detailed plan, the researcher is in a better position to explain the time commitment, risks, and benefits associated with an experiment. Describing the time commitment, potential risks, and possible benefits to potential research subjects is also mandated by human subject protocols. For a more complete discussion on how to minimize the potential harm to experimental research subjects refer to the section titled Minimizing Ethical Dilemmas on page 65.

No matter how willing a research subject is to participate in an experiment, it is still an imposition. Thus, researchers should be mindful of the research participants' time and design the experiment to be as short as realistically possible. Some researchers use enticements to encourage participation. Paying research subjects even a small fee for their time and energy can encourage participation. Some medical researchers even offer free medical checkups. And, sometimes, the possibility of having access to the treatment will entice participants. But research subjects should understand that they might be assigned to the control group and therefore not have access to the treatment during the experiment.

Once you have convinced subjects to participate in the experiment, you have to design a process for assigning subjects to the experimental and control groups. It is absolutely critical in experimental designs to be sure that the experimental and control groups are equivalent prior to exposing the experimental group to the treatment. Otherwise, the results of the experiment could be questionable. There are several strategies for assigning research subjects to the experimental and control groups in a way that ensures that the two groups are more or less the same. One of the most popular methods is called **random assignment**. In this method, the researcher randomly assigns research subjects to the experimental and control groups. Assuming the absence of bias, this method produces two equivalent groups of research subjects. Another method for assigning research subjects to experimental and control groups is called **matching**. In this method, the researcher organizes the research subjects into matching pairs (based on their similarities) and then splits each pair into the experimental and control groups.

These assignment strategies assume that all of the research subjects are available to the researcher at one time. This is not always possible, especially in criminal justice research. For example, during an experiment on the effect of a court-imposed program to reduce impaired driving, the research subjects (individuals convicted of driving while intoxicated) do not enter the experiment at the same time. In this case, the researcher may want to randomly assign subjects into the experimental and control groups as they come through the court system.

Note, too, that in designing an experiment, a researcher should develop strategies for addressing threats to internal and external validity. Some experimental models do a better job of mitigating threats to internal and external validity than others. Table 9.5 compares the different experimental models with respect to their ability to control threats to internal and external validity. In this table, an 'x' indicates that the experimental model is capable of controlling for the threat to internal or external validity. As we can see, the one group no pretest design is the most susceptible to threats to internal and external validity; the Solomon Four Group design is the most capable of controlling these threats.

Table 9.5   Threats to Internal and External Validity Controlled in Different Experimental Models

THREATS	ONE GROUP NO PRETEST	ONE GROUP PRETEST/ POSTTEST	TWO GROUP NO PRETEST	TWO GROUP PRETEST/ POSTTEST	SOLOMON FOUR GROUP
History	NO	NO	YES	YES	YES
Maturation	NO	NO	NO	YES	YES
Mortality	NO	YES	NO	YES	YES
Testing	NO	NO	YES	YES	YES
Instrumentation	NO	NO	YES	YES	YES
Regression	NO	NO	YES	YES	YES
Selection bias	NO	YES	NO	YES	YES
Reactivity	NO	NO	NO	NO	YES
Interaction between selection bias and the dependent variable	NO	NO	?	?	?

Source: Adapted from Campbell and Stanley (1963). *Experimental and quasi-experimental designs for research*. Chicago, IL: Rand McNally.

Developing the Method 9.6 – Designing Experimental Research

Early in the development of their research, Sherman and Berk decided that the best method for their study was to use a true experimental design. Specifically, they opted to use a pretest/posttest control group design. Recall that these researchers wanted to know which response (i.e., arrest, separate, mediate) produced the highest deterrent effect (i.e., reduced the frequency and seriousness of future domestic assault incidents). Therefore, Sherman and Berk decided to create three equivalent experimental groups. Because they had three experimental groups, their design was slightly different than most pretest/posttest control group designs, which typically only have one experimental group.

Another important difference between Sherman and Berk's experimental design and the usual pretest/posttest control group model was the lack of a pretest observation. The domestic assault cases came to the attention of the researchers as the calls for service that met the researchers' criteria came to the attention of the police. Because all of these research subjects were not available to the researchers prior to their exposure to one of the treatments (arrest, separate, mediate), there was really no way to measure the dependent variables (frequency and seriousness) before they were exposed to one of the treatments.

Of course, after the research subjects were identified and assigned to one of the three groups, the researchers were able to determine whether the research subjects had been involved in previous domestic assault incidents. They found that their research subjects had considerable experience in the criminal justice system and with domestic assault in particular. In 80 percent of the cases, the victims had been assaulted by the suspect within the past six months. The police had intervened in 60 percent of these cases. Twenty-seven percent of the couples involved in the experiment were already participating in a counseling program. And among the male suspects involved in the research, 59 percent had been previously arrested for other offenses, 31 percent had been previously arrested for an assaultive offense and 5 percent had been previously arrested for a domestic violence offense (Sherman and Berk, 1984b: 5). This information substituted for the information that would have been provided by a pretest.

You may recall that creating equivalent groups is one of the important requirements for an experiment. In order to ensure equivalency between the three experimental groups, the researchers devised a randomized group assignment plan:

> The design called for each officer to carry a pad of report forms, color coded for the three different police responses. Each time the officers encountered a situation that fit the experiment's criteria, they were to take whatever action was indicated by the report form on top of the pad. The forms were numbered and arranged for each officer in an order determined by the lottery. The consistency of the lottery assignment was to be monitored by research staff observers riding on patrol for a sample of evenings.

> (Sherman and Berk, 1984b: 3)

The final element of this experimental design was the posttest. During this phase, Sherman and Berk determined which enforcement response (arrest, separation, or mediation) had the greatest effect on the frequency and seriousness of future domestic violence incidents. The simplest way to determine which of the three enforcement responses reduced the frequency and seriousness of future domestic assaults was to compare the reoffending rates of the three groups during a period of time following the treatment phase. Sherman and Berk chose to measure the reoffending rates of the three groups within a six-month period of the initial intervention. The decision to use this time frame was based on previous research indicating the frequency of domestic assault reoffending. You may recall that during the six-month period prior to the treatment phase, 80 percent of the victims involved in the experiment had been assaulted by their domestic partner.

Victims are often reluctant to call the police in subsequent cases of domestic assault, especially if their domestic partner was previously arrested and/or was the major breadwinner for the family. Hence, calls to the police for domestic violence were not a perfect measure for reoffending; many domestic assaults may have occurred that did not result in calls to the police. Even when calls were made, official records did not indicate the seriousness of the domestic assault incident. To overcome these challenges, Sherman and Berk chose to conduct follow-up interviews with the victims in addition to drawing on police records. For six months following the initial domestic violence incident, the researchers attempted to contact each victim every two weeks:

> Anticipating something of the victims' background, a predominantly minority, female research staff was employed to contact the victims for a detailed face-to-face interview, to be followed by telephone follow-up interviews every two weeks for 24 weeks. The interviews were designed primarily to measure the frequency and seriousness of victimizations caused by the suspect after the police intervention. The research staff also collected criminal justice reports that mentioned the suspect's name during the six-month follow-up period.

> (Sherman and Berk, 1984a: 263)

The researchers knew that their analyses would require data being collected at various levels of measurement. For example, they wanted to know whether a subsequent domestic assault occurred. This was measured at the nominal level (*yes* or *no*). In addition, they wanted to know how much time had elapsed (in days) between the end of the intervention and the subsequent domestic assault. This variable had to be measured at the ratio level of measurement because it was possible for a subsequent domestic assault to take place immediately after the intervention (i.e., zero days after the intervention). Finally, the researchers wanted to know something about the seriousness of any subsequent domestic assaults. They measured seriousness at the ordinal level by creating three attributes – *actual assault*, *threatened assault*, or *property damage*.

Research involving human beings who are already vulnerable to physical, psychological, and legal harm must be evaluated extensively prior to its implementation to avoid additional harm to the participants. In this case, the research subjects (both the suspects and their victims) were potentially exposed to numerous types of harm. In addition, domestic assault cases often result in injuries to police officers. As a result, this particular experiment was required to undergo considerable scrutiny. The experiment was funded through a grant to the Police Foundation from the National Institute of Justice's Crime Control Theory Program. Approval of the grant required the grantees (Sherman, Berk and the Police Foundation) to present detailed plans on how they intended to avoid potential harm to the individuals involved in the experiment. It is also likely that the researchers themselves were required to submit their research plans for human subjects review in their respective universities (University of Maryland, College Park, and University of California, Santa Barbara). Finally, the experiment was conducted with the cooperation of the Minneapolis Police Department. Chief Anthony V. Bouza was no doubt required to seek approval from the City of Minneapolis prior to agreeing to participate.

To identify and mitigate potential problems before the implementation of the experiment, the researchers decided to conduct a three-day conference. Previously, Sherman and Berk chose to focus on two precincts in the city that had the highest historical incidence of domestic assaults. The 34 officers assigned to these precincts attended this conference and were asked to participate in the experiment for one year. All but one officer agreed to participate. Preliminary conferences like these tend to be very helpful to researchers in that they identify potential problems from the perspective of the individuals who are participating in the experiment. This conference was no exception.

Getting to the Point 9.15 – Experimental researchers should determine which experimental design model they want to use early in the research process. The choice of experimental design depends on a number of factors, including how confident the researchers want to be in their results, what is feasible and ethical in a given research setting, and what researchers want to know about the research subjects.

Collect the Data

The number of data collection opportunities during an experiment depends on the type of model used by the researcher. If the researcher uses a model that includes a pretest, data are collected before the treatment or stimulus is applied. If the pretest instrument is a 'paper and pencil' exercise, the researcher should secure an appropriate space (e.g., a classroom) to administer the pretest. If the experimental model includes a control group, the researcher should avoid cross-contamination of the experimental and control groups. This can be achieved by administering the pretest twice – once to the experimental group and again to the control group.

In addition to measuring the dependent variable, the results of the pretest can provide the researcher with insight into the equivalency of the experimental and control groups. For example, during an experiment on the effect of night shift work on the cardiovascular health of correctional officers, a researcher might randomly assign the research subjects into two groups. The groups are equivalent with respect to age, gender, education, experience, marital/family status, and all other factors known by the researcher to influence cardiovascular health. During the pretest (a heart function stress test), the researcher notices that members of the experimental group are generally healthier than members of the control group. If this difference is significant enough, it might skew the results of the experiment. Thus, the researcher might consider reassigning the research subjects to the experimental and control groups using the results of the pretest.

After the pretest results are in, the researcher should expose the experimental group to the treatment. If the treatment is exposure to some educational or treatment program, only members of the experimental group should be admitted to the classroom. A more daunting task is to keep the research subjects who are exposed to the treatment from sharing their experiences with the members of the control group. Depending on the nature of the treatment, avoiding cross-contamination during the treatment phase can be difficult. Medical researchers have an easier time with this. They simply administer placebos (e.g., sugar pills) to the control group, such that the research subjects have no way of knowing whether they are in the experimental or control group.

After delivering the treatment or stimuli, the researcher should administer the posttest, which normally involves repeating the pretesting process. Cross-contamination is still a potential threat during the posttesting phase. This is especially true if the posttest instrument involves group interviews with the research subjects. In this case, the experimental and control groups should be separated during the posttesting phase.

The actual strategies used by experimental researchers to collect data depend largely on the research design. For example, many researchers use paper and pencil exercises to measure the dependent variable prior to and after they expose the experimental group to the treatment. Other researchers may measure the dependent variable through observations or interviews. In either case, the results from these exercises must be converted into a format acceptable for analysis.

Developing the Method 9.7 – Collecting Data in Experimental Research

Often in field experiments, researchers conduct pilot tests. This is analogous to what survey researchers do when they pretest their survey instrument on a small subsample of respondents. The purpose of this process is to determine whether the survey will function as it was intended to function. A pilot test for a field experiment does the same thing. It is an opportunity for researchers to 'work out the bugs' in an experimental design. Sherman and Berk do not report whether or not they conducted a pilot test. Instead, the three-day conference they conducted prior to the experiment was intended to identify potential problems in the conduct of the experiment. Even with this conference, it is evident in their report that they were forced to make numerous changes in the conduct of the experiment as they confronted problems and challenges.

It is not uncommon for researchers to encounter problems in the field. Seldom do research plans go as expected. Sherman and Berk initially determined that they would need at least 300 cases in order to obtain meaningful results. Originally, they trained 34 officers in two of Minneapolis' four patrol precincts. These two precincts had the highest density of domestic violence reports and arrests, so they were more likely to gather an acceptable sample quicker. In addition, managing the experiment in two rather than four precincts would be easier. The experiment began on March 17, 1981. The researchers estimated that it would take about one year to collect 300 cases. By November of that year, however, the researchers were disappointed with the number of cases they had collected. Thus, they recruited an additional 18 officers to participate in the experiment. And by August 1, 1982, the researchers had collected 314 cases (Sherman and Berk, 1984a and 1984b).

From the beginning, Sherman and Berk were concerned about whether or not the police officers would adhere to the group assignment procedures they had developed. It was logical that a police officer, upon encountering an overly aggressive or non-compliant suspect, might ignore the lottery system's assignment of this person to the mediate or separate group and decide to initiate an arrest. It was equally logical that a police officer, upon encountering a remorseful or compliant suspect, might ignore the assignment of this person to the arrest group and decide to mediate or separate the offender. To monitor this potential problem, Sherman and Berk assigned researchers to ride along with police officers and observe the group assignment process.

Because of the infrequent nature of domestic assault cases and the expenses related to paying these researchers, however, Sherman and Berk eventually abandoned this plan. In its place, they assigned researchers to monitor the police radio and respond to domestic assault calls as they occurred. Unfortunately, even this method failed since the monitors could not determine from the cryptic nature of radio communications which cases were related to domestic assault. The researchers finally settled on an alternative method to ensure that police officers adhered to the assignment method: they printed serial numbers on each of the reporting forms. If an officer submitted a reporting form that was out of sequential order, researchers would know that the officer ignored the group assignment process. Of course, this method did not prevent an officer from ignoring the group assignment process; it just indicated to the researchers if and when the officers ignored the assignment procedures.

Ultimately, Sherman and Berk found that 98.9 percent of the suspects who should have been assigned to the arrest group were arrested, 77.8 percent who should have been assigned to the mediate group were provided mediation services, and 72.8 percent who should have been assigned to the separate group left the scene for the specified eight hours. They concluded that, though "many of the officers occasionally failed to follow fully the experimental design," they were confident that the majority of the officers followed the assignment instructions (Sherman and Berk, 1984b: 3). Compliance with the assignment plan was due in a large part to three factors. First, the researchers encouraged the officers to actively participate in the design of the experiment. The three-day training conference demonstrated to the officers that the researchers were interested in their input and provided the officers with a means to 'buy into' the project. Second, it is likely police officers in the Minneapolis Police Department were as frustrated by domestic assault as the researchers. Providing these officers with a means to make a substantial contribution to our understanding of domestic assault enforcement did a lot to encourage the officers to adhere to experimental procedures. Finally, the researchers committed considerable resources to supervision. Throughout the experiment, members of the research team were available to the officers to answer questions and deal with problems.

A second challenge that emerged in the data collection phase centered on the follow-up interviews with victims. Many researchers were unable to contact the victims for the follow-up interviews. Researchers made up to 20 attempts to contact victims, but many of the victims had either moved or refused to respond to telephone calls or home visits (Sherman and Berk, 1984b: 4). Only 205 of the 330 victims were located and agreed to sit for interviews, representing a 62 percent completion rate. A 62 percent response rate is not terrible, but the researchers were understandably concerned that this attrition rate ('mortality') would affect the validity of the research findings. Had a substantially higher or lower proportion of victims in one group or another chosen not to be interviewed, the strength of the statistical findings would have been threatened. Fortunately, Sherman and Berk found that "there [was] absolutely no evidence that the experimental treatment assigned to the offender affected the victims' decision to grant initial interviews" (1984b: 5).

Getting to the Point 9.16 – The number and nature of data collection strategies used by experimental researchers depend on the experimental design used by the researcher.

Analyze the Data and Interpret the Results

Quantitative results are the most common type of data gathered through an experimental design. The analysis of this data often requires the creation of statistical data sets. During the time between the pre- and posttests, experimental researchers typically create codebooks to organize the quantitative data and begin entering the data into statistical software programs. Sometimes, experimental designs produce qualitative data in the form of words, images, or field observations. Because of its subjectivity, qualitative analysis requires even more preparation and planning.

Most research questions in experimental research are hypotheses of difference, meaning that the researcher alleges that the treatment will make a difference in the group of research subjects exposed to it. In addition, experimental designs tend to include variables that are measured at the interval or ratio levels. These two factors suggest that *t*-tests or **analyses of variance** are the most appropriate statistical techniques for analyzing the data from an experimental design. For information on these statistical techniques refer to the section titled Inferential Statistics on page 362.

As researchers analyze the data from an experiment, they often identify opportunities for additional analysis. For example, they might find, unexpectedly, that two variables are highly correlated. It is perfectly acceptable to capitalize on these unintended insights. Often, these opportunities provide direction for future research.

After conducting a thorough analysis of the data, researchers interpret the results from the experiment. This involves developing an explanation of how and why the treatment affected (or did not affect) the dependent variable. The researcher should also devote considerable time to discussing the possible threats to internal and external validity within the experimental design. Nobody likes to admit their mistakes. But researchers are expected to admit the weaknesses of their study for the sake of advancing knowledge. If the data exist to substantiate the findings, however, the researcher should not be reluctant to argue in support of his or her conclusions.

Developing the Method 9.8 – Analyzing and Interpreting Data From Experimental Research

Sherman and Berk do not report how they prepared their data for analysis. It is clear from their reports, however, that they spent considerable time monitoring the data as it became available (Sherman and Berk, 1984a and 1984b). In terms of the actual data analysis, the researchers used three statistical techniques: a linear probability model, a logit formulation and a proportional hazard approach. A description of these higher order multivariate techniques is beyond the scope of this textbook. But interested readers will find a detailed description in an article published in the *American Sociological Review* (Sherman and Berk, 1984a).

Overall, the statistical analysis conducted by Sherman and Berk revealed that 38.9 percent of the suspects perpetrated a subsequent domestic assault within three months of their treatment. Three independent statistical analyses also indicated that:

- the suspects who were arrested were the least likely to reoffend within six months of the treatment (10 percent reoffended within the reporting period);

- the suspects who were separated were the most likely to reoffend within six months of the treatment (24 percent reoffended within the reporting period); and

- the suspects assigned to the mediation group were less likely to reoffend within six months compared to the suspects who were separated, but more likely to reoffend compared to the suspects who were arrested (19 percent reoffended within the reporting period).

(Sherman and Berk, 1984a and 1984b)

Sherman and Berk concluded that a mandatory arrest policy was the most effective strategy for deterring domestic assault suspects from reoffending.

Sherman and Berk had to have known that the results of this experiment would have profound policy implications. As such, they devoted considerable time to discussing the potential weaknesses of their research. One potential weakness was officer misconduct in adhering to the rules of the experiment. As discussed previously, the researchers were concerned that the officers would ignore the lottery system that was designed to randomly assign the cases into one of the three experimental groups. Again, the researchers went to great lengths to avoid this potential problem. As a result, they were able to identify most cases in which this occurred.

Second, Sherman and Berk recognized that the incapacitation effect of an arrest may have explained the lower reoffending rate. As they explained, "if the arrested suspects spend a large portion of the next six months in jail, they would be expected to have lower recidivism rates" (Sherman and Berk, 1984a: 268). To address this potential weakness, they determined how long each of the arrested suspects in their experiment spent in jail:

> [Forty-three] percent were released within one day, 86 percent were released within one week, and only 14 percent were released after one week or had not yet been released at the time of the initial victim interview. Clearly, there had been very little incapacitation, especially in the context of a six-month follow-up.
>
> (Sherman and Berk, 1984a: 268)

A third problem was sample size, especially when the sample was broken down into various categories (e.g., age, race, employment status, etc.). This made it impossible for the researchers to determine whether some types of offenders responded differently to an arrest. For example, it may be that individuals with more violent criminal histories are less affected by an arrest. Given this weakness, the researchers concluded that it was "premature for state legislatures to pass laws requiring arrests in all misdemeanor domestic assaults" (Sherman and Berk, 1984b: 8).

Fourth, the researchers recognized that the location of the experiment might have produced some external validity problems. Recall that the external validity of an experiment deals with generalizability. Minneapolis has a rather large Native American population, a historically low rate of violence, and low unemployment. Sherman and Berk concluded that "the cultural context of other cities may produce different effects of police actions in domestic violence cases" (Sherman and Berk, 1984b: 8).

Finally, Sherman and Berk acknowledged that the follow-up interviews might have had a "surveillance effect" on the suspects (Sherman and Berk, 1894b: 8). That is, the suspects might have known that their victims were being monitored and therefore might have been reluctant to engage in future offending during the follow-up period. This is an example of reactivity. Sherman and Beck's straightforward discussions about the potential weakness of this research went a long way toward increasing the acceptance of this research among both the scholarly and practitioner communities.

Getting to the Point 9.17 – Experimental designs tend to include variables that are measured at the interval or ratio levels. As such, *t*-tests or analyses of variance are the most common statistical techniques used to analyze data in experimental research. When interpreting the findings from these and other analyses, experimental researchers should be up front about the possible threats to internal and external validity within the experimental design.

Communicate the Findings

How, when, and where the results of an experiment are reported typically depends on who is interested in the results of the experiment. For example, if an experiment is conducted to determine whether an after-school athletic program reduces a juvenile's tendency to join a gang, the results might be of interest to police departments, school administrators, and criminologists.

Developing the Method 9.9 – Communicating the Findings From Experimental Research

The results of the MDVE were published in two places. First, they appeared in an article in the *American Sociological Review*, a scholarly journal published by the American Sociological Association. This highly respected academic journal is distributed widely throughout the Sociology and Criminal Justice academic communities. Remember that articles that appear in academic journals are almost always peer reviewed. Although Professors Sherman and Berk are highly qualified and well respected in their field, their research no doubt benefited from the peer review process. In the report appearing in the *American Sociological Review*, the authors write:

> We wish to express our thanks to the Minneapolis Police Department and its Chief, Anthony V. Bouza, for their cooperation, and to Sarah Fenstermaker Berk, Peter H. Rossi, Albert J. Reiss, Jr., James Q. Wilson, Richard Lempert, and Charles Tittle for comments on an earlier draft of this paper.
>
> (Sherman and Berk, 1984a: 261)

This list of reviewers contains some of the most respected scholars in the field. By communicating this information, Sherman and Berk are letting the reader know that this research was evaluated by others who have expertise in this subject and who know a great deal about experimental design.

In order to reach a wider audience of policing practitioners, a shorter and less technical version of the report was published by the Police Foundation, a co-sponsor of the research. This version of the report was distributed to a large number of police chiefs and administrators. Normally, scholars do not write up a separate report for laypersons or practitioners. But in this case, the research was crucial to the policing community. Note that in writing up their results for two very different audiences, the researchers had to communicate those results a bit differently. For example, the following passages communicate the same finding, but one appeared in the *American Sociological Review* and the other in Police Foundation Reports.

From the *American Sociological Review*	From Police Foundation Reports
"The official recidivism measures show that the arrested suspects manifested significantly less subsequent violence than those who were ordered to leave." (Sherman and Berk, 1984a: 261)	"[The experiment] found that arrest was the most effective of the three standard methods police use to reduce domestic violence." (Sherman and Berk, 1984b: 1)

To be sure, these were not the only times these researchers presented their findings. In fact, for several years following the experiment, Sherman and Berk were asked to make presentations at various scholarly conferences, police organizations, and women's advocacy groups.

Getting to the Point 9.18 – How, when, and where the results of an experiment are reported typically depends on who is interested in the results of the experiment.

Ask Another Research Question

Good research tends to produce as many questions as it answers. These new questions present opportunities to continue the research process. After all, research is a journey, not a destination.

Develop the Method 9.10 – Asking Another Research Question in Experimental Research

The MDVE changed policing procedures in significant ways, especially in the Minneapolis Police Department:

> As a result of the experiment's findings, the Minneapolis Police Department changed its policy on domestic assault in early March of 1984. The policy did not make arrest 100 percent mandatory. But it did require officers to file a written report explaining why they failed to make an arrest when it was legally possible to do so. The initial impact of the policy was to double the number of domestic assault arrests, from 13 the weekend before the policy took effect to 28 the first weekend after. On one day in mid-March there were 42 people in the Minneapolis jail on spouse assault charges, a record as far as local officials could remember.
>
> (Sherman and Berk, 1984b: 8)

One would think that with results this convincing, the controversy over whether a mandatory arrest policy will reduce domestic assaults would have ended. But this is not exactly what happened. One question that remained was whether the results were truly generalizable. Would a mandatory arrest policy reduce domestic assault reoffending in other communities? Subsequent experiments of a similar nature did not produce findings even closely harmonious with the Minneapolis experiment. For example, after the MDVE, the National Institute of Justice and the Centers for Disease Control and Prevention co-sponsored five research programs designed to test Sherman and Berk's findings. These studies, collectively referred to as the Spousal Assault Replication Program, consistently found that the use of arrest was only occasionally associated with reductions in repeat offending. As a result, many police administrators and prosecutors doubt the effectiveness of a 'one size fits all' response to domestic assault.

Sherman and Berk themselves admitted that more research was necessary before the results of their experiment could be generalized to all communities. But they were clear that their results were compelling enough to consider a change in the police response to domestic assaults:

> A replication of the experiment in a different city is necessary to address these questions. But police officers cannot wait for further research to decide how to handle the domestic violence they face each day. They must use the best information available. This experiment provides the only scientifically controlled comparison of different methods of reducing repeat violence. And on the basis of this study alone, police should probably employ arrest in most cases of minor domestic violence.
>
> (Sherman and Berk, 1984b: 8)

To be sure, Sherman and Berk made an important contribution to our understanding of domestic violence and its prevention. But theirs is not the last word in this controversy.

Getting to the Point 9.19 – Good research tends to produce as many questions as it answers. These new questions are opportunities to continue the research process.

FINAL THOUGHTS

At this point, you might be thinking, "Wow! This is complicated. The last thing I ever want to do is an experiment!" Or, you might be thinking, "Wow! This is cool! I would really like to do an experiment!" Both thoughts are correct. Experiments are, indeed, complicated. They require a great deal of planning and management. So many things can go wrong, even in the best planned experiments. Research subjects drop out of the experiment or do not participate fully in the treatment. Research subjects in the experimental group share information with those in the control group. And just when things are going well, something happens outside of the experiment that affects the behavior of the research subjects and masks the effect of the independent variable.

But experiments are also cool. They provide researchers with highly defensible results of what actually happened or could happen. That is, an experiment can tell us exactly how a change in an independent variable results in a change in a dependent variable. This is much better than a survey, which can only tell us what might happen. Experiments are the most powerful explanatory research method and, when done well, can give us insight and guidance in a way that no other research method can.

GETTING TO THE POINT/CHAPTER SUMMARY

- An experiment is a research method that measures the effect of an independent variable on a dependent variable. All experimental design models feature an experimental group, a treatment, and a posttest. More sophisticated experimental design models also include a pretest and a control group.

- The one group, no pretest experimental design only includes the basic elements of an experimental design model – the experimental group, a treatment, and a posttest. This design does not include a pretest or a control group. Because of this the effect of the treatment cannot be accurately measured and the influence of other factors on the dependent variable cannot be identified.

- The one group pretest/posttest experimental design model includes the basic elements of an experimental design model – an experimental group, a treatment, and a posttest. In addition, this model includes a pretest that allows the researcher to measure the actual effect of the treatment (independent variable) on the dependent variable. This design does not include a control group so there is really no way for the researcher to know whether something other than the treatment caused a change to the dependent variable.

- The two group no pretest experimental design model includes the basic elements of the experimental design model – an experimental group, a treatment, and a posttest. This design also includes a control group so the researcher would be able to determine that the independent variable, by itself, had some effect on the dependent variable. However, because there is no pretest the researcher cannot measure how much effect the independent variable had on the dependent variable.

- The two group pretest/posttest experimental design model includes the basic elements of the experimental design model – an experimental group, a treatment, and a posttest. In addition this model has both a pretest and a control group. These two features enable the researcher to measure the actual effect of the treatment on the dependent variable and to determine whether or not other factors might have caused a change in the dependent variable.

- The Solomon Four Group experimental design model includes the basic elements of the experimental design model – an experimental group, a treatment, and a posttest. This model also contains a pretest and a control group. More significantly, this model contains an extra experimental group and an extra control group. These additional features enable the researcher to determine how much, if any, the research subjects' exposure to the pretest affected their performance on the posttest.

- Internal validity refers to the ability of an experimental design to document the causal relationship between an independent variable and a dependent variable. There are six common threats to the internal validity of an experiment: history, maturation, mortality, testing, instrumentation, and regression.

- External validity refers to the generalizability of an experiment's results to other settings and situations. There are two common threats to external validity: reactivity and selection bias. Reactivity occurs when research subjects change their behavior when they become aware that they are being watched or measured. Selection bias occurs when some members of the population are more or less likely to be included in the experimental group, such that the experimental and control groups are not equivalent.

- Experimental research is effective at isolating and measuring the effect of a single independent variable on a dependent variable. Experimental research is also effective at demonstrating a causal relationship between two variables.

- Experimental research requires considerable resources (e.g. time and money). Often experimental research is not feasible because of the amount of control the researcher must exert over the research subjects. In experiments involving human subjects there is a potential for ethical violations.

- Because of their ability to isolate the effect of a single variable on an outcome, experimental designs are most often used in explanatory research. Experiments are appropriate for both pure and applied research purposes.

- In preparing to conduct an experiment, researchers should review the previous literature, paying particular attention to how past researchers measured the dependent variable and what independent variables have been found to affect the dependent variable.

- Because experimental models are used in explanatory research, creating specific hypotheses is an essential step in the experimental research process.

- Experimental researchers should be concerned about conceptualization and measurement of the independent and dependent variables, as well as the variables used to determine equivalency between the experimental and control groups.

- Experimental researchers should determine which experimental design model they want to use early in the research process. The choice of experimental design depends on a number of factors, including how confident the researchers want to be in their results, what is feasible and ethical in a given research setting, and what researchers want to know about the research subjects.

- The number and nature of data collection strategies used by experimental researchers depend on the experimental design used by the researcher.

- Experimental designs tend to include variables that are measured at the interval or ratio levels. As such, *t*-tests or analyses of variance are the most common statistical techniques used to analyze data in experimental research. When interpreting the findings from these and other analyses, experimental researchers should be up front about the possible threats to internal and external validity within the experimental design.

- How, when, and where the results of an experiment are reported typically depends on who is interested in the results of the experiment.

- Good research tends to produce as many questions as it answers. These new questions are opportunities to continue the research process.

CHAPTER EXERCISES

The following chapter exercises are organized into two parts. The first part consists of questions that can be answered using the information from this chapter. This section will test your understanding of the chapter material. The second part consists of research application exercises. These exercises require you to apply what you have learned thus far.

CHAPTER REVIEW QUESTIONS

Respond to each of the following questions using the information from this chapter.

1. The group that is exposed to the treatment or stimulus believed to cause a change in the dependent variable is known as the _____ group.
    a. Control
    b. Experimental
    c. Posttest
    d. Selection

2. The independent variable in an experimental design, or what the researcher is alleging causes a change in the dependent variable, is also known as the:
    a. Control
    b. Effect
    c. Pretest
    d. Treatment

3. Read the following research descriptions and decide which type of experimental design is being described (one group no pretest, one group pretest/posttest, two group posttest only, pretest/posttest control group, and Solomon Four Group).

Description	Experimental design
An experiment has equivalent experimental and control groups; a treatment or stimulus that is applied to the experimental, but not the control group; and pretests and posttests that measure the dependent variable prior to and after exposure to the treatment or stimulus.	
An experiment applies a treatment to a single experimental group and measures the dependent variable both before and after the application of this treatment.	
An experiment includes equivalent experimental and control groups, a treatment or stimulus that is applied to the experimental group and a posttest that measures the dependent variable after the experimental group has been exposed to the treatment.	

Description	Experimental design
An experiment has two experimental groups and two control groups; a treatment or stimulus that is applied only to the experimental groups; pretests that measure the dependent variable prior to the treatment for one of the experimental groups and one of the control groups; and posttests that measure the dependent variable after exposure to the treatment for all groups.	
An experiment has a single experimental group, a treatment or stimulus, and a posttest that measures the dependent variable after the treatment.	

4. True or False: The ability of an experimental design to document the causal relationship between an independent variable and a dependent variable is referred to as internal validity.

5. External validity is related to which of the following?
    a. Generalizability
    b. Instrumentation
    c. Mortality
    d. Reactivity

6. Natural change among research subjects that can be a threat to the internal validity of an experiment's results is referred to as:
    a. History
    b. Maturation
    c. Mortality
    d. Regression

7. When research subjects change their behaviors after becoming aware of an experimental researcher's presence, it is referred to as:
    a. Maturation
    b. Mortality
    c. Reactivity
    d. Regression

8. Read the following research descriptions and decide which threat to internal validity is being posed (history, maturation, mortality, testing, instrumentation, or regression).

Description	Threat to internal validity
During an experiment on recidivism among juvenile offenders a researcher learned that 35 percent of the original participants moved out of state with their families.	

A experimental researcher is attempting to determine if a cognitive intervention technique increases social awareness among violent offenders. To mitigate the potential for pretest bias a researcher used two different tests to measure social awareness. The researcher later learns that the two tests (one used for the pretest and the other for the posttest) were developed to measure separate parts of this concept.	
During an experiment to evaluate the effectiveness of a new public relations program used by a police department to improve its relationship with the community an errant police officer shoots and kills an unarmed teenager.	
An experimental researcher working with chronic adult offenders uses a ten-item inventory as a pretest. He uses the very same ten-item inventory as a posttest. The time frame between the pretest and posttest is less than a week.	
During a multi-year experiment on the effect of an intervention program designed to reduce the potential for domestic violence an experimental researcher learns that there is no difference in the frequency of domestic conflict between the men in the experimental and control groups.	
During an experiment involving young (12–14) juvenile offenders a researcher learns that regardless of the treatment, young juvenile offenders tend to 'age out' of their tendency to commit delinquent acts by the time they are 16 years old.	

9.   Read the following research descriptions and decide which threat to external validity is being posed (reactivity or selection bias).

Description	Threat to external validity
During an experiment a researcher decides to assign participants to the experimental and control groups based on their birthdays. The participants are juvenile offenders. Those born from January through June are assigned to the experimental group. The participants born from July through December are assigned to the control group. The experiment involves an assessment of academic achievement on the onset of juvenile delinquency.	
To test the ability of a racial tolerance program for police officers an experimental researcher 'rides along' with police officers to observe how they interact with racial and ethnic minorities.	

10. Based on your knowledge of experimental design, indicate whether an experimental design would help answer the following research questions.

Research question	Would experimental research be helpful?
How prevalent is bullying in middle school versus high school?	
How do young men and women define and understand rape in the context of dating relationships?	
To what extent does faith-based counseling reduce recidivism among violent ex-offenders?	
Do early intervention programs for academically at-risk students reduce adolescent delinquency?	

RESEARCH APPLICATION EXERCISES

Access to the following articles will be provided by your instructor.

Feder, L. and Dugan, L. (2002). A test of the efficacy of court-mandated counseling for domestic violence offenders: The Broward experiment. *Justice Quarterly, 19*(2), 343–375.

Graziano, L., Schuck, A. and Martin, C. (2010). Police misconduct, media coverage and public perceptions of racial profiling: An Experiment. *Justice Quarterly, 27*(1), 52–76.

Respond to the following question for each of the articles cited above.

11. What was the research question with which the researchers began?

12. What type of experimental design did they use and why?

13. How did the researchers measure the independent variables in their research?

14. How did the researchers measure the dependent variables in their research?

15. What was done, if anything, to avoid potential threats to internal validity?

16. What was done, if anything, to avoid potential threats to external validity?

17. How did the researchers ensure equivalence between the experimental and control groups?

18. In your opinion, did the researchers interpret their results properly?

19. What are some questions that should be asked by subsequent researchers?

20. If you were interested in repeating one of these experiments, what would you do differently and why?

CHAPTER 10

Survey/Interview Research Methods

Surveys are one of the most common social science data gathering techniques. In most cases, the unit of analysis in a survey is an individual. But surveys can also collect information from larger units of analyses, such as organizations and even nations. A great example of a survey is the U.S. Census, which the U.S. government conducts every 10 years. This survey influences election district boundaries, federal budget allocations, and countless other policy decisions.

Surveys are used extensively in the social sciences, as well as in marketing and public opinion polling. They are particularly popular among criminal justice scholars and practitioners. Here is an example of how a police chief might use survey methodology several times during a typical day.

Making Research Real 10.1 – Just Another Day at City Hall

A young intern walked into the chief's office. "You need to see me chief?" she asked. "Yes, I do. It's our turn to host the monthly lunch for city hall employees. We need to know what everyone wants to eat. Their choices are chicken fried steak, Mexican food or fish. Go around city hall and ask the people that work in the offices which option they want," the chief responded.

The chief then grabbed his car keys and left for a breakfast meeting with the Rotary Club. He was looking forward to this meeting because it would be the first time he would hear from local community leaders on the results of a policing project designed to reduce loitering around local businesses. The chief planned to go around the room and have attendees at the meeting give their opinion on how the anti-loitering program was working.

The chief's afternoon was dedicated to a meeting with officers assigned to an interagency juvenile gang task force. The task force had recently contracted with a researcher from the local university to conduct a survey of current and former juvenile gang members. The survey included questions on why these juveniles joined a gang, what they did to maintain their membership in the gang, and the process by which they chose to disassociate from the gang. This research was one of the few projects where time was actually spent gathering information directly from gang members.

At the end of a long day, the chief arrived home and was confronted by his teenage daughter and several of her friends. She had just passed her driver's license exam and was anxious to get her first car. "Daddy, we've looked over all the cars currently for sale on Craig's List and this is the one that we all agree I should have," she exclaimed.

How many surveys did the chief conduct or consult? I count four. Some of the surveys were informal; others were more sophisticated. Some surveys included only one question; others included several questions. A few of the surveys produced quantitative data; others produced qualitative information. One analysis of survey data was as simple as an intern making tally marks in a notebook; another was as complicated as a researcher measuring the psychological factors that attract juveniles to delinquent gangs. Regardless of their level of sophistication, their length, the type of data they collected, and how the data were analyzed, all of these surveys have one thing in common. They collected information by asking individuals or groups of individuals to respond to questions and statements, which, by definition, is what constitutes a **survey**.

This chapter introduces the key terms and concepts of the survey research method and identifies the situations in which researchers should consider using surveys to collect data. Using the steps in the research process discussed in Chapter 2, this chapter then provides detailed instructions on the survey method. As in the previous chapter, you will find the "Developing the Method" feature later in this chapter, which will illustrate how a research project made use of survey research methods.

SURVEY RESEARCH BASICS

I have a confession to make: I am a graduate of the Wilton Cake Decorating Correspondence School. Yes, I know how to decorate cakes. For those of you unfamiliar with correspondence schools, they work like this. You get your assignments in the mail and, when you complete them, you send them in to be graded. If you pass, you get a new set of lessons until you complete the course. Then, you get a certificate "suitable for framing." Correspondence education was very popular before the internet and YouTube. People used to learn all sorts of skills via correspondence. I decided to enroll in the cake decorating course when I was a State Trooper assigned to a five county beat in the remote Texas Panhandle. Believe me, there was not much else to do. And besides, I really like cake.

The first lesson in my cake decorating class required me to make uniform lines, called piping, with butter cream frosting using a pastry bag and several types of tips. When I completed this lesson, I took a picture of my work and sent it in to the company. The final lesson was a three-tiered wedding cake complete with ornate piping on the sides. I passed and received my certificate in the mail. Learning how to do a survey is not much different than learning how to decorate a cake. There are some basic concepts you have to know and some tools you have to master. After that, you have to learn when to apply these concepts and tools so that the survey turns out like you want it to.

Again, surveys are any data collection method wherein individuals or groups are asked to respond to questions and/or statements. For example, you might receive a survey in the mail from your elected representative asking various questions that help him or her identify your position on particular issues. Alternatively, you might be asked to fill out a survey in your Introduction to Psychology class in which you must answer questions about the stresses associated with college. Both of these types of surveys are written surveys. But you might also be asked to answer questions orally either in person or over the phone.

Survey research methods are data collection procedures or processes that involve the use of a survey or interview instrument wherein individuals or groups are asked to respond to questions and/or statements. Any method in which a person is asked a series of preestablished questions would be considered a survey. When we refer to a survey **instrument**, we are referring to the actual questionnaire or document that is designed and administered to a group of respondents. In survey lingo, the **respondent** is the individual or group that is asked to respond to a survey.

> **Getting to the Point 10.1** – Surveys are a data collection method wherein individuals or groups are asked to respond to questions and/or statements. This method involves developing an instrument, which the researcher uses to ask questions and record answers. The individuals or groups that respond to the survey are referred to as respondents.

TYPES OF SURVEYS

There are four basic survey formats. Each has its advantages and disadvantages, as summarized in Table 10.1. The format chosen depends on the researcher's objectives, the research context and the respondents targeted. The first format is the **mail survey**. One of the advantages of mail surveys is that they are low cost. Paper, photocopying, envelopes, and postage can be costly, but overall the costs associated with a self-administered mail survey are comparatively low. Mail surveys also have the advantage of wide coverage. The majority of people can get mail. In mail surveys, respondents do not have to reveal their identity so they may be more willing to be honest. In this sense, they offer anonymity in a way that other formats do not. Finally, mail surveys reduce the potential for **interviewer bias**. By interviewer bias, we mean that sometimes the way an interviewer asks questions affects how respondents answer them.

On the downside, mail surveys tend to have low response rates. In some mail surveys, less than 5 percent of the sample actually responds. This means that the researcher must send out a large number of surveys in order to ensure that a large enough sample will be returned for analysis. In mail surveys, the researcher also does not have control over the conditions under which the survey is taken. A respondent may be distracted while taking the survey, which could affect the quality of the responses. There are also length limitations on a mail survey, since a respondent's willingness to complete a survey decreases as the length of the survey increases.

Another disadvantage of mail surveys is that there is increased risk of miscommunication. If a researcher is not present to respond to questions that a respondent may have about the wording or meaning of particular questions, respondents may skip questions or answer them inaccurately. Finally, there is a risk of data entry error in mail surveys. That is, information from the survey may be entered into a database incorrectly, thus affecting the analysis.

Table 10.1   Advantages and Disadvantages of Different Survey Formats

SURVEY FORMAT	ADVANTAGES	DISADVANTAGES
Mail survey	• Low cost • Wide coverage • Anonymity • Avoids interviewer bias	• Low response rates • No control of the conditions • Length limitations • Possibility of miscommunication • Data entry error
Internet survey	• Lowest cost • Worldwide coverage • Reduces data entry error	• Possible sampling bias • Lack of distribution lists
Telephone survey	• Wide coverage • Higher response rates • Better communication • Reduces data entry error	• More expensive • Length limitations • No visual communication tools • Not possible to interrupt survey • Sampling bias • Decreased use of landline phones
Interview	• Highest response rate • Allows for longer surveys • Control of the conditions • Better communication • Reduces data entry error	• Most expensive • Possibility for interviewer bias • Variation among interviewers

Another survey format is the **internet survey**. The use of internet surveys is growing considerably. They are especially popular for use inside of organizations. Internet surveys are relatively inexpensive to develop and distribute. In fact, they may be the lowest cost alternative. There are a number of commercially available software packages for developing online surveys and many of these are open source (e.g., SurveyMonkey). Internet surveys also provide worldwide coverage since an online survey can be distributed pretty much anywhere in the world. Responses from online surveys can be entered directly, by the respondent, into the appropriate database for subsequent analysis. This eliminates the potential for data entry error.

One of the disadvantages of internet surveys is that they increase the potential for sampling bias. Because the sampling frame is limited to active internet users, respondents will probably be younger than the general population. Internet surveys also face potential distribution problems. It is relatively easy to obtain physical addresses and landline telephone numbers. E-mail addresses are more difficult to obtain. Furthermore, many people have multiple e-mail addresses and may not access these accounts on a regular basis.

A third survey format is the **telephone survey**, whereby researchers survey respondents over the telephone. Like the mail survey, the telephone survey has the advantage of wide coverage, because nearly everyone has a telephone. Telephone surveys tend to have higher response rates than mail surveys because respondents are less likely to hang up the phone than they are to simply discard a mail survey. Unlike mail surveys, telephone surveys lessen the chance of miscommunication since respondents can ask questions about a question's meaning and a researcher can use alternative words when a respondent does not understand a question. In a telephone survey, a researcher can also reorder the questions or slow down the pace when a respondent is having difficulty responding to the questions or statements. Finally, there are fewer data entry errors in telephone surveys because data can be entered directly into the database as it is collected.

A major disadvantage of telephone surveys is that they are more expensive. The labor, technology, programming, and other costs can be considerable. In addition, most respondents are not willing to spend more than five minutes responding to a telephone survey, so it must be relatively short. In fact, as a general rule, a telephone survey must be shorter than a mail survey. Telephone surveys also do not include visual communication tools. For example, when presented with a list of 10 possible answers to a question, respondents to a mail survey can review the list several times before answering. This is more difficult over the telephone because the interviewer has to read and reread the list of responses until the respondent makes a choice. Telephone surveys do not allow respondents to take a break. In a mail survey a respondent can start, stop, and resume the survey at will. Further, because the researcher has no control over who answers the telephone, telephone surveys leave room for sampling bias. For example, in most households, females answer the telephone more frequently than males, which means that females are more likely to be surveyed. Finally, a growing problem with telephone surveys is that an increasing number of households are forgoing landlines altogether, opting instead to use cell phones exclusively. Because cellular telephone numbers are not readily available, there may be distribution problems similar to those found with internet surveys.

The fourth and final type of survey is an **interview**, in which a researcher reads survey questions aloud and allows the respondent to answer orally. Interviews are different from telephone surveys because the interviewer and the respondent are face to face. Like telephone surveys, interviews tend to have high response rates. In fact, interviews tend to have the highest response rate. It is more difficult for a respondent to refuse to participate when a researcher is present and graciously asking *"Do you mind if I ask you a few questions?"* Respondents are also more likely to remain engaged when an interviewer is helping them through the survey. This is especially true if the interviewer is able to establish rapport with the respondent. An interviewer can also control the environment in which the survey is taken. For example, an interview can be conducted in a place where there are few distractions. An interviewer can reorder the questions or slow down the pace when a respondent is having difficulty responding to the questions or statements. An interviewer can also use alternative words in a question when a respondent does not understand a question. Finally, if an interviewer records responses directly into a computer, the chances for data entry error are reduced.

On the downside, interviews are probably the costliest form of survey research. The costs associated with labor, travel, supplies, and sometimes security can be considerable. The presence of an interviewer may also bias the respondents' answers. Again, interviewer bias occurs because we tend to communicate differently depending on who we are communicating with. For example, you probably speak differently to your peers than you do to your professor. Finally, when multiple interviewers are required, like during a big research project, the natural differences in communication styles between interviewers may affect how questions are asked and answered.

Getting to the Point 10.2 – There are four general types of survey formats: mail surveys, internet surveys, telephone surveys, and interviews. Each format has its advantages and disadvantages. The format chosen depends on the researcher's objectives, the research context, and the respondents targeted.

THE BENEFITS AND LIMITATIONS OF SURVEY RESEARCH

There are a number of advantages to survey methods. First and foremost, surveys are good for developing a profile of a community or group. For example, a survey might ask for information on a person's age, height, and weight, which might give a public health researcher the necessary information to devise public health campaigns or outreach efforts. A survey researcher may include a question on a person's race to determine a community's racial–ethnic profile and to see how race–ethnicity is related to other community variables, such as home ownership.

Second, surveys are effective for learning how people behave. For example, the U.S. Census asks people how many minutes they commute to work on a daily basis. The Census Bureau uses this statistic to rank order cities in terms of their level of traffic congestion. Here is another example of how a survey sheds light on individual behavior.

Making Research Real 10.2 – Neighborhood Crime Survey

During a meeting of a neighborhood association, several of the members complain about a recent increase in burglaries. "They've hit four houses so far this year. Something has to be done!" a member complains. The association president appoints an ad hoc committee to contact the police department and ask them for assistance.

The committee chairperson calls the police department and is quickly referred to the Community Services Officer. This officer specializes in helping neighborhoods deter burglars and other types of criminal behavior. The officer asks the committee chairperson, "What are you and your neighbors doing now to deter burglaries?" The chairperson does not have a clue about what her neighbors do to prevent crime. So with the help of the Community Services Officer, she distributes a Crime Risk Survey. Among other things the survey asks:

- When you leave your house for work do you lock your doors?

- Have you trimmed the bushes away from low windows and doors?

- Do you tell your neighbors when you are going out of town?

The answers to these and the other questions inform the Community Services Officer, and the neighborhood association, how the neighborhood residents behave with respect to crime prevention. And they give the Community Services Officer the information he needs to conduct Crime Risk Awareness seminars that teach the neighbors how to deter potential burglars.

Surveys are also useful for measuring attitudes, beliefs, and opinions. For example, political pollsters use surveys to identify the issues that concern voters. Using this information, political consultants might fashion their candidate's message so that it resonates with voters. Likewise, a criminologist might conduct a survey to determine the level of public support for the death penalty. If the survey were repeated over a series of years, we might be able to determine whether support for the death penalty is increasing or decreasing.

Surveys are an excellent method for measuring what people know. You may have watched Jay Leno, the host of NBC's *Tonight Show*, ask people on the street basic questions about history, government, and current events in a comedy segment called *JayWalking*. We laugh when the respondents cannot provide correct answers to the most basic questions. My favorite one was when he asked, *"Who lives at 1600 Pennsylvania Avenue?"* The correct answer is the President of the United States. But a sizable portion of the respondents did not know the answer.

Finally, surveys are used to predict the future. For example, a political pollster may ask likely voters whom they intend to vote for in the next election. The results of these surveys can also be supplemented with exit polls, wherein actual voters are asked whom they just voted for as they leave the polls. This is how news corporations attempt to predict the outcome of an election before the votes are actually counted. Table 10.2 summarizes the uses of the survey research method.

Table 10.2 The Uses of the Survey Research Method

- Developing a community or group profile (i.e., what people look like)
- Learning how people behave (i.e., what people do)
- Measuring attitudes, beliefs, and opinions (i.e., what people think)
- Determining levels of knowledge (i.e., what people know)
- Predicting future trends and patterns (i.e., what people will do)

Getting to the Point 10.3 – Survey research is effective for developing community or group profiles; learning how people behave; measuring attitudes, beliefs, and opinions; determining levels of knowledge; and predicting future trends and patterns.

Though they are useful in certain research situations, surveys are limited in what kind of information they can provide. For example, surveys are not particularly useful for determining a causal relationship between variables. A survey may help you find that two variables, like education and income, are related. But this correlation alone does not establish a causal relationship between the two variables. You may recall the three causal rules from Chapter 5 – temporal order, correlation, and a lack of alternative explanations. If they are taken at one point in time, surveys can provide information on correlation and, to some extent, they can help rule out alternative explanations. But they cannot establish which variable happened first (i.e., temporal order). Carefully controlled longitudinal surveys can provide more insight into temporal order and hence the causal relationship between two variables. But the results are simply not as strong as the results from a well-designed experiment. Here is an example.

Making Research Real 10.3 – The Effect of Marriage on Criminal Behavior

A correctional researcher is interested in the causal relationship between marriage and criminal behavior. She believes that marriage, like other social bonds, deters a person from committing crime. She sends a survey to 1,000 inmates currently serving time at a state prison. Among other questions, she asks them about their marital status. She learns that 80 percent of these offenders are not married. That is, they are single, divorced, or widowed. She concludes that marriage, or the lack thereof, affects a person's tendency to commit criminal acts.

What this researcher fails to consider is the respondents' marital status at the time they committed the criminal offense for which they are serving time. Some of these inmates may have been married when they committed their crime and gotten divorced or become widowed while in prison. Moreover, she fails to rule out alternative explanations. Indeed, a survey like this would not likely be able to ask enough questions to discount all other factors that could cause criminal behavior. For example, we do not know, qualitatively, the nature of these offenders' marriages. They could have been married but not happily so. They might even be in prison because they assaulted their spouse.

At best, the researcher has helped establish some relationship between marriage and criminality. But she has not pinpointed marriage (or the lack of it) as a cause of crime.

Surveys are not always effective for obtaining qualitative information. In most cases, surveys ask questions with preformatted or fixed responses. They do not typically ask respondents to describe something in their own words. And even when they do, surveys may not provide enough space, time or trust for the respondent to answer in a detailed or honest way. Thus, survey research is not particularly effective for measuring complex social phenomena or emerging social issues.

Even when surveys are an effective means to answer research questions, they have the disadvantage of relying on self-reported behavior. In anonymous surveys, there is no way to determine the truth of a respondent's statements or answers. There is also no way to determine whether respondents have answered the questions thoughtfully and thoroughly. They could have been distracted or uninterested while filling out the survey. Or they might not have filled out the survey at all; another person could have provided the answers. In the end, surveys have their limitations and these are important to remember when interpreting survey results.

Finally, validity is often a concern in survey research. Recall that validity means whether or not a measure actually measures what it purports to measure. In survey research we often ask whether a particular question will measure what the researcher intended it to measure. Here is an example. The death penalty is a controversial topic in criminal justice. A survey researcher could simply ask, *"Do you support the death penalty?"* and have the respondents answer *yes* or *no*. Assuming this researcher learned that 70 percent of the respondents answered no, could he conclude that 70 percent of the population would support a repeal of the death penalty? Probably not; this issue is much more complicated than a simple *yes* or *no* response. A small percentage of respondents might fully support the use of the death penalty and another small percentage of respondents might wish it were completely repealed. This researcher's question and answer set are not capable of measuring the largest proportion of respondents – those in the middle that might support the death penalty in some situations and oppose it in others. A lot of these respondents may have answered *no* because they would prefer not to take such a definitive position on this controversial issue. So, this question and answer set are not a valid measure of support for the death penalty. Table 10.3 summarizes the limitations of the survey research method.

Table 10.3   The Limitations of the Survey Research Method

- Difficulty in determining causal relationships between variables

- Inability to measure or illuminate complicated or unknown social phenomena

- Possible inaccuracies and dishonesty in respondents' self-reported behavior, attitudes, and knowledge

- Validity, or whether a survey question measures what it purports to measure, is often a threat

---

Getting to the Point 10.4   Survey research is not effective for determining causal relationships between variables and measuring complicated or unknown social phenomena. Surveys should not be used when the honesty of the respondents is important to the research and their responses cannot be independently verified. It is often difficult to determine the validity of a concept or construct measured through a survey response.

THE SURVEY RESEARCH PROCESS

Learning a new research method is easier when you can see how another person applied the method in an actual research situation. In this section, we will take a look at how a researcher might administer a survey following the basic steps of the research process outlined in Chapter 2. At the end of each research step, you will find the now familiar boxes entitled "Developing the Method." Again, these boxes describe an actual survey that was conducted in the field of criminology. We begin with a general introduction to this case study of survey research.

---

*Developing the Method 10.1 – A Case Study in Survey Research (*The Uniform Crime Reports and National Crime Victimization Survey*)*

Since 1930, the Federal Bureau of Investigation (FBI) has collected information on crimes reported to local police departments under a program called the **Uniform Crime Reports (UCR)**. These data are collected at the local level, summarized at the state level, and sent to the FBI on a quarterly basis. Each year, the FBI uses these data to produce reports on crime and other police administration issues. The most notable of these reports is called *Crime in the United States*. This annual report is widely distributed and used as the national measure of crime. For all practical purposes, each individual UCR is a survey. The FBI asks each police department to respond to questions regarding crimes reported in its precinct and other administrative issues.

Despite its utility, the UCR is limited in that it only provides statistics on crimes actually reported to the police. There are a large number of crimes that are never reported. To supplement the UCR, the

Bureau of Justice Statistics (BJS), part of the U.S. Department of Justice, periodically conducts a survey on criminal victimization. This survey, conducted by telephone, involves a very large sample of residents in the United States. The survey, known as the **National Crime Victimization Survey** (NCVS), asks respondents about their experiences with criminal victimization regardless of whether they reported it to the police. The NCVS includes crimes not reported to the police, but there is no way to verify the accuracy of the information reported by survey respondents. Despite their respective limitations, the UCR and NCVS together provide a fairly good snapshot of crime throughout the United States at particular times.

Ask a Research Question

Whether you choose to conduct an experiment, administer a survey, or interview a group of people depends on what your research question is and what kind of data you are after. As noted in the previous section, the survey research method would not be a good choice of method if you wanted to determine the cause of crime or if you wanted to explore some complicated social phenomena. But it is a good method for profiling particular individuals, groups, and organizations; documenting how people behave and what they think and know; and determining the relationships between two or more variables. Here are some examples of research questions that could be answered through survey research:

- *How has the demographic profile of U.S. religious cults changed over time?*

- *What are the coping skills that individuals use when living in high-crime neighborhoods?*

- *Is there a relationship between educational performance and juvenile delinquency?*

As we can see from the above questions, the purpose of most surveys is to describe a particular group or sub-population, a particular set of behaviors and beliefs, and/or a particular relationship between variables. Thus, surveys produce mostly descriptive data. In some cases, surveys can also be effective for exploratory research. Because survey research is generally not appropriate for establishing causal relationships, they are seldom used for explanatory research.

Surveys are often conducted to determine current conditions or to identify specific problems and needs among respondents. The results of these surveys can influence public policy and lead to change. As a result, applied research relies heavily on survey research methods. But surveys can be used in pure research, as well.

Developing the Method 10.2 – Asking a Research Question in Survey Research

The UCR traces its origins to the 1920s, when the International Association of Chiefs of Police identified a need to measure crime at the national level. In response, the United States Congress authorized the FBI to create a national clearinghouse for statistical information on crime in 1930. This became known as the UCR program. Participation in the UCR program is voluntary, but nearly every university, city, county, state, tribal, and federal policing agency participates (Federal Bureau of Investigation, 2009).

The UCR collects data on a limited number of crimes that are officially reported to the police and crimes that are cleared by an arrest. These crimes are organized into two parts. Part I crimes are the most serious and include murder and non-negligent manslaughter, forcible rape, robbery, aggravated assault, burglary, larceny-theft, motor vehicle theft, and arson. Part II crimes are less serious and include driving while intoxicated, simple assault, and drug-related crimes.

The NCVS was started more recently. It began in 1973 and is conducted by the U.S. Census Bureau on behalf of the Bureau of Justice Statistics. The NCVS collects information on personal and household victimization using a nationally representative sample of households. This information is collected directly from the victims themselves. There are no limits on the types of crimes it allows victims to report, with one obvious exception: the NCVS cannot collect information from murder victims.

Both the UCR and NCVS surveys are descriptive in nature. Neither attempt to explain the reason for crime. Their primary purpose is to collect information so that practitioners, policy makers, and professors have access to data to study crime rates and trends. As such, these data lend themselves to applied and pure research.

Getting to the Point 10.5 – Generally speaking, surveys are effective for describing a particular group or subpopulation, a particular set of behaviors and beliefs, and/or a particular relationship between variables.

Conduct a Literature Review

In addition to the usual objective of the literature review, survey researchers should review the literature with the following questions in mind. First, how have previous researchers defined concepts used in the study? Most research on crime explores similar concepts. Researchers should draw on one another's conceptual definitions to help build a larger body of knowledge on particular topics. For example, recidivism is an important concept in research on correctional rehabilitation strategies. But how should researchers define recidivism? Should they define a recidivist as an ex-offender who commits a new crime within three years of being released from prison? Should they include only crimes that could return the person to jail or prison upon conviction? Should they require that the ex-offender be convicted of a crime before classifying him or her as a recidivist? In answering these questions, researchers should consult the previous literature and make their judgment about what conceptual definition makes most sense and what definition is most comparable for the purpose of building a body of research. Again, when borrowing others' conceptual definitions, it is imperative that you give the previous researcher proper credit.

Survey researchers should also look at the variables and attributes that previous researchers used. For example, you may be interested in measuring the level of public support for the death penalty. You could simply ask: *"Do you support the death penalty?" Yes* or *no?* But in your review of the literature, you might stumble across another measure for support for the death penalty that is more valid, such as:

In which of the following situations do you support the death penalty? (Check all that apply)
- ☐ *When a person is convicted of intentionally murdering a child*
- ☐ *When a person is convicted of intentionally murdering an elderly person*
- ☐ *When a person is convicted of intentionally murdering a police officer, fireman, or paramedic*
- ☐ *When a person intentionally murders more than one person*
- ☐ *When a person intentionally murders another person in a particularly heinous or cruel manner*
- ☐ *Anytime a person intentionally murders another person*

Finally, as you review the literature, you should look at how other researchers have designed surveys similar to the one you are planning. Pay attention to how researchers distributed their surveys and the words they used. For example, police departments often conduct surveys to evaluate how citizens perceive the services they provide. In order to ensure all citizens have an opportunity to participate in the survey, some departments include these surveys in utility bills. If you are interested in targeting everyone in a particular community, you might use a similar format when conducting your survey.

Developing the Method 10.3 – Conducting a Literature Review in Survey Research

Because the UCR and NCVS are ongoing, researchers involved in their administration do not typically conduct extensive literature reviews. The crime categories in the UCR have remained relatively constant for decades. And this is imperative since it allows researchers to compare crime rates from one year to the next. It is equally important for the UCR staff to reconcile definitional differences between jurisdictions so that similar criminal behaviors are defined consistently throughout the survey. Jurisdictions may change penal code definitions and may even decriminalize some behaviors. The UCR staff must be vigilant about staying on top of these changes to ensure the continuity of their survey's results.

One of the most recent threats to the administration of the NCVS, which relies on contacting respondents via the telephone, is the decrease in the number of landline telephones. An increasing number of telephone users are abandoning landline services and opting to use cellular telephone services exclusively.

Cellular telephone numbers are not as accessible as landline telephone numbers. Furthermore, cellular telephone users appear more resistant to responding to telephone surveys. The effect of this social phenomenon on the validity of the NCVS is not yet known. But it is essential that the researchers responsible for conducting the NCVS evaluate the available literature on how this might affect telephone survey research.

Getting to the Point 10.6 – In addition to the usual information researchers look for when conducting a literature review, survey researchers should pay particular attention to how previous researchers defined similar concepts, measured key variables, and designed survey instruments.

Refine the Research Question

Because most surveys are intended to produce descriptive information, hypotheses that predict causal relationships between variables are not usually required in survey research. Instead, your hypotheses should predict whether you expect to see particular relationships emerge in the survey data. If your research objective is merely to explore a particular population or phenomenon, you may not even develop hypotheses at all.

Developing the Method 10.4 – Refining the Research Question in Survey Research

Since their purpose is to produce descriptive data, the UCR and NCVS do not use formal research hypotheses. Further, the research questions that drive both surveys have changed only slightly over time. For the most part, each survey asks the same questions about the same crimes, since the purpose is to produce longitudinal data. But new questions are introduced as new crimes and crime trends emerge. For example, the UCR only began collecting data on hate crimes quite recently. And it would not be surprising to find new questions on the NCVS as new forms of criminal victimization emerge. For example, a decade ago identity theft was relatively rare. Now it is one of the fastest growing forms of criminal behavior in America.

Getting to the Point 10.7 – Because most surveys are intended for descriptive and exploratory research, hypotheses that predict causal relationships between variables are not usually found in survey research. Instead, survey researchers develop hypotheses that predict relationships between variables and/or refine research questions about particular phenomena.

Define the Concepts and Create the Measures

Defining and measuring concepts is especially important in survey research. Conceptual definitions must be consistent throughout the survey research process. And conceptual definitions and measures must be communicated effectively to your respondents. For example, if you define crime as any behavior that can result in a person being sentenced to a term of imprisonment or jail, you must communicate that definition to your respondents. It would not be enough to ask simply: *"Have you ever committed a crime?"* Some respondents would include minor traffic offenses and answer *yes* even though they had never committed a crime as you define it. Many of these problems can be worked out during the pretesting phase of the research process.

Developing the Method 10.5 – Defining Concepts and Creating Measures in Survey Research

With respect to conceptualization, there are differences in how the UCR and NCVS define the term 'crime.' According to the UCR, a behavior is not a crime until it has been reported as a crime to the police. If a crime is never reported to the police or if the local agency does not participate in the UCR program, the crime is never counted. Some crimes, like murder, robbery, and burglary, have a higher probability of being reported to the police. Other crimes, like rape, embezzlement, or simple assault have a lower probability of being reported to the police. Note that the UCR does not collect data from prosecutors or courts. Therefore, there is no way to know whether or not criminal suspects were convicted or sentenced for the crimes that were reported. In 1988, the FBI responded to this flaw by creating the National Incident-Based Reporting System (NIBRS), which collects information on reported crimes, as well as any subsequent arrests, prosecutions, and sentencing for each crime incident.

The UCR requires reporting agencies to determine how their state or local criminal offenses fit into the approved UCR crime categories. But there are some discrepancies between how reporting agencies define certain crimes and how the UCR defines certain crimes. For example, the UCR collects information on forcible rape. The UCR defines forcible rape as "the carnal knowledge of a female forcibly and against her will." Using this definition, the rape of a male would not count as 'forcible rape' for UCR data collection purposes. Decades ago, many states began amending their rape statutes to recognize that a man could be raped. As a result, a discrepancy between state rape statutes and the UCR's forcible rape definition emerged. Currently, the UCR instructs agencies to report male rape as an assault or other sexual offense rather than a forcible rape.

Note that the definition of forcible rape in the newer NIBRS system is broader. Under this program, a forcible rape is defined as "the carnal knowledge of a person, forcibly and/or against that person's will; or not forcibly or against the person's will where the victim is incapable of giving consent because of his/her temporary or permanent mental or physical incapacity or because of his/her youth" (Federal Bureau of Investigation, 2009). This definition includes adult male and child rape victims.

In contrast to the UCR, the NCVS defines crime from the victim's perspective. The NCVS is more interested in the consequences and effects of personal and household victimization and is less concerned about the legal issues of an alleged criminal incident. The NCVS does not collect data from police agencies, prosecutors, or courts. So there is no way to know whether the crime actually happened or whether the alleged offenders were actually arrested, convicted, or sentenced. Instead, this survey collects information about the relationship between the victim and the offender, the characteristics of the offender (if known), self-protection actions taken by the victim during the incident, whether the offender used a weapon, and other descriptive information about the victim.

The NCVS categorizes crimes that are reported by victims, though in a less formal way than the UCR. The NCVS differentiates between personal crimes (rape and sexual attack, robbery, aggravated and simple assault, and purse-snatching/pocket-picking) and property crimes (burglary, theft, motor vehicle theft, and vandalism). But it does not require respondents to use stringent legal definitions when identifying crimes that have been committed against them. For example, if a woman reports that her purse was stolen, it might be classified as a purse-snatching, a robbery (if the offender used a weapon or stole the purse by force), or a burglary (if the purse was taken from the woman's home). How the crime is classified really depends on how much information the victim provides to the survey taker and how the victim defines the incident.

Getting to the Point 10.8 – Defining and measuring concepts is especially important in survey research. Concepts and measures should be consistent throughout the survey research process. More importantly, survey researchers must be sure that the respondents interpret the concepts and measures as they were intended to be understood. This is normally done during a preliminary test of the survey instrument.

Design a Method

At this stage of the research process, survey researchers actually make decisions regarding the format and style of the survey. In a previous section, we discussed four basic survey formats, of which researchers usually select one. Again, the format chosen depends on the researcher's objectives, the research context and the respondents targeted.

Regardless of the survey format chosen, researchers spend a great deal of time developing good survey questions. Indeed, good questions are the heart of an effective survey since poorly constructed questions will produce invalid data. There are three things to consider when writing effective survey questions. First, you should avoid confusion. That is, questions should be written as simply and as clearly as possible. For example, instead of asking *"How many times within an average calendar month do you leave your house for the purposes of obtaining sustenance for yourself or your family?"*, you should just ask, *"About how many times do you go to the grocery store each month?"*

Second, you should consider the literacy, level of education, and experience of the typical respondent when writing questions. For example, if you want to know something about how survey respondents spend their money, you might ask the question differently depending on who you are surveying (see Table 10.4).

Table 10.4 Considering the Respondents' Literacy while Writing Survey Questions

TYPE OF RESPONDENT	EFFECTIVE QUESTIONS
Adults	About what percent of your income is spent on discretionary purchases?
Teenagers	Considering the money you earn, about what percent of it is spent on things like movies, video games and things you want but don't really need?
Children	Do your parents give you money, such as an allowance? If so, how much of that money do you spend on things like candy, soda and toys?

Finally, you should follow the rules of mutual exclusivity and exhaustiveness when writing the response sets for your questions. Again, by **mutually exclusive**, we mean that every question must have one and only one response for every respondent. For example, many survey researchers want to know how old their respondents are. The following response set is not mutually exclusive because respondents who are 25, 40, or 55 years of age could legitimately select more than one box:

Check the box beside the range of ages that you fit into (check only one box)
- ☐ *Below 18 years of age*
- ☐ *18–25 years of age*
- ☐ *25–40 years of age*
- ☐ *40–55 years of age*
- ☐ *55 years of age or older*

This is easy to fix by making a minor adjustment to the age ranges:

Check the box beside the range of ages that you fit into (check only one box)
- ☐ *Below 18 years of age*
- ☐ *18–25 years of age*
- ☐ *26–40 years of age*
- ☐ *41–55 years of age*
- ☐ *56 years of age or older*

Response sets should also include all possible responses. That is, they should be **exhaustive**. For example, many researchers want to know the level of education of respondents. The following response set is not exhaustive because individuals who do not have a high school degree or GED would not be able to legitimately respond to this question.

What is your level of education? (check only one box)
- ☐ *High school diploma or GED*
- ☐ *Two-year Associate's degree*
- ☐ *Four-year Bachelor's degree*
- ☐ *Graduate or professional degree*

Again, this is an easy fix. By adding "Less than high school diploma or GED" to the response set, you would ensure that your response set is exhaustive:

What is your level of education? (check only one box)
- ☐ *Less than high school diploma or GED*
- ☐ *High school diploma or GED*
- ☐ *Two-year Associate's degree*
- ☐ *Four-year Bachelor's degree*
- ☐ *Graduate or professional degree*

> **Getting to the Point 10.9** – In general, survey questions should be written clearly and at a level that is appropriate for the respondent's level of education and experience. In addition, survey researchers should adhere to the rules of mutual exclusivity and exhaustiveness when writing response sets.

Beyond these general considerations, there are a few things researchers should avoid when writing survey questions. First, they should avoid using jargon, slang, and uncommon abbreviations. Consider this question: *"Are the officers that work for the SO generally courteous?"* Many people do not know that 'SO' stands for 'Sheriff's Office.' It would be better to just ask, *"In general, are the officers that work for the Sheriff's Office courteous?"*

Second, researchers should avoid using opinionated or emotional language. Here is an example of an opinionated and emotionally charged question. *"Should a Christian nation such as ours allow the death penalty?"* Not all respondents will be Christian and there are some people who might object to describing our county as 'Christian.' It would be better to simply ask, *"Do you think that our nation should allow the death penalty?"*

Third, survey researchers should avoid asking double-barreled questions. **Double-barreled questions** are two questions in one. Here is an example. *"Indicate whether you agree with the following statement: In order to reduce crime, we should spend more money on education and social services."* What if the respondent believes that we should spend more money on education and less on social services, or more money on social services and less on education? In this case, the question should be split into two separate questions – one about educational spending and another about social service spending.

Fourth, researchers should avoid prestige bias. **Prestige bias** occurs when a question refers to authoritative information that might influence a respondent's answer. Say we asked a respondent whether he or she agrees with the following statement: *"Experts are right that routine police patrols are not an effective crime control strategy."* A respondent is more likely to agree with this statement because it includes the phrase "experts are right." It would be better to simply ask the respondent to agree or disagree with the following statement: *"Routine police patrols are not an effective crime control strategy."*

Fifth, it may seem obvious, but survey researchers should never ask a question that the respondents are unable to answer. For example, if a researcher asked *"Are gangs now worse than they were in the 1960s?"* the respondent would have to know something about how bad gangs are now, as well as how bad they were in the 1960s. The average respondent would not know this information. It would be better to simply ask respondents whether they agree with this statement: *"From my perspective, gangs are worse today than they were in the past."*

Finally, researchers should avoid asking leading questions. **Leading questions** are questions that lead a respondent to answer in a certain way, such as: *"Police* *officers generally make you feel comfortable when you ask them for help, don't they?"* The phrasing of this question will probably lead the respondent to answer *yes.* A better way to ask this question would be, *"Do police officers make you feel comfortable when you ask them for help?"* Table 10.5 summarizes the issues that survey researchers should consider while writing questions.

> **Getting to the Point 10.10** – Survey questions and statements should not contain jargon, slang, uncommon abbreviations, emotional language, and prestige bias. In addition, survey researchers should avoid asking double-barreled and leading questions. Finally, survey questions should be 'answerable.'

Table 10.5   Considerations for Writing Survey Questions

CONSIDERATION	OBJECTIVE
Avoid confusion	Questions should be written as simply as possible so that the vast majority of the respondents will likely understand them.
The literacy of the respondents	Questions should be written to the lowest reading comprehension level that exists within the sample of respondents.
Mutual exclusivity	Response sets (if used) should be written so that each respondent has one and only one answer to a question or statement.
Exhaustive	Response sets (if used) should be written so that each respondent has an option. This may require the use of an 'other' category.
Avoid jargon, slang, and uncommon abbreviations	It should not be assumed that survey respondents will be familiar with terms that may be commonly used by individuals (including researchers) within a particular industry or social group.
Avoid opinionated or emotional language	Questions should not prejudice a respondent's answer.
Avoid double-barreled questions	Questions should ask one and only one thing.
Avoid prestige bias	Questions should not include phrases that suggest the answer is 'already known' by more informed people.
Avoid questions that the respondent is likely unable to answer	Questions should not assume that the respondents have prior or detailed knowledge about a particular issue.
Avoid leading questions	Questions should not include, within them, the answer or an 'obvious' answer.

In addition to the stylistic rules for writing survey questions there are some important mechanical issues that survey researchers should consider when developing their instruments. When writing survey questions, researchers should pay careful attention to **response sets**, which are the ways in which the respondent is allowed to answer a question or respond to a statement. **Direct response sets** allow the respondent to enter specific information into a blank space or box. For example, *"What is your age (in years)?"* allows the respondent to enter his or her age directly onto the survey instrument. Direct response questions are ideal for variables that are measured at the interval or ratio levels, like weight and income. They can also be used for nominal variables whose attributes are well known to the respondent (e.g. gender).

Open response sets also allow respondents to write their own responses to questions, but in a less structured way. An example might be: *"In your opinion, what is the most pressing problem facing our country today?"* Open response sets are useful to survey researchers who want to learn about an emerging social trend or when the range of possible answers is not predictable. Although more difficult to analyze, the responses to these questions often provide robust information.

Finally, **closed-** or **forced-choice response sets** can be used to specify a standard set of responses from which the respondent must choose. Closed- or forced-choice response sets are ideal when the researcher wants to standardize the responses. Here is an example of a forced-choice response set.

What is your race? (Check one of the boxes below)

- ☐ *White*
- ☐ *African American or Black*
- ☐ *Asian or Pacific Islander*
- ☐ *Native American*
- ☐ *Other*

Many closed response sets ask respondents to respond using a rating scale. For example, a researcher might ask survey respondents to indicate the extent to which they agree or disagree with the statement: *"People who murder children should receive the death penalty."* And the response set might be: *"Circle 1 for strongly disagree, 2 for disagree, 3 for neither disagree nor agree, 4 for agree, or 5 for strongly agree."* This type of a rating scale is known as a Likert scale. Often, survey researchers will ask respondents to indicate their level of agreement/disagreement with multiple statements on a particular subject. In these cases, the researcher can create a **composite index number** consisting of the sum of the numerical responses. In this case, a respondent with a higher composite index number would be more in agreement with the statements and vice versa for lower composite index numbers.

You may have noticed that the response set above includes a neutral category 'neither agree nor disagree.' In some survey research, a neutral category is helpful; in others, it is not. Neutral responses are appropriate if you want to measure the level of ambivalence about a particular issue. This is like a 'no opinion' response and would indicate that this particular issue is not very important to that respondent. Alternatively, you might want to force the respondents to take a position either for or against a particular issue. In this case, you would not use the neutral category. You may have also noticed in the response set above that there were five possible responses. Some closed or forced response sets contain only three responses – *Agree*, *Neither Agree nor Disagree*, and *Disagree*. The number of possible responses depends on the researcher's analytical needs. Some researchers want more detail than others. As a practical limit, you should not go over 10 possible responses. Consider the following example:

Using the scale provided, respond to the following statements regarding your experience in this class (circle your response).

	Strongly agree									Strongly disagree
Statements										
This class was interesting.	10	9	8	7	6	5	4	3	2	1
The tests were fair.	10	9	8	7	6	5	4	3	2	1
I would recommend this course to my friends.	10	9	8	7	6	5	4	3	2	1
The exams were unfair.	10	9	8	7	6	5	4	3	2	1
The book and reading materials were boring.	10	9	8	7	6	5	4	3	2	1
I would take another class taught by this professor.	10	9	8	7	6	5	4	3	2	1

Some of the statements in the response set above are written in opposite directions. For example, one statement reads, *"The tests were fair."* In contrast, another statement reads, *"The exams were unfair."* These opposite format questions are called **reversals**. Reversals are used to measure the respondents' attentiveness while responding to the statements. Ideally, a respondent that responded *strongly agree* with the first statement would respond *strongly disagree* with the second statement. If not, it may indicate that the respondent did not commit the time necessary to read and respond to the questions carefully.

> **Getting to the Point 10.11** –There are three basic types of response sets. Direct response sets allow the respondent to enter specific information into a blank space or box. Open response sets also allow respondents to write their own responses to questions, but are more open to interpretation than direct response sets. Closed- or forced-choice response sets specify a standard set of responses from which the respondent must choose.

When designing a survey, researchers should pay attention to the ordering of questions. In general, the questions that are most central to the purpose of the survey should be placed at the beginning of the survey. This is the point in time when the respondent is most motivated, and therefore most likely to be paying attention. Putting these questions at the beginning also helps set the tone of the survey. Questions that are easier for the respondents to answer (e.g., age) should be placed near the end, since this is the point at which respondents have grown tired of questions and are therefore less likely to put thought into their answers. There are exceptions to these rules. For questions that are particularly controversial or sensitive, it might be more advantageous to begin the survey with some easy questions and lead up to the questions that have the potential to offend or upset the respondents. In short, the ordering of survey questions is as much art as it is science. In the final analysis, this is best worked out during a preliminary test of the survey instrument.

Instructions are critical to good survey design. The researcher should not assume that the respondent will just 'figure it out.' Surveys should begin with an introduction that provides information about the purpose, sponsorship, and intended use of the survey. This is also the place where the researcher informs respondents about whether their responses are anonymous or confidential and asks for the respondents' voluntary informed consent to participate. The survey should also include specific instructions that assist the respondent with completing the instrument. Phrases like, *"Using the scale provided," "Check all that apply,"* and *"Circle the best response"* are common instructions. Finally, many surveys, especially mail surveys, conclude with instructions on how to return the survey.

A final consideration in survey design is length. Generally speaking, a survey should never be longer than it has to be. Once the researcher has asked enough questions to test his or her hypotheses or research questions, the survey should end. You should resist the urge to 'just add a few more questions' to a survey. Of course there are exceptions, but the longer the survey, the less likely the respondent will participate.

Getting to the Point 10.12 – Question order, survey instructions, and survey length are critical considerations in survey design. In general, the most challenging and important questions should be placed at the beginning of a survey and the least challenging questions should be placed near the end. Surveys should include an introduction to the survey, specific instructions for answering each question, and concluding instructions on how to return the survey. In terms of length, shorter surveys are better than longer surveys since longer surveys tend to reduce the respondent's willingness to complete the survey.

Once a survey instrument is fully developed, the researcher should conduct a preliminary test to see if it functions as intended. Even the most attentive and well-informed survey researcher will ask a bad question once in a while. **Pretesting** is like a dress rehearsal for a survey. The objective is to test the survey instrument in an environment and with a group of people that closely approximates the actual conditions under which the survey will be taken. A sample of 6 to 12 representative respondents should suffice. Again, the objective here is not to collect actual data, but to determine whether these respondents understand and progress through the survey as you intended them to. The important questions to ask during this process are as follows:

- Are all of the instructions clear and understandable?

- Is the survey instrument easy to use?

- Are the questions written so that the respondents will understand them?

- Are there attributes missing from response sets or that are not mutually exclusive?

- Will this instrument produce the kind of data needed to answer the research question(s)?

Getting to the Point 10.13 – A preliminary test of the survey instrument in an environment and with a small representative group of respondents is essential for ensuring the success of a survey instrument. The purpose of this step is to determine whether the respondents will understand the survey and whether the survey instrument will produce the kind of data necessary to answer the research question(s).

Developing the Method 10.6 – Designing a Method in Survey Research

When the UCR program was being developed, decisions around methodology were heavily influenced by a specially appointed committee of experts and practitioners from the International Association of Chiefs of Police and later the National Sheriff's Association. Before it was officially launched, the program pretested its survey methods through demonstration projects involving a few reporting agencies. With respect to design, the early years of the program had participating agencies using paper forms to tabulate and report the number of crimes reported and arrests made. These paper forms are no longer used. Instead, state-level clearinghouses collect data from the reporting agencies electronically and transmit it in summary form to the national clearinghouse each quarter and again at the end of each calendar year.

The NIBRS began as a pilot project in 1988 involving only one agency, namely the South Carolina Law Enforcement Division. Once the 'bugs' were worked out of the reporting system, the program was expanded. As of 2007, 6,444 agencies contribute data to the NIBRS program. Collectively, these agencies represent about 25 percent of the United States population.

The original design of the NCVS program, which began in 1972, was developed by the National Opinion Research Center and the President's Commission on Law Enforcement and the Administration of Justice. Like the UCR and NIBRS systems, this program was pilot tested before it was fully implemented. The NCVS has always relied upon a telephone survey to collect its data. Crime victims are more likely to be accessible and more likely to share their information via the telephone than on a paper survey. Though face-to-face interviews with crime victims would be ideal, they are too expensive to make them feasible in this case.

Over the years, the United States Congress has asked the UCR and NCVS to expand its data collection to include new crimes, identify emerging crime patterns, and collect data on politically sensitive crimes. In the early 1990s, for example, the UCR began collecting data on crime occurring on university and college campuses. Later, the UCR was asked to collect information on hate crimes. Likewise, the NCVS has expanded its reach to include school violence and attitudes about crime or the police. In every case, program administrators pilot tested the changes they made to their reporting systems well before they were implemented.

Collect the Data

At this stage of the research process, actual data collection commences. The manner in which a survey is distributed depends on its format. Mail surveys are mailed. Internet surveys are published on a website. Telephone surveys are conducted using randomly selected telephone numbers. And interviews are scheduled with the respondents at a specific time and place. As a general rule, a survey should be distributed at a time when most respondents are well informed about a topic. In addition, the researcher should avoid conducting a survey when events are occurring that might affect the respondent's opinion. Historical events, public controversies, natural disasters, and even the season can affect survey responses and response rates. For example, a survey on perceptions of police brutality may produce skewed results if it is distributed after a high-profile case involving police brutality. As well, a survey distributed during the Christmas season is unlikely to produce a high response rate.

The value of a survey depends on the number of respondents who actually respond to it. So it is really important to make sure the **response rate** is as high as possible. Survey researchers can affect the response rate in one of several ways. First, they can choose the best survey format for the population they are targeting. Some populations will respond more readily to a telephone survey than a mail survey, and vice versa. Second, there is just no substitute for good questions. Respondents are busy people and they typically have little patience for poorly written surveys. If they do not understand the questions, they will disengage pretty quickly.

To improve response rates, some survey researchers will send out postcards a few days before the actual survey is distributed. These mailings inform respondents that a survey is on its way and ask for their assistance in filling it out when it arrives. Some researchers also send out reminder cards about a week later to remind the respondents to complete the survey. Another strategy to improve the response rate is to make things as easy as possible for the respondent to return the survey. For example, respondents are more likely to send back a completed survey when a pre-addressed and postage paid envelope is provided than if you ask them to find their own envelope and stamp. Finally, some researchers use incentives to improve response rates. For example, they may include a dollar, a coupon or some other material to increase a respondent's likelihood of responding. I once got a survey with a dollar bill in it as a "small gift to you for completing our survey." I tossed the survey and pocketed the dollar bill. But, later that night, I felt guilty, retrieved the survey from the trash, filled it out and sent it back.

Developing the Method 10.7 – Collecting Data in Survey Research

Because both the UCR and NCVS are ongoing, surveys implementation is constant. Nearly every state has a staff of UCR field representatives who are assigned to assist agencies with reporting the requested data. These field representatives are often part of each state's criminal history records repositories and are paid by the state government. They conduct regular training for the reporting agencies to ensure they comply with the current reporting rules. And each quarter, they compile the information from the reporting agencies and transmit these data to the UCR headquarters. Though participation in the UCR has always been voluntary, all but a few agencies participate since most law enforcement agencies understand the importance of collecting data on crime. Many states have gone so far as to enact statutes or administrative rules to compel agencies to participate. Thus, ensuring a good response rate is less of an issue in the case of the UCR.

In the case of the NCVS, there are no reporting agencies to communicate with since this survey is administered to a random sample of U.S. households. Each year, the NCVS collects victimization data from a representative sample of about 76,000 households, representing approximately 135,000 persons throughout the nation. The NCVS must draw a comparatively large sample because crime is a relatively rare event. As we learned in a previous chapter, when events occur rarely within a population, sample sizes must be large enough to ensure enough cases. In recent years, the NCVS has recognized that an increasing number of people do not have a landline telephone, especially younger people who tend to have higher criminal victimization rates. This has caused some concern over sampling bias since collecting victimization data from cell phone users is becoming increasingly difficult.

Getting to the Point 10.14 – The response to a survey can be improved by appropriately timing when the survey is administered, asking well designed questions, sending reminder post cards, and providing incentives to encourage the respondents to answer.

Analyze the Data

Unless survey responses are entered directly into a database, as in the case of an Internet survey, the researcher will need a system of entering the responses from the survey into a database. We refer to this process as **coding**. Efficient and accurate coding of survey responses begins during the development of the survey instrument. Consider the question below that was used as an example earlier in this chapter.

Using the scale provided, respond to the following statements regarding your experience in this class (circle your response).

	Strongly agree									Strongly disagree
Statements										
This class was interesting.$_1$	10	9	8	7	6	5	4	3	2	1
The tests were fair.$_2$	10	9	8	7	6	5	4	3	2	1
I would recommend this course to my friends.$_2$	10	9	8	7	6	5	4	3	2	1
The exams were unfair.$_4$	10	9	8	7	6	5	4	3	2	1
The book and reading materials were boring.$_5$	10	9	8	7	6	5	4	3	2	1
I would take another class taught by this professor.$_6$	10	9	8	7	6	5	4	3	2	1

Do you notice the numerical subscripts after each statement (e.g., *This class was interesting.*$_1$)? Here, the number 1 would also appear in the data entry screen on the computer, typically at the top of a column in an Excel file. This indicates the spot where the respondent's responses should be recorded. This is easier than writing the actual question in the data entry screen. The responses that are entered into this column would also be numerical, ranging from 10 for *Strongly agree* to 1 for *Strongly disagree*. Because surveys are often confidential or anonymous, most surveys contain a serially assigned document number. In mail surveys, this number is often written at the top of the first page. Numbering surveys with a unique identifier allows the researcher to find and correct possible mistakes caused by coding errors.

Once the survey data have been entered, you can use statistical software programs to analyze the data. Often the first step in the analysis phase is to simply report averages and variations. This is usually done with means, medians, modes, ranges, and standard deviations. For example, the researcher may calculate the average income and level of education among the survey respondents. Most survey researchers are also interested in how variables are related to one another. For example, a survey researcher may want to calculate the correlation between income and education. This is usually done using a **Pearson *r*** correlation, or in the case of ordinal variables, a **Spearman rho**. Some survey researchers use *t*-tests and **analyses of variance** to test the differences between groups of survey respondents. For example, a researcher may use a *t*-test to determine if the income levels between the citizens of two communities are significantly different. Higher order statistical techniques like multiple regression and logistic regression are also common analytical techniques used by survey researchers. During the analysis phase, you should focus primarily on answering your original research question(s). But you may also find opportunities for additional analysis. For information on these statistical techniques refer to Chapter 14.

Developing the Method 10.8 – Analyzing Data in Survey Research

The most well-known statistic available from the UCR is the crime rate, sometimes called the index crime rate. A crime rate is calculated for each type of crime and for different categories of crime. Crime rates are calculated by using the following formula:

$$\frac{Number\ of\ reported\ crimes\ for\ each\ category}{The\ population\ of\ the\ community \times 100,000}$$

The index crime rate for a community, county, region, state, or the nation is always expressed in the UCR program as the number of crimes per 100,000 residents. This provides a standard measure of criminal activity. So if there were 400 aggravated assaults in a community with a population of 200,000, the crime rate for aggravated assault in that community would be 200 per 100,000 residents that year. The NCVS calculates a similar crime rate from the data it collects from a sample of U.S. households.

As the formula above suggests, a change in the crime rate can occur as a result of either a change in the number of reported crimes or a change in the community's population. If both the number of crimes and the population increase, the crime rate might actually remain constant. And if a community's population increases dramatically while the number of crimes remains constant, it might appear that crime is decreasing when it is not. The opposite might also happen; a decreasing population with a stable number of crimes might register elevated crime rates. In situations like these, survey researchers would enter explanatory footnotes next to their results to document the reasons for a change in the crime rate.

Remember that in the UCR program, there is no relationship between the number of crimes reported and the number of arrests. An agency may receive a report of an aggravated assault one year but not make an arrest for that particular assault until the next, if at all. Reporting agencies simply report the number of crimes reported and the number of arrests made that year. Even so, these two variables are used to create a statistic called the clearance rate. If an agency reports receiving 100 aggravated assault cases, but made only 50 arrests for aggravated assault that year, it would have a clearance rate of 50 percent for that year. An uninformed individual may conclude that the agency only solves half of its aggravated assaults. On occasion, an agency reports that it arrests more people for a particular crime than it received reports for that crime. In this case, the agency would have a clearance rate higher than 100 percent and it may appear that the department is solving crimes that have not even been reported! This is a statistical anomaly that cannot be corrected under the current UCR reporting rules. This is one of the reasons that the UCR program created the NIBRS program, which is incident based.

Getting to the Point 10.15 – The use of subscripts on written survey instruments enhances accuracy during the data entry phase. This is known as coding the data. Once data are entered, researchers can use various statistical techniques to analyze survey data.

Interpret the Results

At this stage, the researcher will want to interpret the data and information arising from the survey. This is often more art than science. Calculating a statistic is one thing. Explaining what it means is another. The focus in this stage should be on answering the research question or questions as comprehensively as possible. For example, say you want to know whether sexual promiscuity is related to illegal drug use among juveniles. Your survey results suggest a high correlation between the two variables. But before you conclude that the two variables are related, you should revisit how these two concepts were measured, how each of the measures for your variables are related, and how strong your findings are. It is not uncommon for a researcher to learn during the interpretation phase that a survey did not produce the data necessary to fully answer a research question. Even if a survey is thoroughly planned and pretested, sometimes it just does not work.

Sometimes, discussing what a survey does not say is just as valuable as discussing what a survey does say. Reporting the limitations of your study is critical to helping others interpret your results. Indeed, the most common interpretative mistake survey researchers make is overreaching their data. Say, for example, that your survey reveals that children raised in single-parent households are more likely to participate in delinquent behavior. In this case, you might allege that a lack of parental supervision causes juvenile delinquency. But just because two variables are related does not mean that one is the cause of another. Surveys, particularly **cross-sectional** surveys, or surveys taken at one point in time, are unable to establish a causal link between variables because they are not able to determine temporal order or eliminate plausible alternative explanations. So interpreting these results as evidence of a causal link is an overreach. Instead, you should report the relationship, but caution that this finding should not be read as evidence of a causal link.

Developing the Method 10.9 – Interpreting the Results of Survey Research

Neither the UCR nor the NCVS is designed to measure crime quickly. There is often a substantial time lag between when the data are reported to the clearinghouses and when the data are published. And, often, the final results are not published until well into the following year. As such, the UCR and NCVS data are best suited for tracking crime over time.

Remember, too, that the UCR program only collects information on crimes reported. Likewise, the NCVS program only collects information on criminal victimization. Alone, each data set has its limitations. As a result, many practitioners and scholars use UCR and NCVS in combination. Together, these two surveys produce a powerful measure of crime nationwide. In some years, the UCR reports an overall decrease in crime while the NCVS reports an overall increase in victimization, or vice versa. But other times, these two broad measures of crime report the same trend. Over time, these similar findings lend credibility to each other. With rare exceptions, both the UCR and NCVS have reported decreases in reported crime and criminal victimization since the early 1990s. Taken together, these independent surveys allow criminologists to be more confident in concluding that crime has been on the decrease for well over two decades.

There are other limitations to the UCR and NCVS data sets. The NCVS only measures crime at the national level, whereas the UCR calculates a crime rate for each community and state that participates in the program. The NCVS includes information on a broader range of criminal victimization, whereas the UCR limits its analysis to certain types of crime. The UCR collects additional administrative information from participating agencies, such as the number of sworn and non-sworn personnel employed by each participating agency. In sum, the UCR and NCVS each answer particular questions about crime, but not all questions about crime that we might be interested in asking.

Getting to the Point 10.16 – The interpretation of survey results is often more art than science. The focus of the interpretation should be on answering the research question(s) as comprehensively as possible. To fully interpret survey results, researchers should consider the limitations of their data.

Communicate the Findings

In previous chapters, you learned how difficult it is for social science researchers to measure the concepts they are interested in studying. Concepts like delinquency and even crime are often very difficult to measure. Measurements that might make sense to one researcher might not make sense to another. So survey researchers spend a lot of time describing and defending their measurements to others. And measurement in this case is critical because it determines the validity of your findings and the strength of your conclusions.

Let us consider an example. Say you hypothesize that poverty is related to juvenile delinquency. You define poverty as an inability to procure basic necessities (e.g., shelter, food, and clothing). You measure poverty as earning less than the poverty rate. You define delinquency as any criminal act committed by a juvenile and measure it by the number of convictions occurring before a respondent's 18th birthday. Your research reveals a correlation between these two variables. But what about rich suburban kids who commit crimes but avoid conviction because they can afford good legal representation? In this case, a peer reviewer might have a legitimate issue with your measurements. Of course, it might be too late to fix the survey. But you can at least identify this as a possible limitation when reporting the results of the survey.

In addition to detailing the research methodology and survey instrument, survey research reports often include a table that describes the respondents in terms of demographic features like gender, age, and education. Descriptive tables like this help establish the context of the research. For example, if the researcher reports that the average age of the respondents is 25 years and that the respondents range in age from 15 to 32 years, we know that the results of the survey are only relevant to a young population. Once descriptive information is conveyed, survey reports typically turn to reporting results from various statistical tests. Tables are extremely useful here, but graphs are also effective at communicating results.

The decision about where to report the results of a survey really depend on the intentions of the researcher. Academic researchers often write up their findings in academic articles that they submit to scholarly journals. In large part, this is because our work performance is evaluated by how many articles we publish in a year. Practitioners tend to publish their survey results in trade journals or internal publications. Generally speaking, scholarly audiences demand more complicated and higher order statistical analyses. Practitioner audiences prefer more succinct reports that rely more on tables, charts, and graphs.

Developing the Method 10.10 – Communicating the Findings from Survey Research

Both the UCR and NCVS programs publish annual reports. The UCR publication, *Crime in the United States*, is widely circulated. You often see news articles in local newspapers pick up on this information. Publication of the NCVS report is not as well publicized. Normally the results are released electronically. Both programs provide researchers access to their data and methodologies. Data from both programs are used sporadically throughout the year to demonstrate the current state of crime or trends over a period of years.

Because of their influence on criminal justice policy, both the UCR and NCVS reports are subjected to extensive internal editing prior to their publication. Information provided to the UCR by participating agencies, for example, is evaluated numerous times at the local, state, and federal levels. Although neither report is subjected to a traditional peer review process, they are both extensively fact checked. Occasionally mistakes are made. And more than a few police chiefs have complained of errors in the UCR data when their mayors and city council members use it to question the effectiveness of the local police department.

Getting to the Point 10.17 – The most important part of a survey research report is the section wherein the researcher describes, in detail, the method by which he or she conducted the research. Survey research reports also typically include a table that describes the survey respondents and tables and graphs that report the results of any statistical tests. The decision about where to report the results of a survey depends on the intentions of the researcher and the audience he or she would like to reach.

FINAL THOUGHTS

Several years ago I was asked to help a police department develop a citizens' survey, which is a fairly common survey in the field of criminal justice. The patrol sergeant I was assisting explained that the department was not so much interested in how citizens perceived the police, as it was in the extent to which citizens feared crime. As he described it, crime had actually been decreasing in his community, but citizens continued to complain about relatively minor criminal incidents like graffiti, vandalism, and loitering. The department was concerned that if citizens were fearful of crime, they might not interact with neighbors, participate in community life, and otherwise help ensure a strong social fabric that would prevent more serious crimes from happening.

The sergeant and I developed some questions that measured how fearful the citizens were of crime in his community. And to my surprise, we learned that despite a very low crime rate, most of the citizens in this community were quite fearful of criminal victimization. When they saw graffiti or heard about vandalism from their neighbors, they internalized these events and developed a fear of being a victim of crime. Using this information, the department created several outreach programs designed to make citizens aware of crime and to teach them how to reduce the potential for victimization. Police officers delivered 'crime prevention talks' at community meetings and encouraged citizens to take a more active role in their own protection. The local hardware store sold out of deadbolt locks and the local electrician installed a record number of yard lights. The department developed a reverse 911 system that informed citizens of community threats. In short, this simple survey assisted the department in developing a community-based approach to crime prevention that was quite effective. And it is a great illustration of the value of survey research to scholars and practitioners alike.

GETTING TO THE POINT/CHAPTER SUMMARY

- Surveys are a data collection method wherein individuals or groups are asked to respond to questions and/or statements. This method involves developing an instrument, which the researcher uses to ask questions and record answers. The individuals or groups that respond to the survey are referred to as respondents.

- There are four general types of survey formats: mail surveys, internet surveys, telephone surveys, and interviews. Each format has its advantages and disadvantages. The format chosen depends on the researcher's objectives, the research context, and the respondents targeted.

- Survey research is effective for developing community or group profiles; learning how people behave; measuring attitudes, beliefs, and opinions; determining levels of knowledge; and predicting future trends and patterns.

- Survey research is not effective for determining causal relationships between variables and measuring complicated or unknown social phenomena. Surveys should not be used when the honesty of the respondents is important to the research and their responses cannot be independently verified. It is often difficult to determine the validity of a concept or construct measured through a survey response.

- Generally speaking, surveys are effective for describing a particular group or sub-population, a particular set of behaviors and beliefs, and/or a particular relationship between variables.

- In addition to the usual information researchers look for when conducting a literature review, survey researchers should pay particular attention to how previous researchers defined similar concepts, measured key variables, and designed survey instruments.

- Because most surveys are intended for descriptive and exploratory research, hypotheses that predict causal relationships between variables are not usually found in survey research. Instead, survey researchers develop hypotheses that predict relationships between variables and/or refine research questions about particular phenomena.

- Defining and measuring concepts is especially important in survey research. Concepts and measures should be consistent throughout the survey research process. More importantly, survey researchers must be sure that the respondents interpret the concepts and measures as they were intended to be understood. This is normally done during a preliminary test of the survey instrument.

- In general, survey questions should be written clearly and at a level that is appropriate for the respondent's level of education and experience. In addition, survey researchers should adhere to the rules of mutual exclusivity and exhaustiveness when writing response sets.

- Survey questions and statements should not contain jargon, slang, uncommon abbreviations, emotional language, and prestige bias. In addition, survey researchers should avoid asking double-barreled and leading questions. Finally, survey questions should be 'answerable.'

- There are three basic types of response sets. Direct response sets allow the respondent to enter specific information into a blank space or box. Open response sets also allow respondents to write their own responses to questions, but are more open to interpretation than direct response sets. Closed- or forced-choice response sets specify a standard set of responses from which the respondent must choose.

- Question order, survey instructions, and survey length are critical considerations in survey design. In general, the most challenging and important questions should be placed at the beginning of a survey and the least challenging questions should be placed near the end. Surveys should include an introduction to the survey, specific instructions for answering each question, and concluding instructions on how to return the survey. In terms of length, shorter surveys are better than longer surveys since longer surveys tend to reduce the respondent's willingness to complete the survey.

- A preliminary test of the survey instrument in an environment and with a small representative group of respondents is essential for ensuring the success of a survey instrument. The purpose of this step is to determine whether the respondents will understand the survey and whether the survey instrument will produce the kind of data necessary to answer the research question(s).

- The response to a survey can be improved by appropriately timing when the survey is administered, asking well designed questions, sending reminder post cards, and providing incentives to encourage the respondents to answer.

- The use of subscripts on written survey instruments enhances accuracy during the data entry phase. This is known as coding the data. Once data are entered, researchers can use various statistical techniques to analyze survey data.

- The interpretation of survey results is often more art than science. The focus of the interpretation should be on answering the research question(s) as comprehensively as possible. To fully interpret survey results, researchers should consider the limitations of their data.

- The most important part of a survey research report is the section wherein the researcher describes, in detail, the method by which he or she conducted the research. Survey research reports also typically include a table that describes the survey respondents and tables and graphs that report the results of any statistical tests. The decision about where to report the results of a survey depends on the intentions of the researcher and the audience he or she would like to reach.

CHAPTER EXERCISES

The following chapter exercises are organized into two parts. The first part consists of questions that can be answered using the information from this chapter. This section will test your understanding of the chapter material. The second part consists of research application exercises. These exercises require you to apply what you have learned thus far.

CHAPTER REVIEW QUESTIONS

Respond to each of the following questions using the information from this chapter.

1. What is a survey instrument?
   a. A mechanical device used to determine whether a person is lying on a survey
   b. An analytic technique used to organize answers to particular survey questions
   c. The particular coding method that researchers use for inputting survey data
   d. The questionnaire or document that researchers use to collect survey data

2. Which of the following statements about survey research is accurate?
   a. Hypotheses are almost never developed in survey research.
   b. Individual beliefs can be captured through survey research.
   c. Literature reviews are rarely conducted in survey research.
   d. Surveys are an effective method for measuring cause and effect.

3. For each research scenario below, determine which survey format(s) – mail survey, internet survey, telephone survey, or interview – would be most appropriate.

Research scenario	Survey format(s)
A survey researcher wants to ensure respondents complete anonymity and to avoid any bias that might result from the interaction between respondent and researcher.	
A survey researcher wants to increase response rates and to adjust the wording of survey questions depending on how the respondent understands the questions.	
A survey researcher wants the maximum response rate but might need to provide the respondents with visual images to explain questions.	
A survey researcher wants to reach respondents from different nations and to provide respondents surveys written in the language with which they are most comfortable.	

4. For each survey question below, identify why the question is poorly worded or problematic. The reasons can include: jargon or uncommon abbreviations, emotional language, double-barreled question, prestige bias, respondents' inability to answer, or leading question.

Research question	Problem(s)
Given that crime is such a serious problem in our community, would you agree that taxes should be raised to hire additional police officers?	
Do you think that C.O.P. is a promising crime control strategy in policing?	
In your opinion, should the state legislature increase criminal penalties and remove amenities like cable television from state prisons?	
Do you agree that murderers of children should receive the death penalty for their heinous crime?	
In your opinion, are drug buy/bust operations effective at reducing illegal drug distribution?	
Do you believe that children raised by single parents are more likely to commit crimes, as most experts would contend?	

5. Determine if the following survey questions involve a direct response set, an open response set, or a closed/forced-choice response set.

Survey question	Type of response set
In fifty words or less, describe what you think is the most pressing problem facing criminal justice today.	
What is your age in years?	
What is your race? (Check one of the boxes below) ☐ White ☐ African American or Black ☐ Asian or Pacific Islander ☐ Native American ☐ Other	

6. A researcher develops a survey to measure citizens' perceptions of the police. In one segment of the survey, respondents are asked to indicate their level of agreement or disagreement with a series of statements about the police. Some statements are written so that respondents who perceive the police favorably will agree with the statement; others are written so that respondents who perceive the police favorably will disagree with the statement. In survey research, these opposite format questions are called:
   a. Annulments
   b. Flip-flops
   c. Negatives
   d. Reversals

7. Where should questions about a respondent's age, race, and gender be placed in a survey?
   a. At the beginning so the respondents can get comfortable with the survey
   b. In the middle so the respondents can rest before answering difficult questions
   c. At the end so the respondents have easy questions to answer when they are tired
   d. It does not matter where these questions are placed

8. Which of the following statements about survey length is most accurate?
   a. Longer surveys are better because they are more cost effective to produce.
   b. Shorter surveys are better because respondents are more likely to complete them.
   c. Longer surveys are best for telephone surveys, shorter surveys for mail surveys.
   d. Survey length is unimportant so long as each question is worded correctly.

9. The purpose of pretesting a survey instrument is to:
   a. Determine whether the respondents will understand and be able to respond to the questions on the survey
   b. Figure out how long most respondents will take to complete the survey and return it to researchers
   c. Prepare respondents for the real survey and get them thinking about their possible responses
   d. Provide proof to an Institutional Review Board that the survey will not harm respondents

10. Which of the following is *not* an effective technique for increasing the number of responses to a survey?
   a. Increasing the length of the survey
   b. Providing incentives to complete the survey
   c. Sending out reminder postcards
   d. Timing the survey appropriately

RESEARCH APPLICATION EXERCISES

Access to the following articles will be provided by your instructor.

> Durham, A.M., Elrod, H.P. and Kinkade, P.T. (1996). Public support for the death penalty: Beyond Gallup. *Justice Quarterly, 13*(4), 705–736.
>
> Lutze, F.E. (1998). Are shock incarceration programs more rehabilitative than traditional prisons? A survey of inmates. *Justice Quarterly, 15*(3), 547–566.

Respond to the following questions for each of the articles cited above.

11. Why did the researcher(s) conduct this research? What did they hope to learn?

12. Would you classify this research as exploratory, descriptive, or explanatory? Explain.

13. Would you classify this research as pure or applied? Explain.

14. What survey format did the researcher(s) use? In your opinion, was this the most appropriate format to use? Why or why not?

15. What key concepts did the researchers use and how were they defined and measured in the survey?

16. Who were the survey respondents? And how did the researcher(s) try to improve the response rate?

17. What were the researcher(s)' key findings? In your opinion, did the researcher(s) overreach their conclusions?

18. How did the researcher(s) add to the body of knowledge on this subject? And how would you improve this research or conduct further research to expand this body of knowledge?

CHAPTER 11

Non-Reactive Research Methods

In Chapter 9 (Experimental Design Research Methods), you were introduced to a concept called reactivity. Reactivity occurs when research subjects change their behavior because they become aware that they are being watched or measured. To overcome this common threat to external validity, researchers may want to observe and measure the behavior of their research subjects in a natural setting. 'Natural setting' does not mean in the woods. It means observing how people behave normally in social situations.

To capture human behavior in natural settings, researchers have developed numerous **non-reactive research methodologies**. Non-reactive research is a collection of research methods that unobtrusively gather information from research subjects, that is, without their knowledge. Because the research subjects are unaware that they are being observed, they are less likely to change their behavior. Of course there are certain ethical considerations in this research method, but when done carefully, non-reactive research methods can add to the body of knowledge. We will start with an example from my personal research experience.

Making Research Real 11.1 – Who Buys Gasoline Here?

I am always hungry after teaching evening classes. I know that by the time I get home, everyone in the house will be asleep and, with a family as large as mine, there will not be leftovers from supper. So I often stop at a convenience store for a late night snack and sometimes a tank of gasoline. I have two choices of convenience stores: one near the university and another near my house. Both are part of the same chain and they are nearly identical in what they sell and how they are arranged.

Several years ago, while filling my tank at the store near the university, I noticed that the "Pay Inside Cash" button was noticeably worn while the "Pay Outside Credit/Debit" buttons were nearly unused. That evening, I looked at several of the other pumps and found that almost all of the "Pay Inside Cash" buttons were noticeably worn.

The following weekend, my family and I took a trip to the country. On the way, we stopped at the other convenience store, the one nearest my house. The wear on these buttons was the exact opposite from my previous observations at the other store. The "Pay Outside Credit/Debit" buttons were noticeably worn while the "Pay Inside Cash" buttons appeared to be unused. I deduced that customers at the store nearest the university were more likely to pay cash for their gasoline, whereas the customers at the store near my house paid mostly with credit and debit cards.

Never one to let a good observation go to waste, I shared my observations with my research methods students. They arrived at these hypotheses:

- The customers who shop at the store nearest the university are poor and therefore less likely to have access to debit and credit cards.

- The customers who shop at the store nearest my house are well off and therefore more likely to have access to debit and credit cards.

To test their hypotheses, I called the corporate office and spoke to a very nice person in Customer Relations. I informed him of my observations and of my students' hypotheses. He looked into it and called me back in a few days. It seems that we were right. The differences between the customers that frequent these two locations are quite profound, as we can see from the table below.

	STORE NEAR THE UNIVERSITY	STORE NEAR MY HOUSE
Tobacco sales	A higher percentage of single cigarette package and single cigar sales.	Fewer overall tobacco sales, but a higher percentage of carton cigarette and expensive cigar sales.
Beer and wine	A higher percentage of single can beer and less expensive wine sales. More malt liquor and wine cooler products.	A higher percentage of six-pack and case beer sales. More premium beer and higher priced wines.
Staffing	Higher levels of staffing because cash customers have to enter the store to complete their gasoline purchase.	Lower levels of staffing because credit/debit customers are not required to enter the store to purchase gasoline.

One might assume that the store nearest my house is the more profitable of the two. After all, this store serves a clientele that has more income for discretionary spending. But according to the customer relations person at the corporate headquarters, the store near the university is more profitable overall. As it turns out, convenience stores earn very little profit on gasoline sales. Most of their profit comes from inside sales, like the snacks I purchase on my way home from class. Customers who purchase gasoline at the pump (with a credit or debit card) are less likely to enter the store, and therefore less likely to make an additional inside purchase. Customers who pay with cash must enter the store and are more likely to make an additional purchase.

The findings from my informal research were based on a non-reactive measure. The research subjects (gasoline purchasers) were not aware that their behaviors had been observed when I first noticed the worn buttons on the gasoline pumps. I was 'observing' their behavior without their knowledge and drawing conclusions from my observations. In this chapter, I will discuss how researchers collect information without the knowledge of research subjects and use this information to understand various human behaviors and social phenomena.

Getting to the Point 11.1 – Non-reactive research is a collection of research methods that gather information from research subjects without their knowledge. Because the research subjects are unaware that they are being observed, they are less likely to change their behaviors. These techniques are effective for observing behavior in a natural setting.

NON-REACTIVE RESEARCH METHODS BASICS

Again, non-reactive research is any research process that allows a researcher to gather information on research subjects without their express knowledge or permission. These methods are often described by the kinds of data that they produce. For example, one way to observe human behavior indirectly is to study the **physical traces** that are left behind. Physical traces are sources of evidence that are based on products of past behavior. There are two ways of measuring physical traces: accretion and erosion. An **accretion measure** determines behavior by evaluating the things people possess. For example, a careful observation of the contents of a trashcan might reveal a research subject's eating, spending, and/or social habits. An **erosion measure** determines behavior by evaluating how things are used by people. For example, a worn grassy area caused by pedestrian traffic might suggest the need for an additional sidewalk. Likewise, the worn buttons on a gasoline pump might suggest something about the clientele of convenience stores.

Other non-reactive techniques seek to capture data, but to capture it in an unobtrusive way. The most prominent technique in this regard is **unobtrusive observation**, which is simply observing behavior without being noticed. For example, a researcher might be interested in observing how people protect themselves against possible criminal acts by observing individuals in a crowded bus station. In this context, individuals will not likely know that they are being observed and will act as they normally do. A researcher could count the number of times that individuals touch belongings with both hands; they could observe how many people are reading, talking, or looking around; they could determine how long people stand in one place before moving. All of these data are captured through simple, unobtrusive observation.

Finally, a researcher may look to retrieve **archival data**, which are data that have already been collected and made available by an individual, group, or organization. Archival data might include publicly available records, such as U.S. Census data. Archival data may also be available through private organizations. For example, a researcher may look at newspaper archives to study how newspaper coverage of homicide has changed over time.

Getting to the Point 11.2 – Non-reactive research methodologies have in common their ability to collect information from and about human beings without their knowledge. These methods can include evaluating the things people possess (accretion measures), studying how things are used (erosion measures), observing how individuals or groups behave (unobtrusive observation), and analyzing information collected and made available by someone else (archival data).

TYPES OF NON-REACTIVE METHODS

There are three major types of non-reactive methods: field research, secondary analysis, and content analysis. In **field research**, the researcher observes behavior(s) in a natural setting. For example, we might observe drug addicts to better understand their behavior. Below is another example of field research in criminal justice practice.

Making Research Real 11.2 – Field Research in Criminal Justice

Joe Robinson, Captain of the Patrol Division of a large metropolitan police department, received a call from Margie Mathonican, the President of the Brook Haven Neighborhood Association. Margie was angry about a growing incidence of newspaper thefts in her neighborhood.

"At first it was just one or two of us every other week or so. Now, half of us don't get a paper most of the time. The newspaper company swears they deliver but somebody keeps stealing them," she explained to Captain Robinson. In the overall scope of issues Captain Robinson deals with on a daily basis, newspaper theft, even serial newspaper theft, is certainly not the most important thing to him. But Ms. Mathonican's neighborhood is populated primarily by retired residents. Many of them have lived there for decades. These sorts of minor incivilities tend to bother these residents and cause them to be fearful. He assured Ms. Mathonican that he would have somebody look into it.

Later that day the Captain met with the patrol command staff. He asked the lieutenant and sergeant who supervised the patrol beat that included the Brook Haven Neighborhood to "look into the newspaper thefts." Eventually the order worked its way to Officer Malcolm Adcock, who is the beat manager for the Brook Haven Neighborhood area.

Officer Adcock spoke with Ms. Mathonican and several of the other residents about the newspaper thefts. There seemed to be no pattern within the thefts other than that they were increasing in overall frequency. Together the residents and Officer Adcock decided to increase patrols during the time between when the newspapers were delivered (around 4:00 am) and when most residents retrieved them from their driveways (around 8:00 am). It did not work. Newspaper thefts increased.

Exasperated, Officer Adcock asked the sergeant to approve overtime money so that he could ask the officers to do some stakeouts around the neighborhood. The sergeant agreed, but "only for a couple of nights." At 3:30 am on a Thursday, seven patrol officers sat in unmarked vehicles in strategic locations throughout the Brook Haven Neighborhood. Thirty minutes later the newspaper delivery man drove through the neighborhood throwing papers from the window of his car.

At 4:15 am one of the officers heard the front door to a house across from him open and shut. He observed a young Labrador Retriever emerge from the house and trot to the front yard of the house across the street. After urinating on a tree the dog picked up the neighbor's paper and dropped it into the storm drain in the curb. The dog repeated this process at several houses and then ran between two houses to the adjacent street. The officer at that street observed the dog retrieve newspapers from front yards and drop them in the storm drain on that street. In all the dog retrieved seven papers and dropped all of them into the storm drain before the dog's owner emerged from the house and whistled. The dog returned to his house and the owner petted him as they went back into the house.

The officers who had observed the dog shone their flashlights down into the storm drains. Sure enough there were dozens of newspapers in them still wrapped in plastic bags. In fact, the storm drains were so full that they had to call the Wastewater Department to come clear them.

Officer Adcock interviewed the dog's owner. He concluded that the newspaper thefts began at about the same time the owner had enough confidence in the puppy to allow it to 'do its business' without supervision. The owner had no idea that the dog was stealing newspapers. The problem was solved when the owner agreed to supervise the dog during its early morning constitutional.

This is an example of field research. It involved the unobtrusive observation of behavior in its natural setting. The fact that the 'culprit' in this case was a dog rather than a human being does not change the nature of this research methodology.

Another unobtrusive method is **secondary analysis**. Here, the researcher analyzes previously collected or archival data. Sometimes the data are collected for the purpose of another research project. Sometimes the data are collected and made public for scholars and practitioners to analyze as they see fit. In either case, a researcher would obtain the data set and analyze all or parts of it. For example, we might use census data to understand the changing demographic characteristics of high crime areas. Here is another example of secondary analysis.

Making Research Real 11.3 – Secondary Analysis in Criminal Justice

Janice Armstrong, Warden at the Southern City State Penitentiary, is not at all pleased with a recent proposal from the state legislature to triple bunk prison cells. The state is experiencing severe budget constraints and cannot find enough money to build new or expand existing prisons. Warden Armstrong is worried that increasing the prison population at her facility will lead to more violence among inmates and put her correctional officers at risk.

Warden Armstrong decides to investigate her concerns further. She asks her assistant to gather two pieces of information. First she wants to know the inmate population of the Southern City State Penitentiary each year for the past 20 years. This information resides in the annual reports they submit to the state corrections board. Second, she wants to know the number of correctional officers who were injured on the job through physical confrontation with inmates during the same period. This information resides with the penitentiary's safety officer who keeps these sorts of statistics. Warden Armstrong's assistant provides her with the information and, just as she suspects, as the inmate population increased, the number of officers injured from inmate confrontations also increased. She uses the results of her secondary analysis to argue against an increase in the inmate population at her prison.

A third and final type of non-reactive method is **content analysis**. In a content analysis, the researcher analyzes existing textual information to study human behavior or conditions. For example, we might study the blog posts and website content of a known terroristic organization to predict a future act of terror. Below is another example of content analysis.

Making Research Real 11.4 – Content Analysis in Criminal Justice

Ann Krause, a new Assistant Professor of Technical Writing at State College, is interested in learning more about how police officers communicate in writing. She wants to be able to assist police officers in training with their technical writing skills. To learn more, she decides to conduct a content analysis of existing reports written by police officers.

Professor Krause gathers a sample of 100 case reports from a local police department. She analyzes these reports and identifies the common words and phrases within them. Using this information, she develops a training program to teach police officers how to be more precise in their report writing.

THE BENEFITS AND LIMITATIONS OF NON-REACTIVE RESEARCH METHODS

Non-reactive research methods are highly effective in many research situations, such as when a researcher fears that subjects may change their behavior when they know they are being observed. In this and other cases, researchers must find ways to observe behavior covertly. For example, if we want to understand how prostitutes recognize and approach potential clients, it would be best to observe them without their knowledge, lest they act differently or not at all for fear of criminal prosecution. In a previous chapter, we referred to this as reactivity, which is a major threat to internal validity.

Non-reactive methods are also ideal when the researcher wants to observe behavior in its natural setting. It would be very difficult, maybe impossible, for a researcher to recreate certain situations (e.g., an urban riot) in order to observe certain behaviors or phenomena. In this case, going to the field to observe behavior may be the best option. Finally, in some instances, the data that would be helpful for answering a researcher's question may have already been collected by another researcher. For example, if a researcher wanted to compare the crime rate with the unemployment rate, he or she would find both pieces of information already available. Why collect data that has already been collected? Table 11.1 summarizes these uses of non-reactive research.

Table 11.1 The Uses of Non-Reactive Research

- When research subjects are likely to change their behavior after learning that they are being observed

- When the researcher wants to observe behavior in its natural setting and/or as it naturally occurs

- When the data has been previously collected by a different individual, group, or organization

> **Getting to the Point 11.3** – Non-reactive research techniques are most effective when research subjects are likely to change their behavior when they know they are being observed, when the researcher wants to observe behavior in its natural setting, and/or when the data the researcher needs is already available.

There are some research situations that do not lend themselves to using a non-reactive technique. First, non-reactive methods are not effective when a researcher wants to understand the motivations, attitudes, and beliefs underlying some behavior. For example, a person may behave courteously toward members of another race, but still hold deep racial prejudices. Simply observing her behavior would not provide insight into her underlying prejudice. Second, there may be ethical issues that prevent the use of non-reactive methods. Behaviors observed in public places are generally considered 'fair game' since the research subject has no expectation of privacy. But in other cases, the research subject may have a right to privacy, which would prevent the use of non-reactive techniques. For example, a researcher could not join a support group of individuals whose loved ones had been murdered in order to study the group without their knowledge. This would be a major breach of research ethics. Finally, and perhaps obviously, non-reactive research involving secondary analysis is not possible when the data simply do not exist.

Validity is often a concern in non-reactive research. Internal validity has to do with whether the researcher's measures accurately portray what is occurring. The internal validity of a non-reactive study is sometimes threatened by a researcher's inability to fully understand the meaning of observed behaviors or by a misinterpretation of the observations themselves. In either case the observations may not actually measure what the researcher alleges they measure. External validity is also a common problem in non-reactive research. Non-reactive research often involves observations of very small populations or geographical areas. It is likely that these sample sizes and the manner in which the sample is selected do not produce a truly representative sample of the overall population. So, any conclusions drawn from non-reactive research may not necessarily be generalizable to a larger population or other similar populations. Table 11.2 reviews the circumstances in which non-reactive research would not be appropriate.

Table 11.2 The Limitations of Non-Reactive Research

- Ineffective for studying the internal motivations, beliefs, and attitudes that underlie some behavior

- Potentially unethical if it involves breaching research subjects' right to or expectation of privacy

- Impossible in cases where secondary or archival data do not already exist or are unavailable

- Non-reactive studies are often hampered by internal and external validity problems

Getting to the Point 11.4 – Non-reactive research methods are not particularly effective when a researcher needs to understand underlying motivations and belief systems, when research subjects have a right to or expectation of privacy, and when secondary or archival data do not exist.

THE NON-REACTIVE RESEARCH PROCESS

As in the previous two chapters, we will take a look at the actual research process to understand non-reactive methods in greater depth. Following the steps of the research process outlined in Chapter 2, we will review the process by which a researcher might conduct field research, secondary analysis, and content analysis. To illustrate the process further, I will highlight one research study that involved a content analysis. We begin with a general introduction of this case study.

Developing the Method 11.1 – A Case Study in Non-Reactive Research **(Economic Conditions and Ideologies of Crime in the Media: A Content Analysis of Crime News)**

Several years ago, when my children were young, my wife announced, "From now on, we are not going to watch the evening news! It's too violent." She was right. We were living in a large city at the time and it seemed like the evening news was filled with stories about murder, rape, assault, robbery, and other violent acts. "If it bleeds, it leads" is a common saying in news rooms. In short, crime 'sells.'

The tendency of media outlets to focus on crime and violence has the unfortunate effect of creating false perceptions regarding crime. After a few weeks of watching the evening news, one might think that crime is both common and getting worse. But the statistics indicate that crime is both uncommon and decreasing. In fact, between 2001 and 2012, violent crimes have decreased 13.2 percent.

To better understand media portrayals of crime, Melissa Hickman Barlow, David E. Barlow, and Theodore G. Chiricos set out to conduct a content analysis of media content on crime. They wanted to know whether economic conditions had an effect on how the media portrayed crime. In 1995, they published their research in the scholarly journal *Crime and Delinquency* under the title "Economic Conditions and Ideologies of Crime in the Media: A Content Analysis of Crime News." Their research is an excellent example of content analysis and non-reactive methods in general.

Ask a Research Question

Remember that the method chosen by a researcher should be determined by the research question. Some research questions are best answered by surveys, while others are best answered through experimental methods. Generally speaking, a non-reactive technique should be used when the researcher's presence would affect the research subject's behavior, when the researcher wants to observe behavior in a natural setting, and/or when the data that can answer a research question already exists. Before deciding to use a non-reactive method, however, we have to be certain that we can ethically observe behavior covertly or that we can logistically obtain access to existing data.

A good example of a research question for which a non-reactive method is well suited is: *"What is the average speed of vehicular traffic on a particular residential street?"* Calculating the average speed of vehicular traffic on a residential street would require the use of speed detection equipment, such as RADAR. If RADAR were mounted on an unmarked car parked on the shoulder or on a stationary object near the roadway, most drivers would be unaware that their speeds were being measured. Therefore, they would be unlikely to change their driving speed. The result would be a more accurate measure of vehicular speed on this particular street.

Non-reactive methods are seldom able to document causal relationships and therefore are less commonly used in explanatory research. Indeed, most non-reactive research is of an exploratory or descriptive nature. Exploratory research seeks to document emerging social trends. More often than not, the best way to learn of these trends is to observe them in their natural setting. Descriptive research seeks to describe an existing social process or phenomenon. Again, the best way to describe a social process or phenomenon would be to study it as it occurs naturally. Some examples of exploratory and descriptive research questions for which non-reactive methods are well suited are as follows:

- *How do residents of high-crime neighborhoods carry themselves in public so as to prevent physical confrontations?*
- *What marketing techniques do male and female escorts use when advertising their services in magazines?*
- *Are low-income neighborhoods a major target for sub-prime lenders in the housing industry?*

Developing the Method 11.2 – Asking a Research Question in Non-Reactive Research

Barlow et al. (1995) state that their study is exploratory, which would be appropriate for a content analysis. However, the authors propose that political and economic conditions might help *explain* how the media portrays crime. Thus, it appears that there are pieces of this study that are explanatory in nature. In their own words, they wanted to know "whether media accounts misrepresent crime in ways that support dominant class interest and whether misrepresentation changes in relation to conditions in the political economy" (Barlow et al., 1995: 6). In other words, they are asking whether the media reports on the crimes that most of us want to read about because of what is happening at the time both politically or economically.

Getting to the Point 11.5 – Most non-reactive research is exploratory or descriptive in nature. Because it is often difficult to measure the underlying cause of behavior using a non-reactive research method, non-reactive methods are less often used in explanatory research.

Conduct a Literature Review

One of the things a researcher will look for in a literature review is how previous researchers defined the concepts that they are investigating. This is especially true in non-reactive research. For example, a researcher interested in bullying behavior may choose to observe school children during recess at a local elementary school. But before going to the field, the researcher must first define 'bullying behavior.' This is not as easy as it seems. The threat of physical violence would likely fall within the definition of bullying behavior. But what about ridicule, verbal insults, or peer pressure? As a researcher, you are free to develop your own conceptual definitions and operational measures. But if a previous researcher has developed a workable definition, you may want to use it in your own research.

Reviewing the research of previous researchers who conducted projects similar to yours may also reveal imaginative ways to gain access to certain populations and/or ways of avoiding detection. The mistakes of previous researchers can be instructive, as well. You may recall from Chapter 3 the discussion of Laud Humphreys' *Tearoom Trade*. Humphreys covertly observed the homosexual behavior of 'publically heterosexual' men and then, posing as a census taker, contacted these men's families afterward to gather additional information. Had the identities of these men been revealed, it could have resulted in considerable personal and legal harm to them. As a result of this case, researchers using non-reactive methods are careful to protect the privacy of research subjects.

Developing the Method 11.3 – Conducting a Literature Review in Non-Reactive Research

In their review of the literature, Barlow et al. (1995) discovered a rather robust research history. They found numerous sources that confirmed what we all suspected: "crime news distorts and/or frames crime and crime control in ways that support institutions of power and authority" (Barlow et al., 1995: 3). In short, there are political and economic interests involved in how crime is portrayed in society. Though the literature suggested that media reports on crime painted a distorted picture of crime, previous research had not determined how these distortions changed with changing political and economic conditions. So, the researchers decided to proceed with their study.

Getting to the Point 11.6 – Reviewing the research methods and mistakes of previous researchers who used non-reactive research techniques may help define concepts, access certain populations, and avoid detection in non-reactive research.

Refine the Research Question

In non-reactive methods intended to produce exploratory or descriptive information, traditional hypotheses that predict relationships between variables are not usually required. Instead, you may simply want to pose research questions and/or general statements about what you expect to find in the study. In non-reactive methods intended to produce explanatory information, hypotheses are more appropriate. Here are some examples:

Ha: The presence of a marked patrol car on an interstate highway reduces speed among vehicles.

In this case, the researcher would attempt to determine whether the presence of a patrol car leads to a reduction in speed. This would involve non-reactive field research with a speed detector. Here is a hypothesis for explanatory research using secondary data analysis:

Ha: Specified training programs improve the efficiency of police detectives.

To explore this hypothesis, the researcher might investigate the relationship between the amount of training (measured in hours) and the "efficiency of police detectives," measured as the percentage of criminal cases that result in arrest. This would involve the analysis of training records and Uniform Crime Report data. Here is one more sample hypothesis you might find in a content analysis:

Ha: As media coverage of domestic violence increases, public support for stiffer penalties against domestic violence perpetrators increases.

To respond to this hypothesis, the researcher might conduct a content analysis of media coverage regarding domestic violence over time and compare these findings to public opinion polls regarding domestic violence penalties.

Developing the Method 11.4 – Refining the Research Question in Non-Reactive Research

Barlow et al. (1995) predicted that newspaper coverage of violent crime would not only overstate the problem of violent crime, but that coverage would be most intense during times of unemployment and economic stagnation. Thus, they presented two sets of hypotheses at the outset of their article. The first set of hypotheses focuses on the depiction of violent crime in news articles:

Hypothesis 1: The proportion of news articles that are about crimes of violence is significantly larger than the percentage of violent crimes known to the police.

Hypothesis 2: The proportion of news articles on crimes of violence is greater during high-unemployment years than during low-unemployment years.

Hypothesis 3: The proportion of news articles on crimes of violence is greater during periods of economic stagnation than during periods of economic expansion.

The researchers' second set of hypotheses focused on the "characteristics and images of offenders within crime news articles" (Barlow et al., 1995: 10):

Hypothesis 4: A significantly larger proportion of non-White offenders are depicted in the news articles than the proportion of non-White offenders who are actually arrested.

Hypothesis 5: When the social class of the offender is mentioned, the largest proportion of social class descriptions is in the lower class category.

Hypothesis 6: The proportion of negative images of offenders is greater during high-unemployment years than during low-unemployment years.

Hypothesis 7: The proportion of negative images of offenders is greater during periods of economic stagnation than during periods of economic expansion.

In general, the researchers predicted that newspaper coverage would highlight the non-White and lower class characteristics of criminal offenders during times of unemployment and economic stagnation. That is, the media would focus *disproportionately* on non-White, lower class criminal offenders during economically difficult times.

Getting to the Point 11.7 – In non-reactive research that is exploratory or descriptive in nature, researchers may simply pose research questions and/or general statements about what they expect to find in the study. In non-reactive research that is explanatory in nature, researchers will develop more formal hypotheses.

Define the Concepts and Create the Measures

The process by which a researcher using a non-reactive method develops conceptual definitions is not particularly different from in other types of research. A researcher interested in studying the frequency and intensity of sports violence, for example, might attend numerous sporting events and record instances of sports violence at these events. But before going 'into the field,' he or she would have to define the concept of 'sports violence.' Would it include any aggressive behavior, or just aggressive behavior that exceeds the usual level of competition for the sport? Would it include unusually aggressive behavior between participants in the sporting event, or would it also include aggressive behavior between spectators as well? These questions would have to be answered before proceeding with the field observations.

The challenge in the case of non-reactive research lies in ensuring the validity and reliability of non-reactive measures. Using the above example, it may not be clear whether an instance of aggressive behavior fits our researcher's particular definition of 'sports violence.' This confusion would be even more problematic if there were multiple observers. What if one field observer identified a particular aggressive act as an incidence of 'sports violence,' but another did not? To avoid this problem, researchers may spend considerable time training their research team on what to look for during their observations. For more complicated observations, the researcher may want to assign two to four researchers to observe the same behaviors and then compare their independent conclusions. If all of the researchers reach the same conclusion, they may conclude with more confidence that the measurement strategy is reliable. This is known as **inter-rater reliability**, which we discussed in Chapter 6.

Developing the Method 11.5 – Defining Concepts and Creating Measures in Non-Reactive Research

Barlow et al. (1995) propose that two elements of crime reporting will vary by economic conditions: (1) the *type* of crime that is reported, and (2) the *characteristics* of offenders that are highlighted. In essence, they define the concept of 'media coverage of crime' in two parts.

To measure the type of crime reported by the media, the researchers differentiated between two types of crime: violent and non-violent. Thus, when the researchers analyzed media content, they coded the content as focusing on violent or non-violent crimes. To measure the characteristics of offenders that are highlighted, the researchers included the following variables: age (under 30 or 30+), race (White or Non-White), gender (Male or Female), social status (Lower, Middle, or Upper), employment (Unemployed, Blue-collar, or White-collar), marital status (Married or Not married), family history (Positive or Negative), education (High school + or Less than high school), friends (Has friends or Is isolated) and religion (Religious or Not religious). It is likely that the researchers selected these variables because their review of the literature suggested that factors like age, race, and gender influence whether and how criminals are depicted in the media.

The authors conceptualized 'economic conditions' in two ways: (1) the level of unemployment, and (2) the level of economic stagnation. The authors do not explicitly define what they mean by 'high' or 'low' unemployment. Instead, they decided to analyze media coverage during the year 1953, when there was a relatively low unemployment rate (2.9 percent), and 1958, when there was a comparatively high unemployment rate (6.8 percent). Likewise, the authors do not define what they mean by 'economic stagnation' and 'economic expansion.' Again, they decided to analyze media content during years that are popularly known to be periods of economic stagnation. Those years were 1975, 1979, and 1982, during which the unemployment rates were 8.5, 5.8, and 9.7 percent respectively (Barlow et al., 1995: 6).

Getting to the Point 11.8 – For the most part, the actual process of conceptualization and operationalization is the same in non-reactive research as it is in other research methods.

Design a Method

The principal characteristic of a non-reactive research method is its ability to gather information without the knowledge of the research subjects. In field research, a researcher covertly observes behavior in its natural setting. He or she may also participate in the behavior(s) covertly. In a way, covert observation and participation are like an undercover police investigation, wherein suspects have no idea that their behavior is being observed. The objective of these investigations is to determine whether or not a crime is being committed and, if so, who is culpable. The officers have a hypothesis (i.e., a probable cause) and a conceptual definition of the behaviors they are interested in observing (i.e., criminal violations of the law). Likewise, covert observers should have a very clear idea of what they should be looking for and what observations to make.

Field researchers may consider conducting a pilot or trial run before commencing field research. This involves going into the field, observing, and recording behavior for a short time period to determine whether the method will actually capture the kind of information they need to answer their research question. If it does not, the researcher should revisit earlier steps involving conceptualization, measurement, and design.

Just as in an uncover surveillance operation, it is important to know when to end a field research project. To begin, research is expensive. The more time in the field, the more funds have to be expended for salary, transportation, meals, lodging, and other expenses. Research, especially in the field of criminal justice, can also be dangerous. Having an exit strategy to ensure a researcher will be able to safely disengage is essential. In this regard, researchers should also develop contingencies for events that might interrupt the research process, create ethical problems in research, and/or reveal the researcher's presence. For example, a field researcher observing teenage drinking behaviors may encounter an inebriated research subject about to drive away from the research scene. Should the researcher let the drunken teenager drive? These and other ethical problems threaten the continuation of the research, not to mention the liability of the researcher and his or her sponsoring agency.

Getting to the Point 11.9 – Non-reactive field research involves covert observation of and, in some cases, covert participation in the behavior that a researcher is interested in studying. In this method, it is important to prepare for all possible contingencies that may arise in the field and all possible threats to researchers' safety.

Another type of non-reactive data collection is secondary analysis, which is used when the data a researcher is seeking already exists. In a sense, the use of secondary data is not a data or information-gathering method. The data or information has already been gathered. Instead, the researcher searches for available data sets and evaluates whether the data set is useful to his or her research project. There is no shortage of available data sources. Often, researchers who accept federal funding must agree to file their data in an archive managed by the sponsoring government agency. For example, the Bureau of Justice Statistics, part of the U.S. Department of Justice, maintains archival data sets submitted by previous researchers. The Inter-University Consortium for Political and Social Research also maintains an archive of more than 500,000 files of social science research. These files include data on education, crime, substance abuse, and terrorism (ICPSR, 2011).

A researcher using secondary data must ensure that the data set is both relevant and responsive to his or her research question. For example, data collected by a researcher who studied bullies in 1975 would not likely be useful to a contemporary researcher studying cyber bullying. Even if the data are relevant to a researcher's topic, it might not be responsive to his or her specific research question or hypothesis. For example, if a researcher wants to know the average property damage (in dollars) caused by high-speed vehicular pursuits, previously collected data that merely indicated whether or not a high-speed vehicular pursuit resulted in property damage would not suffice. Note that because the data are already available, pretesting and preliminary analyses are not as critical for researchers using secondary analysis. Assuming the available data is responsive to your research question, it does not make sense to conduct a preliminary analysis.

When using two or more data sets, researchers should make sure that there is congruence between the definitions used in each of the data sources. For example, a researcher studying crime cross-nationally should ascertain how each national data set defines crime and ensure congruence between these definitions. Murder in one nation, for instance, may be considered manslaughter in another.

Getting to the Point 11.10 – The use of secondary data is appealing to most researchers because of its availability and low cost. However, the secondary data must be responsive to the researcher's data needs and research question(s).

Content analysis is a third non-reactive research method. In this technique, a researcher uses previously recorded or written information to study human behavior or conditions. Content analysis is a non-reactive technique because the research subjects are unaware that their behaviors are being observed. In fact, the 'research subjects' may not even be people. For example, television programmers are often criticized for the amount of violence depicted in prime time television programs, especially those programs aired during the 'family hour.' Using a content analysis technique, a researcher might measure the level of violence in these programs. In this case, the 'research subjects' are the television programs.

The most important step in designing a content analysis is to create strong conceptual definitions and operational measures for the phenomena that are being studied. For example, if a researcher wants to develop a list of active terrorist organizations using the internet as a data source, he or she would have to begin with a clear definition of what constitutes a 'terrorist organization.' Failure to clearly define concepts and measure variables will result in not knowing what to look for when data collection commences. In this case, a researcher might define a 'terrorist organization' as a group of two or more individuals who commit violent acts that target innocent civilians for religious, political, or ideological reasons. Using this definition, he or she might go to the internet and look for groups that meet these criteria.

As with field work, it is often a good idea to try out the measures of a content analysis informally to see how they would work when data collection begins in earnest. Pilot tests and trial runs are especially useful when multiple researchers are involved. Differences in how researchers interpret and code data affect both the validity (accuracy) and reliability (consistency) of the information. Using the previous example on terroristic organizations, one researcher may define a group as a terrorist organization, whereas another researcher might not. To reduce such threats to validity, researchers might consider conducting a series of training exercises wherein the researchers and research assistants become familiar with the conceptual definitions and operational measures.

Getting to the Point 11.11 – The most important step in designing a content analysis is to create strong conceptual definitions and operational measures for the phenomena that are being studied. In some cases, this may involve training research assistants.

Developing the Method 11.6 – Designing a Method in Non-Reactive Research

To study media coverage of crime at different periods of time, Barlow et al. (1995) decided to study articles appearing in *Time* magazine. The researchers chose *Time* because it was a widely circulated news magazine and "the best available representative of mainstream media as an influence on and reflection of popular consciousness concerning contemporary social issues" (Barlow et al., 1995: 6). In short, the authors suspected that the magazine might reflect changing public opinion and cultural mores.

An additional consideration for selecting *Time* was that the magazine had a long publication history, making it a suitable source of longitudinal information on changing portrayals of crime. Their selection of this publication enabled the authors to examine "the content of crime news articles ... at different points in the postwar period" and to analyze "media representation of crime in relation to changes and developments in the political economy" (Barlow et al., 1995: 6).

Collect the Data

Again, there is no real data collection that occurs in secondary analysis since the data have already been collected. But for researchers conducting field research and content analysis, data collection can be, and often is, just as rigorous as conducting an experiment or administering a survey. Researchers conducting field research and content analysis often use pre-formatted tables to record information, just as they do in survey research. These are commonly called **coding sheets**. For example, in a content analysis, a researcher might develop a coding sheet to collect data on the frequency and intensity of violent acts depicted on major television networks during the so-called 'family hour' (8–9 pm). The coding sheet might look something like Figure 11.1.

Program viewed: _____

Television channel: _____

Date: _____

Day of the week: _____

Researcher: _____

	Mild violence									Graphic violence
	1	2	3	4	5	6	7	8	9	10
Time[1]										
Time[2]										
Time[3]										
Time[4]										
Time[5]										

Notes:

Figure 11.1 A Coding Sheet for a Content Analysis of Violence on Television

Each individual row on the coding sheet in Figure 11.1 would represent one instance of violence observed on television. Using the scale provided, the researcher would rate the intensity of violence from 1 (mild violence) to 10 (graphic violence). Using the data from this form, the analyst would enter the results into a database. The program's name, television channel, date, day of week, and the name of the research assistant would be entered. Next, the number and intensity of each violent act would be recorded. Using these data, the researcher could develop additional variables to determine overall violence levels for each television program. Recording the research assistant's name and the date would enable the head researcher to reconcile coding mistakes and omissions.

The use of a coding sheet has two important advantages. First, it provides an efficient way to record observations and information. Field researchers or research assistants merely have to glance at the sheet to remember what they are looking for and well-designed tables and blanks provide a space for them to pencil in their observations or data. Second, data sheets provide a concise way to compare the notes made independently by multiple researchers. Such comparisons greatly enhance the reliability of the measure because areas of disagreement can be resolved prior to the analysis.

Getting to the Point 11.12 – Coding sheets provide researchers with an effective and efficient mechanism for recording information in content analyses and field observations.

There are some additional considerations that apply when taking field notes. The most accurate way to record observations in the field is to videotape them. Unfortunately, the overt presence of a camera might cause research subjects to change their behavior. In this sense, the field research would no longer be nonreactive. When possible, researchers can use a video recorder covertly, but they may do so only in public settings where individuals have no right to or expectation of privacy. The same applies to an audio recording. Since hiding video and audio recorders usually poses ethical challenges, many field researchers opt simply to make notes of their observations on paper or a laptop computer while they are observing in the field. This method of recording observations is less accurate, but also less likely to cause a change in the subjects' behavior. The final recording option is for the researcher to make notes after leaving the field, away from the presence of the research subjects. This option is the least reactive, but also the least accurate. Ultimately, researchers must find the appropriate balance between accuracy and obtrusiveness.

Getting to the Point 11.13 – Recording observations is a central part of field research. Video- and audio-taping observations are the most accurate recording methods, but they are also the most reactive and, in some cases, they are also unethical. Recording observations on paper or a laptop are the least accurate, but also the least reactive. Researchers must find the appropriate balance between accuracy and obtrusiveness.

Developing the Method 11.7 – Collecting Data in Non-Reactive Research

During the years on which their analysis focused (1953, 1958, 1975, 1979, and 1982), Barlow et al. (1995) chose articles that were "completely or substantially about crime, criminals, or criminal justice." Only articles that were at least one column in length were chosen. A total of 175 articles met these criteria. Technically speaking, this would be a purposive sample. Only the articles on crime appearing during the years they chose were included in their analysis. The researchers in this case did not use a random sample presumably because no sampling frame existed. In this case, the researchers would have had to identify every article on crime ever published in a written and widely circulated American news source during the selected years. Though this was arguably possible, it was not feasible or efficient. Instead, the researchers chose a representative news source to study media portrayals of crime. Though their sampling strategy was not random, it provided important insight into human behavior.

Once the articles were identified, the researchers turned their attention to conducting the actual content analysis. To do this, they read each article and collected information related to the variables in which they were interested. First, the researcher differentiated between articles about violent and non-violent crime, which was relatively straightforward. Collecting information about the characteristics of the offenders was a bit more problematic. Few articles included information on each of the 10 variables in which the researchers were interested. For example, very few of the articles included information about the offenders' education, relationships with friends, religion, or marital status. In short, their analysis did not yield information about every variable related to the characteristics of the offender.

Although they did not report this detail in their article, it is likely that Barlow et al. (1995) used coding sheets as they read each of the articles. These coding sheets probably contained a list of each variable along with its attributes. As they read the article, the researchers likely made notes on these coding sheets to facilitate subsequent data entry and further analysis. For example, if the article contained a reference to the offender's college degree, the researcher would place a check mark beside the attribute 'High school +' under the education variable.

It is also likely that the researchers read through a few of the articles at first to see if their data collection procedure would work, though, again, they do not report this. For example, if none of the articles contained information about the offender's religion, it would be futile to include this variable in the analysis. If, on the other hand, most of the articles contained information about the offender that they had previously not considered important (e.g., history of drug use), they might have considered adding this variable to their analysis.

Analyze the Data

Secondary analysis is typically of a quantitative nature, though this is not always the case. Criminal justice researchers, for example, might analyze quantitative data from the National Crime Victimization Survey to study longitudinal trends in certain types of criminal victimization. Many quantitative analyses using secondary data use sophisticated statistical techniques, in addition to basic descriptive statistics. Some data sets, however, lend themselves to qualitative research. During the 1930s, for example, interviews were conducted with surviving ex-slaves as part of the Federal Writers' Project. In this case, a researcher might conduct a qualitative data analysis of the interview material to understand how African Americans experienced a life in bondage.

The analysis of field observations and content materials is typically qualitative in nature, but, again, this is not always the case. Researchers might be interested in studying how pedestrians act when approached by panhandlers. In this instance, they might describe different pedestrian responses and/or explore how the race, gender, and age of the panhandler influence pedestrian responses. These descriptive and exploratory accounts would be more subjective and qualitative.

It is also possible to conduct quantitative analyses of data gathered through field observations and content analysis. In our hypothetical research scenario involving a content analysis of violence on primetime television, for example, information on the frequency and intensity of violence on television was collected in numerical form. Likewise, field observations of bullying behavior on a school playground could involve the calculation of frequency and intensity of bullying behaviors.

Developing the Method 11.8 – Analyzing Data in Non-Reactive Research

Barlow et al. (1995) did not include information in their article about how they prepared the information for analysis or how they actually analyzed the content of the articles. It is likely that they entered the information from the coding sheets into a computer program like Excel or SPSS for subsequent analysis. This assumption is based on their use of tabular data within the text of their article.

In terms of their analysis strategy, the authors relied on a statistical technique called chi square analysis, in which they compared percentages. (For more information about this statistical technique refer to Chapter 14.) For example, they compared the percentage of articles that focused on violent crime during periods of high unemployment with the percentage of articles that focused on violent crime during periods of low unemployment.

Getting to the Point 11.14 – The analysis of secondary data, field observations, and content material can be qualitative or quantitative. The type of analysis depends on the research question and the type of data that are available.

Interpret the Results

At this stage of the research process, researchers evaluate their research question or hypothesis using the findings of their research. It is often the case in non-reactive research that there is room for multiple interpretations. Secondary data analysis, for example, might have produced strange and interesting findings that neither support nor refute a research hypothesis. In the case of field work, where researchers often enter the field with research questions rather than strict hypotheses, interpretations of the data can be more subjective. In either case, it is always a good idea to entertain various interpretations of the data and to be up front about the limitations of the data and study design.

Developing the Method 11.9 – Interpreting the Results in Non-Reactive Research

Overall, Barlow et al. (1995) found what we already suspected: crime news is not at all representative of actual crime trends. In other words, the media does not do a very good job of creating an accurate or representative picture of crime. These researchers were somewhat successful in developing a connection between economic conditions and the types of crime stories reported in the media. However, the causal connection between economic conditions and crime reporting is really not known. For example, there is really no way to determine whether the economic conditions existing at the time actually influenced the editorial decision to report on a particular type of crime. These types of causal connections are often difficult in non-reactive research.

Though insightful, this particular study was not without its flaws. Some of these were pointed out by the researchers. First, one could argue that the sample of articles is not representative of the overall media. Other news outlets reported on crime during this period and may have taken a different position from the editors at *Time*. Second, the articles included in the analysis were from five years within a 29-year time frame. *Time*'s editorial philosophy and idea of what was newsworthy may have changed numerous times during this time frame. Finally, though the authors show some relationship between economic conditions and distorted depictions of crime, their analysis did not allow them to substantiate why this might be the case.

Getting to the Point 11.15 – The data or information produced by many non-reactive research techniques often can be interpreted in multiple ways. As such, researchers using these techniques should entertain various interpretations. They should also be up front about the limitations of their study.

Communicate the Findings

Again, if researchers want to engage members of the scholarly community, they should publish their findings in an academic journal or through a university press. If, however, researchers want to appeal to a broader audience, they should publish their findings in a trade journal or other mass media outlet.

In terms of the actual content of the material published, non-reactive research methods may use tables, charts, and graphs if the analysis is quantitative in nature. If the analysis is qualitative in nature, the findings might be written up more as a 'story.' For example, a content analysis of violence in video games might produce quantifiable results like the frequency or intensity of violent acts within the video game. But telling the story of how adolescents behave before, during, and after playing violent video games might also be part of the report.

Developing the Method 11.10 – Communicating the Results of Non-Reactive Research

Barlow et al. (1995) chose to publish their results in a peer-reviewed academic journal. They are university scholars and as such benefit from the publication of their results in this medium. Publishing their research in an academic journal also enhances the scientific value of their major finding that the media provides a distorted portrayal of crime. There has been much debate over media bias between traditional media outlets like ABC, NBC, and CBS and cable news outlets like Fox News, CNN, and MSNBC. Presenting research on this subject in a respected academic journal removes it from the usual muckraking that happens between media providers and contributes actual evidence to the debate around media bias.

Getting to the Point 11.16 – Researchers may use tables, charts, and graphs to communicate the results of their non-reactive research if the analysis is quantitative in nature. Alternatively, if the analysis is qualitative in nature, they may tell a 'story' using quotes, examples and descriptions.

FINAL THOUGHTS

Non-reactive research taps into something that already exists – an everyday behavior, a scientific database, a written document – to answer a research question or test a research hypothesis. Let me illustrate with one final example. I have a reputation for being a bit frugal. In fact, you might even call me a tightwad. I analyze each dollar I spend to be sure I am getting the best deal. As our children reached driving age, I noticed that our automobile insurance premiums rose rather substantially. So I made an appointment with my friendly insurance representative.

As it turns out, we were getting a pretty good deal. We had numerous discounts for safe driving, driver training, and having multiple cars insured by the same company. We even got a discount because our children made good grades. During my conversation with the insurance agent, the agent made a curious comment: "Your rates are also lower because your credit rating is high." Apparently, people with poor credit tend to be poor drivers. The relationship is not causal. But there is enough of a correlation between the two variables that insurance companies in some states establish insurance premiums based in part on an individual's credit history. In this case, and many others, information collected for one purpose may be used for an entirely different purpose. And this is not unlike non-reactive research. The key is to make sure the use of existing information answers the research question and is ethical.

GETTING TO THE POINT/CHAPTER SUMMARY

- Non-reactive research is a collection of research methods that gather information from research subjects without their knowledge. Because the research subjects are unaware that they are being observed, they are less likely to change their behaviors. These techniques are effective for observing behavior in a natural setting.

- Non-reactive research methodologies have in common their ability to collect information from and about human beings without their knowledge. These methods can include evaluating the things people possess (accretion measures), studying how things are used (erosion measures), observing how individuals or groups behave (unobtrusive observation), and analyzing information collected and made available by someone else (archival data).

- Non-reactive research techniques are most effective when research subjects are likely to change their behavior when they know they are being observed, when the researcher wants to observe behavior in its natural setting, and/or when the data the researcher needs is already available.

- Non-reactive research methods are not particularly effective when a researcher needs to understand underlying motivations and belief systems, when research subjects have a right to or expectation of privacy, and when secondary or archival data do not exist.

- Most non-reactive research is exploratory or descriptive in nature. Because it is often difficult to measure the underlying cause of behavior using a non-reactive research method, non-reactive methods are less often used in explanatory research.

- Reviewing the research methods and mistakes of previous researchers who used non-reactive research techniques may help define concepts, access certain populations, and avoid detection in non-reactive research.

- In non-reactive research that is exploratory or descriptive in nature, researchers may simply pose research questions and/or general statements about what they expect to find in the study. In non-reactive research that is explanatory in nature, researchers will develop more formal hypotheses.

- For the most part, the actual process of conceptualization and operationalization is the same in non-reactive research as it is in other research methods.

- Non-reactive field research involves covert observation of and, in some cases, covert participation in the behavior that a researcher is interested in studying. In this method, it is important to prepare for all possible contingencies that may arise in the field and all possible threats to researchers' safety.

- The use of secondary data is appealing to most researchers because of its availability and low cost. However, the secondary data must be responsive to the researcher's data needs and research question(s).

- The most important step in designing a content analysis is to create strong conceptual definitions and operational measures for the phenomena that are being studied. In some cases, this may involve training research assistants.

- Coding sheets provide researchers with an effective and efficient mechanism for recording information in content analyses and field observations.

- Recording observations is a central part of field research. Video- and audio-taping observations are the most accurate recording methods, but they are also the most reactive and, in some cases, they are also unethical. Recording observations on paper or a laptop is the least accurate, but also the least reactive. Researchers must find the appropriate balance between accuracy and obtrusiveness.

- The analysis of secondary data, field observations, and content material can be qualitative or quantitative. The type of analysis depends on the research question and the type of data that are available.

- The data or information produced by many non-reactive research techniques often can be interpreted in multiple ways. As such, researchers using these techniques should entertain various interpretations. They should also be up front about the limitations of their study.

- Researchers may use tables, charts, and graphs to communicate the results of their non-reactive research if the analysis is quantitative in nature. Alternatively, if the analysis is qualitative in nature, they may tell a 'story' using quotes, examples, and descriptions.

The following chapter exercises are organized into two parts. The first part consists of questions that can be answered using the information from this chapter. This section will test your understanding of the chapter material. The second part consists of research application exercises. These exercises require you to apply what you have learned thus far.

CHAPTER REVIEW QUESTIONS

Respond to each of the following questions using the information from this chapter.

1. Non-reactive research is often the best way to gather data when individuals might change their behavior when they become aware of being observed. This behavioral change is a major threat to validity and is known as:
    a. Accretion
    b. Conversion
    c. Reactivity
    d. Selection bias

2. A researcher who studies graffiti to understand relationships between different urban gangs would be using which type of non-reactive measure?
    a. Accretion
    b. Archival
    c. Erosion
    d. Reactive

3. A non-reactive research method that requires a researcher to observe behavior in its natural setting is referred to as _____ research.
    a. Context
    b. Field
    c. Nature
    d. Setting

4. Read the following research scenarios and indicate what type of non-reactive research is represented (field observation, content analysis, secondary analysis).

Research scenario	Non-reactive method
A researcher studies three of the most widely circulated women's magazines over a 10-year time period to explore how they frame the issue of violence against women.	
A researcher uses data from the Survey of Inmates in State and Federal Correctional Facilities, made available through the Inter-University Consortium for Political and Social Research, to study inmates over time.	
A researcher watches the process of jury selection over a one-year period in one courthouse in order to understand the problem of race-conscious jury selection.	

5. Which of the following is a major limitation of non-reactive research?
   a. It can pose ethical challenges when it involves covert observation.
   b. It does not lend itself to descriptive or exploratory research.
   c. Such research removes human behavior from its natural setting.
   d. Research subjects can change their behavior in reaction to being observed.

6. Non-reactive research techniques are *least* useful for which of the following types of research?
   a. Descriptive
   b. Explanatory
   c. Exploratory

7. In field research, it is common to train research assistants on what to look for in field observations and how to code their observations. Such training helps ensure which of the following?
   a. Construct validity
   b. Inter-rater reliability
   c. Predictive validity
   d. Test–retest reliability

8. Read the following research situations and indicate whether the research is an example of non-reactive field observation. Explain your response for each.

Research situation	Non-reactive field observation? (Yes or No)
A researcher from the local university openly observes how correctional officers manage conflict between inmates.	
A researcher poses as a probation officer to understand how probation officers deal with juveniles who violate probation.	
A researcher rides along with a police officer to observe how drivers adjust their driving in the presence of a marked police vehicle.	
A researcher gets permission from a local domestic violence organization to study the organization's outreach efforts while acting as a volunteer.	

9. Researchers conducting unobtrusive observations will often use pre-formatted tables known as _____ to record their data.
   a. Coding sheets
   b. Data books
   c. Field binders
   d. Record tablets

10. The most accurate method for recording information during field observations is to use a video or audio recorder. This method also happens to be the:
   a. Least obtrusive
   b. Least reliable
   c. Most expensive
   d. Most reactive

RESEARCH APPLICATION EXERCISES

Access to the following articles will be provided by your instructor.

> Karp, D.R. (2001). Harm and repair: Observing restorative justice in Vermont. *Justice Quarterly, 18*(4), 727–757.
>
> Wells, W. (2002). The nature and circumstances of defensive gun use: A content analysis of interpersonal conflict situations involving criminal offenders. *Justice Quarterly, 19*(1), 127–157.

Respond to the following questions for each of the articles cited above.

11. What type of non-reactive research technique did the researchers use?

12. Why was the use of this technique appropriate for this research context?

13. What key concepts did the researchers use? How were they defined and measured?

14. Did the researchers encounter any difficulties in their research? If so, how did they handle these difficulties?

15. What were the major conclusions of the article? In your opinion, were these conclusions actually supported by the data? Why or why not?

16. If you were asked to replicate one of these research projects, how might you improve it? Would you use another method? Why or why not?

CHAPTER 12

Qualitative Research Methods

We live in a quantitative world. We want the 'hard numbers,' the facts, the statistics. Indeed, nearly every controversy is debated using statistics. Few people really question how those statistics are generated and even fewer question whether they really tell us anything about the controversy we are debating. But in the end, statistics only tell us so much. For example, I can use my students' performance on exams to measure how well I am doing at teaching them about criminal justice research. But those numbers will not fully capture the effect my teaching has on my students' understanding of crime and research methods.

In the field of criminal justice, many questions can be answered quantitatively. But there are many questions that demand more in-depth and qualitative answers. Some of the earliest criminological studies were qualitative. And though the research has become more quantitative over time, there is something of a resurgence in qualitative measures and methods. Here is an example of how a qualitative measure made a real contribution to my own research agenda.

Making Research Real 12.1 – Learning From My Students

During the fall of 1999, I was asked to mentor an undergraduate student through the McNair Scholars Program. This program provides mentoring to first-generation university students. During the academic year, it was my task to assist this student with a significant research project. The student chose to research racial profiling.

The research on the racial profiling controversy was, at that time, in its infancy. There was not a lot of data readily available and gathering data would have taken more time than we were allowed. So we decided to conduct a content analysis of newspaper articles about individuals who accused the police of racial profiling. The objective of this content analysis was to identify the common features of these accusations. We found about 50 articles nationwide.

One afternoon, while reviewing my student's analysis, I noticed that nearly all of the accusations were based on the fact that the police officer did not issue a citation during the stop. Many of the accusers also mentioned that the officer never told them why they were stopped, though he or she did ask for permission to search the car. "Why is not getting a ticket evidence of racial profiling?" I wondered. It seemed to me that not getting a ticket was a good thing. I also wondered, out loud to my student, why not mentioning the reason for the stop was evidence of racial profiling.

My student looked at me, paused, swallowed hard and asked "Professor, how many times in your life have you been stopped by the police?" "Twice. Once for speeding and once for an expired registration," I responded. "Professor, you've been driving for about 30 years and have only been stopped twice? Would you have a different perspective if you got stopped twice a week or more, never got a ticket, never were told why you were stopped, and always were asked for consent to search your car?" my student asked. "Plus, you used to be a cop, your father was a cop, and many of your friends are cops, right?" he asked. "Well, yes," I responded. "So I'm guessing that you and the people that raised you think pretty highly of cops, right?" he asked. "I suppose so," I responded. "If everyone you knew had a bad experience with the police or if growing up you saw images of people like you having bad experiences with the police, then you might have a poor opinion of the police, right?" he continued.

"Yes, but what's your point?" I asked. "The point is that you have never been, nor will you ever be, an African American man living in the ghetto. So maybe you can't relate to these accusers and their experience," he explained.

This was one of those moments in a professor's life, and believe me there are many, when the student becomes the teacher. My student was right. I was evaluating these stories through a very different and overly quantitative lens. I was merely counting the frequency of the common comments the accusers made in support of their accusations. I was not looking behind the numbers to understand the meaning and significance of their comments. A more qualitative lens could have helped me look at the larger context in which traffic stops and searches occur. It would have also pushed me to consider how and why African American drivers were interpreting these stops and searchers in a particular way.

Qualitative research is a tradition in scientific inquiry that does not rely principally on numeric data and quantitative measures. Instead, it attempts to develop a deeper understanding of human behavior. It is more concerned about how and why humans behave as they do, and how and why they interpret the world as they do.

QUALITATIVE RESEARCH BASICS

The logic of qualitative methods might be best illustrated with an example. In 2007, I took a group of students to London for an overseas learning experience. Our overall objective was to compare the American and British criminal justice processes. But along the way, we also wanted to learn more about British culture. One afternoon, some scientists from the Police Testing Branch invited me to attend a game of cricket. I accepted their invitation and met them at the stadium, which I soon learned is referred to as a 'pitch.'

As a child and young adult, I played a lot of baseball. Although I was never really good at it, I understand and enjoy the game. I figured cricket would be similar. A bowler in cricket is like a pitcher in baseball. A no-ball in cricket is like a balk in baseball. And a bye in cricket is a like a wild pitch in baseball. But almost immediately after the game began, I was confused and never really got back on track. Here are the rules of the game that I wrote down in an effort to understand it:

- Each player that is in the side that is in goes out, and when he is out he comes in and the next player goes in until he is out.

- When they are all out, the side that is out comes in and the side that has been in goes out and tries to get those coming in, out.

- When a player goes out to go in, the players who are out try to get him out, and when he is out he goes in and the next player in goes out.

Got it? Neither did I. To understand cricket, I would have had to have spent more time at the games talking with spectators and players. It was not something I could learn superficially by making a few brief observations. This, in essence, is what qualitative research is all about. **Qualitative research** refers to a broad category of research methods that attempt to produce a more detailed understanding of human behavior, including its meaning and its motivation. In qualitative research, a researcher studies a behavior or phenomenon in depth and from the perspective of the individual or group involved.

Getting to the Point 12.1 – Qualitative research refers to a broad category of research methods that attempt to produce a more detailed understanding of human behavior, including its meaning and its motivation.

TYPES OF QUALITATIVE METHODS

Qualitative research methods include three popular methods in criminal justice research: case studies, ethnography, and grounded theory research. A **case study** is a detailed analysis of a single event, group, or person for the purpose of understanding how a particular context gives rise to this event, group, or person. For example, a researcher might conduct a case study of an organized crime ring. Here is another example of case study research.

Making Research Real 12.2 – What Is a Jack-Roller?

Imagine that you are a sociologist working at one of America's most prestigious institutions of higher learning. You are not famous yet, but in a few years you will be. In fact, your work will influence criminological thought until well into the 21st century. But right now, you are just a highly competent scholar.

Suppose one day you hear an unfamiliar term – jack-roller. "What is a jack-roller?" you ask. Nobody at the university seems to know. You ask around town and eventually learn, from the young paperboy on the street, that a jack-roller is a person who steals money from "drunks and hobos." By now your sociological curiosity is piqued. You decide to learn more.

Unfortunately there is no available research on jack-rollers or jack-rolling. So, you go back to the only source that seems to know anything about it – the paperboy. At first, the paperboy is reluctant to give you the name of a jack-roller, but eventually you give him enough candy to soften his reluctance. He gives you a name and an address. You go to the address to meet the jack-roller, a young man who lives in an inner-city slum. After a while, you gain his confidence. He tells you about his life as a jack-roller, which appears to be his primary vocation. You dutifully write down what he tells you.

The more you learn about this young man, the more questions you have about his activities. You want to know why he chose to be a jack-roller, how he selects victims, how much money he 'earns,' how he avoids getting caught, and what he hopes for the future. Eventually, you have enough to write a short book about this young man's life. The book gets published and becomes the most authoritative treatise on juvenile delinquency at the time.

The above story is actually true, though I embellished parts. I am not sure if Clifford Shaw actually bribed a paperboy into providing him the name of a jack-roller. What I am sure of is that Clifford Shaw's book, *The Jack-Roller*, is a classic criminological text that still remains one of the most influential studies on juvenile delinquency. Professor Shaw's work in this regard is best described as a case study. The 'case' is one juvenile delinquent. But the conclusions Professor Shaw drew from this case helped inform his theory and our understanding of juvenile delinquency.

In addition to case studies, qualitative research methods include ethnographies. An **ethnography** is an in-depth study of a culture for the purpose of understanding that culture and its inner workings. For example, a researcher might conduct an ethnography of a homeless shelter to understand how a particular culture has arisen around the homeless persons who inhabit the shelter and the staff that provides services to them. Here is another example of ethnographic research.

Making Research Real 12.3 – An Ethnography Does Not Have to Be 'Ethnic'

When you hear the word 'ethnography' you might imagine an anthropologist living with a tribe of indigenous people in a remote part of Borneo. But remember that subcultures exist all around us. In 2009, Deirdre M. Bowen published an ethnographic study of one such subculture as it existed in a large urban prosecutor's office. Bowen was particularly interested in the process of plea bargaining, which practitioners and scholars alike had criticized as being inappropriate for settling criminal cases. At this particular prosecutor's office, a new 'rationalized' approach to plea bargaining was being used and Bowen wanted to learn how a particular subculture had grown up around it.

As part of her ethnographic research, Bowen observed negotiations between prosecutors and defense attorneys. She also conducted informal and formal interviews to understand how attorneys adapted to new rules of plea bargaining and how they perceived the reformed approach. She found that the 'reformed' model was not a significant improvement on traditional models of plea bargaining.

A third and final qualitative method is grounded theory research. In **grounded theory research**, a researcher uses the inductive reasoning process to develop a theory that explains observed behaviors or processes. Grounded theory is more of an approach to qualitative research than a specific method. For example, it may involve observations and interviews, which have been discussed elsewhere in this book. What distinguishes this method from other forms of research, however, is its inductive approach of using qualitative data to develop theories of social phenomena. Below is an example.

Making Research Real 12.4 – What Bothers the Homicide Detectives?

In 2011, Dean A. Dabney and a few of his colleagues published a qualitative study on homicide detectives. Up until this point, most of the research assumed that all police detectives experienced the same type of stress. Dabney and his colleagues wanted to develop a theory of stress as it was experienced by homicide detectives in particular. They took an inductive approach. They wanted to understand job-related stress from the vantage point of homicide detectives and to use that understanding to develop a theory of homicide detective stress.

Professor Dabney and his colleagues spent some quality time with the detectives in a homicide unit, interviewing and observing them extensively. They found that the stresses these detectives described were unique to homicide work. The unique stressors were related to such factors as the complexity of homicide crime scenes, time pressures, paperwork demands, and long-term ownership of individual case files. The researchers used this information to propose a theory of homicide investigator stress and drew implications for future research.

Getting to the Point 12.2 – Some of the more popular qualitative research methods include case study research, ethnographic research, and grounded theory research. A case study is a detailed analysis of a single event, group, or person. An ethnography is an in-depth study of a culture. And grounded theory is a methodological approach that uses inductive reasoning to develop a theory to explain observed behaviors or processes.

BENEFITS AND LIMITATIONS OF QUALITATIVE RESEARCH

Qualitative research methods are the most useful in three research situations (see Table 12.1 for a summary). First, when numbers alone cannot capture a social phenomenon, qualitative research methods are useful and necessary. For example, maturity is often measured by chronological age. We may assume that a person who is 25 years old has matured enough to be considered an adult. But, we also know that maturity has different dimensions, some of them physical, emotional, and social. We might consider a person to be physically mature when he or she has stopped growing. We might define a person as emotionally mature when he or she is able to resolve problems without resorting to tantrums or yelling. We might consider a person socially mature if he or she is able to initiate and maintain productive social relationships. In short, qualitative dimensions of maturity can give us a more well-rounded picture of this concept.

Qualitative methods are also effective for understanding how individual perceptions shape human behavior. For example, in a sizable number of cases in which women commit murder, a woman's spouse or intimate partner is killed. A qualitative researcher might want to know how the perceptions of these women influenced their decision to murder their partner. Were they victims of physical or emotional abuse? If so, what did they consider their options to be with respect to ending the abuse? And of these options, why did they make the decision to murder? Understanding these perceptions and motivations would go a long way in understanding this particular phenomenon.

Finally, when existing theories do not give us much insight into social patterns or phenomena, qualitative research can provide data to develop theories inductively. For example, in the wake of the massacre at Columbine High School, in which two students murdered 12 students and one teacher, practitioners and scholars were eager to understand what might have motivated the massacre, especially since existing theories did not do a very good job of explaining the murders. In-depth qualitative analyses of this case helped develop theories of school shootings like this and others.

Table 12.1 The Uses of Qualitative Research Methods

- Providing a nuanced and in-depth picture of a particular phenomenon
- Understanding how perceptions and meanings influence human behavior
- Developing a theory for unexplained social phenomena

Getting to the Point 12.3 – Qualitative research methods are effective when a researcher wants to develop a deeper or more nuanced understanding of a particular phenomenon. These methods are effective at determining how perceptions and meanings influence human behavior and for developing theories for previously unexplained social phenomena.

Generally speaking, the results of qualitative research cannot be generalized to a larger population, and this is one of the major limitations of qualitative research. For example, a researcher conducting an in-depth case study of a gang member cannot generalize her findings to all gang members. Instead, the case study can provide insight into what we might look for in a larger, more generalizable study of gang membership.

In addition to its limited generalizability, qualitative research may simply not be feasible. In some situations, it is not possible for a researcher to observe behavior in its natural setting or to interview members of certain populations. Some research contexts are too dangerous and others may present ethical challenges. For example, a researcher might want to use a qualitative technique to understand how intoxicated drivers avoid detection. This researcher could learn a lot if he rode home with and observed a drunk driver. But doing so would put him in physical danger and it would be unethical to allow a person to drive drunk. Table 12.2 summarizes these limitations.

Table 12.2 The Limitations of Qualitative Research Methods

- Findings cannot be generalized to a larger population
- Research may not be feasible or may pose ethical challenges

Getting to the Point 12.4 – Qualitative research methods are not effective when a researcher wants to generalize findings of the research to a larger or similar population. Some qualitative research may not be feasible because of ethical challenges.

THE QUALITATIVE RESEARCH PROCESS

Let us look now at how qualitative research is conducted within the context of the generic research process introduced in Chapter 2. As usual, I will highlight the stages of the qualitative research process with a section called 'Developing the Method.' Within these highlighted sections, you will read about how two researchers conducted a qualitative study. We will begin with an introduction to this study.

Developing the Method 12.1 – A Case Study in Qualitative Research
(A Study of Crime and Place)

Very many years ago, I was an undergraduate student living in a dormitory. One afternoon, a painting crew showed up at the dorm and repainted the hallways a light shade of green. Actually, I am being nice. It was a hideous shade of pea soup green. One of the residents on my floor also hated the color and filed a complaint with the dorm mother. Ma Bradshaw, as we called her, did not like the color either, but explained that "the folks over at Physical Plant said the color is known to be soothing and will reduce stress among the residents." For whatever reason, my neighbor bought this explanation and dropped his complaint.

Patricia L. Brantingham and Paul J. Brantingham, both professors at Simon Fraser University in British Columbia, Canada, explored a similar issue. They wanted to know whether the physical environment affected criminal behavior. Their article, "Nodes, Paths and Edges: Considerations on the Complexity of Crime and the Physical Environment," appeared in the *Journal of Environmental Psychology* in 1993. Their study was based on case study and grounded theory research and helped establish a research agenda known as environmental criminology.

The Brantinghams made two very important observations at the beginning of their research. First, they noticed that most of the attention on criminal behavior was devoted to explaining individual motivations to commit crime. There was less attention to contextual or environmental factors that influenced crime. Second, they observed that crime prevention strategies that focused on making changes to physical spaces had a very long tradition. Locks, alarms, lighting, and night watchmen have all been used for centuries to decrease the likelihood of criminal behavior. But no theory of the relationship between the physical environment and criminal behavior had ever been established. Thus, they set out to answer questions about this relationship.

Ask a Research Question

Occasionally, one of my students gets really interested in qualitative methods and wants to do a qualitative research project. He or she asks me: "Can you think of a good research question for qualitative research?" I usually answer, "No, not really." As I have reiterated throughout this text, you need to start with a research question and then identify the best method to answer that question. Some questions lend themselves to qualitative research; others do not. Generally speaking, research questions that get at subjective meaning, individual perception, and cultural context are best suited for qualitative research. Here are some research questions that could be answered using a qualitative research method:

- *How do adolescents rationalize their decision to engage in delinquent acts?*

- *What is the process by which petty corruption evolves into serious ethical violations?*

- *What role do race and gender play in jury selection?*

Qualitative research designs are also effective for developing theories to explain human behavior. For example, a researcher may develop a theory that serial offenders are able to remain undetected for many years because of information gaps in the criminal justice information system. To test this theory, he may conduct a case study of an infamous serial offender. In doing so, the researcher may find instances where the offender might have been apprehended had criminal justice agencies been more willing to share information. By identifying information gaps, the researcher can refine his theory of how serial offenders remain undetected over time.

Though most qualitative studies are descriptive and exploratory, it is a mistake to assume that all qualitative research designs are descriptive or exploratory. Qualitative research also has a role to play in explanatory research. Qualitative research can help pinpoint the mechanisms by which a cause leads to an effect. For example, a large body of research suggests that youth and male gender are predictive of criminal behavior. In other words, young men are more likely to commit crimes. But why is this the case? A good qualitative study could shed light on why young men are more likely to commit crimes.

Qualitative research can be used for both pure and applied research. For example, a researcher may want to develop a theory explaining road rage. She learns that individuals convicted of road rage in her community are required to attend a one-day anger management seminar. With the assistance of the traffic court, she obtains a list of these offenders, contacts them, and conducts detailed interviews. Her initial study was done for the purpose of expanding the body of knowledge on road rage. That is, it was pure research. But while presenting her research findings, a traffic court judge asks what causes individuals to overreact in traffic situations. The researcher points out that road rage tends to occur on highly congested roads that add and delete traffic lanes frequently. The constant merging and dispersion of traffic causes some individuals to drive aggressively. She suggests that redesigning roads so that the number of traffic lanes remains relatively constant would likely reduce road rage. In this case, the researcher has applied her findings to solve a present problem.

Developing the Method 12.2 – Asking a Research Question in Qualitative Research

From the outset of their article, the Brantinghams establish that criminal behavior is associated with the physical environment. Even a cursory glance at a map of criminal incidents reveals that crime is not equally distributed throughout a community. It tends to cluster in certain areas. Of course, *association*, or correlation, is not *cause*. Just because criminal incidents are patterned does not mean that the physical space in which they occur is necessarily a cause of criminal behavior. So the researchers set out to understand how crime is related to physical space and to investigate whether there is a causal relationship between the two.

Since the publication of this research in 1993, a considerable amount of research has been done in the area of environmental crime. Subsequent researchers have substantiated the Brantinghams' findings so consistently that many criminologists and criminal justice practitioners routinely accept the connection between environmental factors and criminal behavior. But when this article was first published, the linkage was much more controversial and the research groundbreaking.

In that the Brantinghams took a grounded theory approach, their research was inductive. That is, they used observations to create an explanatory theory for the relationship between crime and the environment. Their research would be an example of pure research, since the Brantinghams were not looking to develop solutions to practical problems. Even so, their research was used by others to develop crime prevention strategies.

Getting to the Point 12.5 – Research questions that require the researcher to probe deeply into social phenomena or to develop new theories for explaining human behavior are best answered using a qualitative research method.

Conduct a Literature Review

The basic literature review in a qualitative study is not much different from that required for a quantitative study. It is important in either case to review both qualitative and quantitative studies on the subject. Indeed, reviewing quantitative research from a qualitative perspective can uncover research opportunities. As previously mentioned, there are some social phenomena that cannot be understood completely with quantitative measures. For example, a criminologist may hypothesize that criminal behavior is caused by *association* with criminal others. He measures *association* by the amount of time individuals spend in close proximity to known offenders. This measure, however, does not explain why correctional officers, who are in daily contact with known criminal offenders, do not commit crime themselves. Maybe there is more to *association* than just spending time with offenders. In this case, a qualitative researcher might look at *how* individuals associate with criminal offenders, which may be just as important as the amount of time they spend with criminal offenders.

Remember that qualitative research looks at specific behaviors occurring in particular contexts. The results of such research are not generalizable to other social settings. Thus, if you find a qualitative study similar to the kind you are proposing, it still might be reasonable to proceed with your research. The historical or geographic context may be different enough to justify another qualitative look at the phenomenon. For example, you may be interested in studying methamphetamine addiction in adults. You find a qualitative study on methamphetamine addiction in Australia. But you know the results cannot be generalized to addiction in the United States. So you decide to use the qualitative techniques and measures used by the previous researcher and replicate the study in a U.S. setting. In this way, you can compare your results to the existing research and contribute to the body of knowledge on methamphetamine addiction.

Grounded theory is distinguishable from other forms of research because the importance of the literature review is somewhat diminished. Grounded theory research does not begin with preconceived notions of how humans or social groups behave. In this sense, a traditional literature review is problematic. Instead, researchers using a grounded theory approach should begin by observing the phenomenon or behavior. This does not mean that researchers should not read up on the subject before entering the field. They may want some background and some sense of the research on the topic before commencing with data collection. But the literature review should not inform the conceptualization process. Conceptualization should be informed by the data and the data alone.

Developing the Method 12.3 – Conducting a Literature Review in Qualitative Research

A substantial part of the Brantinghams' study relied on the previous work of other researchers. This is not typical of most grounded theory research, in which researchers are encouraged to begin observations with an open mind and with little input from the literature. In this respect, the Brantinghams' research should not be considered pure grounded theory research. It also has elements of a case study.

The Brantinghams (1993: 5) drew on three areas of research in their literature review:

- the complex causes or origins ("etiology") of crime;
- individual crime patterns and how the physical environment influences these patterns;
- aggregate crime patterns and how the physical environment influences these patterns.

The Brantinghams observed that none of the previous research 'connected the dots' and considered the relationship between where crime happened, how individuals came to commit crimes, and why crime patterns emerged. Thus, they decided to proceed with their study of how this relationship came together. They used the three areas of research that they reviewed to construct an overall framework for exploring this relationship.

Getting to the Point 12.6 – During the literature review process, qualitative researchers should examine both quantitative and qualitative studies. Existing quantitative research could be enhanced by a qualitative look at the phenomenon; existing qualitative research could be enhanced by looking at the phenomenon in a different context. Grounded theory is distinguishable from other forms of research because the importance of the literature review is somewhat diminished.

Refine the Research Question

If the research is intended to produce exploratory or descriptive information, which many qualitative studies are, traditional hypotheses that predict causal relationships between variables are not required. Instead, you may want to simply explain what you anticipate finding in the research and/or outline a set of research questions. If the research is explanatory, both null and alternative hypotheses are customary.

Developing the Method 12.4 – Refining the Research Question in Qualitative Research

Because the Brantinghams' approach was more inductive, they did not formulate initial hypotheses. Instead, they proposed that a relationship existed between individual crime patterns, aggregate crime patterns, and the physical environment. Their objective was to create a theory that explained this relationship, which subsequent researchers could test through hypothesis-driven research.

Getting to the Point 12.7 – If qualitative research is intended to produce exploratory or descriptive information, traditional hypotheses that predict causal relationships between variables are not required.

Define the Concepts and Create the Measures

The process by which qualitative researchers define concepts is much the same as it is for quantitative researchers, except that qualitative researchers attempt to define concepts at a deeper and more subjective level. For example, studies of violence against women may define battering of women in terms of its prevalence, frequency, and severity. But this conceptualization cannot tell us what the experience of battering means for a woman and what the relationship is between battering and power. Rather than focus on the actual act of battering, a qualitative study might focus on women's perceptions and experiences of battery.

In terms of measurement, qualitative researchers do not rely on quantitative measures. Hence, a qualitative study cannot always be reduced to clearly defined variables. Instead, in-depth observations and interviews attempt to get at subjective meaning and experience. To a quantitative researcher, for example, income may be a useful indicator of poverty. A qualitative researcher may 'measure' poverty at a more experiential level. How do people describe the condition of poverty? What particular experiences do they point to as embodying the experience of poverty? And how do they know when they are living in poverty or moving out of poverty? Again, these are not so much measures as they are descriptions of a subjective experience.

Developing the Method 12.5 – Defining Concepts and Creating Measures in Qualitative Research

Again, conceptualization is critical in qualitative research design, just as it is in quantitative research design. But conceptual definitions may be a little more detailed. Below is a summary of some of the major conceptual definitions used in the study by the Brantinghams (1993: 5).

CONCEPTS	DEFINITIONS
Crime	Crime refers to a broad range of actual behaviors, which may be the result of many different incentives or causal processes.
Individual crime patterns	Individual crime patterns refer to individual criminal acts and where they occur.
Aggregate crime patterns	Aggregate crime patterns refer to where crime occurs, the volume of crime, and the types of crime that occur at a location.

An interesting omission in this list of conceptual definitions is any mention of the term 'physical space.' Although not explicitly defined, physical space in this study refers to a particular area that is distinguishable from other areas in terms of its structure and social interaction. What the researchers imply is that they attempted to differentiate between actual parts of town wherein the residents are socially connected, that is, neighborhoods.

Getting to the Point 12.8 – The process by which qualitative researchers define concepts is much the same as it is for quantitative researchers, except that qualitative researchers attempt to define concepts at a deeper and more subjective level. In terms of measurement, qualitative researchers do not rely on numbers, focusing instead on subjective meanings and experiences.

Design a Method

Again, there are three common qualitative research methods: case study research, ethnographic research, and grounded theory research. A **case study** is a detailed study of a single group, place, or situation. Case studies can either be inductive or deductive. That is, a researcher may conduct a case study in order to develop a theory of why something happened (inductive) or use the information coming from a case study to test the viability of a theory (deductive).

Case studies require the researcher to do more than merely report what is happening. We already know *what* is happening; we want to know *why* something is happening. What are the critical factors in the case? What key decisions were made, who made them, and why did they make the decision they did? What effect did this have on the outcome? Case studies typically involve some combination of in-depth interviews, archival research, and observations.

Case studies can focus on either a typical case or an extreme case. **Typical case studies** focus on cases that are typical or usual. For example, a case study on the death penalty might focus on the events that occur during the investigation, trial, incarceration, and execution of a capital crime offender. **Extreme case studies** focus on atypical or unusual cases. Extreme case studies are helpful for understanding why or how a system did not work the way it was supposed to work. For example, a researcher may evaluate a case involving a chronically abused child in order to determine how the child protective system failed to work on the child's behalf.

Getting to the Point 12.9 – Typical case studies focus on cases that are typical or usual; extreme case studies focus on atypical or unusual cases.

Ethnographic research attempts to understand social phenomena within the context or from the perspective of a particular culture or group. Ethnographic research is very similar to field research, which relies on observations of people and places in their natural setting. But ethnographic researchers move beyond covert observation to become participant observers. In other words, they actually live within the culture or social group they are studying. In doing so, they hope to develop a deeper understanding of the dynamics of the culture. For example, a field researcher may observe homeless people, whereas an ethnographer may actually live as a homeless person. This provides the ethnographer greater access to the research subjects and a more detailed understanding of the group than mere observation would allow.

Ethnographic researchers also use interviews and archival research to develop a nuanced understanding of a particular cultural setting. Ethnographic interviews tend to be longer, more detailed and free flowing than structured interviews since they try to get at the perceptions, experiences, and feelings of individuals in the culture. A great deal of ethnographic research consists of conversations and interactions with individual members of a culture.

Ethnographic research tends to take longer, particularly when the social group being studied is quite different from the ethnographer's own culture or social milieu. In many cases, ethnographic research requires researchers to learn a new language alongside new cultural customs. And this can elongate the research process even more. Perhaps the most difficult challenge for an ethnographer is to approach each research context with an open mind. Individuals develop attitudes and behavioral expectations within their own culture and often learn about other cultures through their own cultural lenses. For example, it may be difficult to understand polygamy, the practice of having multiple wives, when coming from a Western culture where polygamy is not traditionally practiced. To the extent possible, ethnographers must approach the research process with their personal attitudes and cultural beliefs in check so that they can see the world through the lens of another culture. **Ethnocentrism**, the belief in the superiority of one's own culture, has no place in ethnographic research.

> **Getting to the Point 12.10** – Ethnographic research is very similar to field research, which relies on observations of people and places in their natural setting. A major difference is that ethnographic researchers actually live and socialize within the culture they are studying.

Finally, **grounded theory research** is a methodological approach whereby the researcher uses qualitative data and inductive reasoning to develop a theory of some human or group behavior. You may recall that induction begins with a set of observations. These observations are evaluated, compared, and analyzed to achieve some theoretical explanation of human behavior. This is very different from the more commonly used deductive process whereby researchers start with a theory and then gather observations to test the viability of the theory.

In terms of the actual methods used, grounded theory research is not that different from case study and ethnographic research. It involves archival analysis, observations, and interviews. Note that qualitative interviews are quite different from the kind of interviews we explored in our discussion of survey methods. Qualitative interviews utilize open-ended questions and are intended to elicit a more subjective response. For example, in a forced-choice or closed-ended interview question, a researcher might ask: *"Do your friends put pressure on you to smoke marijuana?"* A respondent would be able answer this question with one word – *yes* or *no*. An open-ended interview question might be *"How do your friends pressure you to smoke marijuana?"* The response to this question would be a bit more complicated and would require more thought on the part of the respondent.

Open-ended questions also lend themselves to follow-up and probing questions. For example, in response to the question *"How do your friends pressure you to smoke marijuana?,"* an individual might discuss peer pressure in general terms. As such, a qualitative researcher can pose more probing and follow-up questions, such as *"What happens when you tell them no?"* and *"How do you feel when you succumb to this peer pressure?"* Qualitative interviews are best understood as semi-structured conversations between a researcher and a person about whom that researcher would like to learn more.

> **Getting to the Point 12.11** – In terms of the actual methods used, grounded theory research is not that different from case study and ethnographic research. It involves archival analysis, observations, and qualitative interviews.

Developing the Method 12.6 – Designing a Method in Qualitative Research

The Brantinghams' research has elements of both case study and grounded theory research. They did not conduct observations or interviews. Instead, they drew their data from the published literature to explore why and how people commit crime, where crime happens, and whether or not physical spaces affect crime. They used this information to develop a theory of crime and the physical environment.

This approach is consistent with the grounded theory of research in that it all but ignores what we already know about a topic, such as what one might discover during a literature review, and develops theory from the observations. This approach is a legitimate research method in situations where researchers do not want to be overly influenced by the previous research on a topic. In other words, they want to give the issue a fresh look.

Collect and Analyze the Data

Qualitative researchers must have strong observational and interviewing skills. They must see the world in ways that others do not and they must establish relationships of trust to gain access to other people's perspectives. Police officers are great qualitative researchers because they are usually very skilled at making observations, getting information from people, and figuring out what is most important.

Above all, qualitative researchers must be persistent. For example, researchers conducting a case study may want to access material that may not be readily accessible. This is particularly true of open criminal cases and in cases involving juvenile offenders. Even if access is granted, such access may be limited. Parts of the case, sometimes important parts, may be redacted and therefore unavailable to the researcher. Finally, information about a particular case may not reside in one place. In fact, it seldom does. This requires the researcher to be creative about finding different sources of information.

Persistence is even more important in ethnographic research. Ethnographers have to gain access to a culture or social setting that may be hard to gain entrée to. Ethnographers often rely on gatekeepers to gain such access. **Gatekeepers** are influential people within the culture who can open doors, introduce the researcher, and encourage individuals to speak with the researcher. They sort of vouch for the researcher and assure people of the researcher's legitimacy. Once ethnographers gain access to a culture, they still have the hard work to do of establishing relationships with individuals who can provide a window into that culture. As in all human relationships, these relationships can be complicated and emotionally taxing for the ethnographer.

Effective qualitative researchers develop highly refined methods for recording and recalling the information they gather during the research process. For example, ethnographers write up extensive field notes on their observations and often use personally developed cataloging systems that enable them to organize the information they collect. Interviewers may use audio or video recording devices to be sure they capture as much information as possible.

Getting to the Point 12.12 – Qualitative data collection requires keen observational and interviewing skills, a great deal of persistence, and refined notetaking and recording techniques.

Once the data are collected, the analysis phase can commence. Analyzing qualitative data can be more challenging than analyzing quantitative data. In quantitative research, there is a standard set of statistics that you can run to analyze your data. These statistics will give you and others a meaningful picture of the phenomenon you are studying. Qualitative research does not have such a standard set of analytic tools. Though it is often the case that qualitative researchers will use descriptive statistics to describe their sample of interviewees or the case under investigation, the overall thrust of qualitative research is to explore subjective meanings, perceptions, and experiences.

In most cases, qualitative researchers analyze written information rather than numeric data. A case study of a serial murderer, for example, might involve the analysis of media coverage of the murders, case files from the murderer's imprisonment or institutionalization, and written communication between the murderer and others. Ethnographers also study written information, though this information is usually in the form of field notes and interview transcripts. Likewise, a grounded theory researcher might analyze written archives, field observations, and interview transcripts.

The actual way in which the qualitative researcher goes about analyzing these written documents is very similar to the coding process used in a content analysis, which we examined in Chapter 11. Many qualitative researchers, particularly those who use a grounded theory approach, also use an analytic technique called **memoing**. This involves writing memos or formal notes related to the researcher's understanding of the social phenomenon under investigation and/or the theory that the data seem to be supporting. The purpose of memos is to reflect on the meaning of the data as it emerges in the process of data collection. In the memoing process, researchers make the leap from concrete data to abstract concepts and generalizable theories.

Developing the Method 12.7 – Collecting and Analyzing Data in Qualitative Research

The key to grounded theory research is to use observations to create a theory of some social phenomenon. In this case, the Brantinghams used existing crime data to construct a theory of criminal behavior. Using crime data, they looked to see if certain areas were more or less susceptible to certain types of crime. These data were organized onto crime maps that illustrated community crime patterns. These visual representations enabled the researchers to analyze where crime happens and what types of crimes happen where.

Though the researchers do not provide a great deal of insight into their particular analytical strategies, it is clear that they are using a type of spatial analysis to understand how and where crime takes place. Using maps, they indicate spatially an offender's activity space, which is defined by three major 'nodes,' namely home, work, and recreation. Offenders travel the space between these nodes along what the Brantinghams call 'paths.' It is along these paths, the Brantinghams argue, that crime is most likely to take place. Specifically, most crimes take place at 'edges,' or the boundaries of areas where offenders live, work, and play.

Getting to the Point 12.13 – In most cases, qualitative researchers analyze written information rather than numeric data. Two popular analytic techniques in this regard are coding, in which the researcher identifies major themes, and memoing, in which the researcher reflects on what the data mean.

Interpret the Results

The interpretation of qualitative information is the researcher's informed opinion about what the data mean. Another researcher may interpret the same information quite differently. For any one of these interpretations to be valid, however, the interpretation has to be reasonable and it has to be supported by the data. Say, for example, that a qualitative researcher conducts a study of campus safety using one college campus as a case study. She concludes that the college administration seriously underestimates threats to women's safety on the college campus. In order for this interpretation to be valid, she must present supporting evidence. She could point to quotes from campus personnel, observations of campus policies regarding safety (or the lack thereof), and information from crime reports from the university police.

The way in which qualitative researchers make sense of their data is not unlike how a prosecutor or defense attorney makes sense of the evidence in a criminal case. Both use evidence to make a particular argument about what happened. And both arguments may be valid. But it is the argument that makes most sense and is most supported by the data that is generally considered the strongest. In a sense, qualitative researchers play the role of prosecutor and the defense. They will consider all possible interpretations, but present one interpretation as the most convincing and most valid.

Remember that the purpose of qualitative research is not to generalize about larger social processes or phenomena. The purpose is to focus in on one social context, group, or situation to understand it in great detail. As such, qualitative researchers should be careful not to overreach their findings. Whatever they conclude in their study should apply only to the individuals or groups that were studied. The conclusions should not be applied to any individuals, groups, or institutions outside of that particular context. If qualitative researchers use their results to generalize to a larger population, they are overstepping the boundaries of good qualitative research. The best qualitative studies provide in-depth information that can be tested in future research studies using more rigorous sampling methods and more representative samples.

Developing the Method 12.8 – Interpreting the Results in Qualitative Research

After evaluating the crime maps that they constructed in the course of their study, the Brantinghams arrived at several conclusions. First, they alleged that an individual's knowledge of physical spaces influences his or her decision on where to commit crimes. Specifically, through their in-depth knowledge of the physical space surrounding them, potential criminals know the places that they are least likely to be observed. These are the places they are most likely to commit crimes. Their knowledge of physical space is organized into 'cognitive maps,' which potential offenders use to calculate when and where to commit crimes.

The Brantinghams also reasoned that offenders 'share' these cognitive maps. In other words, offenders seem to agree on the best places to commit crime. This collective but informal knowledge results in consistent crime patterns. That is, crime tends to occur in particular areas that can be predicted.

The interpretation of the data offered by the Brantinghams suggests that urban planners can use zoning regulations to minimize crime. For example, if ingress and egress pathways associated with schools, parks, and youth activity centers are hidden from the casual observation of others, incidents of graffiti are likely to increase along these pathways. If these pathways are opened up to casual observation, the incidence of graffiti is likely to go down (Brantingham and Brantingham, 1993).

Getting to the Point 12.14 – Qualitative researchers can make any number of valid interpretations of their data, so long as the interpretation is reasonable and supported by the evidence. But qualitative researchers should be careful not to overreach their findings.

Communicate the Findings

Rather than rely on charts and graphs to describe social phenomena, qualitative researchers rely on written narratives and/or storytelling techniques. Ethnographers, for example, will often use **thick description**, or a detailed account of their field site and an in-depth description of their field experience, when writing up their findings. Qualitative interviewers will use extensive quotes, giving voice to the people they interviewed. Finally, case studies will often include historical background on the case, detailed contextual information on the case, and in-depth descriptions of how the case evolved over time. Because qualitative research findings are described in narrative form, qualitative research reports and studies are often much longer than their quantitative counterparts.

As with all research, a key component of the research write-up is an analysis of the weaknesses and limitations of the research. Qualitative researchers should be forthcoming about how they collected their data, how trustworthy they think their data are, the contexts in which their data might be applicable, and their own biases in conducting the research. All of these pieces of information help to establish the validity of the research.

Developing the Method 12.9 – Communicating the Results of Qualitative Research

In terms of communicating their major findings, the Brantinghams provide a figure that illustrates the relationship between nodes, pathways, and edges to describe where and how crime patterns emerge. This helps the reader understand conceptually how these features of their theory are interrelated. Beyond this, their article is written in a very approachable manner. It is more conversational than technical in tone.

The Brantinghams do not explicitly state what they perceive to be the weakness of their research. This should not be construed to mean that their research is without fault. For example, they tend to report only the literature that supports their propositions. Admittedly, their review of the literature is extensive and their use of it is superior, but it is reasonable to expect that at least some studies refute the Brantinghams' proposition that physical environment affects crime patterns. It is also reasonable to suspect that certain types of crime (e.g., white-collar crime) are less affected by the physical environment. As such, the theory proposed by the Brantinghams may have its limitations.

Finally, nothing in their theory even attempts to explain how a 'motivated offender' becomes motivated in the first place. They are clear in their characterization of crime as an opportunistic event. Leaving one's wallet in a public bathroom creates an opportunity for crime. But each of us is given dozens of opportunities to commit crime each day. Why do some people pick up the wallet and keep it, whereas others turn it in to the lost-and-found desk? If a predisposition to commit crime is so important to their theory, then it seems reasonable that they should offer some explanation of what causes this predisposition.

Getting to the Point 12.15 – One of the key advantages of qualitative research is its ability to describe and interpret social phenomena at a level of detail that numeric measures cannot achieve. As such, qualitative reports are often longer and more narrative than their quantitative counterparts. They tend to 'tell a story' about the data.

FINAL THOUGHTS

Among researchers in criminal justice and criminology, there is something of a bias against qualitative research. Most researchers in these fields are rather captivated by the quantitative measurement of complicated social phenomena. Numbers are easy to generate, to justify, and to communicate. Qualitative research does not have this advantage. In that qualitative designs nearly always require researchers to get very close to the social phenomena they are studying, criminal justice and criminology scholars may also be wary of taking a qualitative approach. After all, there is a big difference between reviewing juvenile crime statistics and actually spending time with juveniles who commit crime!

These difficulties notwithstanding, qualitative research makes an important contribution to our study of crime and criminal justice. And it should not be overlooked by researchers who embrace a quantitative paradigm. When carpenters build a house, they use an assortment of tools. If boards need cutting, they use a saw. If boards need shaping, they use a plane. Likewise, a researcher must know when to use quantitative methods and when to use qualitative methods. In the end, if the research would benefit from a qualitative design, a researcher should never be afraid to go back to the truck and retrieve that tool. After all, we would probably fire the carpenter who only knew how to use a hammer.

GETTING TO THE POINT/CHAPTER SUMMARY

- Qualitative research refers to a broad category of research methods that attempt to produce a more detailed understanding of human behavior, including its meaning and its motivation.

- Some of the more popular qualitative research methods include case study research, ethnographic research, and grounded theory research. A case study is a detailed analysis of a single event, group, or person. An ethnography is an in-depth study of a culture. And grounded theory is a methodological approach that uses inductive reasoning to develop a theory to explain observed behaviors or processes.

- Qualitative research methods are effective when a researcher wants to develop a deeper or more nuanced understanding of a particular phenomenon. These methods are effective at determining how perceptions and meanings influence human behavior and for developing theories for previously unexplained social phenomena.

- Qualitative research methods are not effective when a researcher wants to generalize findings of the research to a larger or similar population. Some qualitative research may not be feasible because of ethical challenges.

- Research questions that require the researcher to probe deeply into social phenomena or to develop new theories for explaining human behavior are best answered using a qualitative research method.

- During the literature review process, qualitative researchers should examine both quantitative and qualitative studies. Existing quantitative research could be enhanced by a qualitative look at the phenomenon; existing qualitative research could be enhanced by looking at the phenomenon in a different context. Grounded theory is distinguishable from other forms of research because the importance of the literature review is somewhat diminished.

- If the qualitative research is intended to produce exploratory or descriptive information, traditional hypotheses that predict causal relationships between variables are not required.

- The process by which qualitative researchers define concepts is much the same as it is for quantitative researchers, except that qualitative researchers attempt to define concepts at a deeper and more subjective level. In terms of measurement, qualitative researchers do not rely on numbers, focusing instead on subjective meanings and experiences.

- Typical case studies focus on cases that are typical or usual; extreme case studies focus on atypical or unusual cases.

- Ethnographic research is very similar to field research, which relies on observations of people and places in their natural setting. A major difference is that ethnographic researchers actually live and socialize within the culture they are studying.

- In terms of the actual methods used, grounded theory research is not that different from case study and ethnographic research. It involves archival analysis, observations, and qualitative interviews.

- Qualitative data collection requires keen observational and interviewing skills, a great deal of persistence, and refined notetaking and recording techniques.

- In most cases, qualitative researchers analyze written information rather than numeric data. Two popular analytic techniques in this regard are coding, in which the researcher identifies major themes, and memoing, in which the researcher reflects on what the data mean.

- Qualitative researchers can make any number of valid interpretations of their data, so long as the interpretation is reasonable and supported by the evidence. But qualitative researchers should be careful not to overreach their findings.

- One of the key advantages of qualitative research is its ability to describe and interpret social phenomena at a level of detail that numeric measures cannot achieve. As such, qualitative reports are often longer and more narrative than their quantitative counterparts. They tend to 'tell a story' about the data.

CHAPTER EXERCISES

The following chapter exercises are organized into two parts. The first part consists of questions that can be answered using the information from this chapter. This section will test your understanding of the chapter material. The second part consists of research application exercises. These exercises require you to apply what you have learned thus far.

CHAPTER REVIEW QUESTIONS

Respond to each of the following questions using the information from this chapter.

1. A research approach that uses inductive reasoning to develop a theory of some behavior or process is known as _____ research.
    a.   Case study
    b.   Cultural ethnography
    c.   Grounded theory
    d.   Thick description

2. Read the following research descriptions and decide which type of qualitative research is being described (case study, ethnography, grounded theory).

Research description	Qualitative method
A researcher conducts an in-depth study of one white-collar criminal in order to understand how other white-collar criminals operate.	
A researcher lives as a prisoner for a year in an effort to understand the prison subculture.	
A researcher interviews gang members to develop a theory explaining why juveniles are attracted to gangs.	

3. Read the following research scenarios and indicate whether qualitative research methods would be appropriate.

Research scenario	Are qualitative methods appropriate? (Yes or No)
A police officer has discovered that an increasing number of teenagers in her town are using a drug known as 'bath salts.' She does not know where the teens are buying the bath salts or how they are administering bath salts. So she decides to do some research on the matter.	
An assistant professor wants to do a study on the prevalence of posttraumatic stress disorder among police officers in the nation. He is not aware of any study that has attempted to measure this prevalence and thinks the information might be useful to policing agencies.	
A graduate student wants to do research on war rape and war-related sexual violence. He is interested in learning how and why women are raped and sexually assaulted in the context of ongoing military conflicts around the world.	
The assistant director of a homeless shelter is seeing an increased number of homeless families in her community. She wants to learn more about the circumstances surrounding their homelessness and their particular housing and social welfare needs.	

4. True or False: Qualitative research cannot be of an applied nature; it only has a place in pure research.

5. Which of the following qualitative research methods is *least* likely to feature a formal literature review?
    a. Case study research
    b. Ethnographic research
    c. Grounded theory research
    d. No qualitative research method features a literature review

6. Inductive research starts with ____ and moves to ____.
    a. Data; theory
    b. Hypotheses; measurement
    c. Numerical data; written data
    d. Observations; interviews

7. Read the following descriptions of case study research and indicate whether each is an example of a typical or extreme case study.

Research description	Type of case study
A researcher studies a juvenile sex offender to determine how these types of offenders 'select' their victims.	
During a study on police corruption a researcher decides to focus on an officer who is widely known as highly corrupt.	
A researcher chooses to study a serial arsonist who is allegedly responsible for setting hundreds of house fires.	
In order to increase his understanding of this emerging crime trend, a researcher conducts an interview with a teenager who has recently been convicted (first offense) of selling prescription drugs.	

8. Read the following research questions and indicate whether they are an example of a closed-ended (fixed response) question or an open-ended question.

Research question	Closed-ended or open-ended?
Select the box next to the range that includes your annual income. ☐ $15,000–$30,000 ☐ $30,001–$55,000 ☐ $55,001 or more	
How old should one be before one is allowed to purchase alcohol?	
What, in your opinion, is the most serious crime problem in your neighborhood?	
How many times have you been a victim of crime during the past year? ☐ None ☐ 1–3 times ☐ 4–6 times ☐ More than 6 times	

9. When qualitative researchers reflect on the meaning of their data and the concepts emerging from their data, they are engaging in a qualitative technique known as:
   a. Coding
   b. Memoing
   c. Recording
   d. Surveying

10. This term refers to influential people within a culture who can open doors for a qualitative researcher, introduce the researcher, and encourage individuals to speak with the researcher:
    a. Ambassador
    b. Fencesitter
    c. Gatekeeper
    d. Outlier

RESEARCH APPLICATION EXERCISES

Access to the following articles will be provided by your instructor.

Gaarder, E., Rodriquez, N. and Zatz, M.S. (2004). Criers, liars, and manipulators: Probation officers' views of girls. *Justice Quarterly, 21*(3), 547–578.

Gau, J.M., and Brunson, R.K. (2010). Procedural justice and order maintenance policing: A study of inner-city young men's perceptions of police legitimacy. *Justice Quarterly, 27*(2), 255–279.

Respond to the following questions for each of the articles cited above.

11. Why did the researchers conduct this research? What did they hope to learn?

12. To what extent had this subject been studied by previous researchers?

13. How did these researchers conceptualize and operationalize their variables?

14. How did the researchers collect, analyze, and interpret their data?

15. What were the major findings of each article?

16. How would you improve this research and/or conduct additional research to further expand the body of knowledge on this subject?

CHAPTER 13

Evaluation Research Methods

Do you ever wonder why you are spending four or more years of your life earning a Bachelor's degree? It is expensive to go to college and getting more so every year. The costs of tuition, fees, housing, and food, even at state-supported schools, have increased far faster than the rate of inflation. And interest charged on student loans adds to the cost of a college education over the long term, as does the income you lose by attending school fulltime rather than working fulltime.

There are, of course, major benefits to earning a Bachelor's degree. College-educated job applicants have a better chance of getting hired and securing higher starting salaries than high school graduates. Surveys of workers consistently indicate that those with college degrees have higher levels of work satisfaction. Individuals with college degrees have more flexibility and mobility, earning more over the course of their lives than do individuals with high school diplomas. So how do we determine if the benefits outweigh the costs of getting a college education? The answer is a simple cost/benefit analysis.

Just as we can evaluate whether a college education is worth it, we can evaluate whether a criminal justice program or a particular policy is meeting its stated objectives. Here is an example.

Making Research Real 13.1 – These Warrants Are Driving Me Crazy!

Sheriff Joyce Dupree's department has an active speed enforcement program. She implemented this program several years ago following an increase of traffic fatalities on the interstate highway that traverses her county. The program has been effective at reducing traffic fatalities.

In most cases, citizens who receive citations pay their fines. However, about 5 percent of the violators do not contact the court to settle the case. This results in the issuance of a warrant for the arrest of the violator. Currently, there are four deputies assigned to serving these warrants. These deputies attempt to locate the violator and encourage him or her to contact the court as soon as possible. Most violators do so, but a small percentage of the errant violators are very difficult to locate. In one case, a deputy worked for a week to locate a violator only to find out that he had moved out of state.

Sheriff Dupree estimated that it was costing the county about $400,000 in salary, benefits, transportation, and office supply costs to locate 5 percent of the violators. Even if every one of these paid

---

their fine, the county would only collect about $275,000. Therefore, Sheriff Dupree instructed the crime records section to enter traffic warrants into a passive warrant file. She then reassigned the four warrant officers back to the patrol division. Finally, she implemented a policy to not actively search for traffic violators who have not paid their fines, instructing officers instead to, "catch them the next time they get stopped."

One of the deputies suggested that the reason the majority of violators pay their fines is because the department has a reputation for locating them when they do not. "This new policy," the deputy suggested, "might result in an increase of individuals who choose to ignore their citation when the word gets around that we will not come looking for them." The sheriff thought this possibility was reasonable and asked the crime records section to provide her a monthly report on the number of citations and warrants issued each month. "That way I can monitor whether our passive warrant program is working," she reasoned.

Analyzing whether a program or an investment works or whether it is worth our time and effort is at the heart of evaluation research methods. **Evaluation research** considers the effectiveness, efficiency, and the unintended consequences of a program, process, or policy. In this chapter, I will discuss when and how to conduct this kind of research.

EVALUATION RESEARCH BASICS

Again, **evaluation research** is a collection of research methods designed to determine whether a program, process, or policy is achieving its intended outcome. In addition to helping us assess the actual or intended effectiveness of programs, evaluation research methods help us identify unintended consequences of such programs. Such methods are becoming increasingly important in criminal justice agencies. Criminal justice resources have never been unlimited and in some jurisdictions they are becoming scarce. As a result, governments are interested in whether the taxpayer funds they spend on criminal justice are achieving their intended benefits.

For those of you considering a career in criminal justice, learning evaluation research techniques can be a real career booster. One of my former students, we will call her Ann, learned this first hand. After earning her Master's degree Ann took a job as a parole officer. She completed the preservice training program and was assigned a case load of about 50 adult parolees. Over the next year, she observed that parolees who were unmarried, underemployed, and had a history of substance abuse were the most likely to re-offend during parole. Parolees who missed a meeting with their parole officers within the two-month period following their release from prison were also more likely to return to prison. Finally, parolees who were unable to manage their personal finances tended to supplement their incomes with illegal behaviors like drug dealing and burglary. Fortunately, only about 10 to 20 percent of her caseload fit into this category of 'at high risk of re-offending.' So, she focused most of her attention on these ex-offenders.

About a year after starting her job, Ann attended a meeting of parole officers from across the state. At the meeting, the Director of the Parole Commission informed them that the state was about to experience serious budget cuts. This meant that they would not be able to hire additional parole officers or even replace the ones who left the Commission for the foreseeable future. This also meant that recidivism among parolees was likely to increase because there would simply not be enough parole officers to adequately supervise them. After thinking about this problem, Ann pitched an idea to her supervisor. "Look, not all of our parolees need the same level of supervision. Some do fine with limited contact while others need more intensive control. And, with a little more evaluation, we might be able to predict the ones who, by virtue of their actual behavior during the first two months after release, are most likely to recidivate. These we can organize into smaller case loads and instruct the parole officers to supervise them more intensely. The rest can be assigned to larger case loads because they need less active supervision."

Ann's supervisor was impressed. Ann and her supervisor pitched Ann's idea to the Director of the Parole Commission. The Director agreed to let them try Ann's idea, but asked that they evaluate the program after a year. The results were encouraging. Despite a shortage of parole officers, the recidivism rates among parolees did not increase. And, the historically high level of re-offending by high-risk parolees actually decreased. The program is now a major part of the parolee supervision strategy in the state. And Ann is now a supervisor.

Getting to the Point 13.1 – Evaluation research is designed to determine whether a program, process, or policy is achieving its intended outcome and/or resulting in any unintended consequences. Evaluation research is becoming increasingly critical to criminal justice practice.

TYPES OF EVALUATION RESEARCH

There are two common types of evaluation research methods. A **cost/benefit analysis** is a technique that compares the costs and benefits of an existing or future program, process, or policy. For example, if a department wants to implement a new procedure for arrest processing, it might conduct a cost/benefit analysis to make sure the benefits of the procedure outweigh the costs of implementing it.

The **multiple methods approach** involves the use of multiple data gathering techniques to evaluate a program, process, or policy. A multiple methods approach can include a cost/benefit analysis, but most of the time this strategy involves a compilation of various research strategies like experiments, surveys, interviews, and content analyses. Below is an example of an evaluation research study that used a multiple methods approach.

Making Research Real 13.2 – Assessing Megan's Law

State laws that require sex offenders to register and notify public officials of their presence in a community are commonly called Megan's Law. In 2008, Kristen Zgoba, Philip Witt, Melissa Dalessandro, and Bonita Veysey published a report on the practical and financial aspects of Megan's Law in New Jersey. The authors were interested in the effect of Megan's Law on the overall rate of sexual offending over time, its deterrence effect on re-offending, and the costs associated with its implementation and its annual expenditures.

   The study by Zgoba et al. used a multiple methods approach. First, it studied trend data on sex offenses in New Jersey starting 10 years prior to the implementation of Megan's Law (in 1994) and 10 years after implementation. Second, it collected data on 550 sex offenders released from 1990 to 2000 to study various outcomes of interest. Finally, it reviewed implementation and administration costs associated with the law. Among the major findings of the study were the following:

* New Jersey, as a whole, experienced a consistent downward trend of sexual offense rates.

* In all but two counties, sexual offense rates were highest before 1994 and lowest after 1995.

* In the offender release sample, there was a consistent downward trend in re-arrests, reconvictions, and re-incarcerations over time similar to that observed in the trend study.

* Megan's Law showed no demonstrable effect in reducing sexual re-offenses.

* Megan's Law had no effect on reducing the number of victims involved in sexual offenses.

* Start-up costs associated with the law totaled $555,565 and current costs (in 2007) totaled approximately $3.9 million for the responding counties.

Given the lack of demonstrated effect of Megan's Law on sexual offenses, the study found that the considerable costs associated with the law might not be justified.

Getting to the Point 13.2 – Evaluation research typically involves either a cost/benefit analysis, in which the costs associated with a policy or program are weighed against the benefits, or a multiple methods approach, in which various data collection methods are used to evaluate a policy or program.

BENEFITS AND LIMITATIONS OF EVALUATION RESEARCH

Evaluation research is most effective in four types of research situations, as summarized in Table 13.1. First, evaluation research is effective at demonstrating the effectiveness or efficiency of an existing program, process, or policy. For example, for decades, prison-based vocational programs have trained incarcerated offenders in trades like plumbing, welding, and cosmetology. These programs are intended to provide offenders with an opportunity to work in a trade after their release, thereby reducing their potential for recidivism. But do they work? An evaluation of these programs would reveal the answer to this question.

Evaluation research is also effective for monitoring the performance of programs over time. In fact, new criminal justice programs are often required to include plans for the routine evaluation of their performance. In addition to actively monitoring the performance of a program, these evaluation systems are often designed to inform administrators of the need for additional resources or even when to discontinue the program. For example, police departments often receive grants from federal and state agencies to pay overtime to police officers assigned exclusively to enforce mandatory seat belt laws. In this case, independent evaluators might conduct observations at high-volume intersections to measure compliance with the mandatory seat belt law and to determine whether the benefits of the program outweigh the costs associated with it.

Third, evaluation research can identify the unintended consequences of a program, process, or policy. Even well-intended and carefully planned criminal justice programs can result in unintended consequences. For example, many states prohibit the issuance of a driver's license to undocumented workers. Ostensibly, this policy is designed to discourage undocumented workers from living and seeking employment in that state. But there are a number of unintended consequences of this policy. Not having a driver's license or another means of identification precludes an individual from opening a checking account, engaging in routine commerce, and purchasing the required automobile liability insurance. Indeed, some states are reporting increasing percentages of uninsured motorists, the economic effect of which can be substantial. Evaluation research can identify the unintended consequences of laws like this so that policy makers and voters are informed about potential consequences.

Finally, evaluation research can inform public debates on controversial subjects. For example, there is a near constant debate among criminal justice practitioners, policy makers, and scholars on how to address minor drug offending. Some experts advocate a punishment strategy, which would increase criminal penalties for minor drug offenses in the hopes that potential offenders will be deterred. Other experts suggest a therapeutic approach wherein minor drug offenders would receive counseling instead of criminal sanctions. And, a few experts advocate the decriminalization of drug possession altogether. Who is right? Nobody knows for sure. An evaluation project that studies each deterrence strategy would be helpful to this policy debate.

Table 13.1   The Uses of Evaluation Research

- Demonstrating the effectiveness or efficiency of an existing program, process, or policy
- Monitoring the effectiveness or efficiency of new programs, processes, or policies
- Evaluating the unintended consequences of a program, process, or policy
- Informing the debate on controversial programs, processes, and policies

> **Getting to the Point 13.3** – Evaluation research is effective at demonstrating and monitoring the effectiveness or efficiency of new and existing programs, processes, or policies. It can also identify the unintended consequences of and provide objective information about controversial programs, processes, and policies.

Just like all other research methods, there are some situations in which evaluation research would not be beneficial (see Table 13.2 for a summary). First, evaluation research cannot determine the underlying purpose of a program, process, or policy. This purpose must be identified before evaluation research can take place. For example, what is the purpose of prison? Some people believe that prison is intended to incapacitate violent offenders, keeping them in custody so that they cannot victimize others. Others say prison, or the threat of imprisonment, is designed to deter would-be offenders from committing crime. Still others advocate that prisons should be places where we rehabilitate offenders and encourage them to develop more pro-social behaviors. Unless we agree on the desired outcome of a program, process, or policy, there is really no way we can evaluate its effectiveness.

Second, evaluation research is less useful when a program, process, or policy is mandatory or legally required. For example, a police department's promotional system may be determined by a court to be discriminatory to women and racial minorities. In this case, a court order might require the department to change its promotional practices and accept the supervision from a court-appointed monitor, called a master. It would be pointless to evaluate the effect of these practices since they are mandated by the court.

Table 13.2   The Limitations of Evaluation Research

- Cannot determine the underlying outcome or objective of a program, process, or policy
- Pointless when a program, process, or policy is mandatory or legally required

> **Getting to the Point 13.4** – Evaluation research is not effective without agreed upon objectives or when a program is mandated by law, policy, or higher authority.

Before introducing the evaluation research process, it is important to pause and discuss an important ethical consideration. Evaluation research often finds that criminal justice programs are not effective and/or are too expensive, providing evidence for a program's discontinuation. In criminal justice practice, it is not always ethical or possible to discontinue a policy or program, as the following case suggests.

Making Research Real 13.3 – Let's Just Don't Go Down There Anymore

Officer Pete Banner is an experienced community policing coordinator for the Bigton Police Department. His evaluation research projects have identified numerous instances of waste and inefficiency. On a Friday afternoon, he had lunch with his old friend Alan Caffrey. Pete and Alan grew up together in Bigton, attended the same university and married sisters. Alan owns about a dozen food trailers that he operated throughout Bigton.

"Alan," Pete began, "I'm having a problem that I need your business advice on." Alan was surprised. He and Pete never talked business during their monthly lunches. "What is it bud?" Alan asked. Pete explained that he had been evaluating police calls for service and found about 40 locations throughout the city that seemed to call the police to report 'crime' nearly every day. "These are chronic users, maybe even abusers, of policing services. We go there every time they call, take a report, and attempt to solve the underlying problems; but nothing seems to work. These are an immense waste of time." Pete said.

"Well," Alan began, "when one of my food trailers does not produce enough income to justify its placement, we move it to another location. For example, we used to get requests for a food trailer down in Oakmont, but every time we set up one down there we don't sell enough to cover our expenses. So, we don't go down there anymore. I would tell the people that call the police too much to stop calling, and if they don't, I would just ignore them."

Pete thought for a moment. It was an intriguing idea. But after a moment, he realized that as a businessman, Alan has the option of not providing services in unprofitable locations. Police departments, and other public service agencies, do not always have that option. When people call, the police must respond. Pete explained this to Alan. "Well then, old friend, that is just the cost of doing business. No use griping about it. Let's eat. I'm starved," Alan responded.

THE EVALUATION RESEARCH PROCESS

In this section you will learn how researchers and practitioners conduct evaluation research. As before, this section is organized according to the steps of the research process outlined in Chapter 2. And, as before, you will see highlighted sections called 'Developing the Method.' Within these highlighted sections, you will read about how two researchers conducted an evaluation of an important criminal justice resource. I will begin by introducing you to these researchers, although one of them you already know.

Developing the Method 13.1 – A Case Study in Evaluation Research (The Police Protective Custody Process)

In most states, there is a process by which the police can remove abused and/or neglected children from their homes and place them in temporary housing. During this time (usually around three to five working days), the state can seek a court order to have the children permanently removed from the parents' care and placed in state custody pending assignment to a foster home or adoption. This process is known as police protective custody (PPC). In 2003, I conducted an evaluation of this process in Wichita, Kansas in conjunction with a social worker.

In Kansas, the PPC process allows a police officer to remove a child from the care of his or her parents if the officer has probable cause to believe the child is being abused, neglected, or is in need of care. In Wichita, children in this situation are taken to the Wichita Children's Home (WCH). Children admitted to the WCH are interviewed by social workers and representatives from the District Attorney's Office. Sometimes, they are also evaluated by health care providers. During a three-day period following their admission to the WCH, the State of Kansas, through the District Court, decides if sufficient evidence exists to remove the child from the care of his or her custodial parents.

Taking over the care of a child, investigating allegations of abuse or neglect, drawing up a petition for removal of the children from the home, and getting the case heard by the District Court within three business days consume a lot of resources. But the Wichita police know the children will be cared for while they are in the WCH and they know that social workers there will be able to evaluate the child's case properly. Use of the PPC process also reduces the police officer's exposure to liability. No police officer wants to explain why he or she chose not take a child into protective custody when doing so might have saved the child from serious injury or death. Finally, police officers often do not have the time to resolve these issues themselves. They are busy responding to other calls for service.

After being removed from their home in the PPC process, most children are returned and their parents are required or encouraged to accept home-based social services. Only a small percentage of children are permanently removed from their parents' custody. Thus, many children's advocates began to question the efficiency of the PPC process. If most children are returned to the home from which they came, why not just leave them there and deliver services to them while their case is evaluated? These concerns were taken all the more seriously when, in 2002, the State of Kansas faced a severe fiscal crisis. Revenue shortfalls, brought on by tax cuts and a reduction of overall economic activity, resulted in substantial budget cuts for many state services. Increasing costs, particularly for medical care, caused state leaders to look for alternative ways to deliver important state services (Withrow, 2003: i).

In 2003, the WCH asked me and Brien Bolin, a social worker, to assist them in evaluating the PPC process and its effect on the services they provided. At the time, Dr. Bolin and I were Assistant Professors at Wichita State University. Before joining the faculty, I had 20 years of experience as a police officer and administrator and Dr. Bolin had considerable experience as a practicing social worker.

Ask a Research Question

Anytime you evaluate a program, process, or policy, you are conducting evaluation research. As such, here are some examples of research questions you might find in evaluation research:

- *Do new physical fitness requirements for police officers reduce on-the-job injuries?*

- *Do faith-based rehabilitation programs reduce recidivism rates among released offenders more effectively than non-faith-based rehabilitation programs?*

- *Did the saturation patrol initiative reduce or merely displace vehicle burglaries?*

Evaluation research can be exploratory, descriptive, or explanatory depending on the researcher's objective. For example, evaluation research can explore current conditions and provide insight into what types of policies, processes, or programs might be effective in a particular situation. Evaluation research can also describe how individuals or organizations responded or failed to respond to a policy, process, or program. Finally, evaluation research can explain why a program did or did not meet its intended objectives. A recent evaluation research project conducted by the Vera Institute of Justice, for example, examined the cost of prisons to taxpayers in different U.S. states. Researchers found that in the 40 states that participated in the study, the total taxpayer cost of prisons was $39 billion. This particular evaluation project would primarily be descriptive in nature. However, it is entirely possible that after reading it a criminal justice policy maker would want to make changes to the criminal code so that the costs associated with prisons could be better managed.

This form of research is most often done to evaluate a specific policy or program for the purpose of justifying its continuation, change, or abandonment. Hence, evaluation research is almost exclusively applied research. Evaluation research seldom involves pure research because the researcher nearly always intends for the results of the project to affect policy or programming. Note that because of the applied nature of evaluation research, evaluation researchers often overlook theory. They do so at their peril. Theory attempts to explain human behavior in general and can inform how policies and programs might work outside of particular organizations and locations. When evaluators focus on the theory explaining how and why a program works, or does not work, they are in a better position to argue for or against its implementation elsewhere.

Developing the Method 13.2 – Asking a Research Question in Evaluation Research

The evaluation of the police protective custody (PCC) process in Wichita began with a meeting between Dr. Bolin, me and representatives from the Wichita Children's Home (WCH). At that meeting, we agreed upon the following research objectives:

1. To document the PPC process by which a child is referred to and housed by the WCH;

2. To determine what factors affect a child's length of stay at the WCH;

3. To make recommendations for reducing the number of PPC referrals to the WCH;

4. To make recommendations for reducing a child's length of stay at the WCH.

(Withrow, 2003: i)

This evaluation clearly fits the definition of applied research. The first research object was descriptive in nature in that we were asked to describe the process by which a child came to the WCH. The second research objective was exploratory in nature because prior to conducting the research the WCH did not have a solid understanding of what factors played a role in the length of a child's stay at the facility. The last two research objectives, making recommendations, required research of a more explanatory nature. We had to develop causal relationships for why children were referred to the facility before we could make recommendations for changing the system.

At the outset, we all knew that the recommendations would be used to change public policy. One might even argue that the objective of this evaluation research project was action oriented. The WCH wanted to continue to provide housing for abused and neglected children, but they wanted to be sure that the services were targeted at the children who needed these resources the most. Limiting scarce or expensive services to the truly needy is responsible public administration, particularly during times of dwindling resources.

Getting to the Point 13.5 – Evaluation research can be exploratory, descriptive, or explanatory depending on the researcher's objective. It is almost always applied because the researcher usually intends for the results to influence policies and programs.

Conduct a Literature Review

Although there are notable exceptions, most evaluation research does not appear in published form. Instead it resides in the form of reports in the files of criminal justice agencies and in a few practitioner-oriented databases like the National Criminal Justice Reference Service, the Police Executive Research Forum, and the International Association of Chiefs of Police. Since evaluation research is often filed away, subsequent researchers may not even be aware of its existence. The best, and maybe the only, way to access previous evaluation studies is to contact agencies that have programs similar to the one you are evaluating and ask them if they have ever done an evaluation of their programs and if they would share the results with you. Often these can be found on agency websites or by contacting an organization's information office. Generally speaking, criminal justice practitioners are helpful and willing to share information with other practitioners.

Though evaluation research is rarely published in scholarly journals, evaluation research is a legitimate scholarly pursuit and researchers may publish evaluation research in academic journals. In addition to scholarly journals, you may find the results of evaluation research in publications of various government agencies, such as the Department of Justice, Bureau of Justice Statistics, and the Bureau of Justice Assistance.

It is possible that your literature review will produce enough information to answer your research question, thereby avoiding the need to conduct a new evaluation. But be cautious in this regard; criminal justice agencies have a habit of 'borrowing' programs that are effective in other agencies and jurisdictions only to find that the programs do not work for their own agencies or jurisdictions. For example, a program that works well in an urban setting may not work at all in a rural setting. In these circumstances, it may make sense to conduct a formal evaluation of the program even though it has been shown to work in another setting.

Developing the Method 13.3 – Conducting a Literature Review in Evaluation Research

This research study was published in two different reports – one submitted to the Wichita Children's Home (WCH), another submitted to a scholarly journal. Because these outlets were so different, two distinct literature reviews were conducted and developed for the purpose of this evaluation. In 2003, I wrote an initial evaluation report for the WCH. The literature review in this report was limited to a review of police protective custody (PPC) practices in other jurisdictions and evaluations thereof. Specifically, I reviewed how other social services agencies respond to abused and neglected children and compared these practices with the approach used by the WCH.

In 2005, a more scholarly report on this study was published in *Policing: An International Journal of Police Strategies and Management*. This article included an extensive review of the scholarly literature, especially the literature on child protective custody. Within this literature we found numerous citations of research reports on how the protective custody process affects children and families. Interestingly, we learned that the overall effect of protective custody is quite harmful to children. Some researchers even suggested that leaving children in less than ideal conditions was, in the long run, better for them psychologically than placing them in custody.

Following the literature review in each case, there was no discussion of whether to proceed with the research. We were going to proceed with the research regardless of what the literature said because we were under contract to conduct the research and produce a report. Indeed, it would not have been prudent to make recommendations to the WCH based solely on how other jurisdictions were delivering similar social services. Social services are designed to respond to local needs and realities, which are typically unique to each locality. Just because a program works well in one community does not mean that it will work well in another. In short, the WCH wanted a full-scale analysis of *its* program and recommendations that would improve *its* service delivery system. Thus, there was no discussion about whether we would proceed with the research; there was just a review of how other localities were responding to the matter and how other researchers had studied child protective custody.

Getting to the Point 13.6 – Although evaluation research reports can be found in scholarly journals, the overwhelming majority of them are in the possession of various government agencies, privately sponsored research organizations, and individual criminal justice agencies. Such reports are typically available through the internet or can be made available through a direct request to the individual agency in possession of the report.

Refine the Research Question

Again, evaluation researchers are interested in whether policies, processes, and programs are achieving their intended results. Hence, the questions that an evaluation research study might ask are the following:

- *Did the policy, process, or program have its intended effect?*
- *Was the policy, process, or program implemented efficiently?*
- *Did the policy, process, or program result in unintended consequences?*

Although not explicitly stated as hypotheses, these questions are the functional equivalent of and can be formatted into alternative and null hypotheses. Let me illustrate with an example. Many years ago, the United States Immigration and Customs Enforcement (ICE) developed a program called Secure Communities. In this program, local police agencies receive training from ICE on how to recognize undocumented immigrants. In return, the local agencies agree to determine the citizenship status of individuals they come in contact with during routine law enforcement duties. If the officer has probable cause that the person is an undocumented immigrant, the case is referred to ICE for possible deportation proceedings. If a researcher were to evaluate this program, they might start with the following hypotheses:

Ha: *The Secure Communities program results in the apprehension of more criminal undocumented immigrants than would be arrested without the program.*

Ho: *The Secure Communities program does not result in the apprehension of more criminal undocumented immigrants than would be arrested without the program.*

A fundamental question regarding the Secure Communities program is whether it encourages racial profiling. Is it possible that a police officer would focus more scrutiny on Hispanic individuals because he or she suspects them of being undocumented immigrants? In this case, an evaluation researcher might also present hypotheses regarding the unintended consequences of the program:

Ha: *Implementation of the Secure Communities program does not result in the violation of individual civil liberties.*

Ho: *Implementation of the Secure Communities program results in the violation of individual civil liberties.*

The methods by which each of these hypotheses would be evaluated might be different. For example a secondary analysis of arrest and deportation records might provide insight into whether the Secure Communities program resulted in the apprehension of more criminal undocumented immigrants. A content analysis of recently filed court cases might reveal whether implementation of the Secure Communities program resulted in an increase in the number of defendants who allege racial profiling.

Developing the Method 13.4 – Refining the Research Question in Evaluation Research

The research on Wichita's police protective custody (PPC) process was primarily descriptive and exploratory. Specifically, we were asked to document the PPC process and to make recommendations on decreasing the number of PPC referrals. As such, alternative and null hypotheses were neither developed nor explicitly stated. Instead we had a set of specific research objectives. We were asked to:

1. document the PPC process by which a child is referred to and housed by the WCH;

2. determine what factors affect a child's length of stay at the WCH;

3. make recommendations for reducing the number of PPC referrals to the WCH;

4. make recommendations for reducing a child's length of stay at the WCH.

(Withrow, 2003: i)

Though we did not explicitly state hypotheses in this study, we made informal predictions about some of the relationships we were studying. For example, we predicted that children with only one or no parents, children with parents who were not married or used drugs, and children who had been previously abused would be more likely to be removed from their parents' custody. These predictions enabled us to at least begin the analysis. We would later learn that the actual relationships were very different.

Getting to the Point 13.7 – Evaluation research projects may begin with general research questions or explicit hypotheses depending on the nature of the project. In either case, the primary purpose is to investigate whether a program, process, or policy is having its intended results.

Define the Concepts and Create the Measures

At this stage, evaluation researchers must tackle the process of conceptualization and operationalization. In evaluation research, this involves figuring out how to measure policy or program success, efficiency, and/or effectiveness. For example, if a researcher is looking at whether the presence of uniformed officers in marked vehicles deters crime, he must define what he means by crime and explain how he plans to measure it. He might measure the number of calls to the police in beats wherein uniformed officers routinely patrol in marked vehicles versus beats wherein officers do so only occasionally. But are calls to the police a good measure of crime? Many citizens call the police about things that are not criminal and/or think that a crime is taking place when it is not.

Beyond these methodological issues, there is another factor researchers must consider when evaluating policy or program effectiveness. City councils, county boards of supervisors, state legislatures, the United States Congress, and other political institutions create criminal justice policies and programs and may have varied objectives in doing so. What constitutes a successful policy or program to one political institution may be quite different than what constitutes success to another institution. Evaluation researchers should be mindful of the various objectives and indicators of 'success' when measuring policy or program effectiveness.

Developing the Method 13.5 – Defining Concepts and Creating Measures in Evaluation Research

In the Wichita police protective custody (PPC) study, most of the concepts were defined by statute or policy. For example, we merely adopted the statutory definitions of terms like 'foster care,' 'residential care,' 'respite,' 'child in need of care,' 'child in need of supervision,' 'state custody,' and 'police protective custody.' These terms and concepts had meaning within the context of the process we were evaluating.

In terms of our measures, many of the variables we used were dichotomous, meaning that they had only two attributes: family status (two parents/one or no parents), parents' marital status (married/not married), public assistance (no/yes), parents' drug use (no/yes), and previous abuse (no/yes).

We realized pretty early that there were alternative measures of success that depended on the particular demands of the professionals involved in the system. Police officers associated success with the ability to refer a child to the WCH without restriction. Social workers defined success in terms of whether they were able to find a suitable long-term living situation for the child. Prosecutors defined success in terms of their ability to convince a judge to approve a child in need of care petition. Representatives from social services agencies who were concerned about expenditures defined success as the ability to limit services to children who did not need them.

We knew that our research would not satisfy all of the competing demands of the individuals involved in this complicated system. So we focused more on producing accurate descriptions of the system and how it works. We believed that such information would go a long way toward enabling the professionals involved in the system to reach their own conclusions.

Getting to the Point 13.8 – In evaluation research, researchers typically start by defining and operationalizing policy or program effectiveness. Because criminal justice agencies are publically funded, the researchers who evaluate criminal justice programs should be mindful of the various political objectives when developing measures of program effectiveness.

Design a Method

As previously mentioned, the actual method or methods used by evaluation researchers depends on the type of research question asked. Some research questions are better answered by experimental designs; others are better answered by surveys. The use of multiple methods has become particularly popular in evaluation research. For example, an evaluation of a crime prevention strategy might include a survey of public perceptions of safety, a secondary analysis of calls for service, and field observations of police during 'ride alongs.' Each of these data collection methods would answer some aspect of the research question or test one or more of the research hypotheses.

Developing the Method 13.6 – Designing a Method in Evaluation Research

Because the Wichita police protective custody (PPC) study began with four objectives, no single research method would have sufficed. Consequently, we used multiple methods in our evaluation. Initially, we thought that documenting the process by which a child is referred to the WCH through the PPC process could be accomplished through a series of interviews with police officers, social workers, WCH personnel, prosecutors, and judges. As we conducted these interviews, it became very clear that although these professionals were able to accurately describe their responsibilities in the process, few of them had a good sense of the larger picture of the PPC process. Therefore, we decided to conduct a focus group involving individuals from each of the agencies involved in the PPC process.

Among the things we wanted to learn from the focus group were how the police protective custody (PPC) process worked procedurally in each organization, how the work of different agencies impacted the work in other agencies, and what factors affected the processes followed by each agency. We also sought to learn about redundancies in the PPC process and how the agencies worked or did not work together. After listing all the things we wanted to learn from the focus group, we developed open-ended questions, such as *"How do you handle PPC cases?"* We shared these questions with the people we intended to invite to the focus group before the group actually met. Our purpose was to gauge whether the questions would yield productive discussions.

In addition to the focus group, we decided to use archival data to inform our understanding of the PPC process and the problems therein. Among the written documents we reviewed were policies, written procedures, memoranda, statutes, and court rulings. We also relied on secondary data to identify the factors that affected a child's length of stay at the Wichita Children's Home (WCH). Specifically, we used a data set containing information on 6,600 children who had entered the facility during the three years prior to our study. At the beginning, it was not clear whether the data would reveal the factors determining the length of a child's stay at the WCH. But because we did not have the time to embark on a lengthy data collection process, we stuck with the data set to see what it might reveal.

Finally, we decided to conduct interviews with key individuals involved in the PPC process. We scheduled these interviews toward the end of the research study for two reasons. First, they were intended to provide policy makers with an opportunity to express their opinions about the PPC process and offer suggestions on potential legislative or policy changes. Second, these interviews were intended to act as a peer review of the preliminary report. We needed additional confirmation that the PPC process we identified during the focus group was in fact an accurate reflection of what was occurring.

Getting to the Point 13.9 – The actual method or methods used by evaluation researchers to collect data depends on the type of research question(s) asked. The use of multiple methods has become particularly popular in evaluation research.

Collect the Data

Again the process by which data are collected in evaluation research depends on the method or methods chosen by the researcher. There are, however, a few data collection issues specific to evaluation research that bear mentioning. First, gaining full access to data during an evaluation is sometimes difficult. In many cases, individuals who make the policy or work in the program are less than willing to give information, lest the policy or program be found to be unsuccessful or inefficient. In some cases, researchers are denied access to data and/or people by the criminal justice practitioners who are worried about the outcome of an objective evaluation of their program. In other cases, administrators may actually suppress information. While the ethical implications of these practices are substantial, the effect on the quality of an evaluation project can be devastating. Prudent evaluation researchers should refuse to continue a project until they are convinced that they have full and unfettered access to the data they need.

Second, criminal justice information is notoriously incomplete, inaccurate, and inconsistent. It is collected by street-level operatives who are often too busy with other tasks to worry much at all about collecting data. Therefore, it is not uncommon to find large gaps in data or to see changes in how data are collected over time in most criminal justice agencies. Sometimes it is difficult to determine whether the data set has been inappropriately tampered with or just poorly managed. If the data have been poorly collected or managed, evaluation researchers should use other data to supplement this information and/or accept this as a limitation of their study.

Developing the Method 13.7 – Collecting Data in Evaluation Research

Again, the Wichita police protective custody (PPC) study involved four data collection methods: a focus group, a secondary analysis, an archival analysis, and interviews. The focus group especially required substantial planning and forethought. The invitees were busy people, so finding a time when all of them could be together for a whole day was a daunting task. Eventually a day was identified and nearly all of the invitees were able to attend. At this stage, the process of preparing for a focus group is a bit like preparing for a party. To encourage participation in the focus group, we chose an open classroom where the tables could be arranged in a square to create a more intimate environment. The room also had large dry erase boards on each wall, which could facilitate the discussion. We made sure the temperature and lighting were appropriate, set out supplies like writing tablets and pens, ordered coffee and doughnuts, and arranged for lunch to be delivered. Invitations were sent out with directions on how to find the class-room and, because the site was on a university campus, where to park.

I was in charge of running the focus group. When the invitees arrived, I greeted them, offered them refreshments, made introductions, and generally saw to it that they were comfortable. Then, I discussed the schedule and purpose of the day's meeting. Immediately, a hand shot up from the person representing the District Court. This person clearly had an opinion about how the process was working and was not afraid of being critical of how the other agencies were handling these cases. At this point, I had to strike a balance. On the one hand, I wanted this person to express her feelings. If her criticisms were aggressive enough, it might even encourage others to speak, if only to defend themselves. On the other hand, I did not want this person to intimidate others or discourage them from speaking. So I calmly listened and then walked to the dry erase board and drew the process as the speaker had described it. "Have I drawn this accurately?" I asked. This approach communicated to the group that the focus group was not intended to be a gripe session, but a workshop to create an accurate portrayal of the PPC process. Refocusing attention on this objective and away from the complaints gave other individuals 'permission' to speak.

By late afternoon, each representative had spoken and schematic drawings of each part of the PPC process filled all four of the dry erase boards. Throughout the day, my assistant periodically entered the room and copied down the information from the boards, which we used to create a schematic drawing of the entire PPC process. During the last hour, I passed out copies of this figure and asked the members to comment on it. Several did and we made revisions accordingly. Interestingly, most of the participants stayed late while my assistant completed their edits so that they could leave with a clean copy of the figure (see Figure 13.1). The focus group not only produced an agreed upon schema of the PPC process, it allowed me to develop rapport with representatives throughout the PPC system. Later, when I needed to validate infor-mation or ask questions, this rapport would prove useful. It also appeared that this was the first time many of these individuals had actually met. And the meeting showed them the importance of meeting regularly and led to a serious discussion about establishing an advocacy center.

As for the secondary data analysis, again, we relied on a data set maintained by the WCH that con-tained information on 6,600 children who had entered the facility during the three years prior to our study. Data from criminal justice agencies are notoriously incomplete and inconsistent and these data were no exception. For example, in the data set used for this analysis, I found that different codes were used. When entering information on the race of the children, data entry clerks sometimes used 'W' for 'White' and, at other times, 'C' for 'Caucasian.' Likewise, African Americans were sometimes coded as 'A' for 'African American' and, at other times, 'B' for 'Black.' We had to spend some time cleaning the data and adjusting the codes so that the analysis made sense.

To learn about what archival data existed and where it resided, I asked representatives from each agency for information on documents related to policies and procedures for the PPC process. I also asked for statistical reports related to the PPC process. In the end, I ended up with an impressive number of documents. This document review occurred after the focus group exercise. Ideally, it should have occurred before the focus group because it revealed important information about the PPC process. In one case, the process described by the participants of the focus group was refuted by the information that emerged from the document analysis. Phone calls to the focus group members revealed that they all had a misconception about one part of the process. As a result, the schematic drawing of the process was revised.

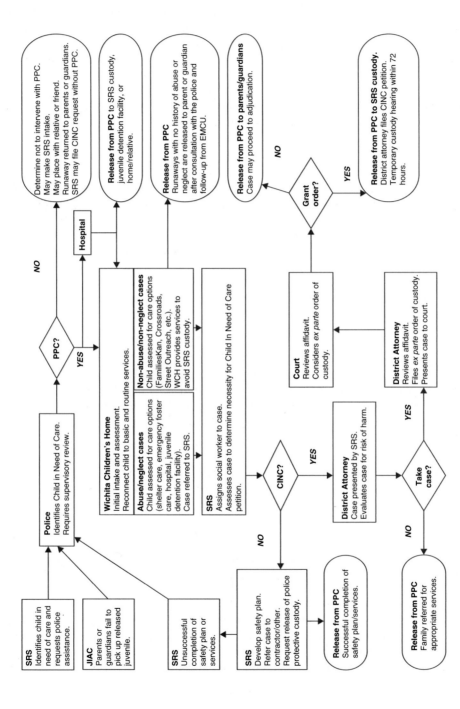

Figure 13.1 The Police Protective Custody Process as Identified Through Focus Groups Involving Participants in the Process

Finally, I conducted interviews with agency leaders, which turned out to be much more difficult than I had anticipated. These are busy people who have little time to speak with researchers. As a result, I was at the mercy of the interviewees' schedules. I had to be flexible and, in many cases, had to meet interviewees after hours or on the weekend. If I could not schedule sufficient time for an interview, I emailed the questions I wanted to ask beforehand so they could prepare for the interview. Most of the interviewees appreciated this and, in many cases, were more generous with their time than they had originally intended to be. The interviews were intentionally scheduled toward the end of the research process so that the interviewees could comment on a draft of the report that I had put together.

Getting to the Point 13.10 – Gaining access to data during evaluation research is sometimes difficult. In many cases, individuals who make the policy or work in the program are less than willing to give information, lest the policy or program be found to be unsuccessful or inefficient. Criminal justice data are also notoriously incomplete, inaccurate, and inconsistent. As a result, evaluation researchers should expect that they will need to spend considerable time preparing the data for analysis.

Analyze the Data and Interpret the Results

The process by which evaluation researchers analyze and interpret the results of their evaluation depends on the nature of the research methods used, the data produced by the research methods, and the overall objectives of the study. Evaluation researchers should bear in mind the point made earlier that criminal justice data are notoriously incomplete and inconsistent. For example, a researcher interested in evaluating how police officers make decisions during high-speed vehicular chases would have to accept the fact that the last thing a police officer has on his or her mind during such an event is collecting data for a researcher. Much of the data produced may be based on the officer's recollection of events, which may or may not be accurate. Acknowledging limitations like these is essential in interpreting the results of evaluation research.

> ### *Developing the Method 13.8 – Analyzing Data and Interpreting Results in Evaluation Research*
>
> Data analysis for the focus group, archival documents, and interviews was relatively straight forward in the Wichita police protective custody (PPC) study. Once the information from these methods was gathered, we merely had to reconstruct the PPC process in narrative and visual form and make note of the various problems and challenges that we uncovered.
>
> Analyzing the secondary data was a bit more involved. For example, we had to differentiate between PPC and non-PPC admissions to the Wichita Children's Home (WCH), since we were primarily focused on

children admitted to the WCH through the PPC process. Once we had prepared the data for analysis, we generated a series of descriptive statistical tables. For example, we compared the demographic features of the children admitted to the WCH through the PPC process with those admitted to the WCH outside of the PPC process. This provided some insight into the differences between these two populations. Interestingly, the two groups were quite similar.

After running some basic descriptive analysis, we turned our attention to identifying the factors that affected the outcome of PPC cases. To this end, we developed a logistic regression model. This statistical technique uses a dichotomous dependent variable. In this case, the dependent variable was called 'State custody' and its attributes were 'no' (coded as '0') and 'yes' (coded as '1'). If the case was coded 0, the child was not retained in state custody and was sent back home. If the case was coded 1, the child was retained in state custody. The analysis revealed that children who were admitted to WCH through the PPC process were more likely to be retained in state custody if:

- they had previously received state social or welfare services;
- they had parents who used illegal drugs;
- they had previously been abused; and/or
- they had limited parental supervision.

The analysis also revealed that children who entered the PPC process because they were abused were more likely to be retained into state custody than if they entered the PPC because they ran away. It was the parents' behavior, not the children's behavior, that determined whether they were retained in state custody.

We were also interested in the factors that affected the length of stay of children admitted to the WCH through the PPC process. Remember that the state must evaluate and decide the fate of each PPC-admitted child within three days. Weekends and holidays do not count. The result is that children admitted on Thursdays and Fridays often stay at the WCH two days longer because the courts are not available on the weekends. The secondary data analysis confirmed that releases were delayed for children admitted on Thursday, Friday, and Saturday.

Inevitably, during the analysis phase, challenges arise. This research was no exception. At one point, the data needed to be converted back to its original form and then recoded into a different format to facilitate a separate analysis. This would have been a tragedy had I not retained an original copy of the data set! These challenges notwithstanding, the results of our analyses led to a number of policy recommendations. Specifically, we recommended that the PPC process be used primarily for children who are most likely to be retained in state custody, namely those who:

- are being or have previously been abused or neglected by an adult;
- have previously received any type of state social or welfare services;
- have limited parental supervision; and/or
- are below an age (<16) when they can reasonably be expected to fend for themselves.

Children that did not fit this description could still be evaluated by the authorities for possible state custody. They would just do so without being housed at the WCH.

At this point in evaluation research a little dose of practicality is in order. We were confident in our analysis based on the data we had, but what about the data we did not have? We had learned during the focus groups that police officers consider dozens of factors while making a decision on police protective custody. Many of these factors are highly subjective and all of them are contextually specific to the situations at hand. So, a bit of caution is in order. The last thing we wanted to happen was to encourage the police officers or anybody else involved in the protective custody process to be overly confident in the statistical model. In other words, we were pretty sure about our conclusions based on the data we had, but had no clue about the effect of the data we did not or never would have.

Getting to the Point 13.11 – The interpretation process in evaluation research is not much different from that required in any research project. But evaluation researchers should bear in mind that criminal justice data are notoriously incomplete and inconsistent. This limitation should always been acknowledged in the interpretation of the results.

Communicate the Findings

It is appropriate for a small group of representatives, advocates, and beneficiaries of the evaluated policy, process, or program to review the evaluation report before it is made available. Often these individuals are in the best position to comment on evaluators' understanding of the problem, their interpretation of the results, and the potential effect of their recommendation(s). Here are a few questions reviewers and researchers should ask when reading a draft report of an evaluation study:

- Does the study cover the areas of concern of those affected by the policy, process, or program?

- Does the researcher have a good understanding of the policy, process, or program?

- Did the researcher do an adequate job of defining the concepts?

- Did the researcher validly and reliably measure these concepts?

- Are the researcher's recommendations reasonable?

Note that some reviewers will attempt to shape the results of evaluation research to serve their own interests. Researchers should never be influenced by a reviewer's agenda if it means departing from accepted research methods and analysis.

Evaluation researchers are often asked to present their findings in multiple formats and to multiple audiences. These audiences may include the public, policy makers, and scholars. The most daunting challenge in communicating the results of an evaluation study is when the media get involved. Generally, the media do not care about the literature review, the methodological design, or the statistical techniques used by the researcher. They want researchers to distill their findings into a headline or a sound bite. Moreover, reporters will often focus on the most controversial aspects of the study. As such, they may ignore the findings that the researcher believes to be the most important.

As in all research, evaluation researchers should be up front about the limitations and weaknesses of their study. This is all the more important in evaluation research since the results of such research are often used to justify a policy or program's continuation or discontinuation.

Developing the Method 13.9 – Communicating the Findings from Evaluation Research

The initial report that we wrote for the Wichita police protective custody (PPC) study was intended for the agencies involved. We attempted to be as brief as possible, so the entire report was only 29 pages, including tables and figures. To accommodate busy practitioners, the report had a two-page executive summary. In addition to writing this report, we were asked to present our findings at several meetings throughout the jurisdiction. For this, we developed another summary report that was longer than the executive summary but much shorter than the full report. We also developed a PowerPoint presentation to accompany these presentations.

In addition to the WCH report, we wrote up a scholarly version of the study, which was written second and was exposed to the customary peer review process. We wrote a more scholarly piece because we believed the findings would be of benefit to other researchers, especially criminologists and social workers. This report was published in the scholarly journal *Policing: An International Journal of Police Strategies and Management*. This version was written to a very different audience, who were quite familiar with the theoretical concepts involved in this research. We spent more time describing our methodology in the scholarly article because such descriptions are a necessary part of scholarly articles. Beyond these differences the articles were essentially the same.

In terms of strengths and weaknesses, we argued that our research did a good job of describing the PPC process. But we also admitted that our research did little to address the fundamental question about whether protective custody is an acceptable response to child abuse and neglect. At some level, removing a child from a dangerous situation is always an acceptable response. Children should never be allowed to remain in abusive or neglectful situations. The research, however, did not identify an alternative to the PPC process to use for children who are discovered in less dangerous situations. Further, the research did not address the liability concerns of police officers. Police officers do not want to be in a position of explaining why they failed to take children into protective custody upon encountering them in 'less than ideal' situations. As one officer commented during one of our research presentations: "Makes no difference to me. I am going to take a kid into PPC even if I *think* they might be in danger. I am not gonna have that on my head if they get hurt after I leave!"

Getting to the Point 13.12 – Evaluation researchers are often asked to present their findings in multiple formats and to multiple audiences. When the media get involved with disseminating the results of the research, evaluation researchers should be mindful of the complicated dynamics of public opinion and messaging.

FINAL THOUGHTS

A few decades ago, the policing profession experienced something of a philosophical shift. Whereas the public historically had been kept out of the policing process, the idea in the mid-1980s was to involve the public in basic police functions. This became known as community policing. We are now entering another philosophical shift in policing, this time toward an approach known as data driven, or predictive policing. This approach uses statistical data to identify small crime problems in the hopes of preventing large crime problems. Part of this process involves the frequent meeting of policing leaders to discuss crime problems and appropriate responses to them. Similar innovations are appearing in corrections.

In sum, the buzz words in criminal justice are 'evidence based practices.' Criminal justice leaders want programs, policies, and practices that are effective and efficient. For future criminal justice practitioners, such as you, the lesson is clear: knowing how to conduct evaluation research will become an increasingly important skill even at the lower levels of the organization. So, if you are wondering whether what you learn in this class will be relevant to you as a criminal justice practitioner, wonder no more.

GETTING TO THE POINT/CHAPTER SUMMARY

- Evaluation research is designed to determine whether a program, process, or policy is achieving its intended outcome and/or resulting in any unintended consequences. Evaluation research is becoming increasingly critical to criminal justice practice.

- Evaluation research typically involves either a cost/benefit analysis, in which the costs associated with a policy or program are weighed against the benefits, or a multiple methods approach, in which various data collection methods are used to evaluate a policy or program.

- Evaluation research is effective at demonstrating and monitoring the effectiveness or efficiency of new and existing programs, processes, or policies. It can also identify the unintended consequences of and provide objective information about controversial programs, processes, and policies.

- Evaluation research is not effective without agreed upon objectives or when a program is mandated by law, policy, or higher authority.

- Evaluation research can be exploratory, descriptive, or explanatory depending on the researcher's objective. It is almost always applied because the researcher usually intends for the results to influence policies and programs.

- Although evaluation research reports can be found in scholarly journals, the overwhelming majority of them are in the possession of various government agencies, privately sponsored research organizations, and individual criminal justice agencies. Such reports are typically available through the internet or can be made available through a direct request to the individual agency in possession of the report.

- Evaluation research projects may begin with general research questions or explicit hypotheses depending on the nature of the project. In either case, the primary purpose is to investigate whether a program, process, or policy is having its intended results.

- In evaluation research, researchers typically start by defining and operationalizing policy or program effectiveness. Because criminal justice agencies are publically funded, the researchers who evaluate criminal justice programs should be mindful of the various political objectives when developing measures of program effectiveness.

- The actual method or methods used by evaluation researchers to collect data depends on the type of research question(s) asked. The use of multiple methods has become particularly popular in evaluation research.

- Gaining access to data during evaluation research is sometimes difficult. In many cases, individuals who make the policy or work in the program are less than willing to give information, lest the policy or program be found to be unsuccessful or inefficient. Criminal justice data are also notoriously incomplete, inaccurate, and inconsistent. As a result, evaluation researchers should expect that they will need to spend considerable time preparing the data for analysis.

- The interpretation process in evaluation research is not much different from that required in any research project. But evaluation researchers should bear in mind that criminal justice data are notoriously incomplete and inconsistent. This limitation should always been acknowledged in the interpretation of the results.

- Evaluation researchers are often asked to present their findings in multiple formats and to multiple audiences. When the media get involved with disseminating the results of the research, evaluation researchers should be mindful of the complicated dynamics of public opinion and messaging.

CHAPTER EXERCISES

The following chapter exercises are organized into two parts. The first part consists of questions that can be answered using the information from this chapter. This section will test your understanding of the chapter material. The second part consists of research application exercises. These exercises require you to apply what you have learned thus far.

CHAPTER REVIEW QUESTIONS

Respond to each of the following questions using the information from this chapter.

1. A systematic technique that compares the costs and benefits of an existing or future program, process, or policy is known as a(n):
    a. Accountability study
    b. Cost/benefit analysis
    c. Feasibility study
    d. Program review

2. Evaluation research generally considers all of the following questions regarding a policy, process, or program except:
    a. Are there unintended consequences?
    b. Is the policy or program effective?
    c. Is the policy or program efficient?
    d. Is there public support for the program?

3. True or False: Evaluation research should focus primarily on intended, not unintended, outcomes of a policy or program.

4. Which of the following could not be said about evaluation research?
    a. Evaluation researchers should steer clear of controversial subjects.
    b. Formal hypotheses are required before starting an evaluation.
    c. It is rare to see evaluations that are descriptive in nature.
    d. The use of multiple methods is becoming more popular.

5. Where would you be most likely to find an evaluation research report?
    a. A scholarly journal
    b. A popular magazine
    c. An academic database
    d. An agency website

6. True or False: Evaluation research is generally not considered scholarly and cannot be published in academic journals.

7. Evaluation research is almost always _____ in nature.
    a. Applied
    b. Qualitative
    c. Quantitative
    d. Theoretical

8. Gaining access to the data necessary to complete evaluation research is sometimes difficult because:
    a. A court order is almost always required to access public records.
    b. Criminal justice programs are, by law, protected from public and private scrutiny.
    c. Individuals may want to avoid an objective evaluation of their program.
    d. The data almost never exist in a form that is unadulterated and unbiased.

9. Which of the following statements about the interpretation and communication phase of evaluation research is most accurate?
    a. It is common to allow agency representatives to put their 'spin' on the results.
    b. It is important to be up front about the limitations of the data used in the report.
    c. It is rare to allow beneficiaries of the evaluated program to review the report draft.
    d. It is not necessary to have the results of the study reviewed before publication.

10. When reporting on evaluation research, the media usually pays particular attention to the:
    a. Controversial findings
    b. Literature review
    c. Research design
    d. Statistical techniques

RESEARCH APPLICATION EXERCISES

Access to the following articles will be provided by your instructor.

Bazemore, G., Stinchcomb, J.B. and Leip, L.A. (2006). Scared smart or bored straight? Testing deterrence logic in an evaluation of police-led truancy intervention. *Justice Quarterly, 21*(2), 269–299.

Esbensen, F.A., Peterson, D., Taylor, T.J. and Osgood, D.W. (2011). Results from a multi-site evaluation of the G.R.E.A.T. program. *Justice Quarterly, 29*(1), 125–151.

Respond to the following questions for each of the articles cited above.

11. Why did these researchers conduct this research? What did they hope to learn?

12. To what extent had the subject of each article been studied by previous researchers?

13. What kind of data did the researchers in each case use?

14. How did the researchers collect, analyze, and interpret their data?

15. What were the major findings of each article?

16. How did the researchers add to the body of knowledge on this subject?

17. How might this research affect the practice of criminal justice?

18. How would you improve this research and/or conduct additional research to further expand the body of knowledge on this subject?

CHAPTER 14

Data and Information Analysis

Analysis is a rather useful word. It can mean some form of examination, study, investigation, scrutiny, and/or testing. In research, we use the term 'analysis' to describe the process by which researchers evaluate the data they gather and formulate an answer to their research questions or hypotheses.

Analysis occurs at the end of the research process, after we have conducted our literature review, designed our research method, and collected our data. But our planning of the analysis phase of research should start at the very beginning of the research process. Without an eye on how we plan to analyze our data, we cannot develop an effective research design. Indeed, concerns about analysis underlie the entire research process since analysis is the essential task in research. Here is an example.

Making Research Real 14.1 – Anticipating Analysis

A high school guidance counselor and school resource officer are concerned about illegal drug use and juvenile delinquency in their high school. They believe that these two factors are positively correlated, meaning that when juveniles increase their use of illegal drugs, they also increase their involvement in delinquent acts.

The most accurate statistic to measure the correlation between two variables is the **Pearson r** correlation coefficient. To calculate the Pearson *r* correlation coefficient, variables must be collected at the interval or ratio **level of measurement**. Unfortunately, our researchers overlook this requirement and develop a survey with the following two questions:

Do you use illegal drugs? (circle one) **YES** or **NO**

Before your 18th birthday, did you commit a violation of the law? (circle one) **YES** or **NO**

The variables in this case (drug use and juvenile delinquency) are collected at the nominal level. Thus, the Pearson *r* correlation coefficient cannot be calculated. Although statistical techniques are available to estimate correlation using nominal data, they are not nearly as precise as the Pearson *r* correlation coefficient.

Luckily, one of the researchers catches this error just before they send out the survey. They correct the mistake by rewriting the questions as follows:

About how many times per month do you use illegal drugs? _____

About how many times per month do you violate the law? _____

The responses to these questions can be measured at the interval or ratio levels. As such, the researchers can now calculate a Pearson r correlation coefficient. The researchers in this case are lucky. Had they gone ahead and collected the data before revising the questions, it would have been too late to conduct the kind of analysis they needed.

The purpose of this chapter is to describe the tools that researchers use to analyze data. The chapter is divided into two parts. The first part focuses on the analysis of quantitative data. **Quantitative data analysis** is a type of analysis wherein the objective values assigned to variables are evaluated. The second part focuses on the analysis of qualitative data. **Qualitative data analysis** is a type of analysis wherein the subjective and interpretive data produced by qualitative research methods is evaluated within the context of a research question. The analytical tools used by quantitative and qualitative researchers are different because the data these researchers collect are different. But generally speaking, analysis is analysis. In both quantitative and qualitative research, considerations about analysis should be made during the design phase of the research process to ensure that the proper analysis can take place.

Getting to the Point 14.1 – During the analysis phase, researchers evaluate the data they gather to answer their research questions or hypotheses. Even though analysis occurs near the end of the research process, considerations of analysis should occur earlier in the research process.

QUANTITATIVE DATA ANALYSIS

Why is it that many people do not like statistics? Well, for one, many people are not particularly fond of math. In math, there are no shades of gray, just right or wrong answers. This can be more than a little intimidating. Second, statisticians use strange words. Exactly what do we mean when we say that "the normal distribution is asymptotic to the abscissa"? But perhaps the biggest reason why people do not like statistics is that they do not trust statistics. Consider, for example, the title of one of the most popular statistics textbooks: *How to Lie with Statistics* (Huff and Geis, 1993).

Though it is reasonable to be scared or distrustful of statistics, there is no good excuse for not developing a solid understanding of statistics. The purpose of this chapter is to provide such an understanding. The beauty of statistics is that they summarize large amounts of data into a single number. In doing so, they enable us to communicate information efficiently. There are two general types of statistics. **Descriptive statistics** tell us the current state of things. With descriptive statistics, we can *describe* what *is* happening. **Inferential statistics** enable us to pinpoint the causes of social phenomena and to predict outcomes. In short, inferential statistics allow us to *infer* what *might* happen. We will cover both types of statistics, which form the basis of quantitative analysis, in the sections that follow.

Note that instruction on the use of statistical software like SPSS, SASS, and STATA is beyond the scope of this book. Instead, I will review some of the most commonly used statistics so that you become familiar with how such statistics are used in quantitative data analysis.

Getting to the Point 14.2 – Statistics summarize large amounts of data into a single number and enable us to communicate information efficiently. There are two general types of statistics: descriptive statistics and inferential statistics.

Descriptive Statistics

Again, **descriptive statistics** describe the current state of something. For example, we may want to describe the characteristics of the prison population or the extent of illicit drug use in a particular community. These statistics provide us a single number that summarizes an entire sample or population.

Measures of Central Tendency   In quantitative data sets, data tend to cluster around a central value. For example, if we were to take the height of all the adults in the world, most of the heights would cluster around one number. A number of descriptive statistics attempt to get at that central value. And in statistics, we call these descriptive statistics **measures of central tendency**. These measures include the mean, median, and mode, which again are all expressions of some central value.

Getting to the Point 14.3 – Descriptive statistics describe the current state of something. An important set of descriptive statistics are known as the measures of central tendency. These measures include the mean, median, and mode.

The **mean** is simply the average of all the values of a particular variable (e.g., height, income, etc.). It is calculated by adding together all of the values for a particular variable and dividing that sum by the total number of cases. For example, if we wanted to know the average age of the 15 faculty members of a Criminal Justice Department, we would ask each of them their ages and add up all the ages. Here is how it would look:

PROFESSORS	AGES
Adams	43
Banes	51
Childes	33
Dunn	43
England	64
Fisher	48
Gaines	50
Harris	34
Isaacson	49
Jones	38
Keller	53
Larson	57
Moore	84
Nadler	43
Owens	51
Total	**741**

Next, we would divide this figure by 15, which is the total number of cases. Below is the actual formula. Σx means the sum of all values and **n** equals the total number of cases:

$\Sigma x/n$

$741/15 = 49.4$

Again, the value of the mean is that we have condensed all the ages into a single number to give us a sense of the group as a whole. Even though the mean is useful, it does have a disadvantage. Specifically, it is sensitive to extreme scores. Notice, for example, that most of the professors in our sample are in their 30s, 40s, and 50s. But

Professor Moore is 84 years old and Professor English is 64. The ages of these two professors pushes the average up and gives the impression that this department is older than it really is. We refer to these extreme scores as **outliers**.

Getting to the Point 14.4 – The mean is calculated by adding together all of the values for a particular variable and dividing that sum by the total number of cases. Although it is a good measure of central tendency, it is sensitive to extreme values, or outliers.

Because the mean is sensitive to extreme values, we might consider using another measure of central tendency, such as the median. The **median** refers to the *middlemost* value; it is the value that is situated in the middle, with half the cases equal to or greater than and half the cases equal to or less than this value. In order to derive the median, you must first arrange the cases in order. It does not matter if they are arranged from highest to lowest or lowest to highest; they just have to be in order. Let us go back to our original list of faculty ages, this time arranging them from youngest to oldest:

PROFESSORS	AGES	
Childes	33	
Harris	34	
Jones	38	
Adams	43	
Dunn	43	
Nadler	43	
Fisher	48	
Isaacson	49	← Median = 49
Gaines	50	
Banes	51	
Owens	51	
Keller	53	
Larson	57	
England	64	
Moore	84	

We derive the *position* of the median by dividing the total number of cases (n) by 2 (i.e., dividing it in half). Here is the formula:

n/2 = the position of the middlemost value, or median

15/2 = 7.5

Then we count, either from the top or from the bottom, to the median's position. Starting from the top with Professor Childes we count down seven and a half spaces and land on Professor Isaacson. Starting from the bottom with Professor Moore we count up seven and a half spaces and again land on Professor Isaacson. Either way, Professor Isaacson is in the middle. There are seven professors younger and seven professors older than Professor Isaacson. Therefore, the median age of the professors in the department is 49.

In general, the median is much less sensitive to extreme values in comparison to the mean. For example, if Professor Moore were to retire, the mean age of the department would fall from 49.4 to 46.9 years of age. That is a fairly significant drop. What would happen to the median in this case? Let us take a look.

PROFESSORS	AGES	
Childes	33	
Harris	34	
Jones	38	
Adams	43	
Dunn	43	
Nadler	43	
Fisher	48	
Isaacson	49	← Median = 48.5
Gaines	50	
Banes	51	
Owens	51	
Keller	53	
Larson	57	
England	64	

n/2 = the position of the middlemost value, or median

14/2 = 7

Starting from the top with Professor Childes we count down seven spaces and land on Professor Fisher. Starting from the bottom with Professor England we count up seven and spaces and land on Professor Isaacson. So, in this case the median exists halfway between Professors Fisher and Isaacson, or 48.5 years of age. Had Professors Fisher and Isaacson both been 48 years of age then the median would have been 48 years of age. It is often the case, however, in distributions with an even number of cases like this one, that the median will be a number that does not actually exist within the original distribution. As we can see, the median did not change much with Professor Moore's retirement, even though Professor Moore is considerably older than the other professors.

Getting to the Point 14.5 – The median is referred to as the *middlemost* value because it is the value that is situated in the middle, with half the cases equal to or greater than and half the cases equal to or lesser than this value. It is less susceptible to extreme values or outliers than the mean.

A third important measure of central tendency is the **mode**, which is the most frequently occurring value in a population or sample. In most cases, there is only one most frequently occurring value. Let us determine the mode in our distribution of professors' ages.

PROFESSORS	AGES	
Childes	33	
Harris	34	
Jones	38	
Adams	43	
Dunn	43	Mode = 43
Nadler	43	
Fisher	48	
Isaacson	49	
Gaines	50	
Banes	51	
Owens	51	
Keller	53	
Larson	57	
England	64	
Moore	84	

As we can see here, 3 of the 15 professors are 43 years old. Thus, the mode in this case is 43. Like the median, the mode is not as sensitive to extreme scores, or outliers. If Professor Moore retires, the mode will still be 43.

Getting to the Point 14.6 – The mode is the most frequently occurring value in a population or sample. Like the median, the mode is less susceptible to extreme values or outliers than the mean.

So which measure of central tendency is best at describing a sample or population? It depends, in part, on whether the data are skewed by extreme scores. If there are no extreme scores, any or all three measures of central tendency should be reported because they will be similar. If the data are skewed by extreme scores, only the median or the mode should be reported since the mean is sensitive to extreme scores. Another factor to consider is how the data are measured. If the data are measured at the interval or ratio levels, all three measures of central tendency can and should be reported. If the data are measured at the nominal level, only the mode should be reported since you cannot calculate a mean or median for nominally measured variables. Table 14.1 provides examples of different levels of measurement and the corresponding measure of central tendency that is typically reported.

Table 14.1   Level of Measurement and Measures of Central Tendency

LEVEL OF MEASUREMENT	MEASURE OF CENTRAL TENDENCY	EXAMPLE
Nominal	Mode	With the exception of the driver, the most frequently injured occupant in a vehicle crash (the mode) is the person in the front passenger seat.
Ordinal	Mode, median	A review of the top scores in the Sergeant's Promotional Exams indicates that the patrol officers who most frequently place near the top of the list (the mode) are those with 10 or more years of experience.
		Of the 11 officers that took the latest promotional exam, six scored 95 percent or higher and six scored 95 percent or lower, meaning that 95 percent is the median score among these test takers. According to this department's promotional policy, only the six officers who scored 95 percent or higher are eligible for further promotional consideration.
Interval/Ratio	Mode, median, mean	The most frequently occurring age (the mode) at which juveniles begin offending is 12 years.
		The median age at which juveniles begin offending is 12 years. Half of all juvenile offenders begin offending at 12 years of age or younger; half begin offending at 12 years of age or older.
		The average (mean) age at which juveniles begin offending is 12 years.

Getting to the Point 14.7 – The decision about which measure of central tendency to use should be based on two factors: (1) whether the data are skewed toward extreme scores, and (2) what level the variables are measured at.

Variability

Measures of central tendency tell us what is usual or typical about the cases in a sample or population. They do not, however, tell us much about the variation that exists within the sample or population. To do this, we need another set of descriptive statistics that relate to **variability**. These statistics are referred to as **measures of variability**. The first descriptive statistic in this regard is known as the **range**, which is the difference between the highest and lowest value in a sample or population. The range is computed by subtracting the smallest value from the largest value. Returning to our list of professors, they range in age from 84 years (Professor Moore) to 33 years (Professor Childes). Therefore the range of ages is 84–33, or 51 years.

Highest value – Lowest value = Range

84 – 33 = 51

Like the mean, the range is sensitive to extreme scores. Again, if Professor Moore (the oldest professor at 84 years of age) retires, the next oldest professor will be Professor England, who is 64. Professor Moore's retirement will reduce the range to 31, a fairly dramatic change.

64 – 33 = 31

Getting to the Point 14.8 – Measures of variability are descriptive statistics that tell us how much variation exists within a sample or population. Among the measures of variability is the range, which is the difference between the highest and lowest value in a sample or population. This descriptive statistic, like the mean, is susceptible to extreme scores or outliers.

To overcome this sensitivity to extreme scores, we often use the **standard deviation**. This measure of variability considers how much each value varies from the mean. Returning to our original list of professors and their ages, the mean age is 49.4 years. To calculate the standard deviation, we subtract each professor's age from the mean. For example, Professor Childes is 33 years old. When we subtract 49.4 from this number, we get –16.4. We do this for each professor, calculating how much each professor's age varies from the mean age.

PROFESSORS	AGES	AGE – MEAN (49.4)
Childes	33	−16.4
Harris	34	−15.4
Jones	38	−11.4
Adams	43	−6.4
Dunn	43	−6.4
Nadler	43	−6.4
Fisher	48	−1.4
Isaacson	49	−0.4
Gaines	50	0.6
Banes	51	1.6
Owens	51	1.6
Keller	53	3.6
Larson	57	7.6
England	64	14.6
Moore	84	34.6
Totals	**741**	**0.0**

If we add all these variations, we get some indication of how much variation exists in our sample of professors. Of course, if we simply added up the numbers, the result would be zero because some of the differences are negative and some are positive (see above). So instead of adding up the differences (and getting zero), we square each difference and then sum the squared deviations from the mean. You may recall from algebra, that the product of two negative numbers is always positive. Consider, for example, the difference between Professor Childes' age and the mean (−16.4). If we square this difference (−16.4 × −16.4), the product will be a positive number (268.96). The table below illustrates what this would look like for every member of our sample of professors.

PROFESSORS	AGES	AGE – MEAN	$(\text{AGE} - \text{MEAN})^2$
Childes	33	−16.4	268.96
Harris	34	−15.4	237.16
Jones	38	−11.4	129.96
Adams	43	−6.4	40.96
Dunn	43	−6.4	40.96

Nadler	43	−6.4	40.96
Fisher	48	−1.4	1.96
Isaacson	49	−0.4	0.16
Gaines	50	0.6	0.36
Banes	51	1.6	2.56
Owens	51	1.6	2.56
Keller	53	3.6	12.96
Larson	57	7.6	57.76
England	64	14.6	213.16
Moore	84	34.6	1197.16
Totals	**741**	**0.0**	**2247.6**

The sum of 2247.6 in the table above is called the sum of squares. Again, we get this sum by squaring each deviation from the mean and adding those numbers together. To calculate the standard deviation, we divide the sum of squares by n, which refers to the total number of cases in our sample. Then, we take the square root ($\surd$) of this quotient.

$$\sqrt{\frac{\sum(x-m)(x-m)}{n}}$$

$$\sqrt{\frac{2247.6}{15}} = 12.2$$

Now that we know how to calculate the standard deviation, how do we interpret it? Higher standard deviations indicate higher levels of variation; lower standard deviations indicate lower levels of variation. Again, consider what might happen if Professor Moore were to retire. In this case, the sum of squares would be 1055.44 and the standard deviation would be 8.7. Without Professor Moore, the ages vary less from the mean (lower levels of variation) and the standard deviation is therefore lower. Because the standard deviation considers both the mean and the total number of cases in the sample or population, it is a much more stable statistic than the range.

Getting to the Point 14.9 – The standard deviation is a descriptive statistic that describes how much variability exists within a sample or population. Because the standard deviation considers both the mean and the total number of cases in the sample or population, it is a much more stable statistic than the range.

Percentages, percentiles, and percent changes are also commonly used descriptive statistics. A **percentage** is a portion of a sample or population. All percentages are based on a denominator of 100. So, if we say that 30 percent of all police officers are members of the National Rifle Association, we mean that for every 100 police officers, 30 are members of the National Rifle Association. Percentages are calculated by dividing the number of like cases by the total number of cases, then multiplying that quotient by 100.

$$\frac{\text{Number of like cases}}{\text{Total number of cases}} \times 100 = \text{Percentage of like cases}$$

So, if there were 257 police officers in our sample of 857 police officers who were members of the National Rifle Association, about 30 percent of our sample of police officers would be members of the National Rifle Association.

$$\frac{257}{857} \times 100 = 30\%$$

Getting to the Point 14.10 – A percentage is a descriptive statistic that describes a portion of a sample or population. Percentages are calculated by dividing the number of like cases by the total number of cases, then multiplying that quotient by 100.

A **percentile** is a statistic that tells us where a value ranks within a distribution. Sometimes this is referred to as the **percentile rank**. For example, if your score on an exam was at the 90th percentile, 90 percent of all the people who took the exam scored equal to or less than you. The formula for the percentile is as follows:

$$\frac{\text{Number of scores below}}{\text{Total number of cases}} \times 100 = \text{Percentile rank}$$

For example, say a police officer scores 83 on a promotional exam. A total of 125 officers took the exam. When the scores are listed from highest to lowest, we learned that 101 officers scored below 83. In this case, the police officer scored at the 81st percentile.

$$\frac{101}{125} \times 100 = 81\text{st percentile}$$

Another way of understanding the percentile is to consider how it relates to the median. The median is the 50th percentile. Half (50 percent) of the cases are equal to or greater than the median and half (50 percent) of the cases are equal to or less than the median.

Percent change is a descriptive statistic that indicates how much something changed from one time to the next. For example, if we learned that the number of robberies fell 30 percent, we might conclude that the police department was doing a good job. We calculate the percent change by subtracting the original number from the new number, dividing that difference by the original number and then multiplying that quotient by 100.

$$\frac{\text{New number} - \text{Original number}}{\text{Original number}} \times 100 = \text{Percent change}$$

Let us apply this formula to a change in stolen vehicles from one year to the next. Last year, 135 vehicles were reported stolen in the town of Bigton. This year, 185 vehicles were reported stolen in Bigton.

$$\frac{185-135}{135} = \frac{50}{135} = .370 \times 100 = 37\%$$

In this particular case, there was a 37 percent *increase* in the number of stolen vehicles. If the number of stolen vehicles had gone down between last year and this year, this percent change would have indicated a decrease in stolen vehicles.

In criminal justice and criminological research, we also use a lot of rates. A **rate** enables us to compare similar behaviors across multiple locations. For example, in 2009, there were 471 reported murders in New York City. That same year, there were 166 murders reported in Dallas, Texas. If you concluded from this that the odds of being a murder victim were higher in New York than in Dallas, you would be mistaken. To compare the incidence of murder between these two cities, we would need to factor in the population size of each city. Crime rates are usually based on reported incidents per 100,000 residents. In 2009, New York had a population of 8,391,881 and Dallas had a population of 1,299,543. We divide each of these numbers by 100,000, which gives us the number of 100,000 units. Then, we divide the number of reported murders by the number of 100,000 units.

CITY	RESIDENTIAL POPULATION	100,000 UNITS (to 2d.p.) (POPULATION ÷ 100,000)	REPORTED MURDERS	MURDER RATE (REPORTED MURDERS ÷ 100,000 UNITS)
New York	8,391,881	83.92	471	471/83.92 = **5.61**
Dallas	1,299,543	13.00	166	166/13.00 = **12.77**

Although New York City experienced nearly three times as many murders as Dallas, when we factor in the size of their residential populations, the murder rate turns out to be much lower in New York. Note that some researchers use smaller base numbers (e.g., 1,000 instead of 100,000). We often see this when the comparisons are being made between communities that have smaller populations.

> **Getting to the Point 14.13** – Rates are a descriptive statistic that enable us to compare similar behaviors across multiple locations. Rates factor in population size and report incidents per *n* units.

The Normal Distribution   A final statistical concept with which you should be familiar is the **normal distribution**. In 1809, a German mathematician by the name of Carl Friedrich Gauss created the concept of the normal distribution, which revolutionized the field of statistics. Gauss observed a high degree of consistency among individuals with respect to their physical features and other attributes. For example, most people tend to be about the same height. Hence, their height clusters around the same number (see Figure 14.1).

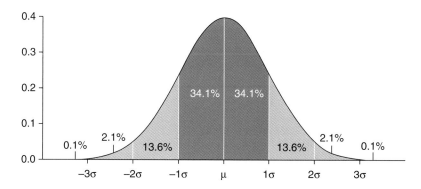

Figure 14.1   The Normal Distribution

Source: http://en.wikipedia.org/wiki/Normal_distribution

In what Gauss called the normal distribution, 68.2 percent of all cases fall within one standard deviation of the mean. Further, 95.4 percent of all cases fall within two standard deviations of the mean, and 99.9 percent of all cases fall within three standard deviations of the mean. In normally distributed data, the mean, median, and mode are equal because all of the data are distributed equally around the same value. We can use this information to predict outcomes. Consider the example below.

Making Research Real 14.2 – How Intelligent Are the Inmates in Our System?

A researcher administers an IQ test to 100 randomly selected inmates. She finds that the average (mean) IQ score is 100 and that the data are normally distributed. The researcher calculates the standard deviation as 10.

Based only on what we know about the normal distribution, we would know that the most frequently occurring IQ score (the mode) is 100. We would also know that half of the inmates have IQ scores of 100 or higher and half have IQ scores of 100 or lower. We would also know the following:

- 68.2 percent of the inmates have IQ scores ranging from 90 to 110 (+/– 1 SD);

- 95.4 percent have IQ scores ranging from 80 to 120 (+/– 2 SDs); and

- 99.9 percent have an IQ score ranging from 70 to 130 (+/– 3 SDs).

If you knew this information and an inmate were assigned to your unit with an IQ of 65, you would know that this inmate's level of intelligence is lower than average. You might use this information when assigning the inmate to the vocational and educational programs available and when making other decisions regarding his or her incarceration.

Getting to the Point 14.14 – In normally distributed data, the mean, median, and mode are equal because all of the data are distributed equally around the same value. In a normal distribution, 68.2 percent of all cases fall within one standard deviation of the mean; 95.4 percent of all cases fall within two standard deviations of the mean; and 99.9 percent of all cases fall within three standard deviations of the mean.

Inferential Statistics

Like descriptive statistics, inferential statistics provide insight into the current state of key variables. But inferential statistics go a step further; they also provide information that can help us predict outcomes related to key variables. Detailed instruction on how to perform inferential statistical techniques is beyond the scope of this textbook. What we will focus on is the logic behind different inferential statistical techniques.

Statistical Significance   The first thing we want to know when looking at inferential statistics is whether the statistic is statistically significant. **Statistical significance** is a measure of the probability that the statistic is due to chance. As a general rule, if the statistical significance of a statistic is .05 or less, we can conclude that the results are not due to chance. The .05 level of statistical significance means that there is a 5 in 100 chance that the results are due to pure chance.

> **Getting to the Point 14.15** – Inferential statistics enable analysts to determine the probability of certain outcomes. When reading inferential statistics, we are concerned with statistical significance, which is a measure of the probability that the statistic is due to chance. If the statistical significance of a statistic is .05 or less, we can conclude that the results are not due to chance.

T-tests   We will start our discussion of inferential statistics with the *t*-test. The **t-test** is a statistical technique used to determine whether or not two groups are different with respect to a single variable. To run a *t*-test, you must have interval or ratio level data. For example, you might determine if two cohorts of criminal justice majors differ with respect to their scores on an assessment exam. A *t*-test produces a **t-score** statistic. Again, if the statistical significance of the *t*-score is .05 or less, we can conclude that the difference between the two groups is not due to chance. Here is an example.

Making Research Real 14.3 – Improving the Self-Esteem of Juvenile Offenders

A juvenile probation officer observes that many of the juvenile offenders in her caseload have very low self-esteem. She believes that if they can improve their self-image, they might be less likely to reoffend. So, she decides to conduct an experiment. She administers a Self-Image Inventory to the 50 juvenile probationers in her caseload. This survey measures how an individual perceives their self-esteem. It ranges from 0 to 100. After administering the survey, she randomly divides the 50 juvenile probationers into two equivalent groups. Each group scores an average of 35 on the Self-Image Inventory. The first group is exposed to a six-week self-esteem workshop. The second group is not.

At the end of the training, the probation officer again administers the Self-Image Inventory to all 50 of the juvenile offenders in her caseload. She learns that the 25 juvenile offenders who were exposed to the training (the experimental group) improved their scores from an average of 35 to an average of 50. The 25 juveniles who did not receive the training, again, scored an average of 35.

On the surface, it would appear that the self-esteem workshop improved the self-images of the juvenile offenders who were exposed to the training. But the probation officer knows that she cannot simply 'eyeball' this. She must conduct a *t*-test to determine if the difference in the scores is statistically significant. After all, the difference could be due to chance. She calculates a *t*-score, which turns out to be statistically significant. She concludes that the self-esteem workshop improves a juvenile offender's self-image.

> **Getting to the Point 14.16** – The *t*-test is a statistical technique used to determine whether or not two groups are different with respect to a single variable. *T*-tests can only be run using interval or ratio level data. If the statistical significance of the *t*-score is .05 or less, it can be concluded that the difference between the two groups is not due to chance.

Analysis of Variance   Another inferential statistical technique is known as the **analysis of variance (ANOVA)**. Like the *t*-test, this technique is used to determine whether or not two groups are different with respect to a single variable measured at the interval or ratio level. But an ANOVA model allows us to compare more than two groups. An ANOVA produces an **F-ratio** statistic, which, like the *t*-score, is tested for statistical significance. If the statistical significance of the *F*-ratio is .05 or less, we can conclude that the difference between at least two of the groups is not due to chance. When comparing three or more groups, it is possible that one group will be different from the others, but the others will be more or less the same. The *F*-ratio only tells us whether or not at least one group is different from the others. In most cases, the researcher must conduct further tests (called **post hoc tests**) to determine which groups are different and which groups are the same. Consider the example below.

Making Research Real 14.4 – Improving the Self-Esteem of Juvenile Offenders – Part II

The juvenile probation officer who ran the experiment on whether self-esteem training would improve the self-images of juvenile offenders is now interested in testing whether the effects of this training are different for different types of offenders.

She administers the Self-Image Inventory to the 75 juvenile probationers now in her caseload. Then, she divides the 75 juvenile probationers into three groups. The first group (drug offenders), second group (sex offenders), and third group (non-drug and non-sex offenders) each scored an average of 35 on the inventory. Each group is exposed to the six-week self-esteem workshop. At the end of the experiment, each of the offenders is administered the same Self-Image Inventory. Here are the results:

OFFENDER GROUP	AVERAGE PRETEST SCORE	AVERAGE POSTTEST SCORE
Sex offenders	35	40
Drug offenders	35	55
Non-sex/drug offenders	35	50

The probation officer determines that the *F*-ratio statistic is significant. At this point, she knows that at least one of the groups is significantly different from the other two. But she wants to know which groups are statistically different. So she conducts a post hoc test. The post hoc test reveals that the self-esteem training improves the self-images of juvenile drug offenders and juvenile non-sex/non-drug offenders, but not juvenile sex offenders.

Getting to the Point 14.17 – The analysis of variance (ANOVA) model allows analysts to compare two or more groups to see if they are different with respect to a single variable measured at the interval or ratio level. An ANOVA produces an *F*-ratio statistic. If the statistical significance of the *F*-ratio is .05 or less, it can be concluded that the difference between at least two of the groups is not due to chance.

Chi Square (X^2)   A third inferential statistical technique is called the **chi square** test. The chi square test is used to determine whether there is a difference between what we expected to happen and what actually happened. This statistical model requires nominal data. The operative statistic is called the **chi square statistic**. If the statistical significance of the chi square statistic is .05 or less, we can conclude that the difference between what actually happened and what was supposed to happen was not due to chance. Here is an example.

Making Research Real 14.5 – Profiling at the Airport

Since the terrorist attacks on September 11, 2001, boarding a commercial airplane has become much more difficult. Travelers are subjected to a higher level of scrutiny and more invasive searches. Over the years, a number of racial, ethnic, and religious groups have complained that they are subjected to higher levels of scrutiny. To evaluate this accusation, a research team decides to conduct an observational study.

After receiving permission from the U.S. Transportation Safety Administration, the team sets up a booth at each of the security screening areas of a major airport. Using a paper tally sheet, they record the race, ethnicity, and religious appearance of the ticketed passengers who pass through the security area. A total of 10,491 ticketed passengers pass through the security area during the three days they observe the security screening area. The passengers are classified as follows:

RACE OR ETHNICITY	NUMBER	PERCENT
White or Caucasian	7,343	70
Black or African American	1,258	12
Hispanic	1,154	11
Asian	629	6
Other or Unknown	107	1
Total	10,491	100

RELIGIOUS APPEARANCE		
Muslim	525	5
Sikh	315	3
Neither Muslim nor Sikh	9,651	92
Total	10,491	100

Of the 10,491 ticketed passengers observed passing through the security area, 1,012 are pulled from the line and asked to submit to a more invasive search of their belongings and persons. These individuals are also classified with respect to their race or ethnicity and religious appearance. Here are the results:

RACE OR ETHNICITY	NUMBER	PERCENT
White or Caucasian	719	71
Black or African American	111	11
Hispanic	121	12
Asian	51	5
Other or Unknown	10	1
Total	1,012	100
RELIGIOUS APPEARANCE		
Muslim	162	16
Sikh	40	4
Neither Muslim nor Sikh	810	80
Total	1,012	100

Comparing the percentages of each group that is observed with the percentages of each group that is searched, the research team finds the following:

FREQUENCIES	WHITE	BLACK	HISPANIC	ASIAN	OTHER	TOTALS
Observed in the secure area	70	12	11	6	1	100
Searched in the secure area	71	11	12	5	1	100
Difference	−1	1	−1	1	0	0
Difference^2	1	1	1	1	0	4

Computed $X^2 = 4$
Critical value of $X^2_{(.05, 4df)} = 9.488$

FREQUENCIES	MUSLIM	SIKH	NEITHER	TOTALS
Observed in the secure area	5	3	92	100
Searched in the secure area	16	4	80	100
Difference	−11	−1	12	0
Difference^2	121	1	144	266

Computed $X^2 = 266$
Critical value of $X^2_{(.05, 2df)} = 5.991$

In these tables, the team has subtracted the proportions searched from the proportion observed. The team would expect these proportions to be equal, meaning that each group has an equal chance of being searched in the screening process. It is clear that they are not. So the team sets out to determine whether the differences are statistically significant. Because the variable of interest is nominal, they conduct a chi square analysis.

The analysis involves a comparison of two chi square values – one that is computed from the frequency table (the computed chi square) and the other that is obtained from a table (the critical value). If the value of the computed chi square exceeds the critical value then an analyst will likely conclude that the difference between what should have happened and what actually happened is statistically significant, that is, not likely due to chance. Alternatively, if the value of the computed chi square is less than the critical value then an analyst will likely conclude that the difference between what should have happened and what actually happened is not statistically significant, that is, likely due to chance.

In our analysis we find examples of both outcomes. For the comparison involving the race or ethnicity of the travelers we find that the computed chi square value (4) is less than the critical value (9.488). Therefore, we conclude that any differences that may exist between the percentages of individuals by race or ethnicity that came through the security area and those that were searched is due to pure chance, that is, it does not appear that the TSA agents are over-selecting individuals based on their race or ethnicity.

On the other hand, for the comparison involving the religious appearance of the travelers we find that the computed chi square value (266) is more than the critical value (5.991). Therefore, we conclude that the differences that exist between the percentages of individuals by religious appearance that came through the security area and those that were searched are not likely to do with chance, that is it appears that the TSA agents are over-selecting individuals based on their religious appearance.

The decision on which religious group is over-selected for a search is based on an inspection of the frequency table and on the analyst's judgment. In this case, 3 percent of the individuals that were observed in the security area appeared to be Sikh while 4 percent of the individuals actually searched appear to be Sikh. Logically, one would conclude that Sikh travelers do not appear to be over-selected by searches. On the other hand, 5 percent of the individuals that were observed in the security area appeared to be Muslim while 16 percent of the individuals actually searched appeared to be Muslim. This suggests that the TSA agents are over-selecting Muslim appearing travelers for searches.

Getting to the Point 14.18 – The chi square test is used to determine whether there is a statistically significant difference between what we expect to happen and what actually happens. The operative statistic is called the chi square statistic. If the statistical significance of the chi square statistic is .05 or less, it can be concluded that the difference between what actually happened and what was expected to happen was not due to chance.

Pearson *r*   The **Pearson *r***, named for its inventor Karl Pearson (1857–1936), is a fourth important inferential statistic. It is used to determine, statistically, whether or not two variables are associated or correlated. It measures both the degree of correlation, as well as the nature of the correlation. In order to use the Pearson *r*, the data must be collected at the interval or ratio level. Numerically, the Pearson *r* statistic ranges from –1 to +1. The closer it is to –1 or +1, the higher the level of correlation between the two variables. The closer it is to 0, the lower the level of correlation between the two variables. If the statistic is positive (+), an increase (or decrease) in one variable leads to an increase (or decrease) in the other. In other words, the variables change in the same direction. If the statistic is negative (-), an increase (or decrease) in one variable leads to a decrease (or increase) in the other. In other words, the variables change in the opposite direction. Here is an example of an analysis using the Pearson *r*.

Making Research Real 14.6 – Keeping Kids Involved

A high school principal believes that the best way to keep teenagers from taking drugs is to provide opportunities for them to participate in extracurricular activities. These extracurricular activities, however, cost a lot of money and school funding is tight. So, he needs some evidence to support his request for additional funding for extracurricular activities.

Partnering with a criminologist from the local university, the principal develops a survey to administer to students. Among other things, the survey asks:

- How many hours per week do you spend in school-related extracurricular activities (e.g., sports teams, school clubs, etc.)?

- How many hours per week do you spend in extracurricular activities outside of school (e.g., Boy Scouts, Girl Scouts, 4-H, etc.)?

- What is your Grade Point Average?

- On average, how many times each month do you partake in illegal drugs or alcohol?

Since the variables were measured at the interval level, the results of this survey were analyzed using a Pearson *r* correlation coefficient. The results are as follows:

	IN-SCHOOL ACTIVITIES	OUTSIDE ACTIVITIES	GPA	DRUG/ALCOHOL USE
In-school activities				
Pearson *r*	**1.00**	0.50	0.90	–.80
Sig.	**.000**	.101	.001	.000
N	**500**	500	500	500
Outside activities				
Pearson *r*	0.50	**1.00**	.035	–.20
Sig.	.101	**.000**	.040	.800
N	500	**500**	500	500

GPA				
Pearson r	0.90	.035	**1.00**	−.75
Sig.	.001	.040	**.000**	.000
N	500	500	**500**	500
Drug/alcohol use				
Pearson r	−.80	−.20	−.75	**1.00**
Sig.	.000	.800	.000	**.000**
N	500	500	500	**500**

The results provide three numbers: the Pearson r statistic (Pearson r), the statistical significance (Sig.) of the Pearson r statistic and the number of cases that were compared (N). In this case, 500 students responded to the survey and all 500 of them answered each of the four questions. So 500 is indicated in each of the cells under N.

To find the Pearson r statistic for each set of variables, the principal can either choose a column at the top (e.g., GPA) and move down the rows to select another variable on the left (e.g., drug/alcohol use). The relevant Pearson r statistic appears in the cell where the two variables meet (−.75 in the case of GPA and drug/alcohol use). Alternatively, he can choose a row on the left (e.g., GPA) and move to the right to select a variable on top (e.g., drug/alcohol use). The Pearson r statistic will be the exact same (again, −.75). Selecting the same variable on top as on the left will reveal a Pearson r correlation coefficient of 1.00. This is because all variables are perfectly correlated with themselves.

The correlation that is most important to the principal is the one between in-school activities and drug/alcohol use. In terms of absolute value, the Pearson r correlation coefficient is −.80. Remember that the strongest Pearson r possible is 1.00. Thus, this Pearson r statistic indicates a strong relationship. The Pearson r in this case is also statistically significant. The relationship between in-school activities and drug/alcohol use is negative, meaning that the more a student is involved in in-school activities, the less likely he or she will use drugs or alcohol. These results are good news for the principal who wants to demonstrate that an expansion of in-school extracurricular activities may help reduce drug and alcohol use.

The principal may encounter some resistance from people who argue that schools cannot do everything and that there are plenty of activities available to students outside of school. But the data suggest that outside activities do not have the same effect on drug/alcohol use as school-sponsored activities. Indeed, the relationship between outside activities and drug/alcohol use is weak (−.20) and not statistically significant (.800).

The Pearson r is a very useful statistical technique. But it has two important limitations. First, you cannot use it to determine which variable is the cause and which variable is the effect. For example, our study found that participation in school-sponsored activities is associated with a decrease in drug and alcohol use. But we cannot say which comes first. It could be that in-school extracurricular activities reduces drug and alcohol use. But, it could also be that students who use drugs and alcohol participate in fewer extracurricular activities. Second, you cannot tell from a Pearson *r* correlation coefficient whether two variables are related directly or indirectly. In our study, for example, in-school activities are significantly and negatively related to drug/alcohol use. But this relationship might not be direct. It could be that in-school activities are related to GPA, which in turn is related to drug/alcohol use. Therefore, researchers should report these results carefully.

Spearman Rho   The **Spearman rho** statistic functions similarly to the Pearson *r*. The Spearman rho, however, is used to analyze the level of correlation of variables measured at the ordinal level. The range of the Spearman rho statistic is also different. Instead of ranging from –1 to +1, the Spearman rho statistic ranges from –.80 to +.80. But, again, both statistics indicate whether two variables are related to one another.

Getting to the Point 14.19 – The Pearson *r* is used to determine whether two variables measured at the interval or ratio level are correlated. The Pearson *r* coefficient ranges from –1 to +1. The closer it is to –1 or +1, the higher the level of correlation between the two variables. Positive Pearson *r* coefficients indicate a positive correlation; negative Pearson *r* coefficients indicate a negative correlation. The Spearman rho statistic is similar to the Pearson *r*, but it indicates the level of correlation between variables measured at the ordinal level and ranges from –.80 to +.80.

Multiple Regression   **Multiple regression** is another important inferential statistical technique. It enables the analyst to measure the individual and combined effects of various independent variables on a single dependent variable. The multiple regression model requires data collected at the interval or ratio levels. The primary statistic produced by a multiple regression is called a coefficient. In most models, there are actually two coefficients. The first coefficient is called an **unstandardized coefficient**. The second coefficient is called a **beta coefficient**, or **standardized coefficient**. The basic regression equation looks like this:

$$y = a + bx$$

Here, y is the value of the dependent variable; a is the amount of variation in the dependent variable that cannot be explained by the independent variable(s); b is the unstandardized regression coefficient for the dependent variable(s); and x is the value of the independent variable. To demonstrate how this works, let us return to our study on the relationship between extracurricular activities and drug and alcohol abuse.

Making Research Real 14.7 – Keeping Kids Involved – Part II

You may recall that the relationship between involvement in school activities and GPA is .90. The unstandardized regression coefficient here, or the b in our regression equation, is .90. If we know how many hours a student spends involved in school activities, we can predict what his or her GPA might be using the regression equation:

$$y_{(GPA)} = a + .90x_{(hours\ spent\ in\ extracurricular\ activities)}$$

Again, a indicates the amount of variation that we cannot explain by the independent variable. For illustration, let us say it is –1.75. (You do not have to worry about how to calculate this. The regression model will do it for you.) If a student says he or she spends five hours per week in extracurricular activities at school, we can multiply .90 by 5, add this product to –1.75, and then predict what the student's GPA might be:

$$y_{(GPA)} = -1.75 + .90(5) = -1.75 + 4.5 = 2.75$$

We conclude that, in the absence of other factors, a student who spends five hours per week involved in school-based extracurricular activities will have a GPA of 2.75.

Remember from the principal's study that some people argued that extracurricular activities outside of school might be just as effective in reducing drug and alcohol use. The Pearson r statistic debunked this idea, showing that the relationship between outside activities and drug/alcohol abuse was weak and not statistically significant. But say that these people want further evidence that outside activities do not have the same effect on drug/alcohol use as in-school activities. To identify the separate effects of these two variables, we could create a multiple regression model. Again, our dependent variable is drug and alcohol use. Our separate independent variables would be participation in school activities and outside activities. Our regression model produces the following statistics:

VARIABLES	UNSTANDARDIZED COEFFICIENTS	BETA COEFFICIENTS	SIG.
Constant	–2.45	–.45	.000
In-school activities	–.85	–1.30	.000
Outside activities	–.20	–.10	.450

Dependent variable: Drug/alcohol abuse $R^2 = .915$

To interpret these results, we would focus on the beta coefficients, or the standardized regression coefficients. The beta coefficient with the highest value (regardless of whether it is negative or positive) is the one that has the most effect on the dependent variable. In this case, the beta coefficient for in-school activities (–1.30) is the highest in terms of absolute value. Therefore, we conclude that this variable has the largest effect on the dependent variable (drug and alcohol use). The beta coefficient for this independent variable is negative. This suggests that when students participate in school-sponsored activities they are significantly less likely to engage in drug or alcohol use.

Participation in non-school-sponsored extracurricular activities has the lowest beta coefficient (–.10) and therefore has the least effect on the dependent variable (drug and alcohol use). In addition, this variable is not statistically significant (.450 is larger than .05, which is the level of statistical significance). This provides further proof that participation in outside activities does not influence drug and alcohol use.

Regression models also include a diagnostic test known as the R^2. This is a measure of how much variation in the dependent variable (in this case, drug and alcohol use) is explained by the independent variables (participation in school-sponsored and non-school-sponsored activities). Our model has an R^2 value of .915. We interpret this to mean that the independent variables explain 91.5 percent of the variation in the dependent variable.

Getting to the Point 14.20 – Multiple regression enables the analyst to measure the individual and combined effects of various independent variables on a dependent variable. A multiple regression requires data collected at the interval or ratio levels.

Selecting an Appropriate Inferential Statistical Technique   At some point during the research process, a researcher must decide which statistical technique to use. To do this, the researcher must know two things: the level at which the data are measured and the type of hypothesis that the study is testing. The level at which the data are measured determines, in part, the statistical techniques that are available to the researcher. For example, if the data are collected at the nominal level, the only statistical technique available to the researcher (of the ones discussed in this chapter) is the chi square analysis. As a general rule, the more precise the level of measurement (interval and ratio are more precise than ordinal and nominal), the more sophisticated the statistical techniques available to the researcher.

The type of hypothesis also determines the statistical technique that should be used by the researcher. Generally, there are two types of hypotheses: association and difference. A **hypothesis of association** alleges that two or more variables are associated with each other. This association can either be positive or negative, but a change in one variable is associated with a change in another. For example, our hypothesis might be that juvenile delinquency is associated with low self-esteem. In this case, we are not alleging that low self-esteem causes juvenile delinquency, just that there is a relationship between the two. A **hypothesis of difference** alleges that an independent variable causes a change in a dependent variable. For example, we might hypothesize that fathers who were abused as children are more likely to abuse their own children. In this case, we are saying that a history of child abuse has a causal effect on the dependent variable. Table 14.2 presents a decision matrix that considers both the level of measurement and the type of hypothesis. This matrix will assist you in deciding which statistical technique to use and when.

Table 14.2 Commonly Used Inferential Statistical Techniques

LEVEL OF MEASUREMENT	TYPE OF HYPOTHESIS	APPROPRIATE STATISTICAL TECHNIQUE
Nominal	Association	N/A
	Difference	Chi square
Ordinal	Association	Spearman rho
	Difference	N/A
Interval/ratio	Association	Pearson *r* (without prediction)
		Regression (with prediction)
	Difference	*T*-test (two groups)
		ANOVA (three or more groups)

You may notice that there are no statistical techniques listed for nominally measured data in a study involving a hypothesis of association analysis. Nor are there techniques listed for analyses involving ordinal measures and a hypothesis of difference. Techniques are available in each of these cases, we just did not cover the techniques in this chapter.

Getting to the Point 14.21 – The decision as to which inferential statistical technique to use depends on the level at which the data are measured and the type of hypothesis that the study is testing.

QUALITATIVE DATA ANALYSIS

The subjective and interpretive nature of qualitative research produces a challenge in terms of data analysis. Human behavior may be interpreted in many different ways depending on the context in which the behavior occurs. The challenge of the qualitative researcher is to understand this subjective meaning, how it arises out of a particular social context, and how it relates to broader social patterns. In this section, we will walk through some of the basic techniques qualitative researchers use to analyze their results. But let us start with an example to illustrate the challenges of qualitative data analysis.

Making Research Real 14.8 – It Wasn't What He Said; It Was How He Said It!

Many years ago, I was an Inspector with the Texas Department of Public Safety. One afternoon, I received a telephone call from an angry citizen. "I want to complain about Trooper Jones [not his real name]. He is very rude and needs to be fired!" the woman exclaimed. It seems that the woman was traveling well over the posted speed limit on an interstate highway in West Texas. She was stopped by Trooper Jones and issued a citation. According to her account, Trooper Jones explained to her the process she had to follow to resolve the matter with the Justice of the Peace Court and ended the contact by saying "Thank you ma'am. Have a nice day." Somewhat perplexed, I asked her why she thought Trooper Jones was rude to her. "Well, it wasn't so much what he said that was rude. It was how he said it," she replied. She felt that the trooper said "Have a nice day" in a mocking manner.

I contacted Trooper Jones to get his side of the story. "Do you remember telling her to have a nice day?" I asked. "No, I don't specifically recall that, but it's likely I did. I always end contacts with that phrase," Jones explained. "In your mind, did you in any way deliver that closing line in a teasing, sarcastic, or joking manner?" I asked. "No! Absolutely not!" he replied.

So who was wrong in this situation? Actually, no one. The complaint was not about the objective reality of the words that were spoken. Everyone agreed that Trooper Jones said, "Have a nice day." What they disagreed on was the intent and meaning of the message. Trooper Jones intended the comment to be, in his own words, a "simple nicety." The complainant perceived that Trooper Jones was being sarcastic and insulting. In this case, there were two valid interpretations of the events.

In the end Trooper Jones apologized to the motorist and explained to her that it was not his intention to be rude. She seemed to be appreciate the sentiment and also apologized for being overly sensitive. I saw Trooper Jones several years later and he recalled the incident. He told me that after that he had changed his habit and now routinely says, "Thank you for your patience. Have a safe journey" at the end of each violator contact.

Rather than give us numbers, qualitative research gives us in-depth information about perceptions, beliefs, and experiences. Qualitative research gives us insight into the 'how' and 'why' of social processes. So analyzing qualitative data can be very different from analyzing quantitative data. To be sure, qualitative researchers, just like quantitative researchers, will often use descriptive statistics to describe their sample and basic research findings. But beyond basic descriptive statistics, qualitative researchers focus more on analyzing words and their meanings.

Getting to the Point 14.22 – Qualitative researchers focus more on analyzing words than they do numbers; they attempt to explain the 'how' and 'why' of social processes.

Transcription

The words that qualitative researchers analyze typically come from interview transcripts and field notes. Field notes are immediately available for analysis because they are already written. Interview transcripts are another matter. In most cases, interviews are tape recorded using an audio or video recorder. These recordings need to be typed up in written form before data analysis can begin. The process of producing a written transcript of video and audio recordings is known as **transcription**.

Truth be told, the transcription process can be exhausting. Computer programs have made the task of transcription much easier than it was years ago, but it can take anywhere from 2 to 10 hours to transcribe one hour of an interview, depending on how fast the people talk and how fast you type. And this does not even include the time it takes to edit the transcript afterwards! Another way to think about it is that each hour of recorded interview equates to roughly 25–50 pages of a manuscript. Given the time-consuming nature of transcription, many researchers will hire a professional transcription service to do the transcribing for them.

Because qualitative research produces such a vast amount of written data, cataloging field notes and written transcripts is essential. For example, transcripts should indicate the date, time, and contact information for each interview. And, these transcripts should be cataloged according to some system that the researcher develops – perhaps by interview date or type of person interviewed.

> **Getting to the Point 14.23** – The process of producing a written transcript of interviews that have been video- or audiotaped is known as transcription. These transcripts provide the written data that qualitative researchers analyze.

Memoing

Field notes and written transcripts are not the only written products that come from qualitative research. Qualitative researchers also engage in a process known as **memoing** throughout the course of their research. As we discussed in the previous chapter on qualitative methods, when researchers engage in memoing, they are basically recording their thoughts and ideas on the research data. Memoing is typically ongoing throughout the data collection process. Say, for example, that you are conducting interviews with street-level drug dealers. As you read through the interview transcripts, you begin to notice commonalities in how the dealers became involved in drug dealing. You write up a memo about these commonalities and reflect on what they might mean for larger patterns of street-level drug dealing.

> **Getting to the Point 14.24** – Qualitative researchers use a process called memoing to record their thoughts and ideas on the research data. Memoing is typically ongoing throughout the data collection process.

As the above example on memoing suggests, a first step in qualitative data analysis is simply reading through the data. As researchers read through these pieces of data, key themes and ideas will likely emerge. Remember that the task of any researcher is to find patterns. Quantitative researchers do this by plugging numerical data into statistical programs; qualitative researchers do this by reading through written data to find recurring themes. This stage of qualitative data analysis basically involves familiarizing yourself with the data.

Segmenting

As researchers read through the data, they begin to organize it into meaningful categories or segments. Researchers refer to this as **segmenting** the data. Often, these categories represent concepts that the researcher is interested in learning more about. For example, a researcher might interview police officers to understand the different paths that led them to a career in policing. He began the research with an idea that family background and formative experiences might play a role in shaping these pathways. So as he reads through the interview transcripts, he might organize sections of the transcript into categories called "family background" and "formative experiences." Here is another example.

Making Research Real 14.9 – A Typology of Violence

Suppose we want to study the use of violence in urban street gangs. We begin our study by defining 'violence' as the use of physical force to injure somebody or damage something. We are interested in distinguishing different levels of violence. So, we also decide to develop a **typology**, or a classification system, of violent acts:

VIOLENT ACTS THAT:	POINT VALUE
Involve the use of an open hand and result in minor physical injury or damage.	1
Involve the use of a closed hand (fist) or feet and result in minor physical injury or damage.	2
Involve the use of a closed hand (fist) or feet and result in moderate physical injury or damage.	3
Involve the use of a non-lethal weapon and result in minor physical injury or damage.	4
Involve the use of a non-lethal weapon and result in moderate physical injury or damage.	5
Involve the use of a non-lethal weapon and result in severe physical injury or damage.	6
Involve the use of a lethal weapon and result in minor physical injury or damage.	7
Involve the use of a lethal weapon and result in moderate physical injury or damage.	8
Involve the use of a lethal weapon and result in severe physical injury or damage.	9
Involve the use of a lethal weapon and result in fatal physical injury or injuries or extreme property damage.	10

With this typology, we could record the intensity, frequency, and duration of different violent acts that we observe in our study. As I mentioned earlier, many researchers rely on descriptive statistics like these in their analyses of qualitative data. But we want to move beyond mere enumeration to understand what our data say about violence. As such, we could also segment our notes into the different categories of violence to try to understand the unique context in which each level of violence is embedded. It could be that urban street gangs have very different motivations and norms surrounding the use of each type of violence.

Getting to the Point 14.25 – Segmenting is a process used by researchers to organize or categorize qualitative data. This stage of qualitative data analysis occurs after researchers have familiarized themselves with the data.

Coding

In the process of segmenting the data, researchers usually apply a particular name or descriptive word to the segments of the data that they identify as meaningful. This process of marking segments of the data with consistent names and terms is referred to as **coding**. In the example we used on discovering pathways to a career in policing, we used two codes: "family background" and "formative experience." A researcher might literally write these codes down in the margins of the interview transcript wherever the interview discusses these themes. If the researcher is using a word processing program, he or she can also highlight or cut and paste sections of the transcript that relate to these themes. In these cases, the researcher is using what we call **a priori codes**, since these codes were established at the outset of the research project.

In the case of grounded research, you do not start with concepts, but discover them in the data. These discovered concepts are often referred to as **grounded codes**. To arrive at a list of grounded codes, researchers would begin with an initial read-through of the written data. Once they become familiar with the data, they read through it again, this time looking for recurring themes, ideas, or issues. They write these down on a sheet of paper. This list could be considered a draft of the final list of codes that will be used to analyze the data. Researchers may do a third read-through of the data to make sure there were not codes that they missed. And to improve the validity of the results, many researchers will ask other members of the research team or other researchers to read through the data and develop their own list, such that they have multiple lists of codes that can be compared and combined.

Once an initial coding list has been developed, qualitative researchers will refine it. Perhaps two different codes really refer to the same theme or idea, in which case they can be combined. Or perhaps one code is too broad and needs to be broken up into multiple codes. Refining the coding list also involves giving each code a meaningful name to capture the idea behind it. Once the coding list has been finalized, researchers read through the data and code it accordingly. So, say you want to understand how motherhood is experienced by women in prison. You conduct interviews with imprisoned mothers, transcribe the interviews, and read through the transcripts for recurring themes. Some of the codes that you arrive at may include: relationships with child caregivers, prison visits with children, and childhood milestones missed. Again, these codes refer to themes or issues that arise from the transcripts.

Getting to the Point 14.26 – After segmenting the data, qualitative researchers go through their data and code it. Coding refers to a process whereby researchers identify recurring themes, label these themes with a descriptive word or phrase (codes), and organize their notes or transcripts according to these themes.

The purpose of coding is to organize your data so that you can analyze it. It is not the final step in the analysis process. Once you have segmented and coded your data, you can analyze the data within each segment to explore particular themes. Using our previous example of studying motherhood behind bars, you might explore the theme of childhood milestones missed. What milestones do the women in the interviews mention most frequently? What do they see as the consequences of missing such milestones? And how do they cope with missing these milestones? Exploring the data in each segment helps you develop a story around that theme, which sheds light on the larger experience of motherhood behind bars.

Diagramming

In addition to exploring the written data within each theme, you want to explore the relationships between various themes. Some researchers do this visually through **diagramming**. Developing a flow chart or a hierarchical diagram to show relationships between different parts of your data will help you develop a visual story of how your data fit together. For example, in exploring the different caregivers of children whose mothers are in prison, you could develop a chart that visually displays the different types of caregivers, such as grandparents, aunts, and foster parents. A mother in prison might have very different relationships with each of these caregiver types, which might affect her experience of mothering behind bars.

Matrices

Qualitative researchers also use **matrices**, or tables, to illustrate relationships between variables. For example, you might develop a table that explores the different coping mechanisms that mothers in prison use when they miss their children's milestones. These coping mechanisms might include watching videos or looking at photographs of their children during a birthday party or high school graduation, providing a letter or a gift to their child to open on the day of their birthday or graduation, and/or listening to stories of the event with their child and caregiver during a prison visit. Your data suggest that these coping mechanisms vary according to the type of caregiver that a child has. So you develop a matrix with coping mechanisms organized by column and type of caregiver by row.

> **Getting to the Point 14.27** – Diagramming is a process by which researchers develop flow charts or hierarchical diagrams to illustrate relationships between different parts of their qualitative data. Researchers also use matrices, or tables, to illustrate such relationships.

There are a number of software programs specifically designed for qualitative data analysis. These programs include ATLAS, Nvivo, NUD-IST, and Ethnograph. These programs are able to comb through large amounts of narrative information to help uncover patterns and themes. And their use is not limited to scholarly analyses. Upon answering a call for service from a burglary, for example, a police officer will complete a case or incident report. These reports are often completed on standard forms that include blanks for such pieces of information as address, time of day, and so on. Often these forms include large spaces for the officers to write additional information in narrative form. This may include a description of how the burglar most likely accessed a residence (*modus operandi*), victim and witness statements, and other information about the crime that does not fit neatly into one of the standard boxes. Normally, these case reports are filed away and never accessed again unless the investigators receive a lead. However, this information may be valuable. Using one of the software programs listed above, an investigator might be able to search these case reports for specific pieces of information or particular patterns, such as common *modus operandi* or stolen items. This process of searching large data sets for patterns is called **data mining**.

> **Getting to the Point 14.28** – There are a number of software programs specifically designed for qualitative data analysis. These programs include ATLAS, Nvivo, NUD-IST, and Ethnograph. Using these and other programs, researchers and practitioners can mine data for patterns and other useful information.

FINAL THOUGHTS

Criminal justice agencies collect an obscene amount of data, almost as much as baseball teams. When I was a State Trooper, for example, we actually had to calculate the number of tickets we wrote for each mile we drove our patrol cars. The guys that worked on interstate highways had high ticket per mile statistics, whereas those of us who worked on less traveled thoroughfares had very low ticket per mile statistics. Our sergeant was always comparing us and usually I was the low man. So, in order to avoid being the subject of ridicule at the monthly meeting, I spent a few days per month writing tickets (a ton of tickets) on an interstate highway about 120 miles from my area. Was I manipulating the statistics? Of course I was.

Though they collect a lot of statistics, criminal justice agencies do not always know how to use the data they have. Indeed, most agencies are in desperate need of people who can make sense of these data. This puts you in a very advantageous position! Using some of the statistical techniques discussed in this chapter, you can now make sense of large amounts of data and use statistics to improve efficiency and effectiveness in various criminal justice agencies. Likewise, you can use qualitative analysis to better understand complex social phenomena like crime. Qualitative researchers, for example, are on the staff of the U.S. Department of Homeland Security and in regional intelligence information fusion centers throughout the nation. These researchers actively monitor communications between individuals and groups who are known to have terrorist connections in order to predict and prevent terrorist acts. In short, the ability to conduct both quantitative and qualitative analysis will make you quite marketable in the fields of criminal justice.

GETTING TO THE POINT/CHAPTER SUMMARY

- During the analysis phase, researchers evaluate the data they gather to answer their research questions or hypotheses. Even though analysis occurs near the end of the research process, considerations of analysis should occur earlier in the research process.

- Statistics summarize large amounts of data into a single number and enable us to communicate information efficiently. There are two general types of statistics: descriptive statistics and inferential statistics.

- Descriptive statistics describe the current state of something. An important set of descriptive statistics are known as the measures of central tendency. These measures include the mean, median, and mode.

- The mean is calculated by adding together all of the values for a particular variable and dividing that sum by the total number of cases. Although it is a good measure of central tendency, it is sensitive to extreme values, or outliers.

- The median is referred to as the *middlemost* value because it is the value that is situated in the middle, with half the cases equal to or greater than and half the cases equal to or lesser than this value. It is less susceptible to extreme values or outliers than the mean.

- The mode is the most frequently occurring value in a population or sample. Like the median, the mode is less susceptible to extreme values or outliers than the mean.

- The decision about which measure of central tendency to use should be based on two factors: (1) whether the data are skewed toward extreme scores, and (2) what level the variables are measured at.

- Measures of variability are descriptive statistics that tell us how much variation exists within a sample or population. Among the measures of variability is the range, which is the difference between the highest and lowest value in a sample or population. This descriptive statistic, like the mean, is susceptible to extreme scores or outliers.

- The standard deviation is a descriptive statistic that describes how much variability exists within a sample or population. Because the standard deviation considers both the mean and the total number of cases in the sample or population, it is a much more stable statistic than the range.

- A percentage is a descriptive statistic that describes a portion of a sample or population. Percentages are calculated by dividing the number of like cases by the total number of cases, then multiplying that quotient by 100.

- A percentile is a statistic that tells us where a value ranks within a distribution. Sometimes this is referred to as the percentile rank. We calculate the percentile rank by dividing the number of cases below the value by the total number of cases and then multiplying that quotient by 100.

- Percent change is a descriptive statistic that indicates how much something changed from one time to the next. We calculate the percent change by subtracting the original number from the new number, dividing that difference by the original number and then multiplying that quotient by 100.

- Rates are a descriptive statistic that enable us to compare similar behaviors across multiple locations. Rates factor in population size and report incidents per n units.

- In normally distributed data, the mean, median, and mode are equal because all of the data are distributed equally around the same value. In a normal distribution, 68.2 percent of all cases fall within one standard deviation of the mean; 95.4 percent of all cases fall within two standard deviations of the mean; and 99.9 percent of all cases fall within three standard deviations of the mean.

- Inferential statistics enable analysts to determine the probability of certain outcomes. When reading inferential statistics, we are concerned with statistical significance, which is a measure of the probability that the statistic is due to chance. If the statistical significance of a statistic is .05 or less, we can conclude that the results are not due to chance.

- The t-test is a statistical technique used to determine whether or not two groups are different with respect to a single variable. T-tests can only be run using interval or ratio level data. If the statistical significance of the t-score is .05 or less, it can be concluded that the difference between the two groups is not due to chance.

- The analysis of variance (ANOVA) model allows analysts to compare two or more groups to see if they are different with respect to a single variable measured at the interval or ratio level. An ANOVA produces an F-ratio statistic. If the statistical significance of the F-ratio is .05 or less, it can be concluded that the difference between at least two of the groups is not due to chance.

- The chi square test is used to determine whether there is a statistically significant difference between what we expect to happen and what actually happens. The operative statistic is called the chi square statistic. If the statistical significance of the chi square statistic is .05 or less, it can be concluded that the difference between what actually happened and what was expected to happen was not due to chance.

- The Pearson r is used to determine whether two variables measured at the interval or ratio level are correlated. The Pearson r coefficient ranges from -1 to $+1$. The closer it is to -1 or $+1$, the higher the level of correlation between the two variables. Positive Pearson r coefficients indicate a positive correlation; negative Pearson r coefficients indicate a negative correlation. The Spearman rho statistic is similar to the Pearson r, but it indicates the level of correlation between variables measured at the ordinal level and ranges from $-.80$ to $+.80$.

- Multiple regression enables the analyst to measure the individual and combined effects of various independent variables on a dependent variable. A multiple regression requires data collected at the interval or ratio levels.

- The decision as to which inferential statistical technique to use depends on the level at which the data are measured and the type of hypothesis that the study is testing.

- Qualitative researchers focus more on analyzing words than they do numbers; they attempt to explain the 'how' and 'why' of social processes.

- The process of producing a written transcript of interviews that have been video- or audiotaped is known as transcription. These transcripts provide the written data that qualitative researchers analyze.

- Qualitative researchers use a process called memoing to record their thoughts and ideas on the research data. Memoing is typically ongoing throughout the data collection process.

- Segmenting is a process used by researchers to organize or categorize qualitative data. This stage of qualitative data analysis occurs after researchers have familiarized themselves with the data.

- After segmenting the data, qualitative researchers go through their data and code it. Coding refers to a process whereby researchers identify recurring themes, label these themes with a descriptive word or phrase (codes), and organize their notes or transcripts according to these themes.

- Diagramming is a process by which researchers develop flow charts or hierarchical diagrams to illustrate relationships between different parts of their qualitative data. Researchers also use matrices, or tables, to illustrate such relationships.

- There are a number of software programs specifically designed for qualitative data analysis. These programs include ATLAS, Nvivo, NUD-IST, and Ethnograph. Using these and other programs, researchers and practitioners can mine data for patterns and other useful information.

CHAPTER EXERCISES

The following chapter exercises are organized into two parts. The first part consists of questions that can be answered using the information from this chapter. This section will test your understanding of the chapter material. The second part consists of research application exercises. These exercises require you to apply what you have learned thus far.

CHAPTER REVIEW QUESTIONS

Respond to each of the following questions using the information from this chapter.

1. The main disadvantage of the mean is that it is:
   a. Difficult to calculate accurately
   b. Less useful than other descriptive statistics
   c. Seldom used in data analysis
   d. Sensitive to extreme values

2. When a researcher's data is collected at the interval or ratio level of measurement, which of the following measures of central tendency are available to use?
   a. Mean
   b. Median
   c. Mode
   d. All of the above

3. Which of the following statistics is a commonly used measure of variability?
   a. The mode
   b. The percentile
   c. The range
   d. The rate

4. Consider the following research descriptions. Identify the descriptive statistic that is being calculated or used in each case (mean, range, percentile rank, rate).

Research description	Descriptive statistic
A researcher administers an IQ test on a sample of 80 juvenile delinquents. She reports the numerical difference between the delinquent that scored the highest and the delinquent that scored the lowest level of intelligence.	
A researcher is studying a sample of teenagers who attend a youth program intended to prevent juvenile delinquency. She is interested in describing the sample and begins by calculating the average age of the teenagers in the program.	

During a conversation between two police officers one comments, "I made an 86 on the last sergeant's exam which ain't bad, but 74 percent of the other officers that took the same exam made a better score."	
A recent study of crime in Bigton revealed that 10 of every 10,000 residents has been a victim of crime in the past year.	

5. In a normal distribution of IQ scores, where the mean is 100 and the standard deviation is 10, what percent of the cases have IQ scores from 90 to 110?
   a. 32 percent
   b. 46 percent
   c. 54 percent
   d. 68 percent

6. Consider the following statistics used in quantitative data analysis. Indicate whether the statistic is an example of a descriptive or inferential statistic.

Statistic	Descriptive or inferential?
T-score	
Rate	
Standard deviation	
Percentage	
Spearman rho	
Chi square	

7. As a general rule, if the statistical significance of a statistic is _____ or less, we can conclude that the results are not due to chance.
   a. .05
   b. .15
   c. .20
   d. .40

8. A statistical technique that is used to determine whether or not two or more groups are different with respect to a single variable measured at the interval or ratio level of measurement is:
   a. A multiple regression
   b. A Pearson *r*
   c. A *t*-test
   d. An ANOVA

9. The decision about which statistical technique to use for analyzing data depends on:
   a.   The level at which the data are measured
   b.   The type of hypothesis being tested
   c.   Both a and b
   d.   Neither a nor b

10. Consider the following descriptions of qualitative data analysis. Identify the technique that is being used in each case (transcribing, memoing, coding, diagramming).

Description	Qualitative technique
A researcher reads through his observations of jury trials involving cases of rape to identify meaningful themes that arise from the data.	
A researcher reflects on how social workers influence the child protective custody process while reading through interview data.	
A researcher develops a flow chart to illustrate the process by which men and women progress through a typical policing career.	
A researcher conducts recorded interviews with minors serving life sentences, which he later translates into a written transcript.	

RESEARCH APPLICATION EXERCISES

The following exercises are designed to provide you with an opportunity to conduct some basic statistical analyses and/or interpret statistical information.

11. Recently, the City of Bigton hired a researcher to determine household incomes among the residents of the city. This researcher collected a sample of households and asked each of them how much they earned each year. Using the income survey data provided on the next page, respond to the following questions:
    a.   What is the mean household income in Bigton?
    b.   What is the median household income in Bigton?
    c.   What is the mode household income in Bigton?
    d.   What is the range of household income in Bigton?
    e.   What is the standard deviation of household income in Bigton?
    f.   If the Bigton City Council decided to impose a tax on all households with earnings above the 90th percentile, at what income level would a household be taxed?

Annual Household Income in Dollars

14000	34000	39000
16000	34000	40000
18000	35000	40000
18000	35000	41000
20000	35000	41000
26000	35000	42000
27000	37000	42000
28000	37000	42000
28000	37000	43000
29000	37000	44000
30000	38000	45000
32000	38000	45000
32000	38000	46000
33000	38000	47000
33000	38000	47000
34000	39000	48000
34000	39000	48000

12. During a recent survey, police officers were asked how many ounces of alcohol they consumed in a typical week. The mean of the responses was 10 ounces per week and the median was 4 ounces per week. Which of the following might explain why these two measures of central tendency are not equal?
   a.   A few of the police officers drink very little.
   b.   A few of the police officers drink a lot.
   c.   You cannot determine this from this information.

2. In a normally distributed sample of 250 adult offenders, the mean age is 32 years and the standard deviation is 2 years. Using this information and what you know about the normal distribution, answer the questions below.
   a.   What percent of these adult offenders are 32 years old or older?
   b.   What percent of these adult offenders are 32 years old or younger?
   c.   What percent of these adult offenders are between the ages of 30 and 34?
   d.   How many of these adult offenders are 32 years old or older?
   e.   How many of these adult offenders are 32 years old or younger?
   f.   How many of these adult offenders are between the ages of 30 and 34?

13. In 2012, the City of Bigton experienced 52 vehicular burglaries. In 2013, the City of Bigton experienced 86 vehicular burglaries. What is the percent change of vehicular burglaries from 2012 to 2013?

14. What is the rate per 100,000 of burglaries in a community with a population of 180,000 that experienced 245 burglaries?

15. Variable x and variable y are correlated. Their Pearson r is $-.90$, which is statistically significant at the .000 level. Using what you know about the Pearson r statistic, identify which of the following statements are true. (More than one might be true.)
    a. An increase in x leads to an increase in y.
    b. An increase in x leads to a decrease in y.
    c. A decrease in x leads to a decrease in y.
    d. A decrease in x leads to an increase in y.

16. Use Table 14.2 to determine which statistical technique would be appropriate for each of the following analyses:
    a. A researcher wants to determine whether or not there is a relationship between poverty and crime. He has data on the annual income of a sample of 10,000 adults. He also has data on the number of times these adults claim to have committed a crime, regardless of whether or not they were caught.
    b. A police chief is concerned about the level of cardiovascular disease among his officers. He believes that participation in an after-work exercise program will improve their cardiovascular health. He divides the officers into two groups and measures their resting heart rate. He then assigns one group to a month-long after-work exercise program. At the end of the month, the chief again measures the resting heart rate of the officers to determine whether or not the exercise program improved the cardiovascular health of the officers who participated in the program.

17. Imagine that you are a researcher interested in how the mainstream news media presents the problem of drug dealing. Go to CNN.com and enter 'drug dealing' into the search box in the upper right corner. Look through the first ten results that are produced by your search. As you read through these ten results, record the following information:
    a. In which section of the website (e.g., CNN blog, CNN World, CNN Opinion) is the news piece featured?
    b. What year was the news piece published?
    c. What kind of code would you use to categorize each news piece?
    d. Looking through your coding list and the prominence of particular codes, what might you conclude about CNN's coverage of drug dealing over the time period in which the news pieces were published?

REFERENCES

Academy of Criminal Justice Sciences. (2012). Code of Ethics. Retrieved from http://www.acjs.org/pubs/167_671_2922.cfm (accessed February 2013).

Alpert, G.P., Dunham, R.G. and Smith, M.R. (2007). Investigating racial profiling by the Miami-Dade Police Department: A multimethod approach. *Criminology and Public Policy, 6*(1), 25–55.

Alpert, G.P., Smith, M.R., Kaminski, R.J., Fridell, L.A. MacDonald, J. and Kubu, B. (2011). *Police use of force, Tasers and other less-lethal weapons.* Washington, DC: United States Department of Justice.

Anderson, D.A. (2002). The deterrence hypothesis and picking pockets at the pickpocket's hanging. *American Law and Economics Review, 4*(2), 295–313.

Anderson, M. and Feinberg, S.E. (2000). Race and ethnicity and the controversy over the U.S. Census. *Current Sociology, 48*(3), 87–110.

Barlow, M.H., Barlow, D.E., and Chiricos, T.G. (1995). Economic conditions and ideologies of crime in the media: A content analysis of crime news. *Crime and Delinquency, 44,* 3–19.

Belmont Report. (1979). *The Belmont report: Ethical principles and guidelines for the protection of human research subjects: Regulations and ethical guidelines.* Washington, DC: National Institutes of Health.

Berger, A. (2004). Dispatches MMR: What they didn't tell you. *British Medical Journal, 329*(7477), 1293.

Bloom, S.G. (2005). Lesson of a lifetime. Washington, DC: Smithsonian Magazine. Retrieved from http://www.smithsonianmag.com/history-archaeology/lesson_lifetime.html (accessed February 2013).

Blumstein, A., Cohen, J. and Nagin, D. (Eds.). (1978). Deterrence and incapacitation: Estimating the effects of criminal sanctions on crime rates: Report of the Panel of Deterrence and Incapacitation. Washington, DC: National Academy of Sciences.

Bonomo, Y.A., Bowes, G., Coffey, C., Carlin, J.B. and Patton, G.C. (2005). Teenage drinking and the onset of alcohol dependence: A cohort study over seven years. *Addiction, 99*(12), 1520–1528.

Bowen, D.M. (2009). Calling your bluff: How prosecutors and defense attorneys adapt plea bargaining strategies to increased formalization. *Justice Quarterly, 26*(1), 2–29.

Brantingham, P.L. and Brantingham, P.J. (1993). Nodes, paths, and edges: Considerations on the complexity of crime and the physical environment. *Journal of Environmental Psychology, 13*(1), 3–28.

Brown v. The Board of Education, 347 US 483 (1954).

Burgess, R., and Akers, R. (1966). A differential association-reinforcement theory of criminal behavior. *Social Problems, 14*(2), 128–147.

Bursik Jr., R.J. (1988). Social disorganization and theories of crime and delinquency: Problems and prospects. *Criminology, 26*(4), 519–539.

Buzawa, E.S. and Buzawa, C.G. (1990). *Domestic violence: The criminal justice response*. Thousand Oaks, CA: Sage.

Campbell, D. and Stanley, J. (1963). *Experimental and quasi-experimental designs for research*. Chicago, IL: Rand McNally.

Chadwick, A. (2002). Remembering Tuskegee. Washington, DC: National Public Radio. Retrieved from http://www.npr.org/programs/morning/features/2002/jul/tuskegee/ (accessed February 2013).

Conan Doyle, A. (2004). *The sign of four*. In Shade, G. (Ed.), *The complete works of Sherlock Holmes, Volume One* (pp. 97–184). New York, NY: Barnes and Noble Books.

Cook, T.D. and Campbell, D.T. (1979). *Quasi-experimentation: Design and analysis issues for field settings*. Chicago, IL: Rand McNally.

Crime Library (2012). Criminal profiling: Part I History and method by Katherine Ramsland. Retrieved from http://www.trutv.com/library/crime/criminal_mind/profiling/history_method/index.html (accessed February 2013).

Dabney, D.A., Copes, H., Tewksbury, R. and Hawk-Tourtelot, S.R. (2011). A qualitative assessment of stress perceptions among members of a homicide unit. *Justice Quarterly*. Retrieved from http://www.tandfonline.com/doi/full/10.1080/07418825.2011.633542 (accessed February 2013).

Davis, R. (2008). The Minneapolis Domestic Violence Experiment. Retrieved from http://www.policeone.com/police-products/training/articles/1690819-The-Minneapolis-Domestic-Violence-Experiment/(accessed February 2013).

Deer, B. (2004). Revealed: MMR research scandal. London, UK: *The Sunday Times*. Retrieved from http://briandeer.com/mmr/lancet-deer-1.htm (accessed February 2013).

Deer, B. (2007). The *Lancet* scandal. London, UK: *The Sunday Times*. Retrieved from http://briandeer.com/mmr-lancet.htm (accessed February 2013).

Federal Bureau of Investigation (2009). *Crime in the United States, 2009 Uniform Crime Report*. Washington, DC: Federal Bureau of Investigation.

Gallup (2011). Gallop Poll on religious preference. Retrieved from http://www.gallup.com/poll/151760/Christianity-Remains-Dominant-Religion-United-States.aspx (accessed February 2013).

Glueck, S. and Glueck, E. (1950). *Unraveling juvenile delinquency*. Boston, MA: Harvard University Press.

Hanson, D.J. (2007). Drug Abuse Resistance Education: The effectiveness of DARE. Potsdam, NY: State University of New York. Retrieved from http://alcoholfacts.org/DARE.html (accessed February 2013).

Henrichson, C. and Delany, R. (2012). The price of prisons: What incarceration costs taxpayers. New York, NY: Vera Institute Center on Sentencing and Corrections. Retrieved from http://www.vera.org/sites/default/files/resources/downloads/Price_of_Prisons_updated_version_072512.pdf (accessed February 2013).

Huff, D. and Geis, I. (1993). *How to lie with statistics*. New York, NY: W.W. Norton and Company.

Humphreys, L. (1975). *Tearoom trade: Impersonal sex in public places*. Piscataway, NJ: Aldine Transaction.

Kelling, G.L. and Wilson, J.Q. (1982) Broken windows: The police and neighborhood safety. New York, NY: *The Atlantic*. Retrieved from http://www.theatlantic.com/magazine/archive/1982/03/broken-windows/304465/ (accessed February 2013).

ICPSR (Interuniversity Consortium for Political and Social Research) (2011). Retrieved from www.icpsr.org (accessed March 2013).

Lamberth, J. (1994). Revised statistical analysis of the incidence of police stops and arrests of black drivers/travelers on the New Jersey Turnpike between exits and interchanges 1 and 3 from years 1988 through 1991. West Chester, PA: Author. Retrieved from http://www.lamberthconsulting.com/page/research--articles (accessed February 2013).

Lamberth, J. (1996). Report of John Lamberth, Ph.D. Washington, DC: American Civil Liberties Union. Retrieved from http://www.clearinghouse.net/ch Docs/public/PN-MD-0003-0006.pdf (accessed March 2013).

Lange, J.E., Blackman, K.O. and Johnson, M.B. (2001). Speed violation survey of the New Jersey Turnpike: Final report. Calverton, MD: Public Services Research Institute.

Langstrom, N. (2002). Long-term follow-up of criminal recidivism in young sex offenders: Temporal patterns and risk factors. *Psychology, 8*(1), 41–58.

Leake, J. (2004). Now adulthood starts at 30. *The Sunday Times*. Retrieved from http://www.thesundaytimes.co.uk/sto/news/uk_news/article233261.ece (accessed March 2013).

Lewin, K. (1946) Action research and minority problems. *Journal of Social Issues, 2*(4), 34–46.

Link, M., McNelly, J. and Withrow, B. (1989). *A comparative analysis of the 9mm semi-automatic pistol and the .357 revolver*. Austin, TX: Texas Department of Public Safety.

Madensen, T.D. and Knutsson, J. (Eds.). (2011). *Preventing crowd violence*. Boulder, CO: Lynne Rienner Publishers.

Payne, R. (2003). *A framework for understanding poverty*. Houston, TX: Aha Publications, Inc.

Plessy v. Ferguson, 163 US 537 (1896).

Quiet Rage (1992). The Stanford prison experiment. Retrieved from http://www.prisonexp.org (accessed February 2013).

RAND (2011). A brief history of the RAND. Santa Monica, CA: RAND Corporation. Retrieved from http://www.rand.org/about/history.html (accessed February 2013).

Sampson, R.J. and Laub, J.H. (1995). *Crime in the making: Pathways and turning points through life*. Boston, MA: Harvard University Press.

San Francisco Chronicle (1998). Obituary of Pierce Brooks. Retrieved from http://www.sfgate.com.

Shaw, C.R. and Becker, H.A. (1966). *The jack-roller: A delinquent boy's own story*. Chicago, IL: University of Chicago Press.

Shaw, C.R. and McKay, H.D. (1942). *Juvenile delinquency and urban areas*. Chicago, IL: The University of Chicago Press.

Sherman, L.W. and Berk, R.A. (1984a) The specific deterrent effects of arrest for domestic assault. *American Sociological Review, 49*(2), 261–272.

Sherman, L.W. and Berk, R.A. (1984b). The Minneapolis domestic violence experiment. Washington, DC: The Police Foundation Reports.

State of New Jersey v. Pedro Soto, 734 A.2d 350 (N.J. Super. CT. Law Div. 1996).

Sutherland, E.H. (1974). *Criminology*. Philadelphia, PA: J.B. Lippincott Company.

Tapscott, D. (2008). *Grown up digital: How the net generation is changing your world*. Columbus, OH: McGraw-Hill.

The Kansas City Patrol Experiment (1974). The Kansas City preventive patrol experiment. Washington, DC: The Police Foundation. Retrieved from http://www.police foundation.org/content/kansas-city-preventive-patrol-experiment-0.

The National Crime Victimization Survey (2012). *Data collection: The national crime victimization survey*. Washington, DC: United States Bureau of Justice.

Retrieved from http://bjs.ojp.usdoj.gov/index.cfm?ty=dcdetail&iid=245 (accessed February 2013).

The Uniform Crime Reports (2012). The Uniform Reporting Program. Washington, DC: Federal Bureau of Investigation. Retrieved from http://www.fbi.gov/about-us/cjis/ucr/ucr (accessed February 2013).

Verano, S.P., Schafer, J.A., Cancino, J.M., Decker, S.H. and Greene, J.R. (2010). A tale of three cities: Crime and displacement after Hurricane Katrina. *Journal of Criminal Justice, 38*(1), 42–50.

Wakefield, A., Murch, S., Anthony, A., et al. (1998). Ileal-lymphoid-nodular hyperplasia, non-specific colitis, and pervasive developmental disorder in children. *Lancet, 351*(9103), 637–641.

Wallace, W.L. (1971). *The logic of science in sociology.* Piscataway, NJ: Aldine Transaction.

Williams, H. (2008). *TASER electronic control devices and sudden in-custody death: Separating evidence from conjecture.* Springfield, IL: Charles C. Thomas, Ltd.

Wilson, J.Q. (1968). *Varieties of police behavior: The management of law and order in eight communities.* London: Oxford University Press.

Winker, M.A. (2004). Measuring race and ethnicity: Why and how? *Journal of the American Medical Association, 293*(13), 1612–1614.

Withrow, B.L. (2003). *Police protective custody: The Wichita Children's Home.* Wichita, KS: The Midwest Criminal Justice Institute at Wichita State University.

Withrow, B.L. (2004). Driving while different: A potential theoretical explanation for race-based policing. *Criminal Justice Policy Review, 15*(3), 344–364.

Withrow, B.L. and Bolin, B. (2005). Police protective custody: A systematic predictive model for the reduction of referrals. *Policing: An International Journal of Police Strategies and Management, 28*(3), 473–492.

Wright, J. and Hensley, C. (2003). From animal cruelty to serial murder: Applying the graduation hypothesis. *International Journal of Offender Therapy and Comparative Criminology, 47*(1), 71–88.

Zgoba, K., Witt, P., Dalessandro, M., and Veysey, B. (2008). Megan's law: Assessing the practical and monetary efficacy. Retrieved from https://www.ncjrs.gov/pdffiles1/nij/grants/225370.pdf (accessed February 2013).

Zhao, J., Thurman, Q.C. and He, N. (1999). Sources of job satisfaction among police officers: A test of demographic and work environment work models. *Justice Quarterly, 16*(1), 153–173.

GLOSSARY/INDEX

Note: 'f' after a page number indicates a figure; 't' indicates a table.

abstract: A commonly used section of a research report, usually about 150 words or less, wherein the researcher summarizes the research question, methods, data, and findings. 40t

Academy of Criminal Justice Sciences 67–69

accretion measure: A non-reactive measure of behavior based on the evaluation of the physical things people possess and/or discard. 271

action research: Similar to applied research, a type of research that focuses on problem solving and involves practitioners in the research design, implementation, and evaluation stages. 10–11

adulthood 115–116

alcohol-related accidents xxxiv–xxxv

Alpert, Geoffrey 29, 100

alternative explanations *see* **lack of plausible alternative explanations**

alternative hypothesis: A hypothesis that alleges a difference or association between two variables. The opposite of a null hypothesis. 149–150

American Sociological Review 206, 224

analysis *see* **content analysis**; data analysis; **secondary analysis**; **unit of analysis**

analysis of variance (ANOVA): An inferential statistical technique used to determine whether or not two or more groups are different with respect to a single variable. 221, 258, 364–365, 373t

Analyze the Data: The eighth step in the research process wherein the researcher uses an appropriate analytical or statistical technique to produce research findings. 37–39

Evaluation Research Methods 339–341
Experimental Design Research Methods 221–223
Non-Reactive Research Methods 287–288
Qualitative Research Methods 310–312
Survey/Interview Research Methods 257–259

anonymity: A form of privacy wherein the researcher does not have sufficient knowledge to connect specific research information to a specific research subject.

as ethical concern 53–54

applied research: In contrast to pure research, a type of research wherein the researcher's initial intention is to apply the knowledge gained to a specific problem or issue. Applied research can later be used to expand the body of knowledge. 10–11

a priori assumption: A statement, written in the form of a rule or guideline, about what the data must reveal for the researcher to confirm his or her hypothesis. 37

a priori codes: In qualitative analysis, predefined concepts established at the outset of a research project. 377

archival data: Data made available by an individual, groups, or organization for the purpose of analysis. 271

Ask Another Question: The eleventh step in the research process wherein the researcher identifies the weaknesses in a research project and then develops another research question that will start the process all over again. 42

Experimental Design Research Methods 225

overview of 66

see also **ethics**

instrument: The actual questionnaire or document containing the pre-established questions or statements on a survey or interview.

for survey research 235

instrumentation: The ability of an experimental design model to document the causal relationship between an independent and dependent variable.

as threat to validity 201, 201–202t

used for experimental designs 208–209

internal validity: The ability of an experimental design model to document the causal relationship between an independent and dependent variable.

threats to 199–202, 201–202t, 216t

Internet survey: A written and self-administered survey instrument that is delivered to a respondent via an electronic medium (such as the Internet) and returned electronically upon completion to the researcher by the respondent. 236–237

interpretive: A paradigm of research that assumes social science inquiry is based on the notion that social science research is fundamentally different from research in the natural sciences. Rather than simply measure human behavior from the 'outside,' interpretive social scientists attempt to get 'inside' to understand the meaning behind human behavior. This involves interpretation rather than simple observation. 81

Interpret the Results: The ninth step in the research process wherein the researcher assigns meaning and practical significance to the results of the analysis. 39

Evaluation Research Methods 339–341

Experimental Design Research Methods 221–223

Non-Reactive Research Methods 288–289

Qualitative Research Methods 312–313

Survey/Interview Research Methods 260–261

inter-rater reliability (method): A method for determining the capacity of a measure to be consistent. Using this method a researcher would ask two or more other researchers to

observe and measure the same thing. Then the researcher would compare the results to see if they generally have the same impression of what they observed. 125, 126t, 281

interval: The second highest level of measurement. Interval variables are also categories like nominal level variables and can also be arranged in a logical order like ordinal level variables. But interval variables have one additional feature that makes them more precise: they have equal differences between their attributes. 118

intervening variables: May occur between independent and dependent variables and change the nature of the causal relationship. In other words, they may intervene in the relationship between an independent and dependent variable. 139–140

and independent and dependent variables 140f

interview: A survey instrument wherein the respondents are contacted face to face and asked to respond to questions and/or statements by a researcher (i.e. interviewer). 237t, 237–238

interviewer bias: Potentially caused when an interviewer's presence or reaction affects the respondent's responses to the questions and/or statements.

and survey research 235

introduction: A commonly used section of a research report that includes an overview of the research, describes the purpose of the research, the research question and the hypothesis, and includes a statement on how the article is organized. 40t

Iraq War 6

IRBs *see* **Institutional Review Boards (IRBs)**

jack-rollers 298–299

jargon 250

job satisfaction 83–84

Johnson, M.B. 106

Journal of Environmental Psychology 302

juvenile delinquency 85

Kelling, George 13–14

the frequency of a value within a sample or population. Requires data measured at the nominal, ordinal, interval, or ratio levels of measurement. 354–355, 362

monograph: A research report that is too long to appear in a scholarly journal but too short or narrowly focused to justify its publication as a book. 13

mortality: One of several potential threats to the internal validity of an experimental design model. Potentially occurs when the loss (for any reason) of a research subject affects the outcome of the experiment.
as threat to validity 200, 201t

multiple methods approach: An evaluation technique that involves the use of multiple data gathering techniques in order to evaluate a program, process, or policy. 323

multiple regression: An inferential statistical technique used to measure the individual and combined effects of various independent variables on a dependent variable. The multiple regression model requires data collected at the interval or ratio levels and a hypothesis alleging an association between the variables. In addition, this model enables the researcher to predict the outcome of the dependent variable when given the values for the independent variables. 370–372

multi-stage sampling: A broad category of sampling technique wherein the sample of research subjects ultimately used by the researcher is the result of two or more sampling steps. 170, 172–173

mutually exclusive: The capacity for a list of variables' attributes to provide a respondent with one and only one response. 143
and survey research 249

National Crime Victimization Survey: A survey of households in the United States conducted periodically by the Department of Justice to determine, among other things, the amount of criminal victimization. 243–248, 255–257, 259–262

National Criminal Justice Reference Service (NCJRS) 14–15

National Incident-Based Reporting System (NIBRS) 247, 255

nature of data: The type of data collected, and in some cases the type of research method used. There are two types of data – quantitative and qualitative. 86–87

NCVS *see* **National Crime Victimization Survey**

negative correlation: A type of association between two variables wherein an increase in one variable results in a decrease in another variable, or a decrease in one variable results in an increase in another variable. 101–102, 102f, 103t

nominal: The lowest level of measurement. Nominal variables are merely names or labels. They are simply things we can categorize, such as ethnicity, religion, and gender. The attributes (i.e. the categories) of nominally measured variables cannot be arranged in any logical order or sequence. 118

non-probability sampling: One of the two major categories of sampling techniques. These techniques do not rely on the random selection of research subjects or cases. As a result, researchers cannot infer that what they learn from a non-probability sample is true of the larger population from which the sample came.
summary of 161t
techniques for 173–179

non-reactive research methods: Any research method that allows a researcher to gather information from or about research subjects unobtrusively, or without their knowledge that they are being measured or observed. 269–271
basics of 271–272
benefits of 274–275
communicating findings for 289–290
conceptualization in 280–281
data analysis for 287–288
data collection in 284–287
interpreting results for 288–289
limitations of 275–276
literature reviews for 278
operationalization in 280–281

Spearman rho: A statistical technique designed to evaluate the level and nature of a correlation between two variables measured at the ordinal level. 258, 370, 373t

split half reliability (method): A method for determining the capacity of a measure to be consistent. This method requires a researcher to split a measure in half and administer each half to two similar groups. The measure is considered reliable if the results from each half are similar. 125, 126t

Spokane (Washington) Police Department 83–84

sponsorship bias: Occurs when the sponsor of a research project attempts to influence the study design and/or interpretation of the data.
as ethical concern 56–58, 64t

Spousal Assault Replication Program 225

spurious: Describes a logical thinking error that occurs when a researcher falsely proposes a causal relationship between two or more variables. 107–108

standard deviation: A measure of variability. This descriptive statistics represents how much each value varies from the mean. Higher standard deviations represent higher levels of variability. 356–358, 362

standardized coefficient: One of two statistics used in a multiple regression model to measure the individual effect of an independent variable on a dependent variable. Also called a beta coefficient. 370
see also **beta coefficient**

State of New Jersey v. Pedro Soto 16

statistical significance: A measure of the probability that the statistic is due to chance. As a general rule, if the statistical significance of a statistic is .05 or less, we conclude that the results are not due to chance. The .05 level of statistical significance means that there is a 5 in 100 chance that the results are due to pure chance. 363

statistics *see* **descriptive statistics; inferential statistics**

storytelling xxiv–xxv

stratified random sampling: A probability sampling technique wherein cases are selected from well-defined strata within the overall population to further enhance the representativeness of the overall sample. 172–173, 173f

stress 300

subscripts 258–259

suppression: Occurs when a research sponsor fails to disclose findings that do not benefit the organization.
as ethical concern 56–58, 64t

surveillance effect 223

survey research method: A data collection procedure or process that involves the use of a survey or interview instrument wherein individuals or groups are asked to respond to questions and/or statements. 235
basics of 234–235
benefits of 238–240
coding in 257–258
communicating findings for 261–262
conceptualization in 246–248
data analysis for 257–259
designing research methods for 248–256
and double-barreled questions 250
exhaustiveness in 249
interpreting results for 260–261
leading questions in 250–251
limitations of 240–242
literature reviews for 244–246
mutual exclusivity in 249
operationalization in 246–248
prestige bias in 250
process of 242–262
research questions in 243–244, 246
response rates for 256–257
validity in 241

surveys: A type of data collection method or research methodology wherein individuals or groups are asked to respond to questions and/or statements.
composite index number 252
considerations for 251t
instructions for 254
Internet 236t, 236–237
length of 254
Likert scales used for 128, 252